The Color of
Strangers
The Color of
Friends

The Color of
Strangers
The Color of
Friends

THE PLAY OF ETHNICITY IN SCHOOL AND COMMUNITY

Alan Peshkin

THE UNIVERSITY OF CHICAGO PRESS
CHICAGO AND LONDON

The University of Chicago Press, Chicago 60637
The University of Chicago Press, Ltd., London
© 1991 by The University of Chicago
All rights reserved. Published 1991
Printed in the United States of America

00 99 98 97 96 95 94 93 92   5 4 3 2

Library of Congress Cataloging-in-Publication Data

Peshkin, Alan.
    The color of strangers, the color of friends : the play of
ethnicity in school and community / Alan Peshkin.
        p.   cm.
    Includes bibliographical references and index.
    ISBN 0-226-66200-4. — ISBN 0-226-66201-2 (pbk.)
    1. Children of immigrants—Education (Secondary)—California—
Case studies.   2. Ethnicity in children—California—Case studies.
3. California—Ethnic relations—Case studies.   4. High school
students—California—Social conditions—Case studies.   I. Title.
    LC3746.5.C2P47   1991
    370.19′342′09794—dc20   90-19765
                                                                              CIP

To my teacher, Wanda Babcock,
to my family, the color of friends,
and to my friends, the color of family

Contents

Preface

Outrage is a matter of history in Riverview and Riverview High School (RHS), the setting for this study of a multiethnic school and community. I explore this history because it provides essential context for understanding Riverview High School today. This school should be understood, for it is the scene of an American success story, albeit not of the Horatio Alger, poor-boy-makes-good type. The school's success is social, not academic, but the rarity of such successes warrants making something of them when they occur. I am pleased to be able to write about a school where strangers and friends are not sorted out by color, where honors and hurrahs are not the exclusive province of a favored few. Would that there were also tales of academic achievement to applaud; I'd return at once to Riverview to track them down and relate the details.

Had I been present in Riverview during the 1975–76 school year rather than the 1985–86 year as I was, I would have had to write about outrage, violence, and disorder, perhaps the greatest share of it ethnicity-based. Ten years later, the *Sturm und Drang* had dissipated, replaced by a much less newsworthy, and much more appreciated, ethnic peace. Thus, it is a relatively quiet story I have to tell; peace, after all, does not provide the stuff of headlines, particularly when it just gradually emerges, almost unnoticed, sans photo opportunities and sound bites.

RHS is home primarily to persons of color. They are black, Mexican, and Filipino, with a very small newcomer group of Southeast Asians. I refer to students as black, rather than African-American, since that was the accepted term at the time of this study. That color at Riverview High School is not a barrier to social interaction I am fully persuaded. And how this has come about I will try to explain. The current salutary status of color is, of course, coincident with the story of ethnic peace. I can describe conditions, I can say what acts preceded what events, and I can underscore what strikes me as the salient features or actions in the story.

I'd prefer to do more than this so I could say as concretely and confidently as one can about complex social events, "If you value this outcome, here is what you ought to do." Unable to write such a prescription, I will nevertheless attest to the possibility that color can be so construed that students, and many parents as well, attend to real rather than ascribed attributes as the basis for who is their friend.

A friend is someone who may be considered—without necessarily being—a suitable mate for one's child or a suitable candidate for political office; a stranger is someone who is not. By extending the concept of friend and stranger, I included all the roles that people could possibly fill with occupants selected on the basis of their ethnicity. For example, consider who is eligible to occupy the social roles of good neighbor, acquaintance, friend, best friend, or mate, and the professional roles of doctor, lawyer, teacher, mayor, or school board member. At times, Riverview residents, young and old, have applied an ethnic criterion as a kind of means test to determine someone's eligibility. The test passed, the person could then be conceptualized as "friend." This designation diminishes one's otherness, one's object-ness, and demands us to accept the burdens (and joys!) of compassion, support, and caring. Persons so conceptualized are not certain to be friends, but now at least they are candidates to become friends, awaiting a judgment that rests on other criteria. And persons so conceptualizing are freed of the opposite burden that comes with holding a group to be strangers.

I didn't go to Riverview in search of a bright spot. I went, as I describe in chapter 1, to explore the play of ethnicity in a school attended by large numbers of students from different ethnic groups. My inquiry began with the question of what the nature of a high school would be that serves a multiethnic community, with no single ethnic group in the majority. In my previous studies, the particular outlook of the relatively homogeneous groups that sent their children to school was reflected in the school's classrooms. Rural Mansfield's school board hired rural-oriented teachers, and Mansfield High School perpetuated the prevailing values and sense of community (Peshkin 1978). Fundamentalist Christian Bethany Baptist Academy did the same on behalf of its host, Bethany Baptist Church (Peshkin 1986). Given what I presumed was Riverview's heterogeneous population, by virtue of its considerable ethnic diversity, I wondered whom RHS served, indeed, whom it could serve? Would it suffer some degree of continuing tension because of an unresolved conflict of values that engendered divergent expectations of the school? Would local authorities in Riverview be pulled and tugged in different educational directions by groups at cross-purposes with each other? Is it farfetched to assume that nonethnic whites and Sicilians and blacks and Mexicans and Filipinos would part company on matters of consequence regarding their children's schooling?

In trying to see how ethnicity operates in the formal and informal life of students and teaches at Riverview High I came upon a bright spot. It pleases me to have found it. By honoring it in the book's title, I do not mean to be underplaying the school's academic failings. They are troubling, and I do discuss them, but they are not unexpected, as we know from the outcomes of education in schools serving poorer youngsters throughout America. Moreover, calling them failings belies the reality of internal comparison. Riverview students have made appreciable progress since its days of turbulence in the 1970s: they attend class more regularly, take school more seriously, score higher on statewide tests, and participate more extensively in school activities. In terms of external comparison, they compete more successfully in county-level events and clearly hold their own academically relative to schools in communities that are equally poor. Success by these measures, however, is not enough. To be sure, it is the basis for local pride, satisfaction, and the sense of being on the way, but the way is truly long and much remains to be done before Riverview High School can celebrate academic victories which approximate those in the social domain.

I first came to Riverview in 1982 when I began my search for a multiethnic site. I looked at six different sites, most of them in southern California. Gordon Cohn and a colleague in the University of Southern California's School of Education arranged my introduction to superintendents of five of the six schools. Such introductions greatly facilitate the researcher's access and I am grateful to have had them.

Riverview was the one place for which I had no introduction. I called the school district's superintendent and received permission to come, first for a two-day visit and later, because Riverview was by then on my short list, for a weeklong visit. All six schools had met my criteria of multiethnicity and of being located in a place small enough to support only one high school. Riverview felt like the right place to be, beginning with the then superintendent, who made all the arrangements I needed to get started. I wrote a letter to the school board seeking approval to spend a full academic year in the high school. The board agreed and the project was ready for serious data collection to begin.

A necessary condition for the implementation of this project was a grant from the Spencer Foundation. As it had with my study of a fundamentalist Christian school, the Spencer Foundation proved to be generous, flexible, and cooperative. I could not ask for finer support. The grant covered my expenses, those of my research associate, Jim

Stanlaw, and the salary of two full-time transcribers. Further support came from a four-year appointment in the University of Illinois' Bureau of Educational Research, which not only provides research time and research assistants, but also outstanding facilitating services from its director, Steven Asher, and its talented secretaries, Carma Diel and Joan Neef. Joan was the lifeline to my university and college during the year I spent in Riverview. By her good work, she helped me to concentrate on doing research. Finally, there are friends and colleagues to thank: Eric Bredo for giving me the idea for this study when I had not even begun the last one; Hank Browne, Vita Browne, Gordon Cohn, Elliot Eisner, Corrine Glesne, Maryann Peshkin, and Nancy Weinberg, who encouraged my work and read and critiqued some or all of my chapters; and June Chambliss and her wonder workers at the word processor. Technophobe that I am, they took my handwritten pages and converted them into legible lines of typesript.

Jim Stanlaw and I shared most data-collecting responsibilities; he tracked down demographic data and I read the local newspaper on microfilm. Jim is particularly adept at working with students who are easily overlooked because they are not leaders or active participants in any part of school life. Their opinions and experiences are worth obtaining, and I'm pleased that Jim did not allow them to be overlooked. Overall, we established a rough division of time, devoting half the school year to participant observation at school and another half to interviewing at school. (This was by no means a hard and fast division.) Accordingly, in the fall semester, we attended classes in every subject-matter department, often returning to observe the same teacher and class at work. We participated as fully as time allowed in the school's curricular and extracurricular activities. The intent was to experience the breadth of activity that occurred in the course of the school year. In the spring semester, we formally interviewed most of our total of about two hundred persons, including teachers, administrators, and counselors; past and present students (varying by ethnic group, age, and academic track); parents (varying by ethnic group); past and present school board members; and other community adults who were or had been active in some phase of public life (e.g., city government and ethnic organizations). We interviewed our out-of-school respondents after school, in the evening, and on weekends. Throughout the year, our efforts to learn about the community of Riverview were generally confined to after-school time.

This book is based on data collected by two white, middle-class males, one in his fifties, the other in his thirties. There may indeed be limitations to what we saw, heard, and understood stemming from our age, sex, and social class. Because I did the selecting, organizing, and writing up of the data, I must take full responsibility for the transformation of the data into this book. Thus it is my version of Riverview's story.

The success of this study depended upon the willingness of people to discuss things they often had never talked about before. To comprehend the nature of school and community, we would ask—sometimes we'd be invited—to enter into the personal lives of our respondents: we wanted to know what their lives were like as student, teacher, parent, native, newcomer, Mexican- or Filipino-American, and the like. Committed to anonymity, I am unable to mention by name either the teachers who ungrudgingly let us sit in their classrooms and return again and again; the several hundred interviewees who on the average we saw for some four sessions; and the many administrators and counselors who, since they do not have free periods, had to make room in their very busy schedules to meet us. In addition, there were secretaries and librarians and others to whom we would say, in one form or another "We need . . . Could you help us with . . . ?" And they did. To all those people I am indebted and profoundly grateful. I began my research feeling that Riverview was the right place to be. I completed it convinced that I had made the right decision. I have returned to Riverview each year since my fieldwork was done in June 1986, and I expect to continue returning.

1

Riverview: The Study, Community, and Stigma

The Study of Ethnicity

At Riverview High School (RHS), color is not the powerfully constraining factor in social interactions that it is almost everywhere else in America. Of course, color is a basis for inclusion and exclusion, but there it is not vested with the negativism typical of other parts of the country. More than this: at RHS, there is an openness to interaction across ethnic boundaries that is cheering to anyone who values an open, integrated society. RHS students revel in this openness; so do I. There is a victory to celebrate at Riverview's high school that is so routine that local people do not take special note of its distinctiveness. I mean to do so in this book as I examine ethnicity as a factor in the historical and contemporary shaping of Riverview's school and community and, moreover, in the creation of a stigma that distorts external perceptions of both school and community.

More than 50 percent of Riverview High School's students are black or Hispanic. Most of them do not drop out, fail, get suspended or expelled, although black and Hispanic students predominate in each of these dismal categories, there as elsewhere. In respect to academic achievement, minority students cannot claim their proportionate place in the school's upper academic track. Riverview High School, in this respect, has done no better and no worse than most American public schools, and this is a sad fact. But it does not dim the school's remarkable social achievement.

By calling attention to the color of the people RHS students call strangers and friends, I emphasize a fact that the students do not: social interactions that normally, elsewhere, occur within an ethnic group, can and routinely do take place across ethnic groups at RHS. This is my major theme. A lesser theme is the persistent, moderate-to-low level of success of black and Hispanic students.

1

Riverview's superintendent of schools, native son Carl Rossi, was himself once a student in the district he now ably administers. He provided me with numerous warm occasions, his coffee pot always ready to pour and his frank words always ready to inform—in response both to questions I thought to ask and those I did not know I should ask. Successively, as we spoke, he would be a young boy growing up in the Riverview of the forties and fifties, a historian, a sociologist, a school administrator, or whatever, ad infinitum. I asked him and everyone else I met, in as many different ways as I could devise, what impact, if any, ethnic diversity has on the life of Riverview's schools. One day he told me:

Our school district—really, sometimes I think we ought to change our name to "Random Sample." If there's ever a report about a multiethnic community, anyone wants to do a study, make a survey, and they need a random sample— that's us. Many urban communities have our kind of mix, but they're too big. We're a nice little size. Look, we've got almost 30 percent black, 20 percent Chicano, 6 or 7 percent Filipino-American. It's a multiethnic community that had some inner-city problems, had a lot of federal dollars coming in, special programs, etc. Larger places, they [i.e., researchers] think they're not going to get any cooperation. They'd get lost in San Francisco or Oakland. "Let's go to Riverview," they say. We get them all the time.

Kind man that he is, he never pointed an accusing finger at me as researcher—and of course, it was not as a random sample of anything that RHS interested me.

Riverview High School is one of the numerous variants of an American high school that local control can create.[1] Indeed, if American schools were subject to the centralized control of a ministry of education, I might find less to study in the school-community relationship that interests me. But they do vary, as I well knew coming to Riverview as I did, fresh from studying a fundamentalist Christian high school that was different in all the ways that a school driven by absolute doctrinal truth can be (Peshkin 1986). In Riverview, I sought a school set in a community where the diversity of ethnicity prevailed, and where ethnic interests manifest themselves in the community's institutional life. Following the exceptional homogeneity of fundamentalist Bethany Baptist Academy, I anticipated considerable heterogeneity in a place where no single group was numerically dominant. It remained to be seen, of course, if my anticipations would be borne out.

---

1. I assume that the prerogatives of most American communities are sufficient to empower them to shape their schools in response to local idiosyncrasies.

I came to Riverview having read that "the persisting facts of ethnicity demand attention, understanding, and accommodation" (Glazer and Moynihan 1970:v), but, I wondered, attention and understanding by whom and accommodation to what in the particular setting of Riverview. I came knowing that though people once "regard[ed] ethnicity as somehow 'Un-American' . . . At present we are busy praising ethnicity out of all proportion" (Pettigrew 1976:15). But would Riverview residents praise or condemn ethnicity, or possibly do both, to different degrees at different times? And I came wondering if Riverview High School would prove to be one of the uncommon places characterized by "institutionalized biracial situations where there is cross-racial friendship [and] racial interdependence" (Pettigrew 1974:16). If so, perhaps there were things worth learning that would apply to other schools and communities.

The Riverview High School that captured my attention certainly possessed the ethnic character that had attracted me to its corner of California in the first place. At the outset of my arrival there in 1982 the statistics existed as a simple matter of record, as data obtainable from the state Office of Instruction in Sacramento. Beyond this record, I learned from the school's old yearbooks that in the yesterday of 1938 the Annes, Williams, Elizabeths, and Richards of Anglo descent attended school with the by then more numerous Rosalies, Anthonys, Salvatores, and Maries of Sicilian descent. By 1948, Mexican Ramonas, Manuels, Carmens, and Luises had joined black Willies, Saundras, Dominiques, and LaShawns, as the Williams and Annes began to leave. Rosalies and Anthonys left later, around 1968—a story worth the telling, as I will do in time—while Filipino Buzons, Cabaddus, Hilados, and Baluyuts increased their presence, with Southeast Asian newcomers, Yong Chu Sims and Lan Phans, as the latest arrivals in Riverview's ethnic procession.

The statistics of Riverview's ethnicity were clear matters of fact, but they remained as flat numbers on the pages of the documents I collected. Not having tried to transform them into three-dimensional figures and faces, I was unprepared for the extraordinary visual diversity that would so impress me on my first visit to Riverview High School and never ceased to impress me until the day I packed up notebooks and tape recorder and returned home to Illinois.

I liked being at Riverview High School. It struck me as a special place, of a sort that did not exist in the America of my father and his friend Art Glass. Art was a bigot. I learned this one day, though never before then had I thought of him or my father or any of their friends in such terms. Art came to visit my father and he was hardly inside the door when he asked, with anger, sarcasm, and irritation in his voice, if we had seen last night's disgusting TV show on which a white master of ceremonies kissed a black actress. Remembering the scene, Art's face contorted, making him look as if he had sipped spoiled milk. Art Glass and my father grew up and lived their lives in one of the many enclosed worlds existing in American society. The worlds did not intersect, except briefly and intermittently in those settings where unskilled labor was needed. I am sure the polychromatic sea of faces at Riverview High would have been reason enough for Art and my father to declare such a school unsuitable for their children.

For me, on the contrary, Riverview High exerted an intense fascination. And because it did, I added further resolve to my commitment to keep track of my subjectivity as I pursued my ongoing interest in school and community in that multiethnic setting. It was an intensification of an earlier awareness I got when, in the course of writing about the fundamentalist Christian school and community, I stumbled upon (and over) the angular contours of my own strong feelings (Peshkin 1985). As a result, I was alerted to the necessity of being mindful—throughout, not at the end of, my inquiry—of what sentiments and values were being evoked as I spent my days immersed in the daily life of Riverview and its high school.[2]

Thus I took note whenever my subjective dispositions were elicited, named them, and organized them into what constitutes the appendix of this volume. To summarize them here would be to express more about my sense of Riverview and Riverview High School than is timely to tell. Much of what I learned about the personal selves that were present in Riverview built upon a central fact of my life: I grew up comfortably, happily, an ethnic child. I attended a public elementary school that was in but not fully of my neighborhood, because the school overlapped a Jewish and a non-Jewish neighborhood. The Bengies, Yossels, Shrooliks, and Chiams I knew at home, became Bernards, Josephs, Irvings, and Harveys at school, and making this home-school shift was basically without strain, since almost everyone's parents spoke English.

We were, as I recall, one person at home, another at school, though these persons were seldom in conflict. Our grandparents were the immigrant generation, but some parents, like my father, had been born abroad and came to America as babies. Thus my friends and I were a

2. Both in this study and in my previous study at fundamentalist Christian Bethany a central aspect of my subjectivity was that I am Jewish. This was not true when I studied a rural school and community; moreover, I do not expect it will necessarily be true in future studies. Different settings and circumstances will evoke different dimensions of one's self; one's subjectivity is situational.

generation removed from the home-school confrontation so characteristic of our parents' past. School irked us primarily when the
Christmas season came and the music teacher had us sing carols. We
balked at "Christ the Lord" and any reference to Jesus, while otherwise
enjoying the melodies, if not the words, of the songs we had to sing. We
never knew we should perhaps be uneasy with "round yon virgin"—I
had no idea what a "yon virgin" was—"mother and child," but we loved
a song in which the three syllables of "gloria" could be melodically extended to eighteen distinct sounds. If anyone I knew felt unpleasantly
different or alienated from the majority society, I retain no memories of
such people. While I knew that being Jewish set me apart from others, I
never wished I were someone else, never envied another group for
being special in a way I'd want to be. It was OK, I thought, to be just who
I naturally was. I was then a seamlessly joined American Jew and figured
that being two things was fine for me and for everyone else, however
their ethnicity happened to be defined and expressed.

Suffice it to say, therefore, that I marveled at the appearance of ethnic
diversity I saw in Riverview; this positive sense undoubtedly will shape
the prose that follows. I join those who believe that value-free research
is a chimera, and who further believe that the researcher's responsibility
is to acknowledge, both to himself and others, how his values have affected his research.

On the Trail of Ethnicity: Research Purposes

In the course of tracking down ethnicity at Riverview High School I
came upon an ordinary, recognizably American school. I saw the boy-
men and girl-women who move in the kaleidoscope of Riverview High,
where some students carry little white teddy bears to which they attach
their earrings and other students carry rubbery squiggles of colored
plastic to which they attach their keys and charms. Students collect and
pore over each other's wallet-size, annually taken photographs, making
of them reverential, fetishlike items that are exchanged and pasted in
albums. Students can judge their popularity by the number they are
asked to give away. They blow bubbles with huge wads of bubble gum,
and they sell candy and jewelry and Christmas decorations to raise money for the myriad causes inspired by class and club needs. The members
of these classes and clubs are enshrined annually in the school yearbook
that serves as the pictorial monument of their adolescent years, storing
away forever the record of each year's good times—the school's academic aspects seldom more than a slight trace in this visual record. That
slight trace may comprise only the group photo of the honor society and

perhaps the messages scrawled on the yearbook's blank spaces where students recall the good times in Miss Doring's English class and the not-so-good times in Mr. Rogosa's post-lunch U.S. history class. Pictured athletes, in both lined-up and action photographs, occupy many pages, forty-eight, to be exact, in the 1985 yearbook. Scholarly activities are less photogenic, and, overall, a less serious enterprise than athletic activities.

Teddy bears and rubbery squiggles and photo exchanges in an institution devoted to learning! Riverview High School's boy-men and girl-women manage to persuade full-grown adults—their teachers, counselors, and administrators—to take seriously what from only a little distance appear to be forms of madness. But after all, these adults have been stewed in a comparable academic pot. Observers from a distance, say from Portugal or Bulgaria, can be forgiven for thinking that what they see is a massive scam perpetrated by collusive adolescents and adults. Local observers know better and otherwise: what appears scamlike is, for better or for worse, the true stuff of American high schools, not all of their stuff, but a lot of it. The play of ethnicity at RHS occurs in an ordinary American high school that in some ways is like many other such schools, but in other ways, quite unlike them.

Having chosen a school characterized by ethnic diversity, I cannot thereby conclude that it is somehow an ethnic school, in the way that a school marked by its devotion to Scripture becomes a Christian school. Ethnicity, unlike Scripture, cannot be seen as a doctrinal thread woven into the whole fabric of a school's formal and informal activities. Still, I reason, devotion to ethnicity, expressed, say, as a commitment to multiculturalism, can be a factor in shaping the school experience. Some advocates may hold their commitment to multiculturalism in a way that compares to the fundamentalist's attachment to Scripture. Barring this degree of attachment, I can imagine the ethnicity of a school expressed in courses, units within courses, clubs, and assemblies.

At RHS, I wondered, in short, if its educators would assume an implicit or explicit mission to take account of their students' ethnicity, to respect and reinforce it when and where they can, so that they could serve the cause of cultural diversity by contributing to ethnic maintenance. In an early visit to Riverview, before I went to live there for a full year of fieldwork, I interviewed an older Mexican couple whose children are graduates of RHS, with children of their own. They spoke of coming from Mexico and of getting married and raising a family in Riverview. I was struck by how being Mexican shapes their sense of themselves. Comfortably, unregrettably American, they still always spoke Spanish with each other, ate Mexican food, supported Mexican causes, and felt

Mexican, albeit not exclusively. Four of their five children, however, married Anglos. Did they care? No, they answered. Did they try to raise their children to do otherwise? Again, no. At this point, the Gomezes began to squirm a bit, aware, as they knew I was, that while they had presented themselves strongly in ethnic terms, they sounded indifferent to the place of ethnicity in their children's identity. Struck by this apparent incongruity, I wondered about the tug between home and school that many families, such as the Gomezes, may have experienced. Who did their children think they were when they went to school, and who did their school encourage them to think they are? I wondered, also, if RHS educators have continued the historic Americanizing mission of our schools. Do they see schools essentially as means to serve the cause of unity by emphasizing those common learnings, language, and beliefs that lead to mainstream socialization, if not to assimilation? Of course, I allow for the possibility that educators value both causes—unity and diversity.

Psychologist Gordon Allport figured that "people adhere to their own families, clans, ethnic groups, [because] the self could not be itself without them. . . . There is no need to postulate a 'consciousness of kind' (1954/1958:29). South Asian–born Ramana, a senior boy at RHS, says he is American. Who are his kind? Do his natal kind have a place in the shaping of his identity? Is it possible that "what is familiar tends to become a value" (ibid.), and the familiar kind at RHS for Ramana and others is American—generic adolescent American—in a way that transcends family, clan, and ethnic group? Accordingly, I will examine what is familiar at RHS and what students and teachers see to value with respect to ethnicity. For example, do students suppress their ethnic selves in a swamp of adolescent concerns in order to be accepted by their peers? Does teacher awareness go beyond understanding the linguistic expression of ethnicity that necessitates special language instruction, to considering what implications the ethnic diversity of their students has for the shaping of school life? Further, what does the daily reality of RHS communicate about who is a full-fledged American? What students learn in response to this question of legitimacy will affect how they visualize their political, economic, and social prerogatives throughout their lives. I will report on student responses to my queries about whether they were subject to name-calling, prejudice, and discrimination; about whether their ethnicity affected their popularity with students and with whom they socialized; and about whether they felt, to the same degree as other students, that RHS was their school. Diverse ethnic groups are juxtaposed at RHS, but I wondered if they had "the type of contact that leads people to *do* things together [in a way that] is likely to result in changed attitudes" (ibid.:264), relative to attitudes that historically have prevailed in the United States. Are students racially separate or together (Pettigrew 1974) is a question that seems especially appropriate to ask at multiracial RHS.

I thought about this question when I read a *New Yorker* article on seventy-four-year-old black trumpeter Roy Eldridge. Looking back, Eldridge recalled the "fun and praise of his performing days" and thought a fifty-year career was "long enough. Anyway, I found out the main doors were always locked. *The color thing*" (emphasis mine) (Balliett 1985: 154). Three little words capture the residue of a lifetime of rejection and denial, the anger now squeezed out, Eldridge's frustration and irritation, however, readily inferred. Color sets barriers between person and desire.

As I learned more about Riverview, I realized that blacks, albeit far from a majority in either school or community, appeared to have disproportionate importance in the perceptions that both outsiders and insiders have of Riverview and its high school. This was one of several matters that emerged after I became more familiar with Riverview. Others were the complexity of cross-ethnic contacts and sentiments, the variable nature of adolescent identity, and the universalist orientation of Riverview High School, with its concomitant pressures to conform and Americanize. Such matters, though not part of my original research plans, are too important not to get treated along with the matters I planned to investigate.

In response to the question, "Why did you pick Riverview for your study?" I would answer, "Because it is a very American place." By this I meant that it was socially complex, in the way that American cities are, containing people diverse in occupation, outlook, and, for my purpose, ethnicity. Riverview, in short, was different from the socially simpler places I'd been before, two of them rural, one fundamentalist Christian.

I thought that ethnic diversity would establish conditions in which it would be hard for teachers either to receive or to maintain a clear mandate regarding whose values to reinforce, whose lives to reflect. Ethnicity was my filter, my yardstick for selecting and rejecting what was available to be experienced and known in Riverview and Riverview High School. If I did not have a specific story to tell—and I did not, in the sense of something to prove or proclaim—I did have a focus. It remained intact throughout my years of fieldwork, which included three one-week visits and one two-week visit in 1983–84, four two-week visits in 1984–85, the full academic year in 1985–86, and thereafter, much thinner contact through a subscription to the local newspaper, telephone calls, and brief visits.

Of course, with ethnicity at the center of my attention, I would not be equally available to perceive and do justice to other possible foci that might invite scrutiny. While flooding one area with light—that of ethnicity—I left others in the dark, perhaps even precluding awareness of their existence. This, I believe, is unavoidable. To give focus to one's investigation is, of necessity, to sharpen the image of one thing, to diminish the image of some others, and to omit altogether still others. A way of seeing is also a way of not seeing.

Most of what I will discuss hereafter relates to my central concern with following the play of ethnicity at RHS. My pursuit of ethnicity was during a relatively quiet time both in Riverview and elsewhere in America, particularly compared with the noisy times of the 1960s and 1970s, when minority issues were daily fare on the front pages of newspapers. I use "play" because it suggests a range of behaviors, from frivolous to serious, that fits the diverse ways that individuals and groups may manifest their ethnicity. Notwithstanding the appearance of diversity, I wondered if a corresponding diversity of belief and behavior were at work to shape the life of RHS. As far as I am aware, my commitment to observing the play of ethnicity carried neither a responsibility nor a wish to find events that cast it in a favorable light, as if I must insure that it is beyond faulting. Just what sentiments my experiences in Riverview might evoke I knew would emerge in time.

At Bethany Baptist Academy, the site of my study of a fundamentalist Christian school, I found myself playing a game I called "When Would a Visitor Know?" By this question I meant to ask what an outsider must see and hear to confirm that he is in an evangelical-fundamentalist Christian school, one committed to integrating Scripture with everything that happens there, as opposed to a school whose Christian identification is limited to bulletin boards, mandatory chapel periods, and prayers before classes begin.

Similarly, by following the play of ethnicity, I hoped to see what it would take to establish ethnicity as a central factor in the operation of RHS. Would I find interests, opportunities, problems, social contacts, and perceptions that derived from ethnicity? Would I see it as a persisting factor? Or would I see it as something that pops up incidentally and unpredictably, an occasional occurrence of no deep consequence, possibly indeed a factor that is ignored when its implications should be heeded?

Specifically, I was interested in learning about educational ethnicization, that is, how far the school had gone, if at all, in making decisions based on ethnicity: Were there entire courses devoted to ethnic studies? Were subject matter and instructional materials chosen with an eye to their ethnic content? Did homework and tests focus on ethnic-related issues, events, groups, and individuals? Were assemblies, bulletin boards, and other forms of recognition devoted to ethnic occasions, holidays, and heroes? Did teachers perceive the ethnicity of their students as a factor in planning lessons, disciplining, counseling, or establishing an effective relationship with students? Moreover, was ethnicity a fact of any consequence in student elections, selection for athletic teams, or in any of the range of decisions for minor and major positions of responsibility and honor that any school makes in the course of a school year? I had no criteria in mind for deciding where the border was between high and low ethnicization. I figured that a year of observing, interviewing, and collecting school documents would prove enlightening on this point.

Furthermore, I was interested in learning about social ethnicization, which relates to the extent to which ethnicity shapes the nature of interpersonal relationships. Specifically, who did students walk to class with, tease, sit next to, party and flirt with, fight, date, marry, play jokes on, and so on down the range of interactions that make American high schools special in nonacademic terms? Again I figured that observation and interviewing would provide some answers.

Were I to learn, via my pursuit of ethnicity, that RHS had been ethnicized, I would answer the question I raise about any school I study— "Whom does the school serve?"—by saying, "The school serves its many ethnic groups by being appropriately sensitive to supporting the ethnic identity of their children. The school serves traditional values, for which parents will be appreciative. The school has not succumbed to relentless Americanization, with its crushing homogenization." This judgment would assume that ethnicization characterized the school in a prominent but not exclusive way, that it occurred within an otherwise recognizably American curriculum.

Were I to learn that social relations within the school had been ethnicized, I would then have to conclude that a capacity for defensive, group mobilization was extant, that prejudice and divisiveness accordingly prevailed, and that much of what is ugly and depressing about American society was being perpetuated. This judgment assumes that ethnicity as a basis for pride and identity is constructive, but when it fosters intergroup hostility and erects barriers, it is damaging. In short, I view ethnicization as positive academically and as negative socially.

By placing ethnicity at center stage in my inquiry I do not mean to claim that it offers the paramount explanation for all that goes on at RHS. It need not be paramount to be important. That ethnicity persists in American society, assuming variable forms and intensities, makes its

play fascinating to observe. I do so mindful that social class, gender, religion, generations of residence in this country, personality, and situational circumstances not only must be taken into account but may be of
greater consequence.[3] These factors, unsurprisingly, not only are present at Riverview and RHS, they often are inextricably linked to
ethnicity. Nonetheless, I follow ethnicity, never meaning to suggest that
if one knows about it, one knows everything that matters, but fully
meaning to suggest that if one does not know about ethnicity, one may
fail to recognize some of the things that matter daily, enduringly, though
differentially, in the life of a multicultural school and community. To see
our complex world only in simple terms is to do it injustice, but to take
one of its terms and use it as a filter through which to view its complexity
may be a contribution to grasping its complexity.

Much referred to here but still unclarified, ethnicity must be discussed so it is at least anchored in a few images that I can expect to use
consistently in what follows. Ethnicity is defined in multifarious ways,
taking its place alongside other words—*values, democracy, freedom*—
whose multiple uses at the hands of a multitude of writers leave one to
wonder if they are examining the same entity. I certainly will not add to
the confusion by offering a new definition. I find sense, rather, in a pragmatic approach that asks what conceptions are useful for understanding
the phenomena that I experienced in Riverview's high school and
community.

Ethnicity, Acculturation, and Assimilation

To Parsons, an ethnic group is one whose members "both with respect to
their own sentiments and those of nonmembers, have a distinctive identity . . . rooted in some kind of a distinctive sense of history" (1975:54).
Isajiw's definition, which complements Parsons, sees ethnics as "an involuntary group of people who share the same culture . . . [and] who
identify themselves and/or are identified by others as belonging to the
same involuntary group" (1974:122). His qualification of "involuntary"
excludes service or interest groups which "are not a product of the basic
socialization process" (p. 121). Ethnic groups have boundaries, shaped
by those inside and outside the group, that serve to define, exclude, and
include (Barth 1969).

Acculturation, the process of taking on the behavior and values of the
dominant culture, is preliminary to and anticipates assimilation, the

---

3. I do so also mindful of those who for different reasons see grounds for downplaying
the importance of ethnicity (see Kilson 1975; Selakovich 1978; and Steinberg 1981).

process wherein the boundaries between groups diminish and people become incorporated into the dominant society. Incorporation can take place in different ways and to different degrees (Yinger 1981).

People manifest different behavior in different situations and at different times of their life (Kiefer 1974; Horowitz 1975; Keyes 1981). Okamura, quoting Paden (1970), writes that "situational ethnicity is premised on the observation that particular contexts may determine which of a person's identities or loyalties are appropriate at a point in time" (Okamura 1981:425). Given role and other constraints, one is never perfectly free to switch behavior, but switching clearly occurs (note code switching, for example, by bilingual speakers), giving ethnicity a contingent nature. "The actor," writes Okamura, "may consider it in his interests to obscure his ethnic identity in a given situation so that the relationship proceeds in terms of other social statuses he holds" (p. 455), such as sex, age, occupation, or class. In a pluralistic, open society like that of the United States, individual choice operating in a context of "competing universes" weakens the impact of ethnicity (Glazer and Moynihan 1970).

Thus, although it may be possible to identify someone reliably as belonging to a particular ethnic group, it is necessary to be cautious about the meanings that follow this identification. Acculturation, a response to the need to adapt to the ways of the dominant culture, always occurs; it is virtually inevitable. The extent of the need is variable and situational. Holding on to one's ethnically distinctive ways of thinking, acting, and believing represents a judgment, sometimes conscious, sometimes not, about the personally necessary limits of assimilation, where the imperatives of absorption may be denied, its opportunities possibly forgone. For some people, ethnicity operates as no more than an accent to their lives, providing a flavor, a comfortable, familiar quality to some occasions. Special food, music, dance, and costumes are examples of such accents. At this low level of ethnic expression, accents are like souvenirs that may be trotted out as needed for public or private use and display. "Hill's devotion to mass was one of the few souvenirs he had kept of Ireland. It was still reassuring," writes author Ernest Gann of a character in his novel Of Good and Evil (1963:14). Souvenirs are important; we make an effort to hold on to them and we often put them away, sometimes for long periods, because they do not occupy a central place in our lives. We might dislike—and be sad about—their loss, should it occur, but we would hardly grieve, because they are not salient in the set of elements that compose our survival. For some other people, often non-ethnics, ethnicity is a basis for financial opportunity. They turn the special food, music, dance, and costumes into ethnic chickenfeed that appeals to customers and audiences.

For still other people, ethnicity operates in a decidedly different way: more than adding souvenirs or chickenfeed, it provides directives regarding what issues to be tough and tender about; when to be shamed and chauvinistic, angry and elated, proud and defiant; and how we will spend our money and where we will pass our Friday nights and Sunday mornings. When ethnicity operates these ways, it engages us at the "deepest psychological level" and is thereby tied to our "sense of survival" (DeVos 1975:17).

Somewhere between the poles of ethnicity as mere accent and ethnicity as defining personal meaning is where I will expect to see it manifest in the behavior of Riverview's young and old.

Ethnicity and Class

In regard to class, or socioeconomic status (SES, as it will be designated hereafter), Gordon writes that it refers to a hierarchy of status groups that differ in terms of wealth, income, and political power (1978:123–24). SES more than ethnicity has figured in social science research of the past, with SES more typically used by sociologists and ethnicity by anthropologists.

In the past fifteen years, a resurgent interest in ethnicity has generated many studies. One senses a concern among some social scientists to legitimate ethnicity as a research variable (see Greeley and McGready 1974, for example), but ethnicity need not either equal or surpass the explanatory power of SES to warrant a central place in a study of American schools. Indeed, the resort to dichotomous thinking—either class or ethnicity, as though they were in competition—is unproductive.

To summarize what clearly will be a continuing debate among social scientists, Rothschild has established ethnicity as an explanatory variable apart from class (1981), and Kobrin and Goldscheider as one that always is linked with class, since all ethnic groups are stratified by SES distinctions (1978:3–4). Bonacich and Modell usefully concluded, based on their study of Japanese-Americans, that ethnicity and SES are two different forms of solidarity that "typically cut across each other" (1980:2), and that their relative importance is an empirical question (see also Gordon 1978:134–36). I share their perspective.

Contemporary Riverview

Riverview is situated between a large river and a spread of low, gently rolling hills. It is neither a city on the make nor a city that has made it. Surrounded by both types of cities, Riverview residents, from civic and elected leaders to business people to ordinary citizens, clearly want to do better. They want growth, progress, development—though, of course, they do not necessarily agree about what the components of each should be. Some Riverview residents want marinas, boutiques, and grand restaurants, others want functioning street lights and un-broken curbs and sidewalks, and still others just want to make it through the day. Those at the marina end of the dream continuum give the impression of racing against time in a world of plans and proposals, outside money, deadlines, and hopes for achieving a critical mass of self-per-petuating civic success.

In the nearly abandoned business section of Riverview's old down-town, once the shopping hub for the area surrounding Riverview, there is a first-class Mexican restaurant. One day its owner became so irritated with the damage to his customers' cars parked on the unsafe streets sur-rounding his restaurant that he threatened publicly to move to Corinth, Riverview's rival neighboring city. He did not move, then or later, but he was clearly vexed. His threat reflected the fear of many that the promise of new business, new residents, new money, might forever be aborted by the lack of safety, the unsightly mess left by failed urban-renewal efforts, and the shortsightedness of downtown landowners.

Incorporated in 1903, just about the time that its coal-mining indus-try shut down, Riverview had a population at the time of its first census in 1910 of about 2,600. Thereafter its population spurted: 1920—5,200; 1930—8,600; 1940—8,200; 1950—13,500; 1960—17,000; 1970—21,400; 1980—36,000; and at present, about 44,000. The current build-ing boom of new homes and apartments promises to exhaust all available land, leaving only the decaying and dead areas in the old part of town as likely space for residential and business expansion.

Cities, like people, get their sense of self from comparisons, so that the answer to the question, "How are we doing?" comes from how we have done relative to some set of others. In the case of small cities, that set of others is likely to be the other cities in one's county. Thus, when Riverview assesses its population growth, often considered one index of progress, it can see a rising curve. But the growth of Riverview's neigh-bors has been far more impressive, a fact all the more galling because most of them are younger and were lagging well behind Riverview until 1950, after which time Riverview grew only modestly and they grew apace.

A fact of consequence for its growth was that by 1950, 7.9 percent of Riverview's population of 13,500 was, as the census noted, "nonwhite." In the 1980 census, the population of the whole country was 9 percent black, 9 percent Hispanic, and 5 percent Asian; in the same census, Riverview's population of 36,000 was 20 percent black, 18 percent Hispanic, and 7 percent Asian. It had the second lowest white population in the county, continuing a trend that had begun by the time of the 1930 census. Riverview's factories attracted minorities and the city did not prevent them from settling in town.

In recent years, Riverview's newcomers have included blacks, Mexicans, and Filipinos, a contingent of Southeast Asians, but even more "whites," defined, as the designation is used locally and as I, therefore, will use it, to include only persons of European origin. These new whites are commuters, a peripatetic lot who seek the good life in California and the best housing bargain they can find, notwithstanding that their new and latest home often is a vast distance from their workplace. They drive so far and for so long that they may be thought of not only as residents of Riverview but also of the clogged-up, often gridlocked freeways that span home and work.

Riverview has worked hard to attract the white newcomers, its leaders feeling the city has done its share for that part of the American population whose income is at or below poverty level. The city has attracted young families whose income places them well above poverty level. One such family was featured in a 1984 newspaper series on Riverview newcomers. The parents were in their midthirties, junior college–educated. The husband worked full-time, the wife part-time. They had moved from a $39,500 house in an "over-the-hill" city (places literally located beyond the hills that surround Riverview), sold it for $42,000, and moved to a $102,000 home in Riverview. The central fact, however, insofar as modifying the image and economic face of Riverview is concerned, is that this family's "expenses usually wipe out their monthly take-home income of $2,200." In comparative terms, Riverview's low-priced housing is striking. In 1985, its typical home price was $99,000, compared to $105,000, $130,000, $155,000, $185,000, and $245,000 in five nearby cities. The low price of Riverview housing was made even more appealing by subsidized mortgage interest rates and lower down payments. With its most recently built higher-cost housing projects, the city hopes to attract newcomers with disposable income, that is, persons with money left over after food, clothing, housing, and medical costs have been met.

The white newcomers have never experienced Riverview's golden age; they are not attached to the city's past. City leaders wonder if they will become attached to its present and future. "They're buying in a little bit," observes a school board member. "The newcomers are going to be the backbone of Riverview," says a city council member. "I respect the dues paid by the older people, but to bring about change, you're going to need new ideas." If many treat the city as just the place they sleep in, not yet joining the PTA or voting in local elections, they still have become a factor in all aspects of Riverview life, with their greatest impact yet to come.

One such impact results from the fact of their numbers. Natives no older than thirty say they remember a time when they knew everyone. What they mean is that since Riverview grew beyond the village status of its early, post-incorporation days, knowing everyone meant, at least, that you recognized a person or knew someone to whom they were related. We lose that sense of knowing everyone when population increases. Nevertheless, in Riverview in the 1980s I heard many of the same caveats that I'd heard and read about in small midwestern villages: "There are no secrets." And "When you're talking to somebody, you're talking to somebody's cousin. If you know those two things, you can live in Riverview." I also heard about the how-dare-they outsiders, those newcomers who dared to speak out in public meetings, who had criticisms and suggestions to offer, without (as seen by those who felt they belonged) having yet earned the right to speak out.

The strongest sense of community prevails among Riverview's native Sicilians, who assemble annually, as they have done since 1979, for their West Side Reunion. All reunion participants once lived within a clearly bounded neighborhood, where now there are poor people, transients, recently arrived minorities, the incipient marina set, and only a trace of Sicilians, old folks unable or unwilling to move. The reunion does what such occasions always do: it reminds those who have left what the old days were like and those who have stayed what they still have in common. Sicilians are a subcommunity within Riverview; overall, the city's other ethnic groups do not enjoy comparable feelings of a shared past and of belonging.

Nonethnic linkages that can join residents also exist. For all native and longtime residents of whatever ethnic origin there is a history and a space they share that transcends the distinctions of their ethnic group. They have attended the same schools, notably the same high school, and experienced the affiliating affect peculiar to American schools. The school colors and nickname and song and football team, all internalized during their memorably vulnerable adolescence, attach students in ways that facilitate developing and perpetuating a sense of community.

In 1986, Riverview had 1,160 unemployed residents, the same percentage (6.8) as in the nation but above the county's 4.8 percent. The city had 15,990 employed residents. Many worked in the dozen or so manufacturing plants, nonlocally-owned, located on Riverview's periphery. These are of the type—steel, chemicals, paper, glass, etc.—that nationwide have suffered declining revenues. Of about 5,400 jobs in these plants in 1979, fewer than half existed five years later.

By contrast, businesses inside Riverview once were almost all locally owned. The prevailing view is that this fact is important in explaining why the once economically preeminent Riverview lost out to its neighbors. It is a story of the shopping mall that got away. In the words of a prominent political figure:

The natives had so much control over property they were able to keep people from coming into Riverview. Everything was mostly locally owned. I remember vividly, maybe around '55 or '56, a developer from Van Nuys wanted to come in and open up a huge shopping center right there near the highway. He wanted to buy that property. The town just fought that guy tooth and nail and he just finally packed his bags and left.

Today, Riverview has no mall that attracts outside shoppers. All its neighbors do.

What Riverview does have are statistics that demonstrate its comparative disadvantages: no matter if the measure is mean or medium household income, Riverview's is at least 20 percent lower than that of its nearest neighbors, and of the county as a whole. Another contrast is in number of residents over twenty-five with a college education—11 percent in Riverview, compared to 26 percent in the county, and about half the percentage of all but one of its nearest neighbors. In short, in regard to these and the other countable matters that are within the ever-expanding domain of the census, Riverview has less of the good things (jobs, money, education) and more of the bad (poverty, poor health, poor housing) than most cities in its county.

What Riverview also has that is not revealed in its statistics are a vigorous chamber of commerce, an imaginative city manager, and a core of people who deplore the image of their city reflected in its statistics and in the old-order outlook of those who kept the mall out of Riverview. The new-order leaders energetically seek enterprising outsiders who can contribute to an economically viable city whose primary problems are not those of decline—prostitution, loitering, drugs, and crime, but of growth—acceptable waste-disposal means, assured sources of clean water, and effective access to work. For the time being, Riverview is dealing with both sets of problems, for both sets stand side by side, revealing the city's two faces.

"Editor," begins Judy Bojorquez's letter of September 4, 1987. She is pleased with the "revitalization" in downtown Riverview (where she has lived for ten years), the renovation of old buildings, and the marina complex of condominiums and berths for boats.

But move over a street or two . . . and see if anything is "on the mend." Dilapidated homes are the rule and I suspect the occupants are glad to have them. It's hard to be against our main street's overpass and underpass project which will benefit everybody. On the other hand, Riverview's low income citizenry has its nose daily rubbed in a massive project patently only for the very well-to-do. A rash of burglaries . . . opened my eyes to the drug and crime problems. In my own case, in addition to the TV and microwave, the thieves took . . . milk, bread, lunch meat, cereal, frozen juices, and even packets of Kool-ade. People so desperate . . . are really at the end of their ropes.

Having struck a note of compassion for desperate thieves, she urges her city to remember that the underprivileged outnumber the boat owners.

Evidence of a new order in economic affairs is clearer than of a new order in political affairs, yet politics also shows the impact of newcomers. In 1983, reform-minded oldtimers joined forces with newcomers in a recall ouster of four of the five city council members, the surviving member remaining in office by a margin of 116 with over eight thousand votes cast. The issue was using, and countenancing the use of, low-interest funds for which they were ineligible. Implicated, also, were the chief of police and city manager, both of whom retain their offices today. In subsequent elections, newcomers of a throw-out-the-rascals outlook gained two seats. Though they have consistently failed to win a majority, it is perfectly clear that the two new members are part of a chorus of voices demanding to be heard; they speak through new neighborhood associations, with no ties or allegiances to old cliques, clubs, bosses, or tradition, however defined. They are nonethnic whites; their affiliations are to nonethnic churches and service clubs, when they are affiliated at all.

Nonetheless, the traditional way to get elected to the city council still works. It involves touching base with the ethnic organizations of the blacks, Mexicans, and Filipinos, appearing before them if they have a candidate's night, getting their prominent members to be included on the paid ad that comes out shortly before election, and signing on a campaign manager and workers whose presence suggests the support of their ethnic group.

Though there are Italian organizations,[4] they do not operate actively in the political arena. Thus, to obtain Sicilian votes, a candidate must work through family networks:

4. Most of the Italian population in Riverview originated in Sicily. An older generation typically referred to themselves as "Sicilians." Local ethnic organizations had and have "Italian" as their ethnic designation. As terms of identity, both Sicilian and Italian are used interchangeably in Riverview. I will most often use "Sicilian" to refer to that group's ethnic identity because it is the term I heard most frequently.

So you go see the head of the family, talk to him. And then, if he likes you, he'll say, "OK, I'll talk to the family." See, like the heads of families here have five-six daughters, five-six son-in-laws, six grandchildren, and lots of aunts, uncles, cousins, stuff like that.

There are "heavyweights" among the Sicilians, one of whom can deliver a reputed 2,000 to 2,500 votes, sufficient in past days to secure a victory, though not today. And the Italian organizations, Sons of Italy and Italian-American Club, "don't play hard politics, [but] you got to touch base with them, go to the functions periodically."

The ethnic dimension of politics is not in itself indicative of either old- or new-order politics, except, perhaps, in the case of the Sicilians, who until recently dominated Riverview's political scene. Since the ethnic groups have never been monolithic, two persons of the same ethnicity have run at the same time and split their group's vote. Loyalty to group has had too many interpretations ever to lead to a successful falling in line by voters within any ethnic group. Still, observers estimate, candidates with the "right" endorsement may get 2,000 to 3,000 Sicilian votes, 1,000 black votes, 600 to 800 Mexican votes, and maybe 200 Filipino votes. The results of Riverview's ethnic structure were revealed in a 1982 study of "influentials" by a reporter from the local newspaper who used the reputational method of sociologist Floyd Hunter (1953). Of twenty-four people nominated as influentials, four were black, two were Mexican, and none were Filipinio. The top three were identified as Italian, as were twelve others of the twenty-four. Only three of the twenty-four were non-Sicilian whites.[5] Five years after this 1982 study of Riverview influentials, controversy over the location of a bowling alley was framed in the polarizing language of a crass commercial venture versus concern for the quality of life. Bowling-alley proponents accused their antagonists of enlisting the support of the city's "most powerful person, . . . head of the most powerful and dangerous political machine that has ever existed in local politics." This person is a woman who in 1982 would not have been known to anyone included in the nominating process that produced the twenty-four influentials. She is a newcomer who heads a new subdivision's neighborhood association, participated in the 1983 recall election, endorsed the two newcomers who got elected, and symbolizes the newcomers' "threat."

This small group of people [concluded the bowling-alley proponent] is trying to remake our city in the images they see as the future. I do not believe the

5. The term "non-Sicilian white," in local and general California usage, excludes Mexicans and all other persons considered to be Caucasian but not of European descent. I am so using it in this volume.

majority of Riverview residents want this. If we don't act now and stand up
and say no to machine politics, we will have no one to blame but ourselves
when they take control.

The hysterical tone of the reference to the newcomers' "machine"
politics suggests at least that Riverview's latest wave of residents is visible and their impact is palpable, if not worrisome, to older residents.
The enduring quality of Riverview's ethnic factor, however, is evident in
the intention of the county supervisor (whose district includes Riverview) to go to Cuernavaca, Mexico, for an intensive course in Spanish; in
the candidates nominated for Citizen of the Year—a Filipino woman, a
Sicilian man, a Mexican woman, a non-Sicilian white man, and a black
man; and in the accusation by the chief of police that the behavior of one
of his police officers can be explained by the officer's prejudice against
people of the "Italian heritage."

I thought a lot about racial togetherness and separation when, in the
early months of my fieldwork, I learned of the extent to which both
Riverview and Riverview High School were stigmatized by neighboring
communities, all of them wealthier and with significantly smaller minority populations. Outsiders perceive Riverview as poor, black, and crime-
ridden, and Riverview High School as a dangerous place, disposed to
race riots. An association between blacks and crime in Riverview could
be seen in the "police notes" of an ordinary day's coverage in the local
newspaper: sixty-seven-year-old man robbed of $90.00 by two men
"described as black, in their mid to late 20's"; pizza-parlor employee
robbed by two men "described as black" who jumped him from behind;
woman's purse stolen from chair in restaurant by a suspect "described as
black."

Riverview's "stigma" seems to be woven into much that happens in
school and community. Once beyond the subject of football, where
Riverview has long been successful, a thick vein of insecurity prevails.
As I learned more about Riverview and its stigmatization, I knew I
would have to explore its negative image and uncover how it may be
affecting the behavior of students at school.

The Community Stigmatized

When Riverview students and adults refer to a condemning "they," they
mean over-the-hill students and adults, usually from the cities of Corinth, Fairview, Dunbar, and Greenbriar, whose words and deeds are
persistent reminders of Riverview's stigmatized status. The point is not
whether Riverview deserves to be stigmatized, but that it is, notwith-

standing the protests of residents that they are the victims of historical events whose onus will not disappear, and of small facts blown up into overgeneralized "truths."

The characteristics seen as stigma-worthy attributes of Riverview and Riverview High School not only describe, they also discredit and devalue. They are the differences that over-the-hill others see as distinguishing themselves, the good ones or friends, from Riverview residents, the bad ones or strangers. These differences stain and contaminate, marking Riverview in ways that the stigmatizers see as unattractive and undesirable, if not hazardous to themselves.

I do not elaborate the matter of stigma in order to invite sympathy or special understanding for a beleaguered community and school; I heard no one in Riverview discuss their stigma in these terms. I do so because it is a central fact of life for the youngsters who grow up in Riverview and for the adults who settle there. It is a fact that residents repeatedly pressed upon me. (I even heard it applied personally by a Fairview shopkeeper who, having learned I was in Riverview on a research project, wondered if I'd gone there to study pollution or crime in the streets.) It is a "bad rep," as RHS students would say, attributable to the disagreeable persistence of racism in American society.

That denigration that is the lot of the stigmatized touches young and old, rich and poor, white and nonwhite. One buys immunity from it only by denying one's status as resident of Riverview or as student of Riverview High School. But even denial might not work, as the experience of a Mexican student suggests. He had gone with friends to a teen dance hall in Dunbar. While walking around outside the building, he said, someone shouted, "'Go back to Riverview where you belong.' I don't know how he knew. I never saw him before. I figured they know how we dress."

Residents repeatedly experience the stigma. "Just like we went to lunch the other day," a woman told me. "Where are you from?" she was asked. "Riverview. 'Riverview!' I know what they're thinking. I want to punch them in the nose." At a high school baseball game played away from home Riverview fans directed some outbursts toward the umpires. A Riverview woman heard one of the umpire's reactions.

The umpire came over to where I was sitting. I think he thought I was from Dunbar. Said something about Riverview kids and that the adults are worse. He was just really throwing daggers. I looked at him and I thought, "He can't say that, he's an umpire. Second, he's talking about my town." I said, "I beg your pardon, sir. I'm from Riverview. I resent what you're saying. You have a few hecklers in the crowd, but that's a baseball game. I resent you telling me

that these Riverview people, which I am a Riverview people, that we're all
that way." I says, "People like you give us a bad name." I also heard the umpires
say they needed an escort to get out of there.

The stigmatizing of Riverview is an event of both past and present
times. Sarah Rasmussen, born and raised about fifty miles from Riverview, came to teach in Riverview in 1943. Her grandfather warned her
not to take the job. She stayed for forty years, notwithstanding her
grandfather's admonitions about the danger to a young woman of being
employed in a rough, tough town.

There were rough and tough Welsh coal miners before the Sicilian
fisherman, and after them came other rough and tough newcomers—
blacks from the South. It is the presence of blacks in Riverview that provides the basis for the city's stigmatization. Says a black Riverview
resident of about sixty years, "It goes back as far back as I go in my lifetime because Riverview was always a community with a lot of minorities.
We had blacks, and Corinth, Dunbar, and Fairview didn't have any."

It may not take many incidents to establish a place as truly rough and
tough; once the reputation exists, a few intermittently recurring incidents may suffice to nourish the reputation. Grist for the mills of stigma
was provided in 1962: "Two Policemen Injured During Grid Game
Fracas," ran a headline in the *Daily Herald*. An editorial followed this
story. It commented on the fights in local parks and at high school games:

Riverview is not a jungle; it is a community of law and order. . . . A general
tightening up of discipline and privileges is needed now before we wake up
some morning to a headline tragedy that will drive more residents and businesses out of this city.

Thus did "rough and tough" get reinforced.

Beth Garrett did not let her daughter "attend school on the day of
rumored trouble" that followed a fight on April 21, 1967, that had "racial
overtones." Rumors flew in all directions, a sense of panic was in the air,
and the *Daily Herald's* editorial begged for calm, for parents to control
their children, for "Negro ministers" to urge their parishioners to block
outside gangs from transgressing Riverview's boundaries, and more:

Residents verbally blasted their town to the published delight of its neighbors
who, basking in their white bigotry, made hay of both facts and rumors . . .
and they undoubtedly dissuaded an unknown number of people from moving
here.

As the writers of both editorials commented, for many years residents
and businessmen did get driven away and prospective residents and

businessmen did not come. These twin phenomena continue to plague Riverview today, despite strenuous efforts to promote a counterforce of progress.

From the time residents are old enough to travel beyond Riverview for shopping, recreation, meetings, education, or socializing, they encounter put-downs. These put-downs assume numerous forms, but they do not vary in tone. At county meetings RHS teachers meet colleagues who are incredulous that anyone goes to RHS to teach and stays there. Riverview adults attend regional meetings of national organizations. Other chapter members are incredulous that anyone as respectable-looking as Mr. or Mrs. X lives in Riverview. Students belonging to a program for youth educators attend a meeting at a nearby college. For some reason, they discuss their respective stereotypic views of each others' school. RHS students, according to the stereotype, are mostly black, poor, dumb, in gangs, and great at basketball. An RHS student at this meeting said,

I told them how it really was. I love living in Riverview. I've grown up here. What can I say? I feel comfortable here. I can't say I've never been ashamed to live in Riverview because at that meeting I felt really low, kind of like I didn't belong there.

Riverview residents, natives and newcomers alike, are fully capable of stigmatizing from within, though they do this selectively because the city has no dearth of boosters willing to swing verbal cudgels at all detractors. The focus of local stigmatizing has the same too-familiar targets: RHS academic standards—"You can't ignore the test scores. I know there are exceptions, but I think it's ridiculous to send your kid there and think he's going to be the exception"; blacks—"I don't really consider myself prejudiced, but when I go to the grocery store . . . and some black people look a lot more meaner than other people . . ."; rowdy—"You walk down the hall and a lot of people will be screaming and stuff. You can go to other schools and they won't do that."

That teachers are like other people is no surprise. Thus, it should be no surprise that teacher judgment falls short of perfection and that they, too, denigrate, most often in reference to their students. A few teachers publicly and unfavorably compare Riverview students to students living over the hill. They commiserate with bright students, and suggest they might be better off at nearby Catholic high schools. They say they will not enroll their own children in RHS unless the moral climate improves. They believe the school's academic quality is limited because it has too many Sicilian teachers who have a second- or third-rate education themselves.

The fullest such indictment was delivered by a veteran teacher, himself an over-the-hill resident, who speaks for those staff members who feel that RHS neglects its academic side. He is among those who, by some lights, are direct and honest, in that he expresses his unexpurgated sentiments to the students, rather than to colleagues in teacher-room, lunchtime catharthic exchanges. Indeed, he is excruciatingly direct and honest:

We give them too much false information that we all are equal, we're all the same. You know and I know that ain't true, baby. I don't see an advantage to going to this school unless you're stupid. It's terrible for the college-bound kid.

I think only in communities like Riverview can a lot of people be somebody. They're nice people here, but they're certainly not somebody. And that's why they return [if they go away to college].

Race isn't such a big issue like it used to be. Why do we even have to worry about the race garbage? Why don't we just get down and educate them socially and academically? The other thing in this school is we give kids 37,000 chances. If their work is not in, we extend the deadline. I just get disgusted. All we're doing is teaching them that everything can be changed. The IRS doesn't change their rules.

Such battering has clear consequences. RHS teachers learn to be defensive—of their students, their school, and their efforts to promote respectable academic standards. Students learn many things, too, some positive and some negative. They develop pride in themselves, their school, and their city. They acquire an impetus to try harder, which sometimes verges on bravado: "If I went to that school [Greenbriar, where student government leaders spent a day], I would ace all their classes. It was so easy. I said 'God, I can't believe they are seniors; they look like sophomores.'" They acquire a tinge of exhibitionism: "our band, for example, they're showoffs, but I like that. They'll do things other bands look at aghast, but secretly wish they were part of." I rarely heard any student react as if, believing the devaluation of outsiders, they should stay put down, feeling that persons like themselves were hopeless.

Like their teachers, students were strongly defensive. "I know I can't change how things have been," wrote a Riverview High School student in a letter to the editor, "but I will stand up for my town and school." She stands with many students. They never denied the problems of their school and community; they also never concluded that these problems had somehow cast a pall of despair over them:

You defend who you are. There's a lot of pride in the city. When we're in the outside world, we'll fight together for Riverview. I think coming from here you learn that everyone looks down on you, and from that you've learned to become proud.

"Fighting together" was an often-expressed concept. It follows naturally from a common sense of rejection, from a sense of being different and needing to stand together in opposition to the notion of outsiders that what makes them different also makes them inferior. Students would not deny they were different; they wanted to make clear that their differences did not merit rejection. Growing up as they did made them special, in that they knew and understood what many types of people were like, and not just the wealthy Caucasians who were their detractors.

Students also acknowledged that they were special in being tough, not necessarily machismo-tough, though there was some of that quality, but physically tough. Without apology or evasiveness, students affirmed what their over-the-hill counterparts believed: RHS students were tough. Theirs was the toughness of "if you put us down, look out" type, or of the "if you push us, expect to get pushed back" type. It is not that most students find fighting appealing, but, rather, that if provoked they will fight back with relative ease.

The overall impact of the personal qualities students develop in response to being stigmatized was stated concisely by a senior boy, Sicilian, a native of native parents: "You don't feel the underdog. Sometimes you feel the outcast." He feels as good as the over-the-hill tennis players he meets at interschool matches. Only they arrive in their Porsches, while he comes in his school's bus, and he knows he lives in a world apart.

"The town has to be a little paranoid, you know. There's people here that say if the rest of the area had its way, there'd be no off ramps [from the highway] into Riverview." "Paranoid" overstates the responses of Riverview residents to their stigmatization. From their children, I most often heard pride, defensiveness, and bravado; I less often heard inferiority, defeatism, and toughness. The city's elected officials, the city council members and its city manager, spoke of image. Each of the city's actual and prospective projects invite reference to Riverview's image, what it has been and what it will be. The *Herald* notes an event as being good or bad for the city's image. Outside developers claim to have been advised to stay away because of the city's image. Student-government leaders commit themselves to "a new image campaign," and former students—given a magic wand—wish for a change in "our image. I wish 'people would feel the way I feel. I love the school." A new image, to its many advocates, seems to mean establishing an impression based on the good things happening in Riverview, on things so good and so extensive that the marks of stigma would be overwhelmed.

Those who write about groups marked by stigma observe that normalization can occur. The stigma can move to the background of consciousness, and the group, strengthened by its shared language and values and united by the external hostility it faces, can go about its business just as any other, unstigmatized, group does. I see Riverview's normalization process in the formal activities of image changing and image creation, and in the informal activities of individuals who in face-to-face encounters try to set the record straight about their city and school. The net effect of these efforts is to communicate that we in Riverview, like you outside Riverview, are normal; when we are unlike you, we are not that different; and when we are that different, it is the least part of us. So, do not condemn the greater (and better) part of us, for that which is true of the least part of us. This is the underlying message of normalization, meant for consumption at home and over the hill. I will not pursue the matter of over-the-hill perceptions, but I will consider how those persons of primary interest to me—RHS students and teachers—conduct their school lives, given the fact of stigma.[6]

In this narrative of strangers and friends, I see Riverview cast in the role of stranger by its neighbors. If the result does not disable, it does bear costs in the form of intangibles relating to individual and collective self-esteem. It is never pleasant to be damned, however much one knows the damning is unjust. For their part, Riverview residents have their own friends and their own strangers and their own opportunity to discredit and devalue.

6. The discussion here about normalization was drawn from the chapter by Becker and Arnold (1986) in the useful collection edited by Ainlay, Becker, and Coleman.

2

Riverview's People: Strangers and Friends

To follow the play of ethnicity as expressed by adults of Riverview's major ethnic groups, I want to sketch each group's coming to Riverview, consider its reception by predecessor groups, and try to suggest the extent of the group's consciousness of its own ethnic identity. The adult expression of the themes of stranger and friend and of ethnic consciousness are point to the counterpoint of their childrens' expressions, which we will hear more of in a later chapter. The children, not surprisingly, know little about the coming of their parents and grandparents to Riverview. They know more, but not a great deal more, about their ethnic identity. They are most knowledgeable about the taboos concerning ethnic boundary lines that should not be transgressed. Elders seldom are silent on these matters, but their taboos seem not to pervade their childrens' thinking or behavior.

On April 23, 1984, the Riverview branch of the Catholic Daughters of the Americas held its regular monthly meeting in the social hall of St. Agnes Church. The meeting was unexceptional; providing no banner news, it was reported next day on the society page of the newspaper. As is traditional in the accounts of such meetings, the newspaper identified all chapter members who had been, are, or were about to engage in noteworthy activity, and what that activity was. So we learn about the Catholic Daughters in one of their springtime sessions; we learn, as well, several facts about Riverview.

St. Agnes Church is the older of Riverview's two Roman Catholic churches. It was built by the river in the community's neighborhoods of first settlement, which now contain the oldest and poorest houses and blotches of failed urban-renewal programs, as well as the bright new condominiums, stores, and marinas, hopeful augurs of old Riverview's renaissance. Once the religious mainstay of all Riverview's Catholics, and particularly of the families of Sicilian fishermen whose little homes surrounded the church, St. Agnes today serves the oldest survivors of the Sicilian families, some Filipinos, and the newcomer Mexicans whose barrio is adjacent to the church. The old survivors may live anywhere in Riverview, many are affluent, and they are strongly attached to the church whose sacraments mark the memorable occasions of their lives. To them, bilingual church documents and masses in Spanish signal clearly that newcomers also possess their church, and they do not take kindly to sharing it. They are as hostile to the use of a foreign language (excluding Latin) at church as at school, joining those who view bilingual education as a sop to newcomers who resist, as they righteously feel they did not, becoming American.

In the progression of names of newsworthy Catholic Daughters, we learn other facts. The multiethnic aspect of Catholicism and its institutions appears in the listing of Daughters who are officers and organizers of events. For example, Mexican Mary Garcia is the second vice-regent; Italian Josephine Borgina will attend the state convention; and Filipino Rachel Coquia cochairs the post-meeting dinner, which happens to be a Filipino meal. Legitimation via cuisine is among the forms that acceptance takes in the passage from stranger to friend.

Of note as another fact are the first names of the women who assisted Rachel Coquia with the Filipino dinner: Busilia, Teopista, Pacita, Toribia, and Oiosa. With the passing of this generation, this arrangement of consonants and vowels will probably never again be used to compose first names of young Filipino-American females; their daughters of Riverview High School are named Kim, Shelly, Eileen, and Jeanna. These women serving traditional food to the Catholic Daughters were born in the Philippines. They never felt impelled to Americanize their names in order to remove one obvious element of their strangerness.

By its many ordinary and special events, Riverview's Catholic Daughters reach out in the best philanthropic spirit to serve needy others: they furnish a room in a home for the elderly, organize monthly hospital visitations, and raise scholarship funds for school children, as does almost every church and civic organization in Riverview. The management of these good deeds reflects the Daughters' ethnic diversity, as does the choice of cuisine served at its post-meeting dinners.

Similar facts could also have been gleaned from reports of other Riverview organizations; the Catholic Daughters of the Americas is not unique in this respect. But I chose to begin a presentation of Riverview's people with a multiethnic organization in order to demonstrate a fact that might otherwise be underplayed: ethnic groups in Riverview are open-boundary collectivities whose members have cross-cutting loyalties, identities, attachments, and commitments that transcend and often conflict with their ethnic affiliations. To be sure, we generally know something worth knowing when we have learned about an individual's ethnicity, but we must always be aware of what we don't know when that is the extent of our knowledge. Riverview's Catholic Daughters allow me to make the point about nonexclusive ethnicity as well as any organization in the community, and also the point about the play of ethnicity.

Non-Sicilian Whites

No residents of Riverview would designate themselves "non-Sicilian whites." Indeed, there is no such formal group, though there are persons who can be identified by reference to what they are not, the point of reference being Sicilian. Of course, Sicilians are Italians, but most of Riverview's Italians come from Sicily, and the historical sense of Sicilians as different from other Italians continues to the present. Moreover, though not a majority, Sicilians are the community's focal group and thus serve other groups as the basis for comparison and contrast in political, economic, and social terms. For the sake of consistency, in this chapter and elsewhere I will refer to Italians as Sicilians, except in quotations and as the context otherwise requires.

Non-Sicilian whites were Riverview's first major, enduring settlers. At first, they were Welsh who came to the area in the 1860s as coal miners and who moved away around 1900 when the coal mines shut down. They were joined by Irish, English, German, and other immigrants, who opened shops, taverns, and hotels to serve first the Welsh miners and later the Sicilian fishing families. Today, few members of these early non-Sicilian settler families remain. We see the old Welsh presence in the names on tombstones in a hilltop cemetery located adjacent to the coal mines, and we see another non-Sicilian presence in Riverview street names and on some still-prospering businesses. Over the years, the size and nature of the white non-Sicilian population has changed; at present, they are Riverview's American, as opposed to Asian and Mexican, newcomers, and its most rapidly growing group.

During much of the time between the departure of the coal miners and the beginning of World War II, Riverview was a two-class, two-group society. Non-Sicilian whites controlled elective and appointive positions in the city and in the school system. Sicilians, as a group, were considerably poorer and had much less political power. Not until 1937 did the city council contain more than one Sicilian. When a third Sicilian was elected in 1946, non-Sicilian whites became the minority for the first time in Riverview history. Yet they continued to occupy most appointed offices save those of police chief and fire chief, which somehow seemed safely filled by Sicilians, even as far back as 1916 when the office of fire chief first appears as a city position.

The story is the same for Riverview's school board, a non-Sicilian white preserve until 1940, when the first Sicilian was elected. He was followed by a second in 1947 and a third in 1949, creating a Sicilian majority that was maintained until 1971.

For most of this century, Riverview's non-Sicilian white professionals and factory managers were preeminent. They lived on the East Side, apart from the Sicilians, attended the Congregational church, even if they were of some other Protestant denomination, and became Masons, Elks, Foresters, and Rotarians. Wives who played bridge had husbands who dined at the Hotel Los Medanos, the occasion marked in the newspaper in a column headed "Elites Annual Confab," organized by the long-defunct University Club Committee. During the decades when Sicilians saw the completion of eighth grade as their academic acme, non-Sicilian white children routinely planned to attend college.

What little evidence exists today does not suggest that ethnicity was important in defining or shaping the identity of the non-Sicilian whites. If asked about their ethnicity, they might have answered, as did one man, a contemporary member of this group, "All that [ethnicity] just swirls around us. I've heard that we're German, but I never picked up on my roots, or anything." His son said, "If someone asks, I just say I'm a white boy, because I know they'll settle for that, and it will make them laugh."

If fathers and sons of the past were casual about their own ethnicity, they and their female kin were not indifferent to the ethnicity of others in Riverview who had not yet assumed, and possibly never would, the status of friend. Distinguishing others as strangers, as not one of us and therefore less worthy and wonderful than we are, if not a threat to us, is so ubiquitous in human behavior as to seem bred in the bone. Riverview's non-Sicilian whites thrust the tag of stranger upon many; eventually, Sicilians would thrust it upon them when they assumed the mantle of power.

Before Sicilians had become more like non-Sicilian whites than like their grandparents, they kept to their place. When the notion of "place" is viable, boundaries exist that include, exclude, and separate. If we want to learn about boundaries and the firmness of commitment to ethnic maintenance, we can ask of each of Riverview's ethnic groups about their place as they and others see it. In octogenarian Mr. Greenspan's day, whites could be civil to Sicilians in their stores, respect them as workers in their factories, but not visit them in their homes, not allow their daughters to join the Rainbow Girls, and not want them as spouses for their own children.

As late as the 1950s, a sense of place still prevailed, however much time and circumstance had moderated its impact and altered old boundaries. By then, however, it was the non-Sicilian whites who were excluded from desirable arenas, from becoming a cheerleader or yearbook editor, for example, and from getting invited to certain parties: "We didn't go to theirs and they didn't come to ours." Rivalry of sorts at school reached out of school to the neighborhoods. Jane Bowman recalls the talk in her white East Side neighborhood when the first Sicilian family moved in. Her neighbors were convinced that their block was going to hell. White residential boundaries had softened, Sicilians had the money, their ghetto was aging, and moving out of their "place" became inevitable—a new story, soon but not easily to be a common old one.

In the 1960s, after more softening and altering of boundaries, Bill Jones was accepted in Sicilian groups, "although not as much as I probably wish I would have been because there was the cliquish thing." Naturally, he says, "I was a lot more comfortable going with the group that I ended up being part of—the generic whites."

From the vantage of the present, non-Sicilian whites still see Sicilians as clannish in their social relations, still clustering together at election time, still part of huge extended families that an outsider cannot break into. "Now, that has become less of a problem, or situation. The Sicilian community isn't as strong." The shoe of strangerness has moved to the other foot, but not completely, for there remains in Riverview a small outpost of female non-Sicilian white worthies whose little group welcomes no blacks, and none but "special" Sicilians. Their pocket of relative exclusivity is less the norm than the picture of Riverview in non-Sicilian Sam Richard's mind. "Who lives in Riverview?" I ask him. "As far as I know, it's mostly Italians, whites, blacks, and Mexicans." "Do you make a distinction between Italians and other white people?" "I guess I just did. When anyone asks me about my town, the Italians always come into my mind because they were some of the first settlers. The few that we know, they let you know they're Italian. They think of themselves as the originals."

Today non-Sicilian whites are attracted to Riverview by its relatively low-priced houses. They are commuters, better educated than most Riverview residents, and detached from the old whites and the Italian originals. It remains to be seen what type of stranger and friend they will prove to be.

Sicilians

The Sicilians came to Riverview in the 1850s and were fishermen until
1957 when the State of California banned all net fishing for salmon in the
local river. No nets, no salmon, and that was that for a way of life that
included not only fishing but also the ancillary businesses of canning,
fish selling, and shipbuilding and repairing. Fishing was a family affair
passed from son to son among the Aiellos, Ferrantes, Cardinallis, Bell-
icis, Davis, and Scuderos, the earliest mid-nineteenth-century immigrants to Riverview from Isola delle Femmine, their Sicilian village.
Much of the tempo and character of life in Riverview before World War
II was shaped by the economic activity of the community's fishermen,
but never as fully as farmers shape the life of their villages, because the
fishing industry shared the local economy first with coal mining and
thereafter with blue-collar jobs in heavy industry.

Valerie Siragusa's grandfather was among Riverview's earliest settlers. He came alone to confirm, as he had heard, that the fishing was
good. He returned to Sicily some years later to get his wife and young
children. Now in her fifties, Valerie remembers with joy growing up on
the West Side. So do many others. Mario Devito, Valerie's junior by
twenty years, also began life on the West Side. He and Valerie spoke
with ease about their lives; their accounts reveal much about Sicilian life
in Riverview. Valerie focuses on respect, both personally and as it relates
to her betters.

Valerie Siragusa
I wouldn't say we were poor but we were treated like we were poor by the
kids from the East Side whose fathers were the big shots in our factories. We
were the best of friends and there never was any resentment. I was raised
knowing my place, just like in England when the queen comes by and people
bow. Some people say they wouldn't bow to anybody, but it's showing a certain respect. It's tradition. It's to each his own. My mother taught us if you're
with the wealthy, you act good, you respect them.

The word respect was the big thing in Italian families that was pounded in
my head more than anything, and that's gone today. There's no such word. If I
was in conversation with my mother and I was telling what my aunt said, I
would not say, "she said." I had to say, "Aunt Anna said," or I'd get slapped.

I always thought I understood about how we lived over here and other
kids lived over there until one summer my girlfriend and I rode our bikes to
the East Side. We were both in high school at the time, and we were riding up
a street when a lady came out of the house. She didn't know us; all she knew
was that we were from the West Side. She stood on her porch and called out
to us, "What are you girls doing on this street?" That was the first time I

realized how hurt you could feel. I knew my mother had told me not to go over there, that you don't bother those people.

We couldn't buy homes over there, even if we could afford it, and my father could. He built a beautiful house on the West Side. My parents were hard workers; they saved their money and minded their own business. Like I said, they didn't make waves and they got above it.

My daughter argues the point with me. I say I didn't feel prejudice; she says there was prejudice. I tell her everybody knew their place, OK? The change came after the war when nobody wanted to know their place. They all wanted to be the same, which is fine. I'm not prejudiced. We knew no difference, so how can you say you're prejudiced if you just think that's the way it's supposed to be?

Mario Devito
We lived on Ninth Street. On the corner I had my grandmother, right next to her was her daughter, two blocks away was another daughter and some uncles. It seemed like our family owned the whole neighborhood. The cousins grew up like brothers and sisters; we met daily in my grandmother's basement. When she died, things were never the same again.

My mom keeps the family pretty tight, too. My sister lives just a couple of doors down. Mom doesn't like to let us leave home. She has the old-time traditions—don't leave the house until you get married. I'm still here. When it's dinner time, we don't eat until everyone is together. If you need help, you go to the family; you use the family connections to get a job. There is that security, and it makes you feel real good to be part of the family. My friends don't understand this closeness, you know, that I have to call if I'm going to be late for dinner.

Even our friends are basically Italian. When a person comes into our home who isn't Italian, there seems to be a little uneasiness. Like if a black were to come into our house—not that they have germs or anything like that—it would just completely throw everybody off. Same way with a Filipino; with a Mexican, too, but maybe not so much. Not that we're prejudiced. Except for marriage. First thing, marry someone Catholic. Second would be Italian. A completely different race they would reject totally.

All of us in the family feel close to Italy. My parents—they're not forcing us to keep in touch. Yet, if something happens in Italy, a tragedy or something, we're always tuned into it, even if it's not in our town. We feel for those people. Day in and day out, I live like everyone else. I don't know of any people who really live by their heritage. I really like the celebrations. That's when I feel especially Italian.

The transplanted Sicilians who settled in Riverview established versions of being Sicilian which to varying degrees they transmitted to their children. Their versions included emphasizing the importance of family, respect, paternal dominance, maternal nurturance, marrying within the religious and ethnic fold, identification with Italy, pride in one's heritage (however defined), special observation of holidays, etc. From these general ideals, real people fashion their lives, both as they see fit and as others allow them.

We more often see the break between generations than we see the type of continuity that Mario Devito describes. In a complex society, the issue is not if there will be breaks, but where they will be, and if they will be so sharp as to disrupt the continuity of family life. The cultural web within which Sicilians lived in Sicily has undergone modification with each generation. What remains varies among individuals and families, though typically what remains are beliefs and practices that do not impede their fitting into American society (see di Leonardo 1984 and Juliani 1988).

So they eat Italian food, but seldom with the predictability of the older generations, when one could reasonably well guess the day of the week from the food that a family ate for dinner. Tommy Davi, at least in his adult reminiscence, remembers walking all the way from church to his grandma's house through uninterrupted wafts of aromatic spaghetti sauce. Yet even today when pasta faces tough competition from pizza and burritos, families may grow garlic, basil, and parsley in their backyards. They remain Catholics and, still faithful churchgoers, may become "modern" Catholics who like the English masses, eat meat on Friday, and practice birth control, if not abortion.

They are far from indifferent to the Sicilian dialect, though it is not an integral part of their lives today. For just as the aroma of sauce once connected one Sicilian home to another, so did the speaking of Sicilian. The necessity of bilingual competency—one language for home and intimacy, another for affairs outside home and family—diminished from generation to generation. Now young persons seldom speak or understand Sicilian. The Italian-language paper that came to Riverview in February 1930 would not flourish today, and good riddance, some would say.

"Speak and act and work and do the American way," says sixty-year-old Frannie Fratano, Riverview native and patriot, to her children. She does not want them to abandon their heritage—"You could still practice what you want at home"—but they should not expect public institutions to promote their practice. Thus, when she got a petition that urged state election ballots be printed only in English, not in Spanish and Chinese, she readily signed it.

Few special holidays remain of the several that Sicilians observed in

the past. At one time, the yearly round was marked by special observances on All Souls', St. Joseph's, St. John the Baptist's, and St. Peter's
days. Seldom observed anymore, the occasions are remembered well
and at first hand only by those over fifty, though a recent St. Joseph's
Benediction brought some 150 men and women to St. Agnes Church. It
was an occasion for an ingathering of the survivors of a rapidly fading
past; they were notable for their gray hair, bald heads, and hearing aids.
Soon no one will know that in the past an image of St. Joseph was
brought down to Riverview's waterfront for the blessing of the fleet by
the priest. Now there is no fleet, so the good patron saint remains inside
the church, no longer serving local people in the old way.

Although the religious festivals have waned, the Columbus Day celebration seems to have a more promising destiny. In 1916, it was,
according to a newspaper account, the "greatest two-day festival ever";
in 1928, the "City [was] Dressed in Gala Attire" for a three-day celebration. Recollection of these three-day events still evokes more nostalgia
than any other single occasions of the past. They are symbolic of a time
when Riverview had been, in a real sense, a Sicilian village. From 1957,
when the festivities ceased, to 1984, when they were revived, only the
high school football games remained as occasions for which all of Riverview turned out. The loss of the pageant in 1957 saddened Sicilians.
They had come to think of Columbus Day as an invariable aspect of life,
like Christmas and Easter. The occasion was declared dispensable, so
the stories go, the year a black girl won the queen contest. The mayor,
always a white male in those days, could not bring himself to plant the
official ceremonial kiss on a black girl. In fact, so it is also told, the year
before, when early counts showed a black girl leading in votes (calcu-
lated by the number of tickets sold by the would-be queen's sponsoring
organization), the mayor bought "a thousand dollars worth of tickets to
make sure he was over the hump." For successfully reviving the Columbus Day celebration, Tony Escalante received Riverview's Chamber of
Commerce 1985 Citizen of the Year award. With plaque in hand and
tears in his eyes he told a crowd of well-wishers, "I just want to bring
back the celebrations and good times I remember as a young child." He
has much company in this sentiment among fellow Sicilians who feel
they have fallen behind other ethnic groups in public expressions of the
ethnicity of their once dominant and still proud group.

Today, old Sicilian men in their seventies and eighties congregate at
the waterfront on nice days, sitting on folding chairs or the steps of the
Riverview Yacht Club. Within their view is the neighborhood where
their golden age was played out; it now is full of run-down homes and
rubble-strewn vacant lots. Social change, parading under one of its

many appellations, will soon replace the rubble and old houses with
dwellings and playgrounds for wealthier newcomers whose disposable
income will so transform Riverview that the golden-agers will be challenged to locate any of the physical landmarks of their past lives. "A lot of
us have died," said one of them when interviewed by a local newspaper
reporter. "We're all in line here waiting for our turn."

For the youth of a generation younger than the men on the waterfront, and not yet in line waiting its turn to die, Riverview was larger,
but still a small place. The feeling of being part of one big family remained, and "I'm not talking of just the Italians. We were tight-knit;
damn near knew everybody," explained one fifty-year-old father. Dad
was boss, and dinner did not begin without him, unlike today "when my
daughter has cheerleading practice and eats before I come home."
People believed that only Catholics would go to heaven. This generation
paints a golden-age picture right out of *American Graffiti* or television's
Happy Days. Eyes shimmer with remembered cruising, dates, dances,
and the drive-in where *everybody* went. Enid Terreza tells me:

If there was a dance coming up and you wanted a date, you hit the Tiger
Drive-In. That was the place to go to see people who might ask you to the
dance. If someone was going to ask you, they could find you and at least get
your telephone number.

High school was fun. All my memories have nothing to do with learning. I
mean it sounds corny to say but it was a wonderful place. A girl should be
engaged a year or two after high school and then married. I think the Anglos,
they were in the direction of college and career more than marriage.

Male contemporaries of Enid share equally glossy-eyed memories. In
the early days, says one, "I can't remember the age when I finally realized there were other people in the world besides Italians." And they
mark 1960 or so as the time by which a "gradual process" produced a
Riverview that no longer had an "Italian flavor." During the good-time
period, the football games were better attended with the then high
school enrollment of 450 than today when it is 1,600; fights were with
fists, one on one, and never with weapons; and school dances featured
the live music of twelve-piece orchestras, rather than the recorded music of disc jockeys.

Since the golden age of the second generation was coincident with
Sicilian political dominance in city and school-board politics, politics is
often mentioned when the reminiscing begins. Horace Breggo captures
a dominant sentiment about voting practice in his recollection below of a
1957 episode with his father. Fresh out of the army, Horace saw promise

in a young man, new to politics, as a city-council candidate. His dad tried hard but failed to dissuade him from supporting the young man.

So my dad, who does not drink, asked me to meet him at a bar later. I had no idea what the old man had in mind until I got there and saw Tony Russo, probably the most influential, behind-the-scenes guy in town. T. R. says to me, "Horace, what has your man done for our people?" "Nothing yet." "Then why not vote for our man? We know what he's done for our people." I knew what he meant. My dad worked for the city at that time.

By 1957, non-Sicilian white political dominance was only a memory. Tony Russo, never a candidate himself, contributed to the establishment of a political dynasty that remained reasonably intact until 1983, when a recall election removed four of the five incumbents. Russo is still a man of power, says his compatriots, willing these days to support an "American," as older Sicilians call non-Sicilian whites, though they'd probably use the vernacular term "Medigani." Horace Breggo says that the question, "What has he done for our people?" is less important than in the past. Times have changed. Riverview's city manger asserts, "I'm not an Italian city manager, I'm a city manager who happens to be Italian." An older non-Sicilian observes, "The cohesiveness is still there. We got a good vote, but now the children of those Italian families are not so goddamn concerned about elections." And a 1986 newspaper interview quotes Riverview historian Ben Antonio as saying, "The Italians have dominated because they've been here, know the town, and know how to get around. In another hundred years, the Italian heritage may be just a memory."

Meanwhile, memory has sufficient impact, emotion, and meaning to establish being Sicilian (or Italian) as a factor in the identity of many local people. Being Sicilian remains a rallying point for political activity, and it is a condition for belonging, if not being a voting member, in one of several organizations whose names—Sons of Italy, Italian Catholic Federation, Italian-American Club—designate their ethnic orientation. The initiation rites of the Italian Catholic Federation require new members to affirm their affection, pride, and allegiance to Christianity, Italy, and America. Together these organizations have about five hundred members.

These organizations are more communal than defensive. They do not function to protect and perpetuate Sicilian rights, territory, or power from non-Sicilian competitors. In assembling members for their regular activities, they remind them of their ethnic affiliation and keep alive the disposition to act conjointly. They help to maintain the boundaries be-

tween ethnic groups. Their acts of boundary maintenance are sufficiently benign as to not threaten or concern others. Still, the boundaries
are maintained.

No Sicilian I met placed ethnic identification above being American.
They are Americans "of Italian extraction," to add a fine point that few
acknowledge; most commonly, they are Italian-American. Also, most
commonly, they attest to pride in their heritage. This is Riverview's
norm for all ethnic groups, though the youngest generation may reject
certain behaviors they associate with tradition, for example, the sexism
and machismo of "old-fashioned" Sicilian males.

The second generation can utter affirmations of being American, and,
in the course of doing so, affirm a complexity they are not mindful of.
Listen to Rose Siino:

If I attend things like concerts, maybe some Hispanic thing, or visit an American family, maybe they have something and I go to whatever they do, I don't
feel Italian. Whatever they're doing, I join in. I can adapt real easy to what
they're doing because I've been raised American and it just doesn't bother
me. The most I feel Italian is like when I went to an Italian festival and heard
Sergio Franco sing. That's when you feel Italian. You're among people, . . .
you're attending your own people's type of thing.

Being Sicilian defines Rose Siino to the extent that she can speak of
adapting "real easy" to what an "American" family is doing, though I
know she would also call hers an "American" family and also refer to
Americans as her own people.

In November 1962 marriages occurred between children of these
families: Davi and Stead, Pirozzoli and Skaggs, Ferrante and Barnes,
and Bruno and Edwards. The resulting "mixed" marriages indicate that
marrying outside one's ethnic group not only happens but may also be
acceptable. Such marriages reflect the rejection of ethnicity as a factor in
mate selection. The prevailing assumption nowadays is that one marries
whomever one loves. Selecting a non-Sicilian mate does not mean, "I
don't want to be Sicilian." It means, "I have met someone I love who is
not Sicilian." Religion more than nationality demarcates who is in the
pool of acceptable mates. It was not always so.

Sicilians, like perhaps all human groups at some time in their history,
held a restricted notion of whom their children should marry: you marry
someone who is of your own people, where friends are to be found. The
changing response to the matter of who is one's people and where acceptable mates are found documents shifting social boundaries and,
thus, the definition of who is stranger and who is friend. In the beginning, arranged marriages insured ethnic solidarity. An older brother in

Italy would send a wife to his younger brother in Riverview. Love, if
it occurred, was a post-marriage phenomenon; divorce was not per-
missible.

Perceptibly, belief and practice changed, with belief even today lagging behind practice. Sicilians eventually married "Americans"—
known variously as whites, Anglos, or Okies—and Mexicans; eventually, it became acceptable to do so. Marrying blacks is thinkable, but
still not acceptable. In the 1950s, Anne Terezza's father drew the line at
marrying a Mexican. "He didn't even mention blacks. That was impossi-
ble. The two Salla sisters did and they no longer existed as people."

The farther they were in time from the settler generation, the more
Sicilians fell in love with and married non-Sicilians. Since the marriage
would take place with or without parental approval, parents began to
develop rationales that would make palatable what, often, they still disapproved. Their rationales sound familiar: "who am I to say otherwise?"
"as long as they love each other;" "as long as they're happy;" "who
he/she picks to marry, that's his/her business;" "you got to go with the
trend because the old way is old-fashioned." Some parents who accept
the new times—when "Americans are accepted as mates"—do so with
barely veiled regrets:

In the old days, people just stayed within their own group. My sister didn't,
but my mother grew to love her husband. My daughter's generation, that's
really changed. Now, it didn't bother me when she wanted to marry out of—
It didn't. To me, that was fine, but I would always say, like my mom always
said, if you're from the same culture, that's one argument you won't have. If
you marry into the same religion, that's another argument you don't have. If
you're not from the same nationality, things come up that he [her daughter's
husband] doesn't understand. We're close-knit, as far as Italian people. American people, not to put them down, they can go off and do their own thing and
think nothing of it.

This is Rosie Valeria reflecting on marriage. She will not give voice to
her disappointment over her daughter's non-Sicilian husband. In seeing
friend in those whom mother and grandmother had declared stranger,
Rosie's daughter gave credence to the propriety of finding friends outside the Sicilian circle. That this circle does not widen effortlessly is
clear as the Sicilians reflect on the non-Sicilian others with whom they
share a common space. Labeling non-Sicilian whites "Americans" testifies to a distinction they make, not yet fully without some prejudice.
Today, Sicilians and "Americans" no longer interact from within stranger
and friend categories.

Still, there is prejudice aplenty. Those who grew up being called

dagos, wops, or macaroni-eaters were not, by virtue of having been vic-
timized themselves, more generous in their view of others who, relative
to them, were poorer newcomers, and different in culture and color. As
late as the mid-1940s, recalls Lisa Carozzi, the Americans living on the
East Side got the breaks: "They got bussed to school; we walked. They
got the scholarships, we weren't even told about scholarships." Twenty
years later, Riverview's blacks would make similar claims, with Sicilians
then cast as the villains. "We were very proud people," Lisa continues,
"in the sense we pulled ourselves up by the bootstraps, did our thing,
and rose above it without asking for help." Ex-victims, we infer from
Lisa's remarks, do not predictably extract a moral of generosity and char-
itableness from their former plight; they extract platitudes for the
uplifting of all victims, as if all were the same, with bootstraps ready for
the tugging.

     With time comes an increasing degree of assimilation and for most
groups the passing of the stigmas that produce the distinctions and sepa-
rations of hardened ethnic boundaries. This applies to the reception of
Sicilians by the non-Sicilian whites, and the Sicilian reception of the
"Mediganis" and other local ethnics. Being Sicilian still constitutes a social distinction, a basis for organizational life, a rallying point for political
activity, and a source for defining and locating one's history and identity.
It is a distinction of consequence, but from all appearances, one that is
waning.

Mexicans

The Mexicans came to America, as did earlier immigrants, fleeing
poverty, oppression, war, and revolution; unlike most immigrants, they
found their haven by crossing a border. "Home" was never far away. It
still isn't. During the post–World War I revolution, Juan Madero's family was caught between battling sides, neither of which they felt strongly
about. They got by trading tequila for wheat, corn, or beans, while waiting for a train to take them north. His family meant always to return
home; in the meantime, the Madero sons and daughters got married,
found jobs in Riverview's mills and canneries, had their own children,
and bought their first little house. Mexico became a place in the heart,
and being Mexican defined them in contrast with Sicilians and others.

     Fred Hernandez came to the United States in 1919, recalling that it
was easy to enter legally at Laredo, where Mexican and Texan towns of
the same name lay on either side of the border. Some people were "con-
traband," coming over illegally. Fred's father was "bamboozled" into a
scheme that put families on canoes crossing the Rio Grande at night.

When Mexican soldiers caught them, they were forced to pay more than they would have if they'd come in legally. For years, Fred felt he could not safely apply for citizenship. In 1942 he decided to "tell the truth," hoping that the authorities would not punish him at thirty-three for his father's transgressions back in 1919.

Paula Bright's mother grew up in Mexico. To the mother, Mexico meant poverty, a childhood spent working for a dollar a month, plus a supply of corn and beans that didn't satisfy the fatherless family's too many mouths; she always believed that no one would have cared if the family starved. This sentiment she passed on to the children she bore in Mexico and those born later in the United States. "Every time you see the America flag," she'd tell Paula and her siblings, "you stand up, take your hat off, and put your hand over your heart." Her mother's gratitude to America and resentment toward Mexico were balanced by her father's belief that everything Mexican was best.

Paula was raised the only way her mother knew how: eat Mexican food, be respectful, dress modestly, practice your religion, and keep your house "spic and span." When Paula got married, her husband-to-be had to see her father to "ask for my hand in marriage." Somehow marriage had lost its hands by the time her own children were ready to be wed. Unlike her mother, Paula does not hate Mexico, Mexicans are "her people," but she loves America too. Her parents never dreamed of returning, as did Juan Madero's family.

Alicia Ocampo, born in Mexico, speaks unaccented English, learned by dint of special coaching in the days before bilingual education, and abetted by a strong desire to avoid the abuse that speakers of accented English earn. Though settled here, with citizenship papers to attest to her legal status, she is rankled by an America that abused her uncles who, when caught entering illegally, lost their money, had their heads shaved, and were fumigated. She is also rankled by an America that "stole" Mexican land in the course of the nineteenth century. Though as fully settled here as Paula Bright, she has never learned to be thrilled when the American flag passes by.

When Mexicans came to California, they followed the seasons and crops as agricultural laborers. Riverview attracted them with its factory jobs; women found work in its canneries. For many years, neither the city nor the school system hired Mexicans. World War II opened up jobs in heavy industry for more Mexicans, and also jobs with responsibility and higher pay.

Fred Hernandez, for example, spent nearly fifty years at the steel mill. They weren't all good years. Fred's story as stranger at work is the story of many of his compatriots. Somehow he acquired the skills required for the job of checker, a rank above his regularly assigned work, yet the company would not appoint him checker. When the regular checker was absent, the foreman asked Fred to do the checker's work. Whenever a new man, always an "American," was employed as checker, the foreman had Fred train him. "There was no future," he says, "no ghost of a chance, that you would ever get ahead—until the war came."

Whenever Fred spoke of fellow workers, he always identified them by their ethnicity: "the president of the steel mill union was another Irishman"; "so the foreman came over and told the checker—the checker was Italian, a good friend of mine . . ."; "there was another American fellow working on the furnace . . ."; "I could see that he didn't like the idea of me, a Mexican, getting onto a job like that"; "there was a Scotchman over there, a young guy, and he was very friendly with me"; "we had a case of a colored guy, he lives down the other side of the road"; "so he got the job and he didn't make the American boys happy at all." As did many men and women of his generation, Fred places people in a group—Italian, American, Scotchman, Irishman, colored. It was natural to sort people out by categories; the people being sorted used the same ones. To be sure, all categories were not synonymous: to Fred, "we" meant Mexican, a consciousness begun at birth, continued by upbringing, and perpetuated by an American "they" which kept him from the jobs he knew his talents entitled him to. A generation later Riverview had changed so much that Fred's children could grow up never knowing their father's Mexican "we" and American "they." Fred, despite the dramatic changes in the life of Mexican-Americans after World War II, could never forget.

Nor could he forget his language, a taken-for-granted fact among the first generation, but never afterward. Yet, Spanish-language use remains an active issue both inside and outside the Mexican community, unlike Sicilian-language use, which dwindles continuously and at best is part of the memory of being Sicilian. When Paula Bright describes St. Agnes Church, she comments with satisfaction on the Spanish Liturgy Committee, the regular Sunday mass conducted in Spanish, the honoring of Our Lady of Guadalupe, the bilingual church bulletins that say both "Merry Christmas!" and "Feliz Navidad!", and all the many ways her church recognizes its Spanish-speaking parishioners. From focusing on the church's "Spanish" features, she turns naturally to speak of the use of Spanish in her life: her grandson studied Spanish in school, but resists attending Spanish mass because he feels he doesn't understand enough; her daughter speaks Spanish "because of her job"; her non-Hispanic husband learned Spanish to be better able to talk to her mother; and Paula's son does not know Spanish, though he mastered Asian lan-

guages during World War II when it was "a matter of survival."
Mastering Spanish never acquired such status.

Parents who established Spanish-only households raised children
who began their first day of school as monolinguals. Juan Madero was
such a parent. His neighbors berated him for what they saw as punishment of his daughter. His other three children do not speak Spanish
because when their elder sister finally learned English, she spoke to
them only in English and they all began to play with kids who spoke English. Children create bilingual homes: Mary Fernando's five siblings
spoke only English to each other and only Spanish to their parents and
other Mexican adults. All are bilingual. Alicia Ocampo, in her thirties,
always speaks Spanish to her fully bilingual son, while riding a bus,
walking the street, anywhere. "I'm speaking to my little boy in Spanish," she says, "and people come up and say, 'You're in America. You're
not supposed to be speaking Mexican.' 'Let me correct you,' I tell them.
'I'm speaking Spanish. There's no such language as Mexican. And I can
speak any language I want. It's my freedom.'" Josie Thompson's parents
spoke Spanish to each other and English to her. Today her Spanish is
"poor and limited." Rosario Salazar's daughters grew up knowing Spanish. Both married men who spoke no Spanish. Her grandchildren speak
only English. Aside from newcomer Mexicans, the only hard-core Spanish monolinguals are grandmothers who could remain sheltered from
the English-speaking world that encompassed them, though even they
had to acquire shopper's English. With the passing of such grandparents, many Mexicans lose their last compelling tie with the Spanish
language. They also lose an impetus for being Mexican in ways that perpetuate the Mexican-as-stranger status.

Though schools were the arenas in which Mexican children con-
fronted their linguistic limitations, many Mexican parents realized they
also were arenas for hooking onto otherwise unattainable opportunities.
Frances Madero remembers with poignancy the occasion for crowning a
queen. Her organization wanted a professional from the Mexican community to do the crowning, but "there was just no professionals. We
couldn't find nobody." When, in time, there were Mexican professionals
"from families that we knew here, you could imagine the emotion that
we felt." No schooling, no Mexican professionals.

In Frances's day in the 1930s, it was enough that a girl learned to read
and write; boys stopped school when they were old enough to go to
work. Frances's mother died when she was young, so her father kept her
home. "I cried and cried when I stopped going. I dreamed of going to
school." And so dreaming, she urged her own children to get educated,
"not so much for social class, but for them to have a better opportunity, a

better way of living, than we had." She worked night shifts at the cannery, going to work when everyone was sleeping. Her husband worked a lifetime in the scrap yard of the steel mill with a craneload of iron hanging over his head.

Frances is of the first generation. Nicholas Miano, of the second, was sent to school by parents who insisted on taking advantage of school. It was not easy to do so: neighbors criticized his father for encouraging his older sister to attend college after high school graduation, rather than to marry. Send her to work, they told him. Teachers criticized Nicholas when he insisted on moving from the noncollege to the college track. Unable to change his mind, they warned him he was too slow and he'd crawl back shamed and begging to be returned to his proper track. He didn't. When he brought the news of his school victory to neighborhood friends, they greeted him with, "Oh, what's the matter? You trying to be white?"

Alicia Ocampo went to school in the early 1960s knowing only the English words for colors taught to her by aunts too timid about their English skills to teach her more. Her first teacher placed all Mexicans in the back of the room. Alicia remembers a fat, jolly teacher who, upon hearing her speak Spanish, observed that she didn't "look like a Mexican." She told Alicia, "I'm going to give you some speech therapy so you won't sound like a Mexican, either." Rejecting the "compliment," Alicia refuses to become "white."

Tom Barcenas trusts that his third-generation children will have an easier time at school than he did, and that their school will have an easier time with them. He was raised by a grandmother whose legacy was neither "money, homes, nor cars," but the insistence that he go to school. He did, having no idea what he would or could do with an education. Having earned a university degree, he sees himself as a role model, in that no school need teach his children to speak English or the value of education. Tom is conscious of social mobility, his own and his children's. He also is conscious that his brown skin places limits on his complete entry into the circle of friends, as it does not for a person of Alicia's complexion.

I hear Mexican children talk in school and they sound no different from my own children. I ask sixty-year-old Luis Herrera if these children remain Mexican in any way. They do, he thinks, but much less than he believes desirable. Parents are too busy to teach them the way he taught his children, "so they talk very small amount of heritage, let's say. And it's unfortunate because they are losing the point of view."

The point of view gets at least public endorsement several times a year when Riverview's Mexican community celebrates Cinco de Mayo, the time of Mexico's victory in 1862 over French troops in the battle of Puebla, and Mexican Independence Day, on September 16, the day in 1810 when Mexico liberated itself from Spanish rule. It also gets endorsed by the Guadalupe Society's annual summer festival, the annual free concert called Concierto de las Americas, and even the Latin Tournament, a combination party and softball tournament to see which of fourteen softball teams qualify for the Hispanic World Tournament. On most of these occasions, queens and kings are crowned, Mexican food is eaten, mariachi musicians play, folkloric dancers perform, and, perhaps most important, Mexican people assemble for hours in a rented place that for a time becomes an ethnic place. On these occasions, Paula Bright wears the dresses and blouses her daughters brought her from Mexico; on these occasions, she says, "I particularly feel Hispanic. I let it be known that I'm there with my people. I am Hispanic and these are my people." More than for festivities, the different events also are a time to raise money for "Hispanic youth to further their education." The "Hispanic" recipients of the money raised need not be more than nominally Hispanic. Indeed, the adolescents eligible for the scholarships seldom attend the celebrations, though they are aware of them; they may see their ethnicity as little more than a matter of festivals.

Juan Madero, Paula Bright, Fred Hernandez, Alicia Ocampo, and their compatriots are little Mexican islands in the American sea, but islands that change their form and substance with time and circumstance. They change, compelled to change, notwithstanding self-admonitions not to forget their roots. They speak of parents being too busy just trying to survive to give attention to being Mexican; of themselves being attuned to getting ahead and the acceptance of American values as abetting the process; of needing to adapt because for foreigners in America that is the right thing to do; of adapting as a natural procedure, so that you went to school and you "became them, just another kid on the block," and you came home and "you're a completely different person"; and of being independent, "not one of the [Mexican] masses," so that when Cesar Chavez came to town and urged people to picket and boycott grapes, Mrs. Ramirez bought grapes, even in the face of accusations that she was not really a Mexican.

Mexican men and women come together in the Latin American Women's League, United Council of Spanish-Speaking Organizations, John F. Kennedy Committee, Latin American Club, and Mexican-American Political Association. Beyond their support for the festive attributes of ethnicity, the organizations defend, intercede on behalf of, motivate for education, and seek political power for those identified as "their people," never quibbling over such matters as whether being

Mexican will be promoted or undermined by the success of these several actions. People who are Mexican are the objects of their activity, though not people who necessarily mean to be Mexican in some ethnically distinct way. They leave the matter of cultural maintenance to families, expect little from the schools, and direct their deepest concerns to the high drop-out rates of Mexican children—30 percent "among Hispanics in the country . . . 13 percent higher than the average rate for all ethnic groups," and to the dearth of "elected or appointed Hispanic officials"—only eight in Riverview's county of 60,000 Hispanics, as reported in the Riverview *Daily Herald* in 1986.

Mexican parents of today are mindful of the fact that their children increasingly marry non-Mexicans. By the out-group marriages of his children, Fred Hernandez sees that the Mexican culture he so studiously cultivated has, as regards his children and grandchildren, started "to fade. That's what hurts, but what are you going to do?" Some Mexican families concede the acceptability of marriage to Anglos, drawing the line at "blacks, orientals, and Indians." Charles Hurtado and his wife draw such a line, joining the extensive company of those who reject blacks as acceptable mates, though Charles worries a bit about interfering mother-in-laws if his children were to marry Italians. But blacks are the strangers, the aliens who constitute the prime "they." Reactions range from the relatively gentle "I don't know how I'd be able to handle that [marriage to a black] with my daughter," to harsh, unmitigated rejection.

Josie Thompson volunteers an explanation for her rejection, hoping that she will be understood, for black children are full participants in her children's affairs and she would like to be seen as a "bigot" only in a limited sense. Not wanting grandchildren of mixed ancestry, she calls herself a bigot. Such children grow up miserable, she says, and this is the point she drives home as she relates the story of her friend Phyllis, the child of a black man and a Filipino woman. Phyllis's mother's second marriage was to a Filipino man. He chased away the black boy who came by for a date with Phyllis. When her stepfather saw the boy, he picked up a large butcher knife and screamed, "You black motherfucker. Get the hell out of my house. I don't want no goddamn niggers in my house." Josie concludes with the words she told her own daughter:

If you ever, ever really felt that you loved a black man so much that he was your life and you wanted to make the rest of your life with him, fine, but have yourself fixed. Don't have kids, because as much as you love your kids, you can't protect them from all the hostility and racism that there is.

Mexicans in Riverview are on both the recieving and the giving ends of hostility and racism. "What we wanted," says Josie plaintively, "is to have more consideration, to be treated like the rest of the citizens in the town." Her lament is the eternal plea of all those who as the strangers see the enviably different and better life of the friends, and, moreover, who do not hold to the idea of having a place to which they must keep. Specifically, they want access to jobs on the basis of skill, not ethnicity; they want non-Mexicans to make no assumptions about their talents based on ethnicity; they want color not to be a factor in the decisions and judgments non-Mexicans make about them; and they want city regulations to apply to them in the same way they do to those whose relatives work for the city. At school they want their children to be treated fairly so that: if something is stolen, teachers don't assume a Mexican child was the thief; if lice are found, teachers don't assume a Mexican child was the original source; if they have a teacher who hugs, they are as likely to be hugged as any non-Mexican student; and if a Mexican fights a non-Mexican child, the same rules and punishments apply equally to both children.

"Is there racism in Riverview?" I ask Josie. "Not a lot like it used to be. It's really mellowed out a lot." Still, she adds, if the Burger King near where a lot of blacks live is robbed, "a damn nigger did it. Instinctively, it comes to mind." "Nigger" refers to "trashy" blacks, she clarifies, not to the ones who do their work and are churchgoers and good neighbors. Mexicans have replaced their near-blanket condemnation of blacks with qualified but far from full acceptance. Few can join Josie in her enthusiastic recounting of her son's black friends, three of whom she thinks of as her adopted sons.

Blacks

Unlike immigrants who come from beyond the borders and get tagged with the label of minority, a black American presence in California is the result of internal migration from other parts of the United States. Riverview's newspaper marked the fact of the in-migration by references in 1919 to "Growth of Colored Church" and to "Colored Masonic Program," which "was a creditable showing . . . revealing as it did the high place of citizenship for which the colored man is aiming and on which he will ultimately land." Some decades later, Martin Luther King wondered when this "ultimately" would arrive.

Few current black families trace their origins to this early period, but those who did live in the Riverview of the 1920s remember that time as do the Sicilians who were their neighbors. Since the nonblack residents of those days were not southerners, they "did not know about discrimination," says Lamar Robinson. "They [whites] treated us fine; there were no racial problems. I didn't know about discrimination until

I came out of the army. I'd read about it, but I had no personal experience with it."

Lamar Robinson's recollections reflect a time in Riverview when the community was divided roughly into the East Side of merchants and managers and the West Side of all the others. Black families were settled among all the others, with no special, ghettoized, residential space set aside for them. That development would come later. Les Baker recalls the Riverview he came to in 1935.

There was a small population of blacks here then, so nobody paid much attention to them. We just blended in with the poor Mexican and poor Italian and poor white. If you was poor, you was poor. It don't matter what color you were. It wasn't a matter of white and black, then. It was a matter of rich and poor. Only two black families in town had homes.

Les Baker reached Riverview after years of stoop labor as a migrant worker who followed the various growing seasons. In his seventies now, he easily recalls the path of his migrant work of fifty and more years ago: hay and watermelons in the Imperial Valley, oranges in the Poorsville area, nuts in the Taft area, peaches in the Hanford area, prunes in the Tulare area—about five months of picking, generally moving northward all the time, with hard, post-picking times a struggle to survive.

At Les's first job in Riverview he handled loads of lead that weighed 500 to 1,250 pounds each. He earned fifteen dollars a week, more than he had ever earned before, doing work that only black men did. By the time World War II began, Les had shifted to a mill whose work the government deemed essential to the war effort. With able-bodied non-blacks drafted into military service, able-bodied blacks constituted a major available source of labor, given that segregation in the military precluded their ready drafting or enlistment. They came to California by the trainload.

Les recalls that the federal government paid the companies doing war-related work "cost plus to get these people." He also recalls that their coming changed Riverview "terrifically, because we had a lot of people here we didn't know and didn't understand." This is the Californian black man reflecting on the southern black men who became his responsibility when his company appointed him to a grievance committee. The newcomer blacks acted different and talked with "a southern drawl," but now, forty-five years later, Les thinks they've blended in. "They're all like us now," by which he implies that having black skin was not immediately sufficient to place the newcomers in the class of "friend" among black oldtimers, though they eventually attained that status.

A second stream of blacks to Riverview developed from the presence of a large, nearby military camp. Young black men stationed at the camp experienced their first taste of life outside the South, liked it, and returned to live in Riverview after the war. Their cousins, aunts, and grandparents followed. In fact, chain migration worked for the blacks, just as it did for the Sicilians and Mexicans before them. Gertie Parson's dad got a job at the steel mill because his nephew worked there and vouched for him; Gertie's brother returned from the military and got a job at the mill because his dad vouched for him. "In those days that's how it was," says Gertie. By a similar route, women got jobs working in the canneries.

The availability of work and the attractiveness of the city and countryside drew blacks to Riverview. This is fact. It coexists with the fact of a pattern of discrimination that other local ethnic groups also experienced at one time or another; for no other group, however, was the discrimination as sustained or pernicious.

As I reflect on the generally positive recollections I heard from older blacks and try to avoid discounting them in the face of the negative recollections I also obtained (often from the very same persons, as well as from others), I reach this conclusion: black residents made peace with constraints that they accepted as the status quo. Defying these constraints was not conducive to maintaining a tranquil life, though for many the time would come when the defying would begin and tranquility no longer could be sustained in the face of constraints that earlier they perceived as endurable.

Defiance did not yet have a voice in October 1930, when the local newspaper ran news items under such headings as these: an ethnically unidentified "Hotel Man Held for Murder in Woman's Death," but ethnically identified "Negroes Held as Pickpocket Suspects Here." Riverview blacks gave voice to defiance about 1939; their target was employment. Later targets would be housing, schooling, and politics. Obviously, blacks could not mobilize in the same way to compel nonblacks to open their social life to them, to admit them as full candidates for the status of friend, though individual personal displeasure at rejection could and would be expressed.

The sum total of these constraints to opportunity—in jobs, housing, education, politics, and social contacts—was enormous. Though they did not have equal impact at any given time, their collective weight compelled blacks to learn how to live without the bitterness and hate that would have been personally harmful. Those who eventually looked at their burden as due cause for bitterness and hate, and turned their sentiments into challenges to change injustice, would soon be heard throughout the nation. Such persons are not a notable part of events in Riverview, though anger and violence persisted as a condition of life in Riverview High School for many years after Martin Luther King's assassination.

Much more common than bitterness and hate would be passivity, a quiet acceptance of the status quo, or a managing of perception that would be passed on from insightful parents to receptive children. Gertie Parson had such a managing parent:

My mom always instilled one thing in us and I tried to do that with my children. She said white people think that they are better than you are, but nobody is any better than you are unless you think so. And that grew up in me. I've never had that inferiority complex like a lot of people. I give my mother the credit.

By such maxims did Gertie and others avoid drawing negative conclusions about themselves based on the unfavorable circumstances of their lives.

Much more common in Riverview than bitterness and hate was the response of Dayton Mitchell. In 1939, when he was a new high school graduate, the then newly organized Riverview chapter of the National Association for the Advancement of Colored People (NAACP) approached him to be a test case to open local factories to jobs for blacks. NAACP leaders wanted him to take the written tests—for which they would tutor him—that were preliminary to employment in four large local factories. Dayton passed all four tests and the NAACP decided to press his case for a job in the steel mill. The NAACP took his case to the mill's national headquarters; Dayton had a job one month later. The victory won the 125-pound Dayton a job on the midnight shift using a 50-pound sledge hammer in the mill's foundry. Over the mill's three shifts, about 325 persons worked in the foundry. Three were black men; the rest were Mexican men.

Getting a job was a victory for the NAACP and Dayton. Being content on the job was another matter: the several hundred Mexican workers refused to shower with Dayton and his fellow black workers. Dayton went to the floor of the union and got booed for his protest against a separate shower for blacks. Dayton went back to the NAACP, which eventually brought the issue before the National Labor Relations Board (NLRB) in Washington, D.C. He recalls that his company's national headquarters accepted the NLRB's ruling of no separate showers. About this "victory" Dayton says, "A victory is not something for me to come back and beat you on the head with. The victory is for me to come back and try to get closer to you and work with you and try to give you a better feel for me."

Dayton learned not only about humility, but also about persisting in pursuit of jobs and improved working conditions for blacks, sometimes in the face of rejection by other blacks. After World War II, Dayton teamed up with other veterans to pressure the locally owned cannery, where many black women worked, to improve working conditions. Police threw them out of the cannery office. On the Sunday following their removal, the pastor of their church admonished unnamed "hoodlums" for bothering the cannery owner. The owner had told the pastor that "if this [pressure] is continued, he will probably fire all of our women."

The issue of housing got joined in Riverview in the 1950s when local authorities, under a federally funded urban-renewal program, removed whole sections of the oldest neighborhoods, where blacks, poor, and elderly persons lived. City government proposals written in the 1960s to get federal funds under Model Cities programs referred to the results of urban renewal as a "huge, barren, weed-filled scar." Most blacks were renters; their houses were torn down. Neither local nor federal government agencies took responsibility for their relocation. Much of the scar was intact in 1986, when the city and developers collaborated on the building of high-cost homes that would cover its remaining traces.

The struggle for open housing continued for many years. Nonblacks drew arbitrary lines beyond which blacks were not to move. Of course, lines gradually did move, from north to south, sometimes from building to building. A prominent east-west road that passes through town is referred to as the Mason-Dixon line, beyond which a minority-free zone was supposed to exist. In 1959, Gloria Nelson bought her house not only beyond the line but in the hills that would soon contain the best of this new area's homes. The owner had a grudge against the city; he got even by being the first to sell a house to a black person. Black residents cheered such victories, but they did not achieve open housing. Over twenty years later, both black and white residents still remember who was first. Finally, two developments changed the housing picture: first, a major local house builder opened his new projects to black buyers, and, second, and more significantly, state and federal laws prohibited discrimination in housing. By the time the housing struggles were over in the 1970s, poor blacks were settled in two areas that became black ghettos, and blacks could and did buy any house in Riverview that they could afford.

In the case of schooling in Riverview, the issue was not equal access for entry into the schools, but equal opportunity to acquire the various academic and nonacademic goods that American schools offer their students. The demands of blacks and other minorities are primarily confined to the period of 1968 to 1980 and will be discussed in a later chapter. For the period before 1968, I will identify one issue that shows the constraints to opportunities for black students.

On May 21, 1965, the local newspaper published a letter to the editor written by Gail Holmes, a black student at Riverview High School. Gail wrote that very few black girls ever passed the tryouts to become cheerleaders and pompon girls; none passed the 1965 tryouts. "It's not because they weren't qualified; it's because the judges were prejudiced." Times had changed in America; public cries of prejudice had become commonplace. The question was not if they would be uttered, but toward what concern that no longer enjoyed the shelter of propriety. Gail Holmes was attuned to the times. She wondered why black males could play on the football team but black females could not cheer them on.

Four days after Gail's letter appeared, the school board met to hear testimony on the pompon issue. The school board concluded that the selection process was fair. The NAACP protested the board's decision. William Council of the Riverview Human Relations Commission urged the board to accept his group as a fact-finding and mediating board. The school board rejoined that it had the facts, whereupon Council got into an exchange with the school board's senior member:

Council: If any violence happens, I want you to have it on your conscience.
Giani: I didn't like that threat.
Council: It wasn't a threat.
Giani: It certainly sounded like a threat to me. My conscience is clear. I've lived all my life in Riverview and with the Negro community. Many are my friends.

The next day's newspaper account observed that Giani's "statement drew laughter and shaking of heads from the audience."

More letters to the editor appeared, the school board convened another meeting, holding firm to its previous decision in the face of an audience of 350 protesters, and the newspaper record of this affair closed with a letter from Evelyn Taylor. After reviewing all details of the case, she concluded that, "As a result [of the selection procedure], the majority of pompon girls are Italians, which is the case every year. . . . Are they qualified, or is it tradition? Yes, tradition. . . . It's time we stopped living in the past."

Though the 1965 pompon choices remained unchanged, the blacks of Riverview had made a point. Thereafter, ethnicity would not be a factor in selecting girls for any of the positions associated with cheerleading.

Open competition would prevail, enforced by administrators who drew a moral from the 1965 incident, though it would take a bit longer before the school board and public would readily accept the moral. Evelyn Taylor had made the point in her letter: in effect, she said, be fair; remove traditional entitlements and proscriptions.

Betsy Hamilton is a younger member of the second generation of blacks in Riverview; her son attends junior high school. I asked her how likely it was for a black person in Riverview to have close friends who are not black. She did not comment, as did older blacks, about "redneck, blue-collar workers who cannot stand to see a black or Chicano or Asian get one step ahead of them"; about having sat down at a family dinner with whites not more than three times in fifty years as an adult in Riverview; or about a black in a mixed marriage remaining "oppressed," notwithstanding being in the "same marriage, same house, same street" with a white partner. What Betsy did speak about, her elders might consider a sign of "progress." The feeling of progress did not resound in Betsy's words.

There are some whites you would call really good friends. There are some you share a common interest with because your kids are on the same baseball team. You may go on a picnic together, they may come over and swim in your pool, but they're not the friend you share your life with. There are friends and there are friends. Most of the people I associate with have friends that are white, but there's a black friend and there's a white friend. Let's face it. There's a difference because they live in a totally different world.

Betsy Hamilton's plaint is not that of Gertie Parson. Gertie's concerns were more fundamental. They relate to the "firsts," all of them accomplishments that were settled aspects of life by the time Betsy was growing up. For example, Gertie can name the first black hired by Riverview's Bank of America, police department, and fire department; and the first black on Riverview's city council, school board, and hospital board. She describes with pride the energy of her friend Gloria Nelson, whose house purchase cracked the previously closed "Mason-Dixon line." "Wherever they didn't want Gertie," Betsy says proudly, "she made sure she was there."

Betsy Hamilton can take for granted changes that began in the 1960s, when federal and state governments began to recognize that they could not ignore with impunity the plight of black Americans. Though government recognition has waxed and waned in past decades, it then still had pronounced meaning for the dispersion of funds and the focus of human resources.

In 1966, Title I authorized the Demonstration Cities and Metro-

politan Act to ameliorate conditions in slums and blighted neighborhoods. Few places in the United States as small as Riverview would
qualify. Popularly called the Model Cities Program, the act offered an
opportunity to numerous cities for a broad attack on the worst of their
neighborhoods. Riverview's application for acceptance as a model city
stated its case in strong terms:

Our lack of explosive violence is probably attributable more to our small size
and the desire of local minority groups to work amicably to solve problems
than to good intergroup relations. This city has welcomed minority groups
from its earliest days. It is in the midst of a heavily industrialized area. . . . This
combination of factors has made us a haven for the low-income families, the
oppressed, the culturally deprived. The presence of these people in large
numbers has influenced the professional and managerial people to live
elsewhere.

The nearly six million dollars Riverview received under the Model
Cities Program covered a range of services to senior citizens, the unemployed, health care needs, family counseling, day care, etc. A condition
for spending the money was the establishment of citizens' committees
that had to approve any plans the city devised. The citizens' committees
always had a majority of blacks and other minority members. Their participation empowered people who were not used to being counted. That
blacks and other minorities were counted is evident not only in the city's
eligibility to receive six million dollars, but also in the school district's
eligibility to benefit from fourteen federal and state programs (as of
1971). By 1970, the city of Riverview was receiving 40 percent of its operating revenues from the federal government.

Moreover, the annual reports that were required as a condition for
receiving federal and state money accustomed cities and school systems
to thinking in ethnic terms. Officially, blacks and other minorities
ceased to be invisible; the money-giving agencies mandated ethnic auditing. All program accomplishments had to be broken down by
ethnicity. For example, the city's community-development coordinator
reported on the loans her program had approved: black—48, Hispanic—6, white—18, and other—1. The city's Small Cities Performance Assessment Report had to present its annual successes in terms
of these categories of beneficiaries: White not Hispanic; Black not Hispanic; American Indian or Alaskan Native; Hispanic; and Asian or Pacific
Islander.

By its connection to money, ethnicity received attention, becoming
an element of strategy in the calculations of organizations and individuals. Listen to white Joseph Flood, who had been active in

establishing an independent community-development agency that required federal funds for its operations:

We determined early on [that] our board was going to be minority-controlled. We made up that policy so when we went for money the government's going to say, "Gee, they're minority-controlled." Also, don't forget, you eliminate any criticism from minority groups.

And listen to Josie Thompson advising her nephew, Timmy, the child of a Mexican mother and Anglo father. Timmy, so Josie explained, had been rejected by companies that told him they needed to hire minorities.

I says, look, put your first name the way you did. I says, and put your mother's maiden name in where your middle name is. Put your father's last name. When they put down what nationality are you, I says circle Caucasian and Latino, or Mexican. He says but my middle name isn't really. . . . I says you put down your first initial of your middle name and then put your mother's maiden name. He got the job he was rejected for before. When he just used his honky name, he didn't get nowhere.

Josie Thompson is not black, but her story demonstrates how ordinary people became attuned to the use of ethnic identity beyond its application to merely private concerns.

"When you are at home," says Linda Jeffries, "it doesn't occur to you. It's just, like, you don't think about color. I had to, you know, say I was black when I went to the outside world." Black Americans go many places where they are not at home. Thus they think about their color, about being black and who they are and, often, who they must be. When the Reverend Hosea Williams, an Atlantic City councilman, spoke at a Riverview church in 1987, he warned the audience of five hundred that black youth must learn the "history of their race," and for how short a time have blacks been able to join the Kiwanis and the chamber of commerce: "A person must understand who he is." But who he is is a variable matter that depends on where he is, who is present, and what is going on. While history may anchor one's identity, it cannot predict what form one's ethnic self will or must assume.

Black adults spend much of their life outside the home in settings where nonblacks predominate, both in numbers and in control. How they manage or adapt in such settings depends on the sense of self they bring with them. Some, like Les Baker, bring an awareness of self fostered by the knowledge of history that Hosea Williams endorsed. His reading has led him to respond with disdain to those who call him a nigger: "The white guy didn't know who I am when he called me that. I'm a

black man. [He laughs.] I'm one of the founders of the world and he
didn't know that."

Gertie Parson, taking her cue from the fact that nonblacks would see
her children in a certain way, taught them that they "are different because of the color of their skin," though never less good because of that
fact. While she did not see assimilation as the destiny of black youth,
other black families did. Their children grew up with white standards as
their ideal. Elsie Gilbert was one such child, but as an adult she realized
that it was more than a matter of losing an accent that stood between her
and total assimilation. "In terms of black history," she says, "one of the
key issues is we just didn't disappear in the masses out there." "Out
there," where Elsie will never disappear, is a white world that impinges
on blacks. "It's true," agrees Gertie, you've got to learn to act white.
"That goes back to another thing my mother taught me—kissing ass.
Well, you have to kiss a little bit, but you don't have to lay there and lick
it. You have to learn how to play the game." Though she will do things
she does not approve of doing, "I let them know I don't like it."

Elsie Gilbert, a single woman in her forties, decided to attend an out-
of-town session of Parents Without Partners. At the meeting, a white
man asked her why she didn't attend the group in a city "where there'd
be more people like me." Some months later, she saw an ad for a meeting of Christian singles, also to be held outside Riverview. Certain about
being Christian and single, she acknowledges that "before I consider
going, the Parents Without Partners situation will pop up again and I'll
wonder what I'll find when I get there. I'm not used to thinking about
that." Yet she is used to having a black viewpoint, and consciously so.
She clarifies this as she talks about her work: "Issues come up, housing,
employment, and so forth, that I bring a different perspective to because I'm black," and she does this in settings where she may be the only
black person present. Clearly, it is not just being black that takes her by
surprise but being black in circumstances where she had not thought of
her blackness as a factor of consequence. Apparently, the twenty or so
years she spent in Riverview, beginning as a young adult in her mid-
twenties, had accustomed her to some ways of being or feeling black but
not to others.

Mexicans speak readily about aspects of being Mexican—language,
food, and music, for example, and, above all, about acclaiming their
Mexican heritage. All Riverview's ethnic groups share this pride in
heritage, expressed as never denying one's ethnic identity. Blacks, more
than Mexicans and Sicilians, seem to want their children to know the
role of their group in American history. They object to history that is
written and taught as if blacks deserve mention only as slaves brought

from Africa, as a factor in the Civil War, as initiators of the 1960s civil-rights movement, and as all-star professional athletes. However, their preference for instruction that shows blacks as co-builders of America is not translated into pressure on the schools to offer such instruction.

All ethnic groups have lived through generations with strong feelings about marrying within one's group and have come to be more casual about choice of mate. Blacks fit this pattern, though their thoughts about propriety vary from those who, like Les Baker, reject what he calls "clannish" considerations. He is pleased that church affiliation does not constitute the barrier to marriage that it used to, and moreover that his grandchildren are from a wide variety of ethnically mixed marriages. Gertie thinks that "God made us all different" and that we should keep these differences. She has no hostility for blacks who marry nonblacks, though she is very pleased that there have been no mixed marriages in her family. Roy Madison joins Gertie in not being antagonistic to what he calls "interracial" marriages; more than this, he would, if necessary, give his blessings to such a marriage—but would not feel right about it. In his explanation, we get a rationale about marriage, identity, and his children that he carries around with him. Parents commonly have them; it is far from predictable, however, that their children share them: "We raise our kids to go to school, to do everything right, to move up and be competitive. If they go out and marry a white or a Mexican, . . . somehow, you're not strictly in your culture when you do that." Given the relative fluidity of American life, it is not always clear where you would be if you try to stay "strictly in your culture."

At present, Riverview's Mexicans have more ethnically based organizations than the Sicilians and blacks, but none with the national stature of the NAACP or with the local political success of the Black Cultural Political League (BCPL). Mexican organizations provide numerous services to newcomer and poor Mexicans; they also do very well in celebrating the two previously described major Mexican occasions, on September 16 and May 5. The black counterparts to these are the various fund-raising dinners and programs different black groups organize, and the observances for Martin Luther King Day and Black History Month. The most significant activities of the black organizations are their watchdog functions on behalf of the black community. We saw the earlier work of the NAACP in cracking barriers to employment. Nowadays, they are not engaged in barrier cracking, though they remain alert, monitoring the affirmative-action committee established by the Riverview School District, inviting candidates for elective offices to present themselves, observing the decisions of the school boards, listening to the complaints of black parents about their children in school, and raising money for cultural activities and scholarships for promising black high school graduates.

Black organizations direct their energies to varied activities. Thus, the Black Political Association (BPA), the day before a recent statewide election, placed an ad that listed its choices for the offices of governor down to the State Board of Equalization, and that declared its position on fourteen different referenda (including Proposition 63, which would make English the state's official language—vote yes, the BPA recommended). It also arranged a Miss Talented Teen contest; the Miss Teenage Galaxy International Pageant; and a cruise—"Dinner on the Bay and All That Jazz," the tickets on sale at Zeeks Beauty Bar or Sheila's House of Hair and Nails.

Some activities, perhaps the most important ones, never become public, in the sense of becoming a newspaper item. The president of the Black Cultural Political League observed that his group is a "watchdog for our school system because our kids often fall in the cracks." Longstanding members of the BCPL believe that there is continuous need to be alert: "They'll [an unspecified "they"] slip back to their old things if you don't keep a steady watch on them." In the past, the BCPL worked alone or with the NAACP to argue for black pompon girls; for black principals, teachers, and administrators; and for black custodians and nonacademic employees. "Today," says a member, "few people will stand on a street corner and yell, 'I hate niggers; I don't want niggers around,' but you know deep down they prefer a white every time. They can't be blatant any more because they know somebody is watching them."

The BCPL and other organizations seem prepared to insure that nonblack organizations and individuals will treat blacks as if they were friends, even though they may not yet believe that blacks really are. It is not easy to remain prepared. The watchdog function requires resources of time, money, and effort that are in short supply. "Some of it is that people like me are burnt out," says Betsy Hamilton. "The people who are really hurting now have not made enough fuss to make those who possibly could lead them look around."

Some of it is that a consciousness of ethnic self that prevailed some years ago no longer exists, or is far less prevalent. For example, in 1972 the local newspaper publicized a summer festival dance sponsored by the Ebony Social Set. Other clubs involved were the Brothers of the Ghetto, Brothers United, Afro-Elites, and Volklords. None of these organizations exist today. Elsie Gilbert recalls when people got very vocal at meetings, pounding on tables, and threatening long, hot summers: "Were that to occur today, people would consider it an unruly, rude interruption of the meeting and would wait until whoever was speaking had their say, and then go on with the meeting."

When Virgil Newfield returned home from his prominent eastern college, a reporter interviewed him. The article concluded with Newfield's view of his black friends who stayed in Riverview: "A lot of them are just not doing anything with their lives. They turned to the streets. They're not my friends anymore, because I can't turn to the streets. The streets are scary." Maybe more Gertie Parsons need to tell their children what Gertie told her children. And maybe more Dayton Mitchells need to tell everyone that "white people and a lot of black people make a mistake" in thinking that black people are all alike. No Riverview organization, black or otherwise, is seriously devoted to cultivating more Parsons and Mitchells.

Filipinos

Filipinos have been migrating to Riverview and its county environs since 1918. Today, 9,000 make their home there, about 1,600 of them living in Riverview, which has the largest Filipino population in the county. And they continue to come, motivated by economic and political problems in their homeland. Their coming is facilitated by familiarity with American life and, often, by competency in English. Since 1975, more than 30,000 a year have entered the United States, making them "the fastest growing Asian population"; soon they will exceed the country's 1.25 million Chinese population (Seligman 1985).

The post–World War I wave of Filipinos were farmers at home and became migrant farm workers here who, like black Les Baker, followed the crops and the seasons. Stephen Hilado was part of this group. With help from an uncle he reached the United States in 1927. After four years of railroad work, much of it knocking in spikes on cross-ties, he had a series of agricultural jobs before coming to California in 1941. During World War II, he found work in the shipyards, but when he was laid off after the war he returned to the railroad and stayed there until he reached retirement age.

Had the matter of Stephen Hilado's presence in California been left to certain others to decide, he'd have stayed in the Philippines. The "others" showed their hand in January 1932, when Riverview's local newspaper carried an editorial stimulated by "racial disorders" in Honolulu:

California has always claimed that they [Japanese and Chinese] were unassimilable. We have had threatened trouble . . . upon several occasions with the Philipinos. Perhaps after a few years and such the rest of the U.S. will agree that California knew what was what when it insisted upon Japanese exclusion. And it wouldn't hurt labor conditions in this country one iota if the Philipinos were kept in the Islands where they belong.

Wartime needs expedite the process of seeing as friends those who recently were strangers. So it was with Filipino men who found careers in the military during World War II, serving in all-Filipino companies under white American officers. These companies were incorporated into the regular United States armed forces during the war and, for their contributions, the government gave the men the option of remaining in the army and becoming naturalized American citizens. It was a much-used option and Filipinos left the islands in even larger numbers than previously. The military wave of Filipinos was accustomed to a life of order and discipline that their children could long remember as trademarks of their fathers.

In the early postwar years, the new Filipino families settled first in the multiethnic residential areas near the mills and later in a new neighborhood consisting of several streets of modest homes that became a short-term Filipino ghetto. When they tried to move out of their "end of town," realtors gave them "the runaround." Still-resident Filipino families well remember the resistance to Filipino home buying, but always in moderate terms: "We were confined to just north of the highway. There was some reluctance—I don't know if it was intentional—to sell us homes south of the highway. There was that natural discrimination. We more or less got along well in proving that we're A-OK to be neighbors next to." Such "proving" captures a widespread sense of the Filipino concept of how to get established in their new country. I would hear comparable language over and over again. I cannot imagine hearing any black or Mexican-American speaking of "natural discrimination."

If they could afford to, Filipino women, like their Mexican counterparts, stayed home to raise families; if they could not, they looked for jobs in the canneries. Their husbands having returned overseas to military service, some women faced the hardship of making a home alone in a new country. Thirty or more years later, the memories of those early years have softened to recollections of earlier settlers helping later settlers, of neighborliness, and of sociable gatherings at dusk at the house of some friend, mothers clustered together on a porch while children played peacefully on nearby streets and sidewalks.

Three generations of Filipinos currently live in Riverview. In general, the first and second generation were born abroad, though the second usually has spent most of its life in the United States. The grandparents, fluent in English, speak their vernacular languages to each other and often to other countrymen. Most speak Tagalog, the Filipino national language. Filipinos retain ties to their homeland by visits, the *Philippine News* (a regional newspaper published in California), and the continuing arrival of newcomers. Thus, to the too-neat image of a three-generation Filipino community, we must add the newcomers, whose children take their place beside Mexicans in bilingual and English-as-a-second-language classes.

Sixteen-year-old Teresa Soberon is one such newcomer. Her description of home life resembles that of the Filipino second generation. The fathers of girls like Teresa just know one way for a young lady to grow up; she, however, learns daily about attractive alternative ways. The result is strongly divergent concerns, the father's expressed as, "What will become of my daughter in this place?" and the daughter's expressed as, "Why won't he let me live my own life?"

You know, I'm wearing shorts and I'm sitting by the door and there are guys walking by. My father said, "Go inside. Don't sit there." I said why. "Because you're wearing shorts and that's it." "God!" I said to my father, "This is America." I don't know what happened to my father. He's not let me date with boys. It's OK with a chaperone. It's OK if my older sister went. But just me only, no. No way. If I tell him this is American, he says you're Filipino.

Teresa has a boyfriend. I ask her to speculate how, if she were married, she might raise her children.

They will be half-Filipino and half-white. For Filipino, they learn respect your mother and teacher; do something in the house; be careful of style; watch her boyfriend or girlfriend. That's it. For American, for starters, clothes. They can wear shorts. No chaperone. Speak English. Tagalog—not really. Better speak English, but tell them all about the Philippines. Some Filipinos born here don't know nothing about the Philippines.

They will have freedom. I don't have freedom. I can't just go out, go to my friends. My father, he says to me, "Be here at 5:00." Like that. It's all my father.

Marry a Filipino, he tells me. I could not marry a Puerto Rican. If I like a Puerto Rican, nobody can stop me. He'll get mad, but it doesn't matter.

Teresa articulates the time-honored practice of ignoring parental preferences for one's mate. She runs some risk of being disowned, but this practice is not sufficiently time-honored to constrain her from concluding "nobody can stop me." Control and independence are at odds in her life, an old story, no less painful for both sides however old it may be. Her father would be surprised by the extent of his daughter's acceptance of his ideas for childrearing.

Carla Estrella, born in the Phillipines like her parents, has children at Riverview High who are Teresa's age and older. She left Luzon too young to remember much about her birthplace; family pictures and stories tell her more than she remembers. Her father, a proud member of the American army at the time of the Japanese invasion in 1942, strongly identifies with the United States, to the extent of permitting only English to be spoken at home. Whenever her father left home, her mother always spoke Tagalog. For some years the family lived away from Riverview. In this period, Carla attended a school where there were no other Filipino children.

I've never considered myself to be exclusively part of a group. When my family came back to Riverview—I was in grade school then—for the first time I realized that I was not American. Here you had to belong to the blacks, the Mexicans, the Italians, the Filipinos, the whites. And I thought, where do I belong? I didn't belong with any of them.

Carla describes feeling separated from her ethnic roots. Just how separated she makes clear as she continues to talk about her life.

I never knew I was a Filipino till I got here. I never felt it. To this day, I don't feel it. I really don't. My father was very proud to be an American citizen. By the time I started school, I thought I was American. I thought I was like anyone else. I thought I was white. I spoke English without an accent. He always said, "You're an American now. Do the best you can." All through my life he kept saying that.

Something else her father kept saying was that Carla should not take an after-school job—"my father was too proud." As a result, she could not afford to attend a four-year college. She commuted to a community college, instead, and soon learned that there was more to ethnicity than language, food, and music. One day a counselor asked her if she would like to go to college because several were sending recruiters to look for minority students under the new Equal Opportunity Program. "Actually," she says, "I had never thought of anyone else as a minority. You're you and that's it." She learned that by being a minority, by accepting a label that she had never thought fit her, she could go to a university for the remainder of her schooling. She learned what Josie Thompson taught her nephew, child of a mixed marriage, about using ethnicity as a means to the ends of education and employment.

Carla's father did not plan what mixture of Filipino and American he would be; she, however, is articulate on this point. Like Teresa's father, her father did not let her go out as she pleased. He controlled her movements, while planting in her the idea that she should accept no limit to her aspirations, and that she was American. When she came to multi-ethnic Riverview, she was compelled to have a label, and "American" was not an acceptable one to her labeled peers. Of course, her fellow students were American, but they also knew they were something else. That something else required specification. As Carla continues to speak, we learn that she probably always felt and acted as if she truly were some nameable ethnic, though she was not accustomed to using the name. To some extent, it still does not sit squarely on her. About being Filipino, she says, "To this day, I don't feel it. I really don't." More than most adults I met, she expressed the several selves we all are, and with no consciousness of conflict among them.

I don't know why I act less Filipino than my parents did. You *don't* know why. I could have stayed just the way they wanted me to, but no one can ever be that way, unless they nail you in a box feeding you those lines so you become almost like a puppet.

My son, he knows he's Filipino. It's just superficial, just what you look like on the outside: he's Filipino, he's Mexican, he's black, that kind of thing. He's like me: I don't know what this Filipino-ness is. I always taught my kids that this nationality thing is superficial. It just helps you to identify who's who.

I have within me the Americanization that I've always had, so that when I go back to my country I cannot understand a lot of the culture. What I do, they frown upon, though for me it's normal. Sometimes I think about the things that are happening in the Philippines [in 1986]. When I think of Marcos, I get embarrassed because he's Filipino like me and he'd do that [create political and economic turmoil]. He took advantage of his country and his people.

For all her denial, in the end she is sufficiently Filipino to feel shamed by the embarrassing behavior of other Filipinos. Every group has a word in its vernacular which refers to that shame: How will it/we look to the neighbors if one of us behaves shamefully? Would it indicate the full loss of ethnic identity if one felt no unease at the publicized misdeeds of one's fellow ethnics? Or would it simply be a matter of self-esteem, of feeling so secure about self that one could not be besmirched however dastardly the deeds of one's fellow ethnics?

Ellis Delgado, like Carla, was born in the Philippines. He came to Riverview when he was eleven, brought by a military father who was pleased to be an American citizen, but did not make a fetish of it. He grew up in Riverview's Filipino ghetto, located just north of the highway. His parents never lived anywhere else, though he joined the

throngs moving to the more desirable homes south of the highway:
"There was no blatant attitude to keep us out. We were recognized as
good people and could move anywhere." No group in Riverview has
been more intent on being so recognized; in this way, Filipinos put effort
into making the passage from stranger to friend. Ellis meant to be seen
and accepted as friend.

Like Carla Estrella, Ellis also presents himself in contrast and reaction to his parents, thinking that he has had the better of life. In
economic terms, he undoubtedly has.

I don't deny I'm a Filipino. I'm always a Filipino, but at the same time I want to
adopt the American way of life. My dad wasn't too pleased with my change in
behavior. For example, when Filipino families visit each other, the kids greet
and acknowledge their seniors by picking up their hand and kissing it. I refused
to do it. This is not American, I say. Sometimes, I find myself doing it now. My
kids don't do it; they don't even know this custom.

There are many customs that Ellis's children don't know about; it is
likely they will not even know they once existed. Ellis and his father
reached young manhood and middle age respectively under circumstances that called their attention to the ethnic fabric of their life: the
father meant to maintain it as he saw fit, making changes in it, also as he
saw fit. Ellis, concluding that his father was not a reliable arbiter of what
was fit, wanted to shape the fabric in his own way.

My parents were strong on good behavior. We thought we had to be good,
while others—the Americans—were cutting up. My father said, "You don't
bring disgrace to the family. You better not be deported." My parents wanted
me to marry our own kind. No blacks, no Americans. Americans in our language refers to the white folks, OK? Nowadays, that's not a material point;
parents on both sides are much more open.

Children compel their parents to redefine who is an acceptable mate. To
Filipinos, non-Filipinos will never be "our own kind," but they become
increasingly acceptable in the range of social interactions that shape a
life, so that the stipulation of "our own kind" as a condition for interaction grows less and less usual.

Ellis is far from the zero point, notwithstanding his definite intention
to be American. Though he did not marry a Filipino woman, he is active
in the Filipino-American Association and in maintaining close ties to the
Filipino friends and families of his youth. He is troubled if the newspapers carry a story showing Filipinos in a bad light. "I don't want
people to generalize about Filipinos," and he resists the disposition of
other Filipinos in business to assume that he will be favorably inclined

toward them because of their shared ethnicity. Also, like Carla, he speaks confidently about the self he is and meant to be.

In my time, we were apprehensive about our identity, about forcing people to accept us for whom we are. We wanted to be accepted but we weren't normal. We were subservient because we were strangers. Now, my kids are accepted for what they are, rather than for behaving right. I wasn't angry because I had to behave; it was natural for me.

When I was younger, and I'd have some issue with my parents, I would decide that I'm not going to live by the same lifestyles as they do. This became a driving force: since I am here in America, I'm not going to live like a Filipino. I'm going to live like an American. I'm going to eat their food, speak their language. If I'm going to die here, I might as well be one of them. The aspiration was there to better my self, using my parents as a minimum and looking at the white neighbor as the optimum.

Donald Baclig, in his seventies, has lived all of his years since 1946 in the United States, most of them in Riverview. He joins the many Filipinos—they seem to be the majority—who believe that a combination of education and intention are sufficient for success. He reasons that since the U.S. Army had accepted Filipinos, it would simply be a matter of time before their adopted countrymen also would. "After all, Filipinos are a law-abiding people."

Donald draws a contrast between blacks and the Filipinos, disclaiming "discrimination against the blacks." Filipinos did not feel "left out of things" before "President Johnson signed the civil-rights law," but the blacks, "they feel that Uncle Sam owes them something." He speaks the tough language of self-sufficiency, of scorning welfare, of joining those of his immigrant predecessors who were poor when they arrived and "now are the mainstream" because they came to America to "prove themselves." Donald's words are a paean to his adopted country. They sound as if he had read some of the scores of pages exalting the land of opportunity and decided, "That's my story, too. A Filipino voice should be heard telling it."

Donald and his wife are active participants in the Filipino-American Association. They have taken their turn as leaders and as members of committees. They go to the organization's regular bingo nights and would never miss any of the group's special events, one of which I will describe in a moment. It is uncommon to see a Filipino under thirty at the special events. It is not that the youngest generation prefers dancing to the beat of other music. (In fact, they do, as do younger people in general.) They just prefer the beat of another way of life, having consigned the traditional behavior of their parents to the category of those "sentimental nicknacks" Carla Estrella does not want around to clutter up her home. "We just tried to stress the culture with our children," says Donald. "That's all. Don't forget. We want them to know the dances, songs, customs. They are adapting to some of them, but they aren't really very much into it. They lost that." He speaks matter-of-factly, as if to say that in acquiring the fruits of freedom, you give up your old ways and that's just how it is in America.

A common news items in the *Daily Herald* is one that mentions the activities of the Filipino-American Association (FAA), the largest (with 250 to 300 members) and most inclusive of the several local Filipino groups, in that persons from all regions of the Philippines will join. "Welcome to Our Cultural Fiesta," reads one side of the FAA's printed program. The other side hopes that you'll "continue to join us each year" for the dinner, traditional dancing, fashion show of traditional clothing, and, as always, dancing to the popular music of a live band or orchestra.

For its Bataan Day observance each year, the FAA organizes a ceremony to commemorate the Death March in 1942 of the thirty-five-thousand Filipino and American soldiers who had surrendered at Bataan. Along with the ceremony, there is a dinner and a dance. For this event, members decorated the Filipino-American Cultural Center with banners naming famous Pacific Theater battle sites—for example, Leyte, Iwo Jima, and Corregidor. And they honored the marchers in a candle-lighting, flower-laying ceremony held before a color guard standing at attention. Widows of the marchers came forward to receive a rose. Some wept lightly, touching their eyes with Kleenex. Both the Filipino and United States national anthems were sung, the latter first, though the oldest persons did not sing it at all.

"I know everyone is waiting for the dancing," said the FAA president before he launched into his comments on freedom and its relationship to Bataan. Remembering Bataan and its significance faced stiff competition from the long evening of dancing ahead, and even stiffer competition from the dancing enjoyed by Filipinos adolescents, notably absent on this occasion, as they were for the Cultural Fiesta. The night before, dressed in rented formal wear and newly bought gowns, they were very much present for their junior prom.

The FAA raises money for scholarships and serves as a contact point for newcomer Filipinos interested in taking English-as-a-second-language classes. Perhaps most important, it joins Filipinos in formal and informal activities that serve as reminder, reaffirmation, and reassurance of their community's still cherished singularity. Out of these community feelings they discuss Filipino interests: Do they exist? What are they? Do they get their share? Is it a fair share? When the school district hires a Filipino counselor or administrator, what relationship, if any, do they have with the Filipino community? Is the Filipino on the city council a representative of the Filipino community? Of the community at large? "Let's face it," says Angelica Cuyo, "a black feels different from a white, and maybe from Filipinos. Filipinos might feel different from blacks on one matter or another." Therefore, she concludes, the different ethnic groups need their own representation, but, she adds, it would be an "injustice" if such representatives only saw the "good points" of their own group, rather than "things as a whole." Ellis Delgado, to the contrary, says, "We don't have any beef, so to speak. For me to think, 'Yes, we need a Filipino voice,' runs counter to my feeling," though he thinks that the school district, the police department, and the city government ought to hire Filipinos, but not because they are Filipino but because they are qualified. He wants young Filipinos to have role models in Filipino adults employed in responsible positions throughout Riverview.

The Filipino-American Association joins the Black Cultural Political League, the United Council of Spanish-Speaking Organizations, the Sons of Italy, as well as the many other smaller ethnically based groups, in giving voice to the concerns and interests of its members, sometimes to the concerns and interests of its ethnic group in general. Here is how Riverview's ethnic voices sounded to non-Sicilian white Pete Murphy:

You've got some ethnic-oriented groups around this town. The school is not just isolated by itself. We're in the middle of a town that has had representatives out there walking up and down the street that are proclaiming themselves for the NAACP and from the Mexican-American Society [there is no such group]. We've had members run for public office in this town whose major thrust in what they proclaimed themselves to be is, "I think we should have Filipino influence on the school board." "I think we should have Mexican influence on the school board." What the hell, the school is right in the middle of this. It's bound to reflect. Italian, too, by the way.

Pete Murphy is part of the contemporary contingent of Riverview residents who see strangers when they look at people who do not quite look and sound as they themselves do, who resent what Pete calls the "thrust" of the ethnic groups. His sense of propriety is violated by the success of those who perpetrate the thrusts. Filipinos, and the other ethnic groups, have had their share of Pete Murphys since they arrived in America. Of all Riverview's settled ethnic groups, perhaps the Filipinos have had the least of that sort of thing to contend with.

Today, says Angelica Cuyo, unlike fifteen or twenty years ago, a Filipino can expect to have close friends drawn from all the ethnic groups, because Riverview is a "melting pot," which is her personal shorthand way of indicating that the social barriers between ethnic groups are lowered. However, when the Filipinos reached Riverview after World War II, they saw a community that contained two groups: "the Italians and the others." Italians "didn't want what I call outsiders in here," recalls Carla Estrella. Italians constituted the "we" against whom non-Italians measured themselves as "they." Carla perceived them as having prestige and money, and being in a position to be the agents of discrimination: "I just think we were the others."

In 1957, when Donald Baclig looked for a house, realtors offered only those that were "out in the boondocks or in the black community. We called it racism." It was also racism when Carla's father would tell stories which concluded with his saying, "Oh, I hate those blacks" or, "They're all . . ." indicating a prejudice that still exists. For example, the Filipino-American Association stipulates that their members be either Filipino or married to a Filipino, but it does have non-Filipino honorary members. A few years ago it rejected for honorary membership the man who was Riverview's first black city councilman and mayor, while accepting an Italian politician and his mother.

The FAA rejection of a black man as honorary member represents one facet of Filipino opinion toward blacks; there are others. Among the most generous is Ellis Delgado's:

I would like to show the black community that we appreciated very much what they had done. Their movement, their caucuses—we benefited from them, although we were not out in the forefront supporting them. I'll be the first one to admit that. They opened up the way, they opened up eyes and made people understand as to where not only blacks but the minority groups in general, they got the short end of the stick.

Among second-generation Filipinos, I did not hear harsh antiblack sentiment. They seemed to show the impact of the relatively easy acceptance they received at the hands of their predecessors. "I don't look at race," says Angelica Cuyo, "as when we do things together." Her observation about adult social relations is true enough. Her contact is with professional blacks—middle-class, as she is—and in such circumstances race often matters little. When, however, the circumstances involves their children's serious romantic relationships with blacks, race becomes a more prominent factor.

"Filipinos, I guess they're well known for not making a fuss, or going around parading," observes Angelica. "There's got to be something in this race—the Filipino race—that everybody accepts." And there's got to be something in the black "race" that compels adults of all ethnic groups to draw the line somewhere in their relationship to it. Adults are restrictive in their application of the status of friend to blacks: denying it altogether, restricting it in the interests of mixed-race children, or subtly exulting in the integrated successes of one's children that do not progress beyond innocent boy-girl contacts.

Third-generation Filipinos, the students now at Riverview High School, are being raised by confident, self-assured parents. Since the world they know is friendly to people like them, they can believe there is a relationship between hard work, ambition, and success. This world calls attention to their ethnicity, but acculturation is more valued than ethnic maintenance. They do not have grandparents who serve as guardians of tradition in the special way that elders do who never mastered English. Their grandparents speak English, play bingo, and fox-trot with the best of the Americans.

As a group, Riverview Filipinos spent a relatively short time in the status of minority. For a brief time, they were joined in political causes with Mexicans and blacks, the more enduring and officially designated minorities. Mexicans and blacks, notwithstanding common political, economic, and educational problems, find that which separates them more important than that which joins them. All three groups are, to varying degrees, distinguished from the majority population by language, behavior, appearance, and color. To be accepted in mainstream American society, all three groups modify some of the ethnic attributes that distinguish them; some they retain as a matter of pride; some, like color, resist modification, though the meaning that others attach to color is affected by the overall context of language, behavior, and appearance.

The members of each ethnic group rarely express reservations about being American. Indeed, becoming American proves to be so consuming that it requires special effort to retain one's cultural distinctions. Those most readily retained are associated with a holiday (Cinco de Mayo), the church (who to marry), the kitchen, or entertainment (music and dance). Anthropologist Edward Bruner (1961) wrote about different manifestations of group extinction. While none of Riverview's ethnic groups risk the extreme case of biological extinction, "when there are no living members," they do risk linguistic and social extinction, whereby they "stop speaking their own language" and "lack a distinctive society" (p. 259).

The notion of "extinction" fails to capture the amorphous attachment that individuals have to their ethnic identity. The nominal ethnic tie reflected in answer to the question, "Who are you?" may be just the surface of an assortment of feelings, loyalties, sympathies, and the like that can be the basis for social, traditional, or economic reaction given the right precipitating events. Thus, individuals who ordinarily are not assertively ethnic may become so, as they did in the Riverview of the 1960s and the 1970s. Arriving there for the first time in 1982, I just missed that Riverview. When my interviews and reading of the *Daily Herald* uncovered the heightened ethnicity of those decades, I found them hard to place in the calm Riverview I was daily experiencing just a few years later.

Ethnicity went public in the 1960s and 1970s. Politics and education in Riverview have never been the same. Though no one I met would wish to return to the turmoil of the recent past, the ethnic revitalization provided a force for social change that suited those times. Ethnophobia was no longer publicly acceptable; ethnics came out of the closet. The nonincidental fact of poverty, injustice, and prejudice animated legislation and Supreme Court decisions. Riverview and Riverview High School experienced twelve very uneasy years from 1968 to 1980. These years provide a critical transition between an old and a new order in Riverview and Riverview High School. A decade and more of ethnic assertiveness cracked a longstanding status quo of placid, easy-going, bounded place so that the nature of social interactions could be redefined.

3

History and Ethnicity: From the Riot of 1968 to the Boycott of 1980

The children of the Alicias, Daytons, and Carlas, whose voices we have just heard, have their own decisions to make about the place of ethnicity in their lives. They must mediate between the worlds of home, school, and peers in coming to terms with what distinctions to value and perpetuate. This process of mediation varies in response to a number of circumstances, and one of particular importance is the place of ethnicity in national affairs.

During the years of my contact with Riverview and its high school, 1982 to 1987, the fires of the civil-rights movement burned lightly compared to the 1960s and 1970s. If black remained beautiful, the words were heard and read less frequently throughout the land. Whether activists were tired from the stress of previous years, as I heard expressed in several communities in 1982, or the Reagan presidency had cast a pall on social movements in general, voices were calmer, confrontations generally a thing of the past, and social injustices, never in short supply, failed to stir widespread, deep-seated, concerted alarm.

In contrast, during the period 1968 to 1980, ethnicity was like a virus. It infected the body of Riverview High School, spreading throughout the system. As long as the virus remained active, no event escaped its impact, at least to some degree. Though blacks, whites, Mexicans, and Filipinos were actors in the drama of this period, black energy and concerns occupied center stage. As one school district administrator put it, this was the "black era." His reference is to color not to mood, though many Riverview residents would also think it an apt designation of the mood.

Accordingly, I continue my pursuit of the play of ethnicity by exploring the period just before I came to Riverview. I believe that the subdued, constrained perceptions of ethnicity that I observed during

71

the years of my inquiry, a matter for subsequent chapters, are to be understood, at least in part, by the excruciating salience of ethnicity in the
previous years.

School-district concentration on ethnicity is embodied, albeit by implication, in a 1976 proposal to reduce and prevent crime and disruption
in Riverview High School. "This project," the proposal writers stated,
"reflects the feelings, attitudes, frustration and anxieties as a microcosm
[of the ethnic-based disorder] in the community and modern day society." In short, the writers were saying, Riverview is not alone. Indeed, it
was not, as we shall see when we consider briefly what was happening in
the country—before and after 1968—that set the mood for events in
Riverview.

No Riverview resident or educator ever thought to tell me that the
most nagging concerns of the 1968–80 period were connected more with
money than with ethnicity. For this once-affluent school district was continually pinched, first, by a tax base drawn from declining heavy
industry and second, by the stringencies of Proposition 14, with its
lowered real estate rates of assessment. Less revenue, failed tax referenda, and escalating salaries, fringe benefits, and cost of living combined
to create a backdrop of fiscal hardship against which ethnicity-related
issues were played. Coincidentally, as local sources of money con-
stricted, special federal and state programs for minorities expanded.
These financial circumstances, as one person, a school board member of
that era, told me, led to a certain

white backlash of, "Well, gee, those [minority] kids are getting it all. Why
can't mine have it?" The demands were on the school to be everything to
everybody. There was just not enough money. Try to explain this to a basically
workingman's community. All they know is that this kid over here is getting a
lot of things in the way of monies.

Clearly, during the 1968–80 period, ethnicity wound its way through
Riverview High School. Ethnicity was omnipresent for over a decade;
when it ceased to be, educators whose tenure spanned the entire period, as well as afterward, would remark on the quiet that had descended
on their lives: something, they'd say, had changed. It took several years
of quiet before they could say what it was that was happening.

In retrospect, local observers trace the onset of quiet times to 1980,
when a Hispanic boycott rocked the city and school in what turned out to
be a sort of ethnic last hurrah. Thus, 1980 marks the end point of this
historical preface to my study of Riverview High School. The beginning
point, in 1968, was what local observers call the riot, none of them, to
my knowledge, yet taking the revisionist point of view that would de-

mand a less emotional term for the disturbance or take a more charitable view of its causes and its possibly salutary consequences. Events in America preceding April 1968 had not conditioned Riverview residents to be charitable or sanguine in the matter of angry black Americans; later events angered and frustrated them and when all that simmered down, they were simply glad it was over. Charity seems always to be in short supply.

The Old Order: Before 1968

Riverview residents did not wake up one morning in the spring of 1968 and discover over night that "negroes" had become "blacks," that people the government had designated "minorities" were angry, that injustice, like a shroud, covered the nation, and that nonminorities were suddenly and unexpectedly pressed to rethink what practical consequences freedom and equality had for life in America. Waking up, in the sense of becoming knowingly aware, is a complex matter. It occurs unpredictably, over time, and the enlightenment it brings is not linear: we neither get predictably smarter over time nor do we get as smart as we can be in orderly fashion. It would be easy to subscribe to a big-bang theory of enlightenment, that if you want people to listen to whatever they have been ignoring, make a great crashing noise. Such a noise may startle us into a state of temporary attention but have no enduring effect on us; or it may indeed genuinely capture our attention so that building upon the lesser sounds we've been hearing, we can actually tune in and respond to the messages clamoring for response.

Historians can easily substantiate that on the national scene both lesser and greater sounds had been broadcast prior to 1968. At times, the domestic news read like reports from the battle fronts of a raging war. Take 1962, when James Meredith became the first black in this century to attend the University of Mississippi:

September 26: Meredith Fails in Third Attempt to Enter School
September 27: Meredith Fails in Fourth Try at Miss. U.
October 1: Military Equipment Dominates College Scene: Meredith Under
    Guard: 15,000 Troops on Hand
October 3: Meredith Takes Aptitude Test: Troops Remain

These are headlines from Riverview's *Daily Herald*.

The new year, 1963, began with the announcement that "First Negro Registers at Segregated Clemson," one headline in the profusion of those that announced the progress of blacks to gain admission to historically segregated institutions. Later generations, having missed the stunning news of the 1960s as it unrolled in the daily newspaper, might well wonder what was going on then. Why the fuss about keeping blacks out of colleges and universities, and why the fuss about preventing their entry at that late date in our history? It is instructive that Riverview residents would rarely read about any other non-Anglo group making headlines for breakthroughs on the education front or on other fronts of antidiscrimination action.

Birmingham, Alabama, became the scene of protest in the spring of 1963, with one week in May illustrating in capsule form a course of events that in general would be repeated elsewhere:

May 3: Police Loose Dogs on Negro Gathering [when Martin Luther King was speaking]
May 4: Negro Leaders Plan More Demonstrations
May 8: Race Demonstrations Halt [after 2,200 protesters were jailed and King was in the midst of spending eight days in jail]
May 9: Firemen Hose Negros [who were part of a group planning to desegregate lunch counters and other facilities]
May 10: Alabama Race Strife Ends [because after five weeks of demonstrations, lunch counters are open, job opportunities are expanded, etc.]

On June 12, 1963, Mississippi black civil-rights leader Medgar Evers was shot in the back. Six days later he was buried in Arlington Cemetery, a symbolic action that was within the competency of the federal government to make at a time when our social order seemed poised to explode. On the day Evers was buried, in a season customarily devoted to baseball and other late spring pleasures, black students staged a "freedom strike" in Boston; NAACP's Roy Wilkins led 150 "freedom marchers" in Englewood, New Jersey; the restaurant association of Fayetteville, North Carolina, agreed to sixty days of desegregation if blacks would end their demonstrations; the mayor of Chattanooga, Tennessee, said a biracial commission would work to "promote peaceful and equitable" race relations; 105 blacks were charged with contempt of court for violating an injunction against "unruly protests" in Danville, Virginia; 500 blacks staged antisegregation demonstrations in Gadsden, Alabama; and 800 blacks marched in Savannah, Georgia, to desegregate restaurants. Within a month, the rallies, demonstrations, and protests would break out in northern locations—Philadelphia, Miami, Chicago, and Prichard, Iowa.

In this season of discontent, two black residents of Riverview wrote letters to the editor. James J. Graves applauded the rise of "angry young Negro leadership" in America. Will W. Brown wondered if there was a civil war on in the South. "Let us give the Negro a chance," he wrote. "He is at least the equal of a dog and the law protects the dog." And

Dayton Mitchell stood before Riverview's city council to insist that its members announce a policy on nondiscrimination in housing, or he would organize a march.

Throughout the summer of 1964, Riverview residents could read more stories drawn from the vein of distress in their society:

July 14: First Negro Serves on County Grand Jury [in Riverview's own county]

July 21: Harlem Boils: Another Night of Hell Seen

July 22: Racist Agitators Fan Brooklyn Riot

August 3: Negro Mob Battles Jersey City Police

August 12: End to Racial Violence, Disorders Asked by LBJ

August 17: Police Restore Calm in Chicago Area After Riots

August 25: Mayor [of San Francisco] Names First Negro Supervisor

And they could continue to read such stories in 1965, close to home in California, when "Over 100 Men from [Riverview's National Guard] . . . Sent to Riot Scene" (in Watts).

The drama of events in America during the six years preceding King's 1968 assassination had no close counterpart in Riverview. Still, many of its black residents identified with the activities of the national civil-rights movement, and we hear their voices not on the newspapers' front pages but typically in letters to the editor. From these letters, and also from the occasional article, we get a sense of prevailing sentiment. To be sure, we do not know the full extent of the sentiment; we know, however, from its familiar ring, that it was not just the feeling of some idiosyncratic individual.

In these years we see the intersection of the personal and the political, with individuals decrying undeserved evils inflicted upon them, and organizations pressing the appropriate political institutions, by those means within their purview, to remove the evils. It was indeed a time for decrying and for political pressure. On the same day in September 1963 that Christine Greenhouse was crowned Riverview's queen of the Mexican Independence Day Celebration, Vera Davis wrote a letter to express her distress that one must be white to qualify for decent jobs. "What are we going to tell our children when they ask us someday why we are not free?" Much would be done by local, state, and national governments to respond to her distress: too little, by some lights, and too much, by others. A comparable point could be made for the manifold distresses of the numerous Vera Davises whose long-silent suffering was given voice by the emboldening circumstances of the civil-rights movement. They never had to be told they were enduring injustices, but they did need encouragement to oppose them openly.

In 1965 Riverview's NAACP set out to uncover the full extent of de facto discrimination in the Riverview school district. Accordingly, they asked the school board to do a "racial census" of teachers, administrators, counselors, secretaries, and janitors. Board members doubted the legality of such a census and the superintendent said the Fair Employment Practices Commission prohibited it. Soon afterward, ethnic auditing became a routine fact of life and a condition for obtaining state and federal money. What the FEPC had once prohibited in the name of one sense of fairness interfered with acquiring the data to document the magnitude of the considerable unfairness that existed.

For every person like city manager Hank Ward, who, when he spoke at Riverview's first citywide prayer breakfast in March 1968, acknowledged the culpability of white Americans for the plight of black Americans, there were more like the woman whose letter thanked the local newspaper for its editorial upholding "law and order." From her perspective, protest connoted instability and disruption. The local police were accused of discrimination in hiring, brutal treatment of minorities, and general insensitivity in their response to nonwhite citizens. But they, too, eventually moved toward ethnic auditing and other responses to the charges against them, but not until after 1968. Until then, an old order generally prevailed in Riverview, no less so in its schools.

Perhaps nowhere was the old order more deeply enshrined than on the school board. Its five members, chosen in at-large elections, were not of one mind in all matters, but they all were white. Indeed, all of the board's five members had been white since the school district's inception. Until 1940, white meant non-Sicilian, or what Sicilians called "American." In 1940, Tommy Costa, the first Sicilian, was elected, ending the "American" monopoly of school control by a handful of men who were landowners, businessmen, professionals, industry executives, and bank presidents. Costa tried to run with the blessing of the incumbents, which was the established procedure. Unable to get their blessing, he ran anyway. After the election, the incumbent "friends," making sure Costa knew his place, did not speak to the winning "stranger" for two months. Costa remained a board member for over twenty years, most of them years when Sicilians dominated the board.

As indicated earlier, Sicilians dominated the school board from 1948 to 1973. While in power, they were overseers of a school system that neither knew how to be responsive to nonwhites nor thought it was necessary. Before 1968 high school teachers were predominantly "American," although as openings occurred in nonacademic positions, the district filled these with Sicilians. One oldtimer boasted that he got sixty-three persons hired in nonacademic positions. In time, favoritism would become an

issue in school board elections, as the board became a forum for contend-
ing ideas of how the schools should be run and by whom.

It has always been the case that if there is ethnic diversity in a city
with one high school, that school, barring white flight, will be the scene
of the community's greatest, continuing cross-ethnic contact. Depending on time and circumstances, the school, accordingly, can be a place of
considerable ethnic peace or ethnic discord. From all indications, ethnic
peace of a sort generally prevailed in Riverview before 1960. Peace is not
to be confused with equity between whites and nonwhites in the distribution of the goods a school can offer; it was peace in the sense of an
established order, of an accepted way of doing things, of people knowing
their place and keeping to it.

That peace is not necessarily contentment became obvious. White
citizens—speaking from the standpoint of the present—would reflect
on the 1968 riot with astonishment that black citizens had been so angry
at that time. Only by virtue of the selective hearing and seeing that all
humans are capable of could they have failed, both then and now, to note
and name the discontent of their black counterparts at RHS, and its
basis.

Even if we confine our knowledge of RHS in the 1950s to the recollections of white adults still resident in Riverview, we can draw a picture of
a social life that, when perspectives changed, as they did in the following
decades, could be seen as galling. Anglo and Mexican students were
friendly with, but not friends of, black students; years of proximity had
shaped a circumscribed intimacy that defined acceptable and unacceptable zones of contact. Says Sylvia Rizzato of her high school years in the
late 1950s:

Everybody got along fine. As far as dating, everybody stayed in their own
group—the color barrier. But as far as friendship in classrooms, lunchrooms,
and dances, everybody was fine. I remember in my junior year there was
some black boys we were very, very good friends with. We all started dancing. I remember going home and saying, "Gee, did we make history?" because
we had never danced with a black boy. Never.

She and her friends did make history. Teresa Piccolo and her friends
did not. Teresa was the head pompon girl about the same time Sylvia was
in school. As I described in the previous chapter, the absence of black
pompon girls on the spirit squad eventually became a public issue.
Teresa's experiences help to understand why.

I never was on a squad with black people. I don't know if that was because
Laverne Thomas [the only black girl to try out] was just too fat or because she

was black. I think it was both. I was one of the main judges because I was the head pompon girl. My statement to her was "I don't care what color you are, you aren't any good." I don't know if she was any good. Well, she couldn't be because she was much too heavy. I was never tested in terms of someone trying out who was thin and really good. Laverne had the nerve to try out. At that time, she was a group of one.

Teresa and her friends did what white girls always did: exclude blacks.

Further, in regard to the "astonishment" of nonblacks by the anger of blacks expressed on April 5, the day after King's assassination, I turn to several events and statements from the period preceding King's death. For example, before April 1968, teachers and teacher aides had had three years of inservice courses and lectures under such titles as "Reading and Language Foundations of Culturally Disadvantaged Youth," "The Mexican-American Cultural Heritage," "The Meaning and Stigma of Cultural Deprivation," "Negro Culture and Contributions of American Negroes to Our Society," "Intergroup Relations," and "Nuevas Vistas" (on the instruction of the Mexican-American student).

In 1967, well over a year before the riot, Riverview's Model Cities application included a section on "School-Community Relations." The section spoke of the "racially tainted conflict and near violence" of RHS, and of "some school officials" who resist help for "the trouble-maker, the social outcast, the delinquent," preferring to tighten discipline and increase the number of expulsions.

In February 1968 the president of the local NAACP chapter wrote to the school board "demanding the following improvements": that a school in the black ghetto be integrated and that "Negro History" be taught at RHS. The assistant superintendent claimed that RHS already taught "Negro History" in its U.S. History and Problems of Democracy courses. A school board member in 1968 recalls the NAACP letter:

It was like the gnat that's annoying you. It wasn't taken with any great impact. I don't think that anything that any of the black community said was taken with much regard until after Martin Luther King's assassination. Then we went into a whole different era.

"A Whole Different Era": Post-1968

"We had a riot here in 1968. I can remember that day. I remember going home and loading my gun," says Rico Ferrante, who was working out of town when he got a call from his mother-in-law about a riot at the high school. Blacks were marching and they were going to burn up everything behind the elementary school near his house. Rico told her "like hell they will," and he came home.

I put a rifle at every window. I sat there and waited. I called my neighbor and said, "If they come this way, you take them, and if they come this other way, meet them in a cross fire." Then I'm thinking, "God damn, what am I doing? Is this worth killing somebody over?" At first it was, "I don't give a damn what your justification is." Then, "No, this is wrong." I unloaded all my guns, got my family in the car, and went to visit my brother in Corinth.

Rico Ferrante was worried and angry and defensive. To varying degrees, many Riverview residents would feel this way for the next twelve years.

The riot damage at RHS was assessed as forty-two broken chairs, twenty-one smashed window panes, four injured persons (one of them hospitalized), and one principal aching from a blow to his back. This is one way of specifying the damage. Repairs to the school's property cost about $4,600. There would be other ways of calculating the damage and its costs; in time, it might even be possible to identify some benefits.

The simple fact of the matter was that following the news of King's assassination, about two hundred black RHS students gathered and moved toward the lunchroom area where for five minutes they broke chairs and windows, fought with nonblack students, and "shoved and jostled" teachers. The newspaper's language fit the mood of many Riverview residents: "mob tears up school cafeteria"; "Negro youths went on rampage"; "a melee at the high school"; and "the April 5 disorders." The April 5 incident engendered considerable emotion; individual and collective venting of this emotion was necessary. The venting began immediately and continued for months; the search for solutions by RHS personnel, the school district, and other community agencies continued for years.

"Why did it happen?" everyone asked. Commissions were appointed to find out; private theories were expounded. All answers and theories rang with rationality; none fully satisfied the urgent need to know. Clearly, if one knew why students became angry, gathered in large numbers, and attacked people and property, then one could prevent a repetition of this behavior. Each possible explanation carried implications concerning the practices and policies of the school and community. An immediate consequence appeared in the results of the city council election of April 10. It followed so close on the heels of King's death and the extraordinary local and national reactions as to establish a causal relationship. Voters elected a second Mexican and the first-ever black, and they rejected the incumbent mayor, a Sicilian, who sought reelection.

The next day, 11,600 federal troops "occupied" Washington, D.C.; ma-
chine-gun emplacements stood on the front steps of the Capitol, and
troops took up positions on the White House lawn.

Following the events of April 5, an immediate issue was what to do
about the sixteen black students whom teachers, police, and students
had identified as the riot leaders. The school district chose to expel
them. All but one of the fifteen demanded that his expulsion hearing be
conducted in a public session, with lawyers present to represent both
sides, and the school board sitting as judge and jury. The hearings re-
sembled formal court proceedings; emotions surged on both sides. The
newspaper dutifully reported the latest results. "More Expelled in
Hearing," was the heading for the May 9 article that reported on cases
numbered nine and ten. To date, the board had reinstated only one of
the sixteen accused students. Five more remained to be heard. At the
May 9 hearing, the defense lawyer looked for mitigating factors in the
provocative behavior of a rival gang of Mexican-Americans, and also of
the high school principal, who, the night of King's murder, was alleged
to have said, "They [also] should have shot Rap Brown and Stokely Car-
michael—but that's one down and two to go." The principal confirmed
that he had been at the bar but denied he had spoken as accused. The
matter was left at that.

By May 10, the hearings were complete. Multiple charges had been
directed against each student, including fighting, profanity, willful diso-
bedience, defiance of authority, and threatening to use force or violence;
each charge met the state of California's requirements for expulsion.
The school board expelled thirteen, reinstated two, and dropped one
from the rolls due to "underachievement." In reaction, a group of thirty-
five students and mothers picketed outside the high school. Four days
later, an unknown arsonist burned tables and chairs in the same cafeteria
where the earlier damage had been done. Before the month of May was
over, an interracial group planned a series of six one-hour workshops,
the school board approved the recruitment of minority teachers in the
South, and the wife of the man who headed Riverview's NAACP concluded that the students had been expelled to teach a lesson: white
interests should not be questioned. Before the summer of 1968 was
over, both the high school principal, with sixteen years' local experience, and the school district superintendent, with twenty-two years'
local experience, resigned their positions.

In time, the spotlight would shift from the sixteen students. While
they were in it, their cause inspired letters to the editor. The mood of the
letters reflected a nation in conflict. Wrote one man about the "April 5th
rioters": not "race, religion or color, or any other reason" offer "mitigat-

ing circumstances for these offenses. Let law and order prevail now!"
The letter of a black woman accompanied his: "Is the problem in Riverview unruly students? Or is it the same sickness that has been growing
uncontrolled in other parts of our nation? Long as there's racial prejudice in the halls of RHS, none of us are safe." Lest readers feel torn
between these two views, one seeking punishment, the other understanding, several days later the paper's editorial column (every editor's
personal "letter") took clear sides: accusations of racism in Riverview
were unfounded, and racism could not explain the violence of "young
rowdies" who pushed to see how much they could get away with, while
claiming their grief "for a man [King] they never knew anything about."
The authority for this latter fact, said the editorial, was local "senior
Negroes."

There were indeed black persons in Riverview whom the newspaper
could, for its purposes, designate "senior Negroes." Their relatively
moderate position, together with that of nonblack persons still resident
in Riverview, helped create what became the community's dominant
mood. Here is the voice of "senior Negro" Ralph Benson, who had one
child in RHS in 1968:

When people are rioting, they lose their sense of perspective. You can either
go out there and get with them or stay away. They're the most dangerous
animals there is. I'm sympathetic to rioters nowhere. There was a justification for them to be angry, but not for them to be rioting.

Though Benson would not join the chorus of protesters at the hearings of
the sixteen black students, he would continue to encourage and lead organized efforts for change in housing, education, jobs, and politics.
Benson's preference to achieve change through concerted organizational pressure rather than through demonstrations seemed to be the
norm for Riverview's black residents. His work was endorsed by Frank
Cary, a white RHS teacher.

By his own acknowledgment, Frank was among the innocents in 1968
who could not have imagined a riot was possible. Only when it happened and he learned of the anger and the charges did he notice that his
school had no minority administrators, coaches, or counselors. "I don't
know how a black feels," Frank says. "When he goes to my school, I don't
know how he feels. I'm not black. And when you got this many, and the
administration weren't really paying any attention." Following the riot,
Frank immediately joined a cadre of teachers who determined to listen
and pay attention. In his own way he continues to do so today. His papers
from 1968, the artefacts of the hours he spent "doing what I could," are
still in his desk drawer at school. He readily locates them some eighteen

years later as he unsentimentally discusses his and his school's trying times.

Bill Garcia was a high school student in 1968 and thus lacked the perspective of a Ralph Benson or Frank Cary. As an athlete and a resident of the end of town where minorities lived next door to each other, he had literally spent all of his young life playing with black boys. On April 5, his black friends wanted him to join them in their defiance:

"Hey, are you going to join us?" this one guy says after the announcement came over the loudspeaker that we should go home as soon as we can. I said, "I'm sorry, I'm with nobody." I was so angry because these black people, they were my friends. I played with them. To this day, I just can't see why they did it. It still drives me crazy. Maybe they seen something I didn't see. I was a Mexican kid; I didn't see their side.

Garcia cannot find mitigating circumstances that condone violence; he pretends to no knowledge of history that offers insight on the status of blacks in Riverview or anywhere else. But still resident in Riverview, he is part of the group that never saw blacks as "them," and thus excludable from the status of friend. Different people make different contributions.

The contributions of 1968 school board member Phil Colin join those of Benson, Cary, and Garcia to provide a foundation upon which normalcy slowly developed and a new climate of opinion and practice eventually emerged. While gunshots were normal sounds on the streets of Riverview's major ghetto, and sixteen black families lamented the fate of their sons before an all-white school board that their friends and neighbors had labeled racist, the board members themselves lived with trepidations and doubts of their own. Phil Colin recollects that:

Fear is not the word I want because we went ahead and did it [conduct the suspension hearings], never knowing if something was going to happen to us the first couple of sessions. Then security was set up. The more hearings we went through, the more commonplace they became, and the fear diminished. Then I got curious. What prompts people to get to a point in their life before that's the only way they can lash out? Two groups of parents called meetings with me; they didn't want their names used. They didn't condone the violence, and they knew that the [sixteen] children had to be punished, but they wanted to know, was there something that could be done to make the system change. That's when I thought, "Hey, something's going on." These people cared about their kids as I care about mine. After the expulsion hearing, I knew things had to happen: the system funnels their kids out and they don't get jobs, our counseling wasn't what it should be, and our tracking system was there.

The normalcy and the new opinions and practices formed slowly in the face of tension and violence that persisted for years. In 1969, when Ray Taymor ran for president of the RHS "student body," one of the many publicity posters he pinned around the school had "nigger" scribbled on it. In 1974, Model Cities personnel surveyed 259 RHS students, of whom 67 percent said there was racial tension in Riverview and 76 percent in the schools. In 1976, students were polled for information to include in the high schools' accreditation report. One question asked, "Are there racial/ethnic tensions in your school?" Of 1,117 respondents, 634 answered yes, 156 no, and 327 don't know. In 1982, the same question was asked for the same purpose. Of 882 respondents, 217 answered yes, 323 no, and 342 don't know.

Before conditions improved at Riverview High School, years would follow that school officials, school board members, parents, and the newspapers most often described as violent. No particular care was taken in the application of the term, so violence encompassed a range of events all accepted as disagreeably disruptive, and all relating to fights between and within ethnic groups. When teachers chanced to become the target of student assault, as happened if they tried to break up a fight, the reaction of the local teachers' association would be added to that of administrators and school board. When the target was an innocent student who had been "jumped" while walking the high school corridors, parental indignation would be joined to that of the district officials. And when the targets included athletes from an opposing team injured by Riverview players and fans in the course of a game, then anger shaped decisions regarding whether or not to include Riverview on next year's schedule, and, if so, where, outside of Riverview, to hold the contest.

Though violence was not a continuous occurrence at RHS in the years following King's death, it was both sufficiently common and sufficiently remarkable to appear regularly as a school board agenda item; a spur to devising yet one more plan for controlling what always was declared to be the misbehavior of a small minority of students; and an item in local and county newspapers, and, occasionally, in newspapers outside the county. Bad news travels indecently well and lodges in the memory, as Riverview residents later recalled with great regret when they felt they had outgrown their reputation as a "riot school." Nonetheless, it still hangs on.

The seventies were a memorable decade, the succession of events labeled "violent" insured that it would be. "It was very tough times," says teacher Tom Buckley. "I hurt inside when I think about it." The times were not tough because Riverview's parents, educators, and school board members were indifferent to what was happening at RHS. To the contrary, fully paralleling the assaults and threats of teacher walkouts were years of efforts that persisted throughout the 1970s, despite a degree of failure and frustration that severely tested the will of the many who struggled to find solutions. In one way or another, much of the energy expended by persons and groups from inside and outside the school district was directed to personnel: who would be elected to the school board, who would be appointed principal or dean of students, or who would be hired as teacher, cook, or custodian. The widely accepted view about old-order Riverview was that those who controlled the school board dictated who would be appointed and hired. Less widely accepted, but garnering increasing support, was the view that the school district should hire more minorities, not only because it was the just thing to do, but also, it would be argued unto the present, because it was the educationally sound thing to do.

The pre-1968 school board majority was accustomed to quiet meetings, with very few "irregulars" present, the regulars being the board members and the district administrators, who always attended. Interest in the hearings of the sixteen students was so great that the sessions were moved to an auditorium at the high school, as were many other sessions of the 1970s. Thereafter, variably motivated interest in board meetings continued; for the time being, the era of quiet, poorly attended meetings was over. Some parents attended as watchers. They attended every board meeting, believing that the school board, if other consciences are present, does better than it otherwise would. Indeed, school board watching by some who began years ago continues to the present.

Perhaps the first major occasion to focus on personnel arose at the junior high school with the vacancy of dean of students. Though obviously not directly a high school matter, this issue escalated into a heated controversy that affected the entire school district. Simply put, the school board, by a three-to-two majority, appointed as dean of students a white man who had not been recommended by the committee the board had designated to screen candidates and make a recommendation. The committee had advised hiring a particular black man.

Reaction to this controversy spurred people from all ethnic groups to organize a recall of the two men and one woman who constituted the school board majority. Never before had a recall been attempted. Antagonists aligned themselves with Citizens United for Recall Election (CURE) or with Citizens Against Recall Effort (CARE), the former trying to cure the school district of "favoritism, cronyism, pure politics," and the latter trying to establish that if one cared about Riverview, one opposed busing, supported the neighborhood-school concept, favored two high schools, one on each end of town, and preferred not to create a "Berkeley-like atmosphere" in Riverview. As an adjective, "Berkeley-like" was synonymous with "radical." On the eve of the recall election of September 16, 1970, a paid ad appeared in the newspaper that captured the sense of many CARE supporters: the recall plot "is so sinister as to be almost unbelievable" that it is happening in Riverview, rather than in Santa Barbara or Berkeley.

In what was probably the largest percentage of voter turnout in Riverview's history of school board elections, 5,012 of 8,973 possible voters (55.8 percent) went to the polls. "Trio Keeps School Seats," announced the headlines in the next day's paper, including a statement by the board member who led this little group of winners: "What you have done today," he said to Riverview residents, "is spoken to keep the community the way it was a few years ago."

Voters may have rejected CURE's recall efforts, but they did not mean to keep the community the way it was. Several things happened. In 1971, they elected a black man to the board for the first time. The other two members of the three-person majority did not seek reelection when their terms expired in 1973. Replacing them was the first-ever Hispanic board member and a very young man, Sicilian, a Riverview native recently graduated from RHS, who took a most liberal view of school district policy and practice.

As black, Hispanic, and youth joined the old board minority of two, Riverview voters clearly signaled their readiness for a new order. A newly cast board was a necessary but not sufficient condition for a new order to emerge in Riverview's high school. After all, it is far simpler to select new persons who promise to construct new policies than to reorder a social system that had been shaken and shaped by the force of social change in the nation at large. A new board was a beginning. Its members would fight and split among themselves, and reveal sharp distinctions of principle, but the old guard never again gained power in school district affairs.

If the new-guard board was not always of one mind, it still could coalesce around the notion of hiring nonwhite administrators just as soon as openings were available. Between 1973 and 1976, the school district hired four minority principals, three black and one Mexican, an asymmetry that created considerable consternation within the Mexican community. As of 1976, when the new board formally committed itself to an affirmative-action program, the continuing issues would be from which minority group the new employees would come and, always a serious matter, whether any "qualified" minorities would be available. By their approval of affirmative-action programs the board fully removed the onus of "stranger" from the consideration of who is qualified to be a teacher but, also, of who it is desirable to have as a teacher.

The issue of being qualified is the simple technical matter of who has the educationally correct degrees and experience. The issue of desirability is the truly tough matter, since it draws upon feelings that govern whom we will grant the status of "friend" to. Formal programs are not necessarily the best means for influencing feelings (indeed, they may be counterproductive), but affirmative action created a reality—the hiring of minorities in all occupational categories the high school contained— that stood a chance of being usefully educative. Given that the reality was to be planned, rather than emerge naturally over time, its dimensions were specified. The plan was to have the percentage of minorities in all job categories equate the percentage of students in each minority group.

By this principle, the "distortions" of the pre–affirmative-action period were retrospectively evident. They had been detailed in the 1970 suit that Riverview's Black Political Association filed with the Fair Employment Practices Commission. Of the school district's then 6,156 students, 28 percent were black, 21 percent Spanish-surnamed, and 4 percent Asian; but of 295 teachers, only 5 percent were black, 2 percent Spanish-surnamed, and 3 percent Asian. By 1982, of RHS's 78 teachers, 15 percent were black, 5 percent Spanish-surnamed, and 4 percent Asian, a clear gain over the district figures of 1970, but a long way from the district's goal of equivalency.

Affirmative action in hiring was perhaps the most concrete and enduring policy that emerged from the turbulence of the 1960s and 1970s. Of course, it was not the only response to the turbulence, nor were increased numbers of minorities employed by the school district the only hoped-for outcome. In light of the belief in Riverview that its disorder was due to shortcomings of communication, understanding, respect, and sensitivity, various actions were taken. Here are some of them.

Within one week of the 1968 riot at RHS, a newly organized Human Relations Commission met and urged the district to hire a specialist in intergroup relations. "While we all mean well," reported the commission's chairman, "without the guidance of professional staff members we don't know how to put it into effect." In fact, the district did hire an intergroup specialist, a black man, who was replaced one year later by another black man who still holds this position. At one time, his staff, swollen by the flow of federal dollars, contained eighteen full-time persons; his staff today consists of one secretary whom he shares with another school district official.

Within three weeks of the 1968 riot, the teachers' professional organization formed the Teacher Human Relations Committee. They adopted a four-point program: (1) establish face-to-face communication; (2) eliminate rumors; (3) reduce distrust; and (4) work with all interested groups. This teachers' group sought a middle ground that would avoid the extremes of believing, on the one hand, that "wrongdoers" must be punished in order for "law and order to prevail now!" or of believing, on the other, that ours is a society sick beyond redemption.

This teacher-organized committee held informal meetings with parents, set up a weekend retreat for thirty students and ten teachers, disseminated resolutions in support of integrating schools, and, in general, tried to clarify the fact that they were willing to listen to aggrieved parents and students. By this intent, teachers were legitimating the voices of students and parents, two groups that typically were not often heard, or, if heard, were not necessarily taken seriously.

"Human relations" became a slogan of the times. It was incorporated into the names of teacher, school, and city committees and commissions. It seemed to speak of an incapacity of people of all ages to do successfully outside their own ethnic group what they managed to do successfully within it: that is, to establish a way of being together that was mutually satisfying. Older Riverview residents, invariably non-minorities, would affirm how well everyone always used to get along, generally unaware that the terms of getting along had changed, and the changes necessitated redefining what "getting along" entailed.

Central to the efforts taken to improve human relations were the encounter group and sensitivity training. These two activities had many practitioners who capitalized on the prevailing intergroup unease. At their best, they brought face-to-face people who had confused, mistaken views and angry feelings about each other, and they pursued the development of sensitivity to the feelings of others, especially when people did not realize they were being insensitive. It was no small challenge to teachers to know just how to respond to even young children who, in the early days of busing in Riverview, said to teachers who urged them not to dawdle as they boarded the bus, "Take your fucking white hands off me." Black teachers also faced challenges from black students who had a "bro, you owe me" outlook. These students expected special treatment from black teachers: "Bro, help me. Bro, you owe me. Hey, I'm a bro; let's get over. What they were asking for was, 'Hey, just let me be lazy because we're [both] black-skinned.'" This was how one black teacher described one aspect of the times during the 1970s.

"We went down on Friday and came back on Sunday"—this is how Riverview adults and students would characterize their weekend retreats spent "learning to be sensitive" to "the diversity of cultures."

These occasions produced more talk than many people could tolerate, particularly if they could not equate talk with "doing something." To be sure, then as now more than talk was needed, but there is tangible evidence that some talk for some people proved to be beneficial. For example, of thirty-seven participants (about two-thirds students and one-third teachers) in the "Weekend of Laying It on the Line" that met at White Sulphur Springs in Napa Valley, thirty-six said "yes" to the prospect of planning "other weekend encounters"; one said "maybe." They answered the question about what they like most about the weekend by saying that "they truly understood their own inner feelings for the first time." An example of "inner feelings" emerged in an exchange between a white parent and a Mexican student during a meeting held soon after the Napa Valley weekend. The student had attended the weekend.

Parent: When the leaders told the kids to go in their own racial groups, where did you go? To the brown or white group?
Student: To the white group.
Parent: See? You didn't separate brown and white.
Student: Will you ask me why I went to the white group in the beginning?
Parent: No, it doesn't matter to me.
Student: Let me explain.
Parent: All right, why did you go in the white group?
Student: Because I was confused. For the first time in my life I was thinking.
Parent: So you classified yourself!
Student: I was indoctrinated in the beginning to go white. When I went to the white group, it was the other Mexican kids who told me to go to their group.
Parent: Was it a crime to go to the white group?
Student: Yes.

This Mexican student had come to a sense of himself that violated the white parent's conviction, expressed prior to the above exchange, that "There is no such thing as brown, Chicano, or La Raza. There are only three races. We must teach our children that their loyalty is to their country as Americans and to their family and God."

A white school board member came to a sense of himself when he joined a group at another such weekend. It happened after a black parent yelled at him to ask, in effect, how had he dared expel the students involved in the 1968 riot. "I yelled back, 'What else would you have done?'" Board member and parent exchanged views, had a drink together later that night, and began a friendship that still exists. What also still exists is this board member's discovery: "I came to find a lot of people, great, wonderful human beings, they were black. We're no different than they. We have the same feelings, the same cares."

White teachers at RHS in 1968, and still there today, are inclined to make a distinction: though they did not like what many black students were doing in the 1970s, they learned important lessons from that period of disorder, notably that there was a reasonable basis to the frustrations of blacks and that they had to learn which words and deeds were inflammatory. The football coach learned that to minimize accusations of racially based favoritism he had to introduce a careful system of grading the performance of all players, backed up by film records, so that each player, by knowing his grade and the basis for it, would understand his possibility of playing in the next game.

The benefits of the many meetings—by whatever name—that brought together educators and students and adult minorities extended throughout the school system, from teacher aides to district administrators. A member of the latter group characterizes the evolution from the post-1968 days to 1980. In the beginning, he says, we could not "communicate without battling," because whenever blacks came before the school board, their style would be confrontational. Later, the feeling grew that "if we could feel they were reasonable, we could be reasonable, too." This change, he adds, "didn't happen over night." In between were the weekend retreats composed of people who in public meetings took issue with each other but who had learned "to respect one another as human beings." People learned to see the human beings who lived behind the much-used, distorting labels of "militant" and "bigot." A local black activist of the 1970s, a participant in many retreats and meetings, sums up their results:

We'd go somewhere with the [white] school people and tell them what we disliked. They'd tell us their viewpoint. At the end of the session, we'd analyze what we did and said, and try to reach a mutual agreement to make things better. Some of it came out; some things got a little better. You know, you don't straighten everyone out. You accomplish something. It's not a waste.

His assessment is far from glowing, but there is today a residue from this period, as I infer from an event that occurred long afterward. Recently, a spokesman for the local Hispanic community approached the district's central administration with an offer to help in anyway possible to remedy the alarming dropout rate of Hispanic adolescents. The man took pains to clarify that the local branch of the Mexican-American Political Association (MAPA) wanted to be involved, but they wanted the district to understand that they were not the old MAPA. Therefore, the district should not get defensive, as he knew the district always did in the past when MAPA approached with a request. Times had changed, organizations had changed, and school leaders had learned lessons, namely, how to listen to requests made by people who had learned something about how to make them.

If ethnic organizations heightened ethnic consciousness in order to enhance self-image and appropriate awareness of their group's identity and its rights and opportunities, a host of state and local agencies served as their counterparts to heighten the consciousness of the educators whose professional lives were affected by the new ethnic awareness. Owing to several decisions that had been made recently, reasoned a 1969 memo from Riverview's superintendent of schools, there would be a "school-community planning workshop." It would not be a "continuing of the sensitivity or encounter groups that took place earlier in the school year. The purposes of the workshop are to better prepare our teachers to have the children less concerned and to get the parents more at ease for the entire integration process." "Less concerned" and "more at ease," indeed! This soft language obscured the hard uncertainty about a world changing too fast. Everyone needed a workshop to learn how to play their new parts in the drama of rights and race and responsibility.

The need for teachers to be better prepared was generated by what seemed at times to be an endless stream of possibilities brought forth with federal money. The Riverview school district not only had hired an intergroup specialist, who as needed would promote understanding and smooth often-troubled waters but had also engaged a full-time director of federal projects. This grant-proposal-writing, project-coordinating specialist became a new fixture in school districts across the country. The range of opportunities available for getting federal money not only created habits of dependency, it also served to sensitize educators to children and needs that otherwise might have been ignored. It is far from true that the resulting proposals were well-conceived and that their implementation was well-executed with enduring, salutary results. Nonetheless, at the very least, the federal plans—relating to bilingual-bicultural education, to "educationally disadvantaged youths," to Indian education, and the like—were part of nationwide formal and informal acts that focused on formerly under-seen and under-heard Americans. A Riverview administrator recalled when the district received money under the Indian Education Act:

Never saw so many Indians in my life, all of a sudden. I don't mean to be derogatory about it, but people who had never really felt Indian became Indian.

A great deal of it was not as a way to get money, but was encouraged by the fact that this [being Indian] was acceptable now.

It seemed, in fact, that a spotlight was beamed on matters of ethnicity to a degree that would seem extreme only when one looked back from the perspective of a later time.

Another effort of RHS educators, clearly intended to be positive, paralleled the negativism and disorder of the period. It related to changes in the substance of the students' school experience. Local, state, and national pressures converged to insure that no school with even a small black or Mexican population could resist making some type of curricular responses. One of the most common is called "ethnic studies." Several days after the April 1968 riot, the RHS principal announced that school would open in September with a new elective: "American Negro Cultural History." This elective soon became Black History; it was joined by Mexican History and the teaching of Tagalog, the official language of the Philippines. All of these classes proved to be ephemeral. Declining student interest led to their removal from the curriculum, though educators claim that rewritten United States history texts obviated the need for special ethnic classes. RHS could not have resisted the introduction of ethnic-oriented electives, but it is doubtful that there was any way the school could have retained them.

Ethnic courses suffered from the students' generally declining interest in electives and from their preference for more obviously job-related classes, as well as from their feeling that they did not need special instruction about themselves. Ethnic courses also suffered from the faculty's belief that they were not necessary, that it was best to integrate ethnic content into traditional English and social-studies offerings. In retrospect, the ethnic course seemed to be primarily of symbolic consequence: minorities needed to "demand" them to demonstrate their attentiveness to their singular identity; school districts needed to offer them to demonstrate their sensitivity to minorities. The enduring necessity of the courses did not seem to have been internalized by either the minorities or the educators; the courses were readily outcompeted by other courses and considerations for the use of student time.

In contrast to the ethnic courses, bilingual education was not elective in the sense of being one in a series of optional offerings. Students of limited ability in English could take the English-as-a-second language class. Similarly, they could take special science, mathematics, or social-studies classes that were taught with the help of aides who were competent in English and Spanish. I will elaborate elsewhere on the bilingual program at RHS. I refer to it now because it not only was mandated by state legislation and facilitated by federal support, it also was a response to ardent demands from the Mexican community. At its best, bilingual education was responsive to the special linguistic and cultural needs of non–English-speaking youth; at its worst, it was just an occasion for expanded job opportunities, in that the more the programs expanded, the more jobs became available for speakers of Spanish, the only language group for which special aides were hired. Distress over the sufficiency of the school district's support of bilingual education would culminate in the events which close this period of uneasy years.

Ethnic courses did not exhaust RHS's post-riot curricular reactions. When minority pressure alerted the school to the inequity of its three-track academic ranking system, the school abolished tracking. The frequency with which minority students got low grades led to an informal practice of grade inflation; this muted a possible political reaction from unhappy parents and their defensive organizations. It also kept athletes eligible to play who otherwise might have been disallowed, a crucial issue in a town so devoted to its football team. With the abolition of the tracking system, as well as the high incidence of academic failure by minority students, grade inflation notwithstanding, the school needed a curricular alternative. It found one in an arrangement it called the Opportunity Program, a school within a school under the direction of four teachers and one school-community liaison person. In time, alternative arrangements would abound, as if to suggest that academic sorting is inevitable: if one means of tracking students is abolished, a vacuum is created that must be filled by some other means.

Student-organized ethnic clubs were introduced as extracurricular activities in this period. In time, there was a Black Students Union, La Raza, and Fil-American Club. In reaction, other students organized an Italian Club, now defunct. At this club's inception, recalled one of its founding members, "We said, 'Hey, why don't we form an Italian club?' There were Mexicans in La Raza, and there were other clubs. So we made our own club, but we never organized to try to better our ethnic group, like La Raza. They seemed to be a radical group." At no time have these clubs attracted more than a small number of students; each club occasionally attracts persons from other ethnic groups.

Once one ethnic club was in existence, it was probably inevitable that there would be others. In a multiethnic society, the behavior of ethnic groups is reactive to the behavior of others. It was probably also inevitable that countervailing reactions would arise from persons inside and outside the ethnic groups. Here is the view of a Mexican man expressed in a letter to the editor shortly after the riot when the air was thick with views in support of an ethnically relevant curriculum. He did not want the school to emphasize Mexican history, to have it singled out in any way. He could teach his own children about their heritage. "I wanted to be assimilated," he concludes, "and become an integral part of the community. Now, you people stand there and point a finger and say, 'Look there goes a Mexican.'" To him, if someone said, "There goes a Mexican," they would not be saying, "There goes a friend."

Here is the view of a school board member whose years embraced the period when ethnic studies were afoot. His reservations derive in part from his sense of being American, and in part from his sense of the function of schools. He quotes approvingly the words of a European exchange student who attended RHS in the 1970s: "You're all Americans and have so much to be proud of. Why are you so busy trying to recognize the heritage from where you came?" To this board member, going beyond food and festivals in the observance of one's ethnic identity is going too far. This was not a popular view to express in the 1970s, and he did not express it publicly at school board meetings. What he could express, because it did not reflect directly on the propriety of ethnic maintenance, was the belief that the high school already is jammed with too many things to do. Thus, when schools undertake ethnic-oriented instruction they assume a "role beyond the role of education." And thus was engendered a backlash in support of the three Rs.

Long before the curricular backlash occurred there was the backlash from white families who decided that neither Riverview nor Riverview High School were secure places. They fled town, hoping to find in nearby communities what they believed Riverview had forsaken. This flight was wrenching to many who had grown up in Riverview, felt deep affection for it, and thought of it as home. They left when they no longer could perceive it as the home they knew and loved; their departure cleaved families and friendships. Those who stayed felt abandoned; those who left often felt guilty.

I'll tell you why I moved. At the time, my son was eight. He couldn't go to the Boys Club without having a knife stuck in his neck, afraid the kids would ask him for money and stuff. We started to have a situation with the blacks. These were people that were coming in from the outside. They were not Riverview blacks, no. I just told my wife, I said, "I can't handle this anymore. We gotta do something."

They moved to Corinth, though even today they belong to Riverview organizations and are defensive about their exodus.

The exodus from Riverview began long before parents felt threatened by the post-1968 "climate of fear" at RHS. Wealthier non-Sicilian whites had moved away as they saw Riverview become increasingly a town of minorities, most particularly of the black minority. Their move reflected the usual disposition of the wealthy for a community and school where their values predominate. Riverview was not such a place. The exodus was accelerated later by fear of what they perceived as poor, hostile, violence-prone minorities. Parental passions were aroused. Commenting on the "animal behavior" of students at a football game, an Italian woman expressed sentiments in her letter to the editor that had much support: "I for one will never send my kids to Riverview High and I'm sure that I'm one of a large group of parents who feel the same way."

In the school year that began immediately following the 1968 riot, legal and illegal student transfers out of RHS were substantial, exceeding one hundred. The pre-riot fall enrollment of 1,307 in 1967 dropped to 1,175 in the post-riot fall of 1968, and remained there (at 1,174) in the fall of 1969. The football coach estimated he lost nine of thirteen returning lettermen because of transfers. Teachers commented on the decreased size of their post-riot college-prep classes. Some parents then drew their case for departure from the high school's diminished academic environment: "I moved when my son was ready for high school because I wanted a place where it was not easy to get a C, a place where he'd have to work for it." School district administrators lamented the loss of such parents: "We lost a good chunk of the middle-class whites, a good chunk of the better students and parents who got involved in school."

Those who could not leave joined other white parents in clamoring for an emphasis on "the basics," Americanism, and discipline, while decrying the school system's emphasis on ethnicity. It was OK for the school district's intergroup specialist to quiet racial conflict. His ethnic calendar was another matter. He distributed it to all schools. Informing students and teachers of the occasions for celebrating the deeds and birth dates of successful minority persons was not what the back-to-the-basics parents thought schooling should be about.

The Hispanic Boycott

I have written this account of the 1968–80 period mainly from the standpoint of reactions to and from black Americans. This emphasis reflects the fact, prevalent both in Riverview and nationwide, that blacks were preeminent in the civil-rights movement; they took the lead in articulating the injustices they and other minorities lived with, and in pressing the case for justice to be done. Mexican-Americans shared these injustices, and had several of their own. They never elicited the degree of hostility and obloquy directed at blacks by those who were put off by minorities, nor were they as successful as blacks in stating their cause and organizing to promote it.

That they had a cause, that they endured indignities, that they felt the schools slighted their children—of this I have no doubt. That they would get vocally, publicly angry—Riverview had no doubt: "My name is George Sonoma. I'm here on behalf of my son, George Sonoma." These are the opening words of a father whose son the football coach removed from the team for possession of alcohol. The Sonoma case occurred in September 1980. Four years earlier, in 1976, the district aroused Hispanic ire when it hired a black rather than a Hispanic administrator; in response, the Mexican-American Political Association composed and submitted a five-point statement of "educational needs" to a special meeting of the school board. The points related to hiring Hispanic and Spanish-speaking principals, teachers, counselors, aides, and nonacademics. By the time of the Sonoma case, the needs had become demands and hiring had become just one of several issues.

Sonoma spoke eloquently, movingly on behalf of his son, a sixteen-year-old lad who was the victim of bad luck and school rules. Young George chanced to be sitting by a bus window when the father of a teammate handed George a bottle of champagne. The bottle was intended for the man's son, not for George. George held on to the bottle for some time after the bus started its journey to an away game. As he handed the bottle to another player for the purpose of throwing it out of the bus, the bottle broke open. When the bus driver smelled the alcohol, he stopped the bus. The coach, as school rules dictate, removed George Sonoma from the bus and the team, and he never again played football for RHS, where football is the king of sports.

Sonoma did not deny that his son had held a bottle of champagne. He tried to establish that what his son was doing when he did not at once report receipt of the bottle to someone in authority was protecting both the boy for whom the champagne was intended, and the boy's father. Mr. Sonoma continued:

Apparently, what they [the coaches] were going by is the rule. A rule is a rule. And they have to go by that. I think this rule, as far as my boy is concerned, is too severe. I think they did not pay any attention to the circumstances involving the incident. . . . My son showed bad judgment, really bad judgment. But, yet, you've got to stop and think: this is a young, young adult, sixteen years old. His alliances, his thoughts, aren't completely what they should be.

In the next month, many would articulate arguments for returning George to the team. None of them would be more convincing than those of his father. All of them failed. To demonstrate their resolve, the entire RHS coaching staff of nineteen men and women voted on the matter of Sonoma's exclusion from the team; seventeen voted affirmatively. Appeals to the principal, the superintendent, and, ultimately, the school board failed, the latter in a split vote, with one board member abstaining on the grounds that his son was the football coach who ousted Sonoma.

The Sonoma case triggered a long list of demands and some of the longest school board meetings in the history of the district, meetings at which George Sonoma alternately would be forgotten, as other issues assumed primacy, and remembered, in appeals for justice which acknowledged that though a rule is a rule it should not be applied rigidly to an innocent boy. On behalf of the issue and George Sonoma, Jaime Mendoza, an officer of the Mexican-American Political Association, and a resident of a nearby town (never, at any time, did he live in Riverview), was the main speaker. Nobody involved on any side of the events of that fall ever felt indifferent to Jaime Mendoza; nobody ever felt neutral about him. He could sniff out a potential issue and present it in a public arena, ideally one where press and television coverage were on hand, in tones so dire that the audience cheered and applauded. He accused the coaches of being inconsistent in their treatment of student rulebreakers, and the principal of backing up the coaches:

The reason this Chicano case came to you [the school board] is indeed because it's Chicano students who get the short end of the deal. That appears to me just from what I've seen tonight. And also when I approached the principal at the high school a few minutes ago, he was defensive, he was hostile, he was uncommunicative, giving me the impression that he's hiding something. He's not being open and honest with the community people.

Mendoza made this observation at the first of a series of board meetings devoted totally or largely to Hispanic concerns.

In the course of this and other meetings, MAPA set forth their demands, always including a reversal of the coaches' decision to keep Sonoma off the football team. Talk of a boycott surfaced now and then, until MAPA declared such displeasure with the school board's dilatory reactions that only a boycott would suffice to express their consternation.

Little handwritten posters in English and Spanish announced the basic fact: "Boycott"/"Huelga," to begin on Monday, October 14, 1980. An estimated 110 students, 40 percent of the high school's Hispanic enrollment, marched with placards outside their school building. "More bilingual teachers and aides" was a common message. As they marched they chanted, "Let's stop racism." The next day, according to plan, they paraded outside the superintendent's office; the day was rainy and fewer students marched. The superintendent, like the principal the day before, readily conceded the need for more bilingual teachers. "The problem," he said, "is that the labor market doesn't reflect the needs." The principal had earlier explained to reporters that the school had interviewed sixty applicants for the 1980–81 school year; three of them were bilingual, and all three accepted jobs elsewhere. It took an extended meeting with the school board on Wednesday night to end what had become a three-day boycott. MAPA leaders heard their requests put in the form of motions and voted on by the five-person board; the audience booed, whistled, hooted, cheered, and clapped, depending on the eloquence and bias of the speaker.

In the relatively quiet years that followed the three-day boycott of 1980 that he helped promote, MAPA spokesman Jaime Mendoza retained his performing skills; he would lack, however, a stage on which to perform. When he had a stage, he and others raised so many issues, made so many accusations and demands, that perhaps the most fundamental concern of the Hispanic community got obscured. It was expressed by another MAPA leader after a meeting held a week before the boycott began. Commenting on the importance of education, the MAPA member said, "We want our kids to be taxpayers, not a burden on our society." As much as local participants and onlookers could infer from MAPA's roster of concerns that its primary interest was in ethnic maintenance, it seemed most to want to remove obstacles that impeded Hispanic youth from becoming successful in American society. I believe this point was not evident in Riverview's local newspaper when, at year's end in 1980, it ranked the community's top stories and placed the boycott fourth, behind a water fight and its curfew violation, a large fire, and seven murders.

In 1973, a community agency interested in promoting the city's economic interests ran an ad inviting people to submit appropriate items for its newspaper and radio publicity campaign. The ad ran under the title, "Riverview's Good News Report." In 1974, RHS students performed *Hair*, the first high school in the nation to do so. At the play's end, students from the audience joined the cast in dancing on the stage and singing, "Let the Sun Shine In." That year's seniors ended their graduation ceremonies the same way. The next year, the RHS drama teacher decided to follow *Hair* with a production of *Barefoot in the Park*. For the play's husband and wife, he cast, with their approval, a black girl with a white boy. The boy's father disapproved and the boy withdrew from the play.

I am uncertain which of these several RHS events the ad-running community agency would have perceived as "good news." In fact, I see the period of 1968 to 1980 as one in which Riverview residents, young and old, were rethinking what constituted good news. As in the song from *Hair*, they were discovering what the sunlight was that, in a manner of speaking, they would let shine into their lives. It was a traumatic time, a period of education in and through turmoil. The same general set of events would move previously indifferent people in opposite directions. Here is one teacher:

Our own legislature said before you suspend a kid, you've got to have a hearing. Jesus Christ, do you know what you're asking for when you say that? Every minority was clamoring for its own rights, but never talking about it own responsibilities.

And here is another:

Today we're much more aware of color. Maybe that's why the ugly seventies and late sixties were a necessity. A lot of people had a right to rebel because they were being ignored or shut out. So maybe the ugliness was necessary. I'm glad it's over.

In 1969, an editorial in the local newspaper reflected on the school board's decision to dismiss their newly hired superintendent, conjecturing that this resulted from the superintendent's efforts to integrate schools and from his preference to hire people based on their qualifications. It is a measure of the changes that had occurred in Riverview that such objections, by 1980, sounded quaint and antiquated. Ethnic alertness had become enshrined, as had an elaborate candidate-selection process.

In June 1979 the school board conducted a public hearing "To Determine if any Riverview School District Schools are Racially or Ethnically Segregated and to Adopt Criteria Related Thereto." The board president declared the hearing open and asked for questions from the audience. Hearing none, he declared the hearing closed. Thereupon, the board voted unanimously to approve the conclusion that its schools were not ethnically or racially segregated. Busing and desegregation were non-issues; here was one basis for turmoil gone. At other school board meetings, students were reported to have stopped jumping other students, and to be less mean, angry, and bitter. Here were other bases for turmoil gone. The community's ethnic organizations stopped their routine monitoring of school board meetings. "There wasn't as much controversy going on," one regular monitor put it. Also, the school board seemed to have become worthy of trust because of the lessons it had learned. A trusted school board reduces the prospect of turmoil. In the years following 1980, the board members, administrators, teachers, and nonacademic employees whose lives were most closely associated with the schools would remark with relief and satisfaction that times had changed for the better at Riverview High, that a welcome quiet had settled in.

If in October 1980 the resolution of Hispanic demands brought an end to the era of ethnic unease, the high school had other grounds for distress. It was shocked by the news it received the very next month. Indeed, the point of the news would prove to be a recurrent theme, as each fall the school district received test results which showed its students' academic achievement within the context of all county and state school districts. The heading of the story that carried the news read, "Riverview Test Scores Lowest in County"; the scores placed Riverview at the fifth percentile in the state. Each year when the results were made public, an assistant superintendent would appear before the school board to declare that the sad test results were fairly understood only if compared with those from other school districts with a comparable so cioeconomic status. Nobody present at such meetings doubted that Riverview's high percentage of poor minorities was, somehow, an explanatory factor; yet nobody voiced this explanation.

4

Riverview High School: Demographics,
Curricular Alternatives, and Academic
Underachievement

If the turmoil of the 1968–80 period did not end all at once in 1980, the feeling that it was ending was perceptible. By then, the ameliorative responses had taken effect, the nation had quieted, and healing took place. Board members and administrators had an easier time: their telephones rang less often and the tones of the callers were less strident. Not since the boycott has the school board faced an issue so momentous as to necessitate the use of the high school's large auditorium. These days when board members hear about the ethnic mix of the cheerleading squad— in the unlikely event that they hear anything of this sort—it may be a query about the underrepresentation of white students.

Of course problems remain, but they are not the thorny ones of those uneasy years. Now, teachers say, students work together rather than fight, and activists from the minority community comment on the recent succession of good years, pointing to teachers' better understanding of students from different ethnic backgrounds and to the absence of race as a factor in student fights. In the past, teachers commonly worried "about keeping my kids under control. Now, I worry about getting homework done. Our students act better." In recent school board elections, incumbents and challengers mostly discussed matters relating to growth. Race, human relations, ethnic courses, busing, and ethnic strife seem not to be part of any candidate's program or any constituent's pressure.

Riverview High School Students: What Are They Like?

Riverview's approximately six thousand K–12 students are located in six K–5 elementary schools, two 6–8 middle schools, and one 9–12 high

Table 1. Riverview High School Students, 1970–87, by Ethnicity

Year	White		Black		Hispanic		Asian		American Indian		All Students (= N)
	Total No.	%	Total No.	%	Total No.	%	Total No.	%	Total No.	%	
1970	530	42.3	370	29.5	303	24.2	50	3.9	1	0	1,254
1971	596	47.8	379	30.4	262	21.0	9	.7	0	0	1,246[a]
1972	755	44.6	506	29.9	365	21.6	64	3.8	1	0	1,691
1973	711	44.1	462	28.7	363	22.5	75	4.6	1	.6	1,612
1974	671	39.8	482	31.8	374	20.7	80	5.0	2	.1	1,609
1975	730	45.6	467	29.2	360	22.5	36	2.2	8	.5	1,601
1976	632	40.0	505	31.8	329	20.7	119	7.5	5	.3	1,590
1977	640	40.3	490	30.8	328	20.6	126	7.9	6	.4	1,590
1978	593	38.2	496	31.9	334	21.5	126	8.1	5	.2	1,554
1979	562	36.5	474	30.8	348	22.6	142	9.2	14	.9	1,540
1980	541	35.3	496	32.4	347	22.7	146	9.5	1		1,531
1981	473	32.9	496	34.5	331	23.0	132	9.2	4	.3	1,436
1982 1983[b]	466	31.9	491	33.6	321	22.0	179	12.2	5	.3	1,462
1984	507	32.4	512	32.7	332	21.2	207	13.2	6	.4	1,563
1985	519	33.5	456	29.4	352	22.7	209	13.5	9	.5	1,546
1986	521	31.5	509	30.3	358	21.7	258	15.7	5	.3	1,651[c]
1987	504	30.9	478	29.3	365	22.3	286	17.5	0	0	1,633[c]

SOURCE: Riverview Unified School District files.

[a] I am inclined to disregard all these 1971 figures (possibly even those for 1970) because the Asian total of nine is improbable, and because of the great disparity between the totals in 1970 and 1971 and the total in 1972.

[b] No figures are available for this year.

[c] Excluded are one Pacific islander in 1986 and 11 in 1987 because ethnic counting did not include them in previous years.

school. In town there are one Catholic and several Christian elementary schools, and in an over-the-hill town there are two Catholic high schools. Together these nonpublic schools claim about six hundred of Riverview's children; district officials do not know their exact dispersion across the K–12 spectrum.

Since 1970, the school district has collected data on the ethnic identity of RHS students. Following changing directives from external sources, the district has used various ethnic designations, such as white, white not of Hispanic origin, black, black not of Hispanic origin, Hispanic, Spanish-surname, Asian (including Filipinos), Asian (excluding Filipinos), Filipinos, American Indian or Alaskan Native, and Indian. Table 1 uses those headings that best subsume the figures the district compiled over the period from 1970 to 1987: white, black, Hispanic, Asian, and American Indian, omitting just one additional heading currently in use—Filipino.[1] Most Hispanic students are Mexican and most Asian students, Filipino. In 1985, for example, of 209 Asian students at RHS, 142 were Filipinos; we know these numbers because for the State of California's ethnic accounting "Filipino" is a separate designation.

Whereas Riverview's overall population has grown steadily since 1970, its high school population has not. It reached a high point of 1691 in 1972, then declined steadily for the next twelve years, rising again only at the end of our period. Several trends stand out in the 1970–87 period, when enrollments ranged from approximately 1,200 to 1,700: American Indians are a negligible component of the student body; black enrollment has fluctuated but basically increased, while remaining at about the same proportion of the total (30 percent); Hispanic enrollment has grown more slowly than that of blacks and their proportion of the total has declined (from about 24 to 22 percent); Asian enrollment has grown most dramatically, their proportion of the total increasing from about 4 to more than 17 percent; and whites, always the largest single group, crested in 1972 (I am not confident about 1971 figures) and after peaking again at 46 percent in 1975, declined to about 31 percent in 1987. California has a large and growing nonwhite population. Still, RHS is more heavily "ethnic" than the state at large, whose public-school population stands at 53 percent white, 10 percent black, 28 percent Hispanic, 8 percent Asian, and about 1 percent American Indian.

Given the antipathy many parents direct toward RHS and their relative comfort with the district's K–8 educational provisions, I conclude that most of the six hundred local students not attending Riverview schools are of high school age. These students have begun to trickle back to RHS, their parents reassured by the succession of quiet years since 1980. The trickle may become a torrent when the city's many new home-building projects are complete, for they will bring in mostly white and Asian families who can better afford the cost of the new homes. Space in older, low-cost housing correspondingly decreases as the new projects are built upon old housing sites. A general consequence of these demographic changes is that children from more affluent families will increase as a proportion of the total student body. The number of blacks and Hispanics also is growing, although at a lesser rate. They will remain a stable if relatively smaller component of the school and community, unlike the situation common in other cities where one ethnic group replaces another and in the process totally changes the nature of the school and community. RHS is not about to lose its multiethnic character. Some

1. I omit Filipinos as a category because for many years, before they became a separate category, Filipinos were placed under "Asian." I cannot extract them from the Asian total.

families will prefer nonpublic schools; most will not. The net effect of
these newcomers is felt in school board elections and in parental pressure for a more academic orientation than in the past. In its several
meanings, the complexion of Riverview is changing.

Riverview's schools serve a large population of children drawn from
families that receive Aid to Families of Dependent Children (AFDC).
During the years for which data are available (1967–84), some 25 to 30
percent of all K–12 children were from AFDC families, with high school
percentages tending toward the upper end of this range. In 1984, Riverview's 27.5 percent AFDC students placed it at the top of the list for all
seventeen school districts in the county; only one other school district
was over 20 percent. All the others were less than 15 percent.

The district's schools serve a small number of children whose language skills place them in the "limited English-proficient" (LEP)
category. About 6 percent of Riverview's K–12 children are LEP, with a
somewhat lower percentage at RHS. These children are primarily Spanish speakers, but also includes those who speak languages from their
native Vietnam, Laos, and the Philippines.

The school district's most complete survey of students was made for
the high school group that entered in 1981 and graduated in 1985. A
total of 579 entering students had to be accounted for: 285 graduated,
leaving 294 others. Of these, 115 took one of the school district's several
main alternate routes (continuation high schools—discussed below—
independent study, or adult school) to complete high school, and 133
transferred out of the district to other schools. Of the remaining 46, 21
could not be traced, and the 25 others ran away, died, or were expelled.
What the State of California calls "attrition" takes a harsh toll among
high school students. Using 1983 data (California Dept. of Education
1983), we see that 29 percent of 335,000 students who began high school
in 1979 did not graduate in 1983.

For the class of 1985, school district officers also inquired about the
academic qualifications of the surviving 285 students. RHS is ever sensitive to the readiness of its students to attend the state's prestigious
university-level institutions (UCLA, UC-Berkeley, UC-Davis, etc.), for
this achievement can be used to slay the dragons of detractors who see
RHS as academically hopeless. Data on the class of 1985 do not obviously arm the dragon slayers nor do they testify to the school's
hopelessness. Only 46, or 16 percent, of the total number (reduced,
somehow, from 285 to 279) of seniors studied took the particular pattern
of courses required for university entry; a lesser 26, or 9 percent, had
high enough SAT scores plus the necessary courses to qualify for admission. Thirteen students actually registered in California's university-

level institutions, 5 of whom were Hispanic; the ethnicity of the remaining 8 was not identified.[2] But an ethnic accounting is provided for the 46 who took the "right" courses to attend a university; they are in the group known generally as "college prep" and constitute an academic elite at RHS. Of the 46, 54 percent are white, 20 percent black, 15 percent Hispanic, 7 percent Filipino, and 4 percent other (probably Southeast Asian). All ethnic groups except whites are underrepresented in the 1985 college-prep elite. (This is not usually true for the Filipinos, nor is it for other Asians who do not seem to have been identified in the 1985 survey).

The Curriculum and Its Alternatives

Long gone is RHS's vast array of elective courses, a curricular hallmark of American high schools in the 1960s and 1970s. Such choice as exists today within a particular subject is based more on student skill than on student interest. To begin with, for many years the required courses in social studies, mathematics, science, and English had a college-prep level and a general level, with only English having a third or "honors" level. After the successful trial in 1985–86 of CORE, an honors program for a select group of sophomores who took special English, social studies, and science classes, there now is an honors group of about twenty-five students in each of the school's four grades. With an honors level added to the previous college prep and general levels, RHS has returned to a triple-tiered tracking system. Tracking had been a casualty of the academic and civil-rights activism of the 1970s.

Mathematics offers the greatest number of options. Its twelve or so different courses range from consumer math to calculus, as the school strives to insure a satisfactory experience with numeracy for all its students. Science includes the usual general science, biology, chemistry, and physics; social studies, in addition to world history and United States history, includes psychology, economics, government, and, occasionally, sociology. Vocational choices are broad—cooking, sewing, drafting, woodworking, electricity, typing, accounting, business skills, and auto repair. The arts are amply provided for in its art, crafts, photography, choir, piano, band, jazz ensemble, beginning and advanced acting, and stagecraft courses. Three foreign languages—Spanish, French, and Italian—are taught.

Within the ambit of Riverview school district, as well as admin-

---

2. In 1968, 10 of 133 graduates attended California's high-level universities, as did 7 of 309 in 1969 and 7 of 236 in 1970.

istratively within RHS, there are many alternatives to the regular programs RHS offers as its general, college-prep, and honors tracks. The alternative programs are designed for students who, because of their intellectual limitations, their persistent misbehavior, or their personal circumstances, are placed outside the mainstream programs by either RHS educators or the students themselves. Indeed, it could be argued that in the district's and the county's special educational opportunities there exists an abundance of curricular arrangements for reluctant, unwilling, or handicapped learners.

Beyond the three mainstream channels are ten alternative channels. Seven are within the Riverview school district—continuation high schools, independent study, adult education, high risk, opportunity, resource, and special day. Three are under county control—regional occupation program, county day school, and a residential school.

These ten alternatives are by no means parallel academic opportunities. Some are restricted by the age at which a student can enter, some by the breadth of the curriculum, some by whether or not they offer a diploma, some by how long a student can remain in the program. Each is designed to respond to the particular circumstances or characteristics of the students eligible to register. Most have their counterparts, under the same name, in school districts throughout California, and counterparts under other names exist throughout the country. Their local names— "Opportunity," "Resource," "Special Day," "GRASP (Gaining Resources and Surveying Potentials)"—are at once euphemisms and invitations to succeed in some way, at some level, offering students a chance, so educators reason, that might not be available if they had to be assigned only to one of the three regular programs.

The honors-track CORE program class is for self-selected students who apply and then are chosen on the basis of "achievement test scores, grade point average, teacher recommendations, and a writing sample." In its first year of operation, CORE assembled about twenty-five bright sophomores who during three common periods each day developed an esprit that set them apart from all other sophomores and cheered teachers about the prospects for academic high flying at RHS.

Nonwhite teachers fear that CORE will facilitate the process of dumping minority students ever farther away from the school's academically prestigious heights. Older teachers, who recall past pressure to abolish tracking, wonder about its return. CORE teachers welcome the emergence of an elite that deserves the challenges of a special program. Most CORE students and their parents would agree, and as long as the program can produce rhapsodic students, its detractors will be hard put to contain its expansion. Here is such a student:

Last year when I was a freshman the work assigned to me was too slow. I was getting bored. CORE was needed so that students will learn, not just strive for all A's. I want to learn; I mean, shit, I learned a lot this year. I think so. Like last night, I had a dream. I was dreaming I was at a museum. I never had a dream like this [probably because before he took CORE, he had never been to museums]. Some kid asked, "What's an impressionist painting?" I explained it to the kid, and while I explained it, I was painting impressionist paintings. I was saying, like, "It's different because it didn't follow the orthodox style." I was saying, "See, look at these dibs and dabs, smears and blotches." Then, I woke up. I go, was it for real or was I watching TV?

By virtue of their problems and needs, alternative-education students are separated from mainstream-education students. Educators believe that the resulting process of mutual isolation and insulation best serves the interests of both groups. It is most unlikely that the alternative education programs will ever be candidates for use in the school and community's new-image campaigns. The adolescents whose problems and needs establish their eligibility for these programs may touch our hearts, but they do not look good "for the record."

Entry to the continuation high schools, independent study, and Opportunity School is established through the deliberations of a group consisting of an assistant superintendent of schools, continuation school principals, independent study director, high school counselors and deans, and others. The group takes testimony from students and parents, and from the high school personnel who have had contact with the student. For example, sixteen-year-old white Clara voluntarily sought admission to independent study. She and her mother explained that Clara did not get along well with students, that she did not like physical education, particularly the compulsory showers. When boyish-looking Clara and her mother left the room, the dean, who supported Clara's request, told the "last straw" story. One day, Clara went to the girl's bathroom, but the girls threw her out, accusing her of being a boy, and reported her to a dean. The group agreed that she could report to independent study, where she could set her own hours, work at her own pace, and earn the necessary credits for graduation. In 1985, of seventy students in independent study, 3 percent were Filipino, 19 percent Hispanic, 37 percent black, and 41 percent white.

At the same meeting when Clara's case was heard, sixteen-year-old Mexican Paul Hurda voluntarily sought admission to one of Riverview's two continuation high schools. His aunt said he was not used to attending a school as large and as ethnically varied as RHS, and that he had got into fights. Paul had cuts on his forearm. The counselor present was suspicious of these cuts. The continuation school principal agreed to accept Paul, though his admission was contingent on Paul's willingness to meet with a counselor.

The continuation high school offers Paul a setting with a capacity for eighty students, carefully monitored attendance, a half-day program that leaves students free to work outside, and an opportunity to earn credits necessary for graduation. To enter, students must be at least sixteen; typically, they have had attendance or discipline problems. Each teacher is responsible for regular contact by phone or personal visit with the parents of fifteen students. In 1985, of sixty-one students at one of Riverview's two continuation schools, 3 percent were Pacific Islanders, 3 percent Filipinos, 10 percent Hispanic, 20 percent white, and 64 percent black. Of 61 students at Riverview's other continuation school, which took less serious cases, 3 were Filipino, 15 percent white, 31 percent Hispanic, and 50 percent black. Each year, about eight to ten students transfer back to RHS.

The Opportunity Program is the counterpart of the continuation school for students under sixteen who are freshmen and sophomores. About seventy-five students participated in the program's English, social studies, mathematics, and science classes. Tracy Rivera teaches in this program.

I once had Billy Peters in my class [says Rivera]. I had to decide what strategy I'd use with him. I said I would try regular progress reports and involve him in weight lifting. We got his period truancy—how many classes he cut—reduced in one grading quarter from 232 to 10. His quarter grades went up from .67 to 1.33 [in a system where 4.0 is an A]. Roger, another student, his grades went from .36 to 1.24 and his 122 unexcused period absences went down to 27.

We set up concrete goals for each student at the outset and then we monitor. I try to get to know each student, their family, what their likes are, what bothers them. Our students usually come in after referral by a counselor. Very few of them, I would say, could compete [in the academic mainstream], and maybe that's why they were truant or were behavior problems.

The County Day School accepts twelve- to seventeen-year-old students in a four-period school day. It aims to get students returned to their regular high schools by getting them back on course with regular attendance, a quiet presence in class, and academic progress toward earning credits for graduation. A police officer picks students up if they're not at school. It tries to keep students from being shipped off to the Ranch (another county-run program), which is a residential school for hard-core problem students whose behavior falls just short of meriting a prison sentence.

In 1987 Riverview introduced an off-campus, last-chance program, located in a local black church, for high school freshmen designated "high risk." They are at risk for being admitted to the County Day School. Some Riverview school board members greeted this program with serious reservations, seeing it as one more "dumping ground" for teachers who "don't want to deal with students who are difficult to teach."

Two other alternatives within the school district are for students who have learning difficulties, with the most severe students assigned to Special Day Classes. Students whose test scores show a difference of two and a half years between tested ability and tested achievement are assigned to Resource Program classes. In 1985, the Special Day Classes had fifty students, most of them black males;[3] the Resource Program Classes had forty-four students drawn from all ethnic groups and containing somewhat more males than females. Special Day students take up to five special classes each day and they can obtain a regular high school diploma; Resource Class students can take no more than two of their classes in this program, and are expected to graduate with mainstream classmates. Three full-time teachers staff each of the programs.

From one perspective, these many academic alternatives are opportunities that enable students to stay in school and obtain an education that is "suitable" for them. If left only to one of the three mainstream tracks, some students would be out of place, and others, having already demonstrated their unwillingness or inability to fit in, would leave school. From another perspective, the one reflected in the dumping-ground designation some school board members applied to Riverview's new high-risk program, the alternative programs weed troublesome students out of the mainstream garden. Since school districts cannot discard their student "weeds," they house them in little curricular patches of their own, leaving the mainstream blooms free to benefit from the "regular" curriculum. In fact, the weeding-out perspective can be applied as well to each of the two tracks below that of the new honors program. Once the sorting-out process begins, it has no end. With a little imagination educators can devise more and more student categories, each warranting another curricular alternative, in a perpetual quest for purer and more teachable groups.

Between the good of honoring individual differences and the bad of

3. Studies show that "blacks are more than twice as likely as whites to be placed in special education classes" (Snider 1987:20).

creating dumping grounds, there are conflicting facts. Teachers proudly report their victories: students saved by alternative programs, pulled back from the brink of academic extinction, boredom, or suffocation. Yet in Riverview, as elsewhere throughout the nation, a disproportionately large number of minority, mostly black, students populate the alternative programs and don't gain entry to the upper academic tracks.[4]

RHS Educators

RHS principal Fred Borcher refers again and again to the events of 1968. He experienced the turmoil following the King assassination not only as an educator but also as a Riverview native who had graduated from RHS and returned from college to make his career within Riverview's school system. Borcher guides RHS as both educator and native, attuned to expectations and needs that arise from both statuses. RHS is not merely the place where he works, it is his school in the sense that loyal graduates possessively proclaim a school to be their school. Fred Borcher is a loyal graduate. By his own account, 1968 both shocked and instructed him, though I do not think his outlook is locked in time, limited to those lessons and realities of life at RHS that emerged from the events of that year.

He speaks at length in the following pages to this point, more so than anyone else. Borcher is, after all, the high school's prime "teacher." Notwithstanding that some teachers may contest his views or disagree with his interpretation of events and their implications, he has been RHS's principal since the early 1970s. Accordingly, the broad issues of curriculum, the selection of teachers, the numerous daily decisions that together constitute the judgments that help shape a school's ethos—these have long been fully, though not exclusively, in his domain. Other voices will be heard soon enough to reinforce, take issue with, and, possibly contradict outright what Borcher says. The point here is not to identify where the truth lies but rather to consider the multiple realities within which RHS teachers, students, and administrators dwell. For the high school abounds with realities. Fred Borcher speaks from a privileged position, and I take seriously his perspective.

The principals in our district meet once a month, together with our coaches and athletic directors. The reason for getting together is for athletics. Of

---

4. Snider's study of "173 large urban school districts" confirmed the sorting of black students into alternative programs. He further found that as the number of black teachers in a school increases, the number of black students placed in special classes, suspended, or expelled decreases (1987:1).

course, when we're there, we're always discussing other things. It gets into grading, it gets into lots of things. No one would have my job, if that's the question you're going to ask.

I don't think I can distinguish between the different ethnic groups in what they want the school to do for their children. Just the contacts that I've had from parents, it's usually, "I want them to have something that I didn't have or at least to have what I did and more." I really don't see any great differences between a black or a Chicano or a white. I think their expectations are all the same. They all want what's best for their particular kid. I think some of them have higher expectations for their kids than they should, but that's a parent, too. No one wants to admit that their kids don't have the ability to be a doctor.

I hope we give students that basic knowledge that they would need to be able to function in life. We try to give them a vocational background, or at least an understanding of the different choices that they have. I think that's why the push for the career center and all of the vocational areas that we have. Then, of course, there's the academic, and what we're doing right now is working on the CORE program, because I think for so many years we've done so much as far as the low end of the scale.

I get pressures from different groups. What we don't get is the Filipino-Americans or the NAACP or the Sons of Italy coming in. Not any more. We used to, yes. We had the NAACP. They wanted black studies. The Mexican-American association wanted certain things put in the curriculum. No more. We don't have those things. I haven't had anything like that for probably ten to fifteen years.

We had a black-studies program. After two or three years, the students stopped taking it. We had Mexican-American history, we had black history, and we didn't have enough students to sign up for the classes. So we had to drop the classes. Right now, every once in a while we even offer Spanish for Spanish speakers. Some years we get three sign-ups; some years we get four. Those were all put in the curriculum as a result of meeting the needs of the community, the students, and the requests from the different organizations.

See, it depends on who's running these organizations. If Lamar Robinson is running an organization, then you would hear from him because he knows what's going on in the school. He has connections. Some of these organizations, right now, for instance, the Mexican-American, they're almost nonexistent, anymore. Up until a couple of years ago, they were very strong. Those people who have a concern will come in and do a one-to-one basis, rather than a big show at a board meeting. The only call from an organization this year has been from—I don't know if it was from the Black Political Association or from NAACP—they were questioning what we were doing with some of those kids on suspension, are we handling them any different. After we explained to them what we were doing, it was great, they approved of it and they liked it. Someone had brought it to their attention and rather than come to a board meeting, they called the superintendent and asked the question and that ended it.

There is a continuing legacy in the school with the way people operate as teachers and principals and counselors going back to those days of '68. Subconsciously, I think I do everyday. There's always—back of your mind, no matter where I go, even if I'm off campus to a meeting—there's always that feeling when the telephone rings, "Is it for me?" because it happened so many times years ago. With the mixture that we have, it can happen. You want to believe that it won't because we think everyone is working together and everyone understands and accepts each other, but it's there. There's always that potential, which you're not going to have at Fairview High School, which is 100 percent white. When you deal with people you always ask yourself, "Did I do it this way last time?" That's where you have to be extremely careful, but I don't think I have to talk to a black person any different than I talk to a white person.

I have to be very conscious of my administrators, what they say and how they react, because when the parental complaint comes in, then they're calling me to complain the way they were treated by so and so: he talks down to me just because I'm black. As principal, I'm being tested in terms of my prejudice all the time. I think the classroom teacher is, too. Was I mindful of this in '67? In 1965? As a student here? No, never. This is the legacy of '68. But, again, there was nothing wrong with that happening. We thought we didn't owe an explanation and I think, many times, in many cases, we do owe an explanation. But up until probably '68, we never had to explain to parents. We certainly do now.

Riverview seems to be oriented to keeping their particular cultural heritage. I think that some of the clubs that we have on campus would encourage that—the La Raza club for the Latinos, the Filipino-American club for the Filipinos, the Black Student Union. I think that the bilingual program somewhat does that too, but I think sometimes to an extent where we hinder the learning of, well, I can't say the learning, but I think it slows down the process of mainstreaming them. I've seen kids in the bilingual program for six, seven, eight years. And I am against that. . . .

About ten years ago we had the Italians who were upset. We had the Swedish people who would say, "Why don't you do anything for us?" Or the Greek people . . . So, we got to a point where every day on the bulletin we were reading something. We had a whole calendar kept and every day we would have to say something about whose [ethnic heroes' and celebrities'] birthday it was and recognize every ethnic group. We did it because the pressure started with the blacks and then it went into the Latinos. The pressure is no longer there.

There's nothing wrong with infusing in the home economics class the backgrounds and the cultures of the different kids, whether it be blacks or Italian or Mexican. That's beautiful. See, I think in history we did neglect to teach about blacks, to teach what all the different cultures have added to the United States. Not only in United States history, but in the government and world history classes, too. If what people tell me is really what they believe, it doesn't matter what color the teacher is as long as the respect is there for the student. I agree. I don't care what color you are.

It's all gone today: the black studies, the Mexican-American history, etc. It's all gone as a result of lack of enrollment. We went through that period. It was the thing to do in the seventies. You know, it's no longer the thing. I think we're getting back to what we were in the fifties.

What is not all gone today is Borcher's deep-seated grasp of the fact that his school serves several constituencies, and though in general they hold similar expectations of the school, their needs at any given time are never identical. Moreover, he believes that where complaints exist, he must be prepared to hear them as the expressions of an individual or a group with legitimate claims to shape the experience of students at RHS. Like most administrators, he prefers the style of some petitioners to that of others, but the style he prefers is not a function of ethnicity.

Borcher had his "consciousness raised," as they say, regarding the nonwhite youth who attend his school. Now, he means to be attuned to their fate, their requests and expectations, and to the implications of their presence in the school's instructional program. More than just being acceptable, it is desirable that home economics, for example, be infused with "the backgrounds and the cultures of the different kids." But he is no less attuned to what he sees as the preeminent fact about the socialization of students: they must be able to fit into society, which means that they must be able to talk and conduct themselves in ways that mainstream America endorses. Few parents or teachers would contest this point. That he welcomes the presence of "backgrounds and cultures" is not to suggest that he actively pursues their inclusion anywhere in the school's program. That would not be his style. Recollecting the disorder of a time when schools were unresponsive to minority group wants, he is prepared to consider them seriously, much as a merchant will provide goods that a market demands and stop providing them when the market no longer demands them.

Having survived the turmoil of the 1968–80 period, Borcher is cred-
ible in the eyes of Riverview adults. He meets them with a depth of
insight, understanding, and sensitivity that would be hard for an outsider to match. Yet few of his teachers are aware of the range of views he
expresses above, having had little or no occasion to hear them. Even
knowing them, teachers would not at once, if ever, subscribe to them.
Tradition does not confer such legitimacy and authority upon school administrators. In contrast, when the principal of the fundamentalist
Christian school I studied (1986) expressed his views, I had no doubt
that his teachers not only knew about them but also that they basically
held the same views and accepted them as guidelines for their teaching.
For better or worse, Christian schools have a mission that is clear,
known, and controlling. For better or worse, public schools usually do
not.

I asked teachers if they ever discussed schoolwide or departmental
goals. Most said they never had. Some said they vaguely recalled such
discussion on the occasion of accreditation visits, but they were not sure.
A few of the oldest teachers recalled such meetings but said they were
ineffective, explaining that nobody pays attention to such meetings:
"They've [teachers] already got their own opinions for what it's
[education] about." Indeed, they do have their own opinions, and they
express them freely, if seldom eloquently. For teachers, once beyond
their formal training, and possibly not even there, are not compelled to
articulate the general ends for which their instruction is the means.
Thus, they have little opportunity to become experienced in stating
what purpose their teaching serves. They readily acknowledge that
those purposes they do express are personal: they made them up
themselves.

Clearly, the principal's views have an impact when he meets with any
of the community groups that are interested in schooling, as they do also
when he meets with parents or teachers who come with requests or concerns. Otherwise, he seeks no occasion to promote a Borcher agenda for
RHS. Such schoolwide agenda as there is derives from state requirements and tests, University of California admission requirements, and
the textbooks and workbooks currently in use. To some degree, teachers
of a particular subject matter (for example, English, mathematics, or
social studies) meet to plan and coordinate the scope and sequence of
their instruction, or the emphasis to be given to a particular skill, such as
critical thinking. From these several sources, classroom instruction
acquires a broad, general form within which teachers may shape their
own and their students' conduct. The commonality of this broad, gen-

eral form creates instructional similarities among American schools. Dissimilarities arise from the particularities of a school's setting, its clientele, and its educators.

Perhaps under ideal conditions the teachers who work in a certain school would be those who have chosen to work there because, knowing what the school is like, they've judged that they could make their best contribution there. For the most part, this is not the case at RHS, any more than it is at most public schools. While their reasons for coming to RHS are not identical, the teachers speak primarily of needing a job, often in a school located in an area where they were committed to living because of a spouse's job. What they do not speak of, barring a few exceptions, is being attracted to RHS because of the opportunities provided by a multiethnic population. Indeed, most teachers learn of this attribute at the time of their interview, often by the intention of Mr. Borcher, who feels obliged to ascertain that the candidate not only is qualified, say, for teaching English, but is prepared to teach it to a multitude of poor, nonwhite youngsters.

A notable exception to the large group of teachers who have come to RHS because it meant merely getting a job are the twenty (of a total of eighty) who are graduates of RHS. These teachers returned home to work, accepted by a school board and administration as particularly welcome school district employees. These returned-home teachers do not necessarily desire their hometown jobs because RHS promises the opportunities of a multiethnic setting. They generally do not focus on the presence of ethnicity in their community and school unless their attention is called to it; to them, ethnicity is just part of the fabric of life in Riverview. They happen to like Riverview, feeling comfortable and good about being at home with family and friends. As one teacher explained,

I was working somewhere else for a while, but I knew I was going to live in this community. I liked it; it grew on me. Being away from it, I still used to come back and look at the people, and look at the town. It's not that they were my type of people, or my this or my that. There weren't any of those mys to it. It was that I liked it.

For most of its history, RHS had no hometown teachers. This changed after World War II when some Sicilian boys attended college and came home to teach. Other teachers perceive the native contingent as a cliquish group, joined by the easy ties of place and birth—most are Sicilian—and of upbringing. The hometown teachers think they bring a special commitment to their school—"We bring the blood of the town to the classroom"—as well as a level of understanding of students and parents surpassing that of colleagues who reside outside Riverview and simply commute there to work. Though the hometown teachers do have a strong attachment to RHS, of the sort that only a former student may have, they are not otherwise identifiable as distinct in the conduct of their professional responsibilities.

Most teachers are likely to have had exalted motivations for becoming teachers in the first place; some volunteer that such motivations still provide impetus for their work. Under the routine circumstances that prevail at RHS and most schools, however, exalted motivations are very difficult to sustain. These circumstances include the isolated, segmented nature of the teacher's job.

Isolation derives from several basic facts: teachers perform behind closed doors, with minimal and, at best, perfunctory supervision, and they typically relate to fellow teachers in nonprofessional terms during brunch, lunch, and free-period breaks. Teacher breaks are occasions for relief from teaching, not for the "cross-pollination" that one teacher said she missed, and the absence of which, she thought, necessitated everyone "reinventing the wheel" for themselves. Moreover, when they do meet with fellow educators for professional purposes, it is at the bidding of superiors, both within and outside the school system, and for agendas they seldom are party to establishing.

Accordingly, teachers are not inspired or sustained by a shared mission. They commonly refer to their peaceful, closed-door autonomy. Their autonomy remains peaceful as long as they do not "make waves," by which they mean not allowing their classes to get out of control and not failing too many students (which leads to phone calls and unwanted attention from superiors).

A sense of being socially segmented, or polarized, as many teachers put it, prevails generally among the faculty. They lament the many small groups that contain their colleagues and the corresponding lack of a sense of community that would engender widespread caring and support. The segmented feeling is a concomitant of large size. It is not, however, inevitable that a large faculty be fragmented by dichotomies such as native-nonnative, Riverview–non-Riverview resident, male-female, white-nonwhite, young-old, experienced-inexperienced, sports fan–nonsports fan, ad infinitum—and the social groups that can form on the basis of these factors.

A consequence of isolation (which I mean to convey as a relative, not absolute fact of life for teachers at RHS) is that teachers do not ordinarily benefit from, or provide benefits to, their colleagues. Teachers are discrete, parallel performers, and their classrooms are fortresses of independence, the welcoming drawbridge routinely down only to those who are eighteen and under, and only for official, narrowly specified purposes to anyone else.

Educators' Views of Parents

Parents, as RHS teachers perceive them, do not normally become involved with the school in ways that threaten teacher autonomy. To be sure, during the 1970s, individuals and groups lobbied for "relevant" courses; their efforts succeeded, as school board members, administrators, and teachers responded with appropriate, albeit ephemeral, curricular changes. Such intensity of effort and organization was not ordinarily present either before this period or afterwards. Today, parental inactivity and uninvolvement—never to be confused with indifference—are the norms. Their behavior says, in effect, that as long as teachers don't make waves, parents will stay away from school. Since wave-making has little or nothing to do with the quality of teaching and academic achievement, the norms by inference leave teachers behind their closed doors fundamentally free of parental constraints.

Rather than celebrating this freedom, most teachers feel abandoned by parents. On those several nights each school year when teachers are in their classrooms ready to receive them, parents do not come: "I have 140 students; during the last open house 7 parents showed up." "This year was my best year. I had 15 or 18 parents show up from my 90 students. In years past I was lucky to see the parents of 4 kids." "I've averaged maybe 10 parents a year over the past sixteen years. That's out of five classes, say 30 in a class."

Moreover, only forty of five hundred invited parents came to meetings called to discuss the proficiency test their children had failed. Passing this test is a condition for graduation. Similarly, parents ignored invitations to meetings where counselors would discuss financial aid services or where state college and university representatives would be present. And parents did not generally attend theatrical and musical performances in which their children appeared. The only occasions that guaranteed a large parental presence were football games and graduation ceremonies.

I asked teachers what they thought parents expected from the high school and if there was any conflict among the expectations held by the different ethnic groups. They did not know what parents wanted (and therefore could not know about conflict) because they had never heard parents, barring the odd individual, speak about their expectations.

Perhaps the chief wishes of RHS educators with regard to parents are not that they should be more sophisticated about what to expect from their children's school. Teachers, rather, would like to see parents acting as allies in support of their endeavors, alert to offering praise for especially praiseworthy efforts. By their lights parents should in effect support the everyday demands teachers place upon their students (doing homework, for example, and doing it seriously); they should rally to provide the support necessitated by exceptional circumstances, such as when teachers have a special problem in getting a child to perform at a satisfactory level; and they should know what teachers do so they can offer them encouraging comments.

This year was the first year I ever heard a parent tell me, "I've heard some good things about what you're teaching the students." I was thrilled to death. I mean, my ego was out to here. I didn't even think that my students discussed what they learned in class. I was thrilled. But the majority of parents, I don't know, they want a place for their children to be, and they don't want them in trouble.

In the same breath wherewith they lament the lack of parental support, many teachers explain that a high percentage of the parents are too busy or too tired to accept the school's invitations for the meetings designed to benefit their children. Some parents just do not know that there is anything they should do about their children's education beyond sending them to school; for such persons, the role of parental supporter is one they have never seen played. Other parents, teachers say, lead such personally troubled lives that they have little capacity for attending to the concerns of their adolescent children, whom they are likely to see as grown up and thus beyond the need for vigilant parental attention.

There are "on-our-backs" parents who want to know, as one teacher put it, "what we are teaching, why we are teaching it that way, and why we are not doing it a different way." Such parents are uncommon at RIIS. Most Riverview parents are so far from being on the backs of teachers that teachers can only see their classroom efforts as being enhanced by more parental interest and support: "If we cannot get the families of these kids to encourage them, I think we're kind of beating a dead horse. We, as teachers, can't handle the whole situation."

Educators' Views of Students

When I first came here I asked a veteran teacher how come if you tell the students you are going to have a test on Friday, they don't study for the test. He said, "Welcome to Riverview High."

The change teachers would most like to see at Riverview High would be that students take seriously their school's academic charge. The college-prep group, a small fraction of the student body, is, not surprisingly, disproportionately represented in elective leadership positions and in other positions of responsibility. They do not, however, set the academic tone of the school, for they, too, are part of the student culture, and not immune to the prevailing low level of academic aspiration and achievement. Could it be otherwise? Given our tradition of local control and the fact that students are prone to bring to school those attitudinal and behavioral dispositions they unwittingly internalize from home and neighborhood, a school, basically, will mirror its host community. To do otherwise requires a level of time, effort, resources, and personnel which, in combination, is difficult to attain.

A teacher whose appointment lies primarily in the college-prep track spoke with irritation and frustration about the reality that RHS reflects.

Even though I've coached all my life, I'd like to see less emphasis on athletics. When I see all the money spent on athletics, such as the football field, the scoreboard, and the goal posts—those things you could get by without . . . I wanted new books; I waited for years for them. This shows that we care about the field we play on (even though they could play on any kind of field); we don't care about students having a new textbook, even though the old ones are fifteen years old.

A top school district administrator, himself frustrated by the district's limited success in convincing newcomer parents that their children are academically "safe" in Riverview's schools, said about students: "We don't have a large percentage of kids who are motivated to do well at the high school. Those who are motivated and those who apply themselves will do well. We don't have a large number."

In the absence of a large number of such students, and not powerfully compelled to the contrary by pressure from other sources, teachers adapt their classroom conduct to the extant norms of student effort and expectation and thereby contribute to the perpetuation of these norms. "Kids," in the frank opinion of one teacher, "tend to respond to the dominant culture here—which is lazy." Such adaptation is one element of several (parental and administrator behavior are other major elements) that are part of the unplanned conspiracy to maintain limited academic accomplishment at RHS.

Unmindful of their part in this pageant of mediocrity, teachers seem to yearn for changes in their students. They want students to be "more studious," "college-oriented," "receptive to learning," "concerned about achieving," and "proud of academic success." To be sure, a sizable group of teachers want these behaviors applied to vocational classes, as, in their opinion, befits the predominantly blue-collar nature of Riverview's population. Still, regardless of whether the focus is on traditional academic subjects (English, science, etc.) or vocational subjects (home economics, auto mechanics, office skills, etc.), teachers want industrious students who are bent on learning.

Teachers obviously cannot plan who their students will be; they get the ones they get. Over the years, their perceptions of these students coalesce into judgments that pass as their own (possibly collective) conventional wisdom about what they should and should not do with students. These judgments, however much they may be drawn from "data" on students, are likely to say as much about teachers—their character, their commitment to teaching, their sense of what constitutes academic achievement, and their ideas about the promise of schooling—as about students.

Though I believe that the best way to grasp what teachers are like is to watch them teach for an extended period of time, I also believe that observation cannot reveal much about their values, hopes, perceptions, and the like. Thus, I asked RHS teachers to talk about students, my questions purposely general to avoid unwanted structuring. The results of their talk constitute a self-drawn portrait of the faculty, one with a cast of characters that can be found in schools anywhere in the country. The set includes the tender-hearted, the flinty, the sensitive, the cynical, the wise, and more, for there is no limit to the types of human beings who elect to become teachers, and there are no controls from within the teaching profession—nor should there be—that would admit only certain personality types.

The following excerpts are not intended to illuminate the character of a particular teacher, but, rather, to portray the variety of pedagogical signatures or trademarks characterizing the instructional aggregate that is the RHS faculty. For the purpose of at least simple identification, I preface each excerpt with the teacher's gender and ethnicity, whether they attended RHS (noted as local or nonlocal), and how long they have been at RHS (noted as newcomer—under five years; or veteran—over five years).

Male, Non-Sicilian White, Nonlocal, Veteran:
Some of the lower [achieving] kids, they bug me, but I love their being very human. You can really relate to some of them. They're just so natu-

ral and unpretentious that you catch yourself even liking the jerks, you know.

Male, Black, Local, Veteran:
These are probably the nicest kids you'll ever run into. We get resistance, hardening, but all you have to do is massage that heart. You got to get in there and work on it. When you do, you'll find that most of these kids, they'll protect you to the very end. They'll do your work, they'll argue for you, they'll do the whole thing. They'll nurture you while you're nurturing them.

Female, Sicilian, Local, Veteran:
I want students to know that I love them and I want them also to be independent and free of anything that I've taught them in terms of attitudes. After they graduate, I love to see them, but only if they have a job or are going to college or have some, you know, goal in mind. I don't want to hear about all the hard times they've been running into. I don't want to hear that they quit their job because it's boring. Life is as boring as you choose to make it. I don't want to have to put up with their stories, showing up at my house at two in the morning—I've had it happen—to tell me horrible things.

Female, Non-Sicilian White, Nonlocal, Veteran:
The students become very close to you if you are close to them. You have to show them that you are interested in them. Like I have kids that will call me Mother. They don't mean that in a derogatory sense because they know me, their parents know me, and they do get close to you.

Four teachers, four ways of relating to students, four choices in the faculty grab bag for students to select from for those non-academic, nonclassroom needs they have learned will elicit a response at school. The first teacher identifies his preferred students by their natural, unpretentious qualities, as he judges these qualities, the second by their willingness to engage in mutual nurturance, the third by the rationality of their lives, and the fourth by their feeling of closeness to the extent that they call her Mother. All four may or may not teach effectively; the point is that each may be selecting with whom they will invest their effort and concern in terms they may not be cognizant of. Moreover, each of them focuses on self, so that when I ask them to talk about students, they begin with an "I" statement, though this is only by implication in the words of the black male and the white female. In contrast, while the next two teachers do not say less about themselves in their statements, they do focus more directly on the students.

Male, Non-Sicilian White, Nonlocal, Veteran:
Most of the kids are conniving schemers who will use anybody they can to get what they want. A lot of them are liars, cheaters, thieves; they can justify it in their minds. Outside here this used to be a good-looking garden—until the riots. Then everything kind of went to hell.

They feel that they don't really have to work to obtain a grade. I don't know what it is; I can't put my finger on it. I don't think you can say that all blacks or all Mexicans are that way. Just, maybe, it's the lower . . . I do know that when a kid goes to kindergarten, he is spoon-fed and they pass him along. I found most kids in Riverview are babies.

Female, Black, Nonlocal, Veteran:
I find that the kids are very mature. As far as relating to students of all colors and walks of life, they do this very well. They have learned how to cope with life in a very mature way.

A lot of them have jobs. A lot come from homes where there's only one parent. They've learned to come out of this environment. Some of the environments are turbulent.

When it comes to the ways of the world and life, they are sophisticated. Now, in taking care of homework, that might be another thing. They have a lot of outside things calling them—jobs, home problems, and everything, so it may be difficult to get them to do homework on a continual basis.

Two more teachers, two more ways, one particularly negative, the other not so much positive as understanding. Each looks at the same youngsters and sees distinctly different personal qualities in them, wicked babies, on the one hand, and differentially competent persons, on the other. Clearly their perspectives color their interactions with students; equally clearly, students learn different things about themselves from each teacher.

Soon after novice teachers get the first chalk smudge on their clothing and administer their first test, they begin to acquire lore about what students are like and how to manage them. The lore accumulates as they leave their novice status and become veterans. Here are several illustrations of such lore.

Male, Non-Sicilian White, Nonlocal, Veteran:
Kids here, more than anywhere else I've been, like consistency. So, whatever you choose, stick to it, unless you see a certain reason you must change a rule. Explain to the kids why you're changing, but get a set of rules down and stick to it. The black and the white and the Hispanic—you teach them all the same. You treat them all the same as far as tardies and all that. They will respect

that. When you try to pretend that they're not black or Hispanic, you're got a problem on your hands.

Female, Black, Local, Veteran:
A lot of students here, they get their outside forces working on them. When they get here, sometimes they lash out at the teachers. I find that this occurs quite a bit. I try to back off from it; I don't try to put them in a corner. If the student is going to get to the point where they are going to put me all down in the ground, I mean just totally disrespectful, then I have to do something because of the other students.

Female, Non-Sicilian White, Nonlocal, Veteran:
What I hear over and over from other teachers, and from people in general, is that our students experience a lot of yelling at home. They hardly ever hear any yelling in my classroom. They experience a lot of irrational behavior at home, I hear. I don't think they experience it in my classroom. So, it must really be kind of like night and day for them. I'm creating an atmosphere that I hope is calming for them.

Male, Non-Sicilian White, Nonlocal, Veteran:
At RHS, you have to be relaxed with the fact that there are differences in values, differences in style, you know. For example, laughter. Sometimes, it's very loud. You have to understand that you can't put a person down for that. The whole school is not going to be a regimented, quiet school. It is absolutely not even appropriate here because a lot of the students have not learned . . . Students say something before they think. I think there has to be tolerance. Such behavior is not necessarily disruptive; that's something you have to understand.

Be consistent, don't back students into a corner, be gentle and understanding—is this not good sense that extends beyond RHS? The consistency advocate closes his observations with a point that I will explore later: teach and treat all ethnic groups the same—this is how he speaks of consistency—but don't forget that a black is black or a Mexican is a Mexican. He does not say how he manages this distinction. The other three teachers identify the impact of out-of-school factors on in-school behavior. For these three, such factors constitute data of consequence, though they, and their many other colleagues, may not see the same implications for their personal responses to these factors. Out-of-school factors are material everywhere, though RHS teachers see their influence as generally negative, and, in light of this, urge varying degrees of forbearance and understanding.

The next set of teachers comments on what is undoubtedly a fact about RHS students: many do not come to class with the materials—

pen, pencil, notebook, textbook—their teachers expect them to have. So I am not surprised that when I ask teachers what students are like, this is something they nearly always tell me about. Also, unsurprisingly, teachers do not sound alike when they comment on this fact.

Male, Non-Sicilian White, Nonlocal, Veteran:
I see an awful lot of sit-on-their-assism. It's black and it's brown and it's white. When I see a kid come in here with books in his hand, I'm not going to have much problem. I know that already. The chances of his being a discipline problem or unwilling to work, it all but disappears. It's the ones that come in without the textbook . . . I bet you in my classes there's not five of them that carry notebooks out of twenty or twenty-five.

Female, Black, Local, Veteran:
A lot of the kids say, "Are you gonna give us a lecture today?" I do a lot of that; it's never planned. A recent one was on the issue of not bringing materials. I just can't see a child coming to class on a regular basis without a book or anything to write about. So, I find myself getting on the phone. I really need to cut it [lecturing] out because I'm getting tired of listening to myself.

Male, Non-Sicilian White, Local, Veteran:
How many of the kids walk around with books in their hands? They don't. They don't come to class with pencils and paper either. They just kinda show up. That's it. That's the only kind of responsibility I think they have. Somebody said I had to go to school and here I am. How much education do you need to stand in a welfare line? How much education do you need twice a month to get your welfare check? It's automatic. You have welfare workers take care of you. If you miss a day in line, they come to your house.

The first of these teachers expects good behavior of students who come prepared to class. Well and good, but those who do not come prepared he expects to misbehave and do poorly. His expectations understandably shape student behavior already oriented toward indifference to classroom success; moreover, unlike the second teacher who lectures students and calls their parents, he does not seem to take concerted measures to redress the student behavior that he dislikes. The tradition of teacher autonomy, in the absence of a sense of school mission or of established means of bringing vexing problems to a responsive forum, leaves teachers to stew in the juices of their not-so-splendid classroom isolation.

The third teacher makes a too-easy association between the appearance of student indifference at school and the behavior students learn at home. By so doing, he can excuse himself from finding other explanations and, possibly, from accepting any responsibility for what, admittedly, is a disturbing problem.

The next and final set of teacher views about RHS students contains a causal connection, as teachers see things, between the home conditions of students and their classroom conduct. The first excerpt sets the case for deficiencies in the students' home; the next three express the consequences.

Male, Non-Sicilian White, Nonlocal, Veteran:
We have in our district a lot of youngsters from minority areas and from low-income areas. Many of them do not understand, nor do their parents understand, the value of an education. The majority do not come from homes where there are books, magazines, encyclopedias, or even a newspaper. Therefore, you have to take that into consideration.

Your job is to present an education to the group and not allow any individual to interrupt that education process for the rest of the group. If they're interrupting that process, talk it over with them. If that doesn't work, you send them out of the classroom. If that doesn't work, you send them to the office till somebody recognizes that there's a problem and will take further steps.

Female, Non-Sicilian White, Nonlocal, Newcomer:
There's a lot less pressure teaching here because the kids aren't out to kill for their grades. "Oh, I got a C. That's good enough." The teachers I see are cycling down to the kids, and that really distresses me.

I like the kids; I love the kids. I think they're wonderful. They're not real motivated, but they're real nice kids. When I first came here, I lowered my standards because I thought, "Oh God, I'm not going to pass anybody." Then, after being here a year, I said I'm not going to lower my standards. They're not stupid. They're not trained, but they're not stupid. So I raised my standards for what is a passing grade. You know what? I didn't have any worse a failure rate with higher expectations than I did with lower expectations.

Male, Non-Sicilian White, Nonlocal, Newcomer:
Kids here, compared to other schools, are not as hungry, not as keen. The only ones that are, I'd say, are the Vietnamese or Asian students. Other schools, kids won't show each other their homework. I try to keep my standard. The only thing I hold back on is extracurricular projects. I don't see that little extra drive for me to put out the effort to say, "Ok, if anyone wants to do a project, I'll be here. I'll help you design something." There are times I really feel bad about it, too, that I don't put my little extra to encourage that. But I don't see that sparkle and depth in the kids' eyes to warrant it.

Male, Non-Sicilian White, Nonlocal, Newcomer:
Let's say that if I want to teach a topic, I have to do it logically and give the whole picture. It doesn't work with these kids. Most of the kids I get are not college-oriented, so they are satisfied just with knowing how to do things, not why.

The proposition is that if students come from a certain type of home (i.e., one that lacks the products of the written word and a high regard for schooling), then they will be unmotivated, lazy, and unable to handle logical characterizations of problems. (The list of disabilities could be expanded.) In the face of this proposition, one teacher, after a year's lapse, keeps her standards high and feels rewarded for doing so. Other teachers adjust their style of teaching and retreat from the fullest offering of instructional opportunity (albeit feeling some guilt in the process). The consensus among teachers is that they respond to students more often with scaled-down standards than with instructional adjustments that reflect a wish to find alternative routes to unscaled down academic success. Students confirm that this is true, saying: classes should be harder, the homework is too easy, the school should be more academic, teachers should stress the importance of getting an education. Their point, however, is the same, and it is made both by college-prep and by general students. That they make it does not mean that they would eagerly welcome tougher classes. It does mean that they realize that it is easier to get by at RHS than it should be, and that it would be to their benefit if it were not so easy.

Teachers everywhere know that students work best when their self-esteem is high. Some teachers are more attuned to this aspect of student behavior than others. Mrs. Messina is one of them, though it is obvious that she also has other attributes that distinguish her teaching, admirable ones that lead her, for example, to respect a student's nonstandard English even as she insists they master standard English. Her reasoning is that knowing only nonstandard English severely limits a student's life choices. So does an absence of self-esteem, she strongly believes, and that is why she has made fostering it one of her trademarks.

I want students to feel they can do. Sometimes, I think that is what I teach best of all. I sound like a football coach, I know. I teach them they can do and sometimes they come back to me the next year in tears. Other teachers don't do what I do. I don't care if it's in grammar or literature or poetry — my job is to teach them that learning is possible and they're not stupid.

Mrs. Messina teaches with considerable energy and drive. Her teaching lasts until the end of each period; she is not one of those who routinely assigns workbook-seatwork "activity." Activity is a misnomer for these too-frequent classroom events, which, at their best, keep students occupied and free teachers from teaching. Riverview taxpayers get their money's worth from Mrs. Messina.

I emphasize what I see as her commitment to teaching to preface what she replied in answer to my question about what she thought was the outcome of schooling at RHS. As did many parents, students, and other teachers, Mrs. Messina mentioned the special opportunity a multiethnic setting provides to learn how to "interact with everybody," as she put it. "For some," she added, "it's the only place they have to go. For others, it'll be the only moment they ever starred in something." In social terms, she felt reasonably certain of what the school contributed. In educational terms, by which she meant the cognitive consequences of instruction, she would not even speculate.

I'm not going to think about it; I don't know. You know, I never have students from ten or fifteen years ago come back and tell me they remembered learning helping verbs. They'll always say, "I'll never forget the time . . ." and the time is never really related to learning.

Yet RHS and its sister schools throughout California fairly abound with tests. Like a battleship bristling with guns that jut strategically in all directions, tests thrust into the lives of students and teachers. They, too, can shoot down and destroy: sometimes a teacher at whose doorstep poor examination results are laid; sometimes an individual or group of students whose scores earn them the label of "substandard" or "deficient"; and sometimes a school whose comparative test numbers reveal it to be less "successful" than its neighbors. This judgment turns away prospective homebuyers who, sensitive to their children's future, measure goodness by a school's standing in the annual examination marathons the state conducts. Since the test results for all schools are public and, as in Riverview, a matter of front-page if not banner-headline news, it is easy to know and compare a school's ranking.

For Mrs. Messina, tests do not reveal what education her students have received. They do establish a "report card" of sorts, which some educators construe as one element in the picture of accountability that current notions of responsibility require be painted for all schools. They do encumber teachers with demands on their time and with instructional chores that remove them from classroom activities they value. And they do put administrators on the defensive to explain to their school boards why the results are the way they are when they are disappointing.

A 1980 study, summarized in an *Education Week* column (1988b), revealed the expanding scale of standardized-test use by public schools. It concluded that the "trends pose a danger . . . since such tests may be inaccurate and biased against women and minorities"; in addition, they "may narrow the curriculum and loosen local control over education." Most predictably, RHS's test results remind anyone who pays attention to them of the stigma that overshadows Riverview school and community because the results, when they are good, are only good when considered within Riverview's "socioeconomic comparison group." The comparison group concept also communicates to Riverview that if it does very well, it has the dubious distinction, one I remember from elementary school seating arrangements, of being one of the smartest kids in the dummy row.

In recent years, RHS has scored in the top 25 percent of its socioeconomic comparison group; among all schools statewide, however, it has scored in the bottom 25 percent. It has received such scores for decades. A 1947 survey of RHS observed that twelfth-grade achievement levels were below state norms in all tested areas and concluded that "There appear to be many pupils in Riverview who are not stimulated toward school achievement by strong scholastic motives and educational traditions." A current mathematics teacher reported:

Students say to me, "You aren't going to fail me because I don't do well on that [standardized] test." They don't even try. They don't care about what it does to the image of the whole school district. Now, if they're out on the football field, everyone of them will try hard because they want Riverview to win.

A couple of years ago, a student had just got through studying fractions, common denominators, and numerators. Then she took one of the standardized tests that had this same stuff on it. She added all the denominators and all the numerators. I said, "Why did you do that?" She said, "You showed me how [to do it right], but this was easier to do." She couldn't have cared . . . just to get through.

When the state arranged a monetary incentive for schools whose test scores improved from one year to the next, RHS mobilized its seniors to teach them how to take the test and to take it seriously. Now, money was at stake; it could be spent for any legitimate school purpose, including student wants and in keeping with their priorities. Teachers rallied to the cause of upping California Assessment Program (CAP) scores. All parents of seniors received letters that stressed the test's importance. All seniors went to a full-period meeting to hear a special CAP-test cheer led by the cheerleaders, and speeches by, among others, the principal, superintendent, and school board president. These collective efforts earned RHS $74,480.

Similarly, teachers increasingly rally to the cause of improving SAT scores. They teach test-taking techniques. They adjust their personal teaching plans to respond to the reality that tests are not merely important, they are crucial to the educational futures of the small group who plan to attend college. RHS teachers are getting accustomed to making such adjustments, as they are subjected to the continuous process of gradually eroding local control. But they are not yet accustomed to routine, systematic, concerted effort to redress a tradition of academic underachievement. The school's nagging failure is like a fishbone caught in one's throat, only the bone has been there so long that the pain is acceptable and almost everyone takes its presence for granted.

5

Teachers and Ethnicity: Respect, Universalism, and Avoidance

The Impact of Student Ethnicity

Ethnicity appears in different guises for different people in the world of RHS. The words of one outsider and two insiders suggest something about the differences. Selakovich, a writer on American education, concluded that since there was too much to know about minority cultures, teachers could not be expected to work "such understanding into their teaching." It was more than enough, he said, that they assist a student "to ultimately become a self-supporting adult." Still, he thought, "Anybody with any sense who has to work with large groups of minority children soon discovers what pleases and what insults them" (1978:141). This view is one part of RHS's landscape. Another is expressed by a veteran RHS teacher: "You know, I just work here and never really think about some of this stuff [my questions about ethnicity]. And I assume that the other people don't either." And a third is from a student who was answering my question about whether, if I were a new student, I should expect RHS to be different from my previous high school. "Gosh, yeah, we're different. Not only because of the races involved. . . ."

All three perspectives operate simultaneously. Teachers, parents, and students do give preeminence to becoming "a self-supporting adult"; the ramifications of ethnicity fail to occupy even a distant second place. Most everyone does learn "what pleases and what insults," which is another way of expressing the fact that acquiring knowledge to conduct effective, appropriate social interaction comes with the territory in Riverview. Moreover, in ways that I don't think I fully grasp, most everyone appears both to disregard ethnicity at the very moment that they clearly have it in mind—"Gosh, yeah . . . races . . ."—when I ask a

129

question. In some sense, it is simultaneously taken for granted and not taken for granted.

One counselor remembers the pressure to abandon the three-tier tracking system as "the only time I was aware of demands put upon the school. It was right after the riots. Parents thought there were more black kids in the C track," as, indeed, there were. What this counselor commits to history—"demands put upon the school"—is contemporary and persistent for many who work with the Riverview Unified School District. Although minority electorates do not exact promises from school board members who seek their support at election time, board members who hope to be reelected do not forget their electorates.

You have to be cognizant in a way of who the hell you are dealing with at all times. It's just that when we make a decision, or when I see a group or talk to a group, it might have effects on these other groups, too. I think all board members are aware of the feelings of the different [ethnic] organizations.

What this board member identifies as a general awareness is particularized by central administration personnel who daily relate to their public through phone calls, personal visits, and letters. According to district administrators, a high proportion of the issues they deal with relate to minority parents and children, and most often with black parents and children: "usually in confrontations between students it's everybody against the black child or the black child against everybody." Black students more than any other group run afoul of school regulations; they dominate disciplinary referrals. Black parents, more than others, believe their children "aren't given a fair shake," and white parents refer to problems with black children as the most common explanation for requesting that their child be transferred out of the school district (while they still are living in it). One parent seeking a transfer explained that she tried hard to make things work out: "I wanted my child to grow up in this kind of community," she said. "I wanted her to get the exposure to all kinds of kids, but I can't let this go on [her daughter's fear of a group of black girls who beat her up]." She got the transfer.

A Riverview administrator speaks of the special challenge of his job:

In another community you may be accused of being unfair, or of being an incompetent administrator, but you're not going to be accused of being a racist. You're not going to fear one of the public agencies coming in to conduct an investigation because you're receiving federal funds and someone has accused you of violating federal regulations. I take all calls and see all people just for that reason that I don't want anything to escalate. People don't understand, and it's not limited to this office. The principal [at RHS] has to deal with it every day.

And so he does, as I learn when I ask him about ethnicity as a factor in his work. In response, he begins with a recounting of the previous three days. On Monday, he met with the NAACP, which a parent had called to look into the charge of a teacher kicking her child. (The principal explained, however, that parental use of the NAACP in this way has been uncommon since the 1970s.) On Tuesday, he attended a meeting of the parents' advisory board for bilingual education. He also received a call from Mexican parents whose son had been stopped by the police and questioned about his green card (which verifies that one is a legal immigrant). The family was upset because the principal hadn't heard about the incident. Parents believe he should know everything. On Wednesday, white parents called to criticize his rigidity in accepting medical excuses. They felt that he would not have been so strict if their daughter was black or Hispanic.

RHS principal Fred Borcher also is alert to prevent the escalation of problems with an ethnic basis, recalling too well the 1970s, when escalation seemed to be routine. Borcher makes clear to his faculty where his sensitivities are, as one of his teachers vividly recalls. The teacher was at a meeting with the principal and other members of his department to discuss a problem.

I made an observation. All I did was say, "Well, it's interesting to me that the student and counselor involved are black and the teacher is white." Man, the boss, when I say yelling, he was yelling, "I don't want to hear another remark like that." He thought I was being, you know, smart ass and blatantly prejudiced against blacks. I wasn't. I was just asking was that part of the problem.

As times change, so do sensitivities. For the decade following 1968, administrators kept alert to the ethnic composition of appointive school-based groups, intent on avoiding charges of racism of the type they had received earlier about pompon girls. In general, their concern was neither to be nor appear to be racist regarding the distribution of students in both the rewarding and unrewarding aspects of the school. Administrator concern readily transferred to teachers who might oppose the concept of balanced representation of ethnic groups, while understanding the political necessity of balance. Educators prefer the universalist concept of merit or talent when required to make academic selections. Thus those involved in the CORE project that returned the school to a three-track academic system were pleased to see the successful operation of universalism, as the school defined it.

As it happened, the first CORE group of about thirty sophomores contained no blacks, at least as far as anyone knew. One of the CORE teachers spoke about this fact. While the selection process was underway, she recalled:

We came across some names and I said, "This sounds like a black name." The group [selection committee] said it doesn't matter. They have to meet the criteria. I guess some black people, when the letters were sent out about who was accepted into CORE and there were no blacks, they went to the district office. But things are beginning to change: they [administrators] did not capitulate. Ten years ago they would have said, "Oh my God, you'd better get some in there." I think we would've all quit if they'd said that. I mean, we're not in here for a race thing. On the first day of school, though, one of the girls in the CORE class said there are no blacks in here. That's when Scott said, "I'm the token nigger." He's only half black. If he didn't tell you that, you would never know.

Administrators make judgments all the time, more often, surely, than they make policy. Clearly, at the time of CORE's inception, they felt that as things stood in Riverview, they could sanction a special new program that seemed to contain no black students. If the program never admitted any black students, that, of course, would be an entirely different matter. What has changed in recent times is not whether it is good judgment to be mindful of ethnic composition—it definitely is—but when to apply the judgment.

Administrators and teachers are attuned to the fact of ethnicity at RHS at the very point of being hired. When administrator candidates seek a job in the Riverview school district, they first face a panel of interviewers and then write an essay. One of the two topics on which they can choose to write asks them to complete this statement: "The principal should be able to successfully communicate and coordinate educational programs to a racially and socially diverse population because . . ."

When teacher candidates are being interviewed, they are told about RHS's ethnic makeup, usually stated as 65 percent minority and 35 percent nonminority, and invited to react to this fact, which many of the candidates have not been aware of. Borcher carefully monitors their reactions to these percentages and to the prospect of teaching in a school that is probably unlike any they ever attended or worked at. Veteran RHS teachers reason that the shock value of the ethnic statistics helps prepare teacher candidates for the "reality" of RHS. It is by way of saying, "Do you know what you're getting into?" Once hired, new teachers are not allowed to forget about ethnic percentages. Both the school and the local newspaper deal in the figures of ethnicity. "Districts lagging in effort to hire minority teachers," read the heading of a long September 1987 account devoted to the percentage of minority teachers and students in the seven school districts in Riverview's part of the county. Not surprisingly, Riverview had more minority teachers (36 percent) and students (65 percent) than any other district, the next closest having 14 percent and 36 percent, respectively.

Riverview's school board and central office administrators are eager to employ minority teachers; they never find enough to satisfy their needs. Their interests extend beyond affirmative-action commitments to include the strong belief that minority children require minority role models. I inquired about the ethnicity of teachers, inviting them to reflect on their own ethnic identity as a factor of any type in their work. Of course, they did not all see this fact in the same way, any more than students and their parents see their own ethnicity in the same way.

Some took a "teachers are just teachers" position, as many do when they think about the ethnicity of students, saying "kids are just kids" and, therefore, they are color-blind. When they discount their own ethnicity as a personal attribute of consequence, they are giving centrality to their role as generic teacher, as when Joe Rich tells me:

If the kids are mad at you, I mean it doesn't matter whether you're black or white. I've heard them call me, "Oh, that bastard." And the same with Tommy Harris. I never heard students say, "Oh, that black bastard." If they're angry, I think they're angry at the teacher, not at our color, whatever.

Joe Rich speaks of what he thinks is generally true about teachers. Some of his colleagues make the same point, saying, in effect, that they see no difference in the way students from different ethnic groups relate to them. Such an acknowledgment may reflect their skill at being inviting and available to all children in the range of ways students call upon teachers. "What's important to kids is the person, not their ethnicity," they say, which may be taken to mean "I'm the type of person that all students can relate to."

Still, in different ways at different times, teachers feel themselves or their colleagues being addressed or perceived in terms of their ethnicity. White teachers felt that nonwhite students were disposed to seek out teachers from their own group. They never made this observation in strong or invariable language. It was more a case of some students trying to get into a particular teacher's class because of his reputation as being friendly with or understanding of his fellow ethnics, or some teachers attracting students who come by during free-time periods for informal talk, counseling, and the like. "Take, Roberts, for example. She is the black mother. So long as she doesn't try to be too strong, she's got it made with the black kids. Blacks tend to be very maternalistic."

Filipino and Mexican teachers thought that some students sought them out because of their shared ethnicity, feeling that they might get a more sympathetic hearing or be better understood (particularly when limited facility in English was a factor). Teachers also spoke of the sympathy they felt when they had grown up in circumstances similar to those of the students: "This kid's father sounded very much like my father: the military background, the thinking this is my house, this is the way things are."

Black teachers were most often singled out and most often singled themselves out as those for whom ethnicity might be the basis of a special relationship with students. They felt a particular need to look into matters in which black students might not be getting a fair deal (as in being admitted to CORE); they advised students who were taking the CORE admission tests not to write in "lingo" (black dialect), knowing they would be marked down for doing so. They took exception to the public behavior of black students that might reflect poorly on all black students (and on themselves):

Gereane called somebody a whore. I just, you know, looked at her and said, "Girl, I can't believe that is coming out of your mouth. What if your momma were here?" She said, "Well, my momma uses it, too." Well, I know her momma does not say that. I told her it is not cool to make your family sound like that. I had to point out to her that white kids look at you . . . If it had been a Filipino or white student, I guess I would have said the same thing, but I felt closer saying that to her because she was trying to put this over as a black thing. I resent that.

And they feel they successfully use their knowledge as black persons to manage potentially unpleasant incidents in class.

There's some black students in my third period, they'll start to say something. I look at them and they back down. They know that if they cross me, I'm liable to really cut up on them. They back off, I think, because I'm black: "You want to get smart with me? If you want to get down, I'll get down."

Moreover, they also use their role as black women:

I can get away with saying something, you know, that their mother would say to them. It's the way in which I say it, and maybe a slang word or a cut of the eye. In other words, "You'd better get in place or else you're going to hear from me."

Some white students charge some black teachers with being too black in their language and outlook, and favoring black students. Others comment on black teachers as being the only teachers "that treated everybody fair." Students may or may not agree with the perceptions of those black teachers who, like their white counterparts, see themselves just as person or as teacher, without an ethnic or gender qualification. (Only black female teachers ever mentioned their gender as a factor in relating to students, and the reference was not to students in general, but to black students.) "I never think of myself as a black teacher," I was told; "I think of myself as an educator. I try to relate to all of my students as people. In fact," she added, "I get less visits from my own people than I do the other races."

Doris Washington provided the most elaborate response to my question about the identity of teachers. (Indeed, black teachers generally offered the longest answers to this and all questions relating to ethnicity.) I asked her who she was at school: teacher, female teacher, or black female teacher?

I think it depends on who's looking. If you're talking about the students, some of them I can tell are pleased when they see me because I am black. I've noticed the same thing with parents. There's a commonality, you know. Sometimes, when I make these little phrases, it's something they hear at home. I hear them say, "Well, that's what my mother says." Now, I don't know [she says, having second thoughts about this point]. The white kids say that, too. I don't think it's so much that it's black as it's a mother.

When I go to faculty meetings, I think of myself as teacher. I don't think of necessarily being a black teacher because we all get the same rules. We all look at the same things. There are always color lines. There are some things I would tell a black teacher that I wouldn't tell a white teacher. There are some things I have seen around here with students that I wonder if color has anything to do with it. Maybe it wasn't the color thing; maybe it was the sex thing, or the attitude or the socioeconomics thing.

With parents, I'm Doris Washington, teacher. Sometimes, the race thing comes in, especially if it's a parent I know. Well, I don't know, maybe it's more the personal connection. It's like, "Watch my kid. If he gets out of line, don't tolerate it." I don't know if they would tell a white teacher that. You know, it's always good to see people of color, especially when you're one. Generally, I'm the teacher. When we have our little meetings, I tell everybody the same thing.

I think I'm probably more black outside of school. My social activities are mostly with black people. When I read things, when I see things, I'm relating to them as a black person.

The ethnicity of teachers could conceivably have an impact on their teaching assignments, their relations with others within their teaching departments, and their informal associations during those times within a school day and year when teachers assemble. Aside from the usual animosity that exists between some teachers and their department heads and principals, and between pairs of teachers in any school, RHS teachers did not identify ethnicity as a point of any consequence in the professional side of their work. Teaching and other assignments are made on the basis of credentials and equity. Teachers do not generally form ethnic groupings; it is as ordinary and easy for them to conduct their daily activities in the midst of ethnic diversity as it is for students, notwithstanding that most spent their pre-RHS lives in places that basically were ethnically homogeneous. Black teachers confirm the observation of their nonblack colleagues that ethnic amity prevails: "For all practical purposes, we could all be mainstream Anglo. I have not found any singling out, you know, 'Well, you're black, so you're not going to be able to do that.'"

Beneath this ethnic amity lie ogres of uncertainty, reservation, and bias that may never surface at school. Unlike so many RHS students who have never experienced anything but the normalcy of cross-ethnic interaction, most teachers have both learned and experienced the elements of racism and its concomitant results. Veteran nonblack teachers have faced the charge of racism from black teachers; they also experience classroom disruptions that more often than not implicate black students. Thus, the reactions of nonblack teachers to black students and teachers is complex. We can get a sense of this complexity when teachers move beyond polite responses and speak frankly, as did Burt Borman. He has taught at RHS for more than fifteen years, coming here from a small midwestern town where he was raised and later taught. He explains that "it doesn't put any pressure on me if a teacher is Jewish or Mexican or Filipino," but it does if the teacher is black. He runs through the school's black faculty, thinking out loud about the pressure he has just mentioned, and realizes his reactions depend upon the "blackness" of a particular teacher. Mr. A. he doesn't "think of as being black"; Ms. B. makes him feel "edgy" because she has a "chip on her shoulder about being black, so around her you feel superconscious of just being a nice guy. Let me be very up front," he says after going over his reactions to his black colleagues. "Sure, I'm prejudiced against blacks, but it's something we work out together." I do not believe that the working-out process he refers to here involves a "we" in a literal sense. It is, rather, that he has learned to make accommodations that are suitable for a multiethnic environment containing almost one-third black students and many black co-workers. He and other nonblack teachers have mastered the essentials of accommodation that permit a school to function not only without tension, but peacefully in all respects. Borman had "never met a black in my life, really," before coming to Riverview, a handicap that constrains him from having blacks move readily from the category of stranger to friend. Still, from what he sees every day at RHS, and what he learned from his own children who had been students at RHS, he knows that blacks clearly do occupy the category of friend, even if only thinly in his own life both in and out of school. He describes Doris Washington as "the only black teacher that I really, truly care for. I just wouldn't do anything to hurt our relationship and I don't know that I could." Burt Borman is unusual not in the sentiments that he expresses, but in his ability to disclose them to others and to admit them to himself.

Universalism

RHS principal Fred Borcher knows from long experience that not all teachers, otherwise qualified, fit in a multiethnic school. But what it takes to be effective, let alone just get by, in such a school, are not issues that he systematically brings before his faculty. Teachers say that neither schoolwide nor department faculty meetings have examined the implications of RHS being primarily a school of nonwhite students. "There is no discussion as far as ethnic groups and all that. Our department tends to be more into the academic thing." This is Doris Washington again. She refers to a recent meeting where "I think if the teachers had started talking about color, I think they would have got down to what they really wanted to say." Informally, teachers also claim not to discuss ethnicity.

You know, I can have lunch with a lot of the black teachers and they talk about the same stuff that I talk about—rotten classes, terrible kids, de dah, de dah. The exact same thing. It doesn't matter if they're black or whatever.

Over the years, Borcher actually did arrange workshops that addressed issues of teaching ethnic students. Interestingly enough, very few teachers recall participating in them. They remember learning about interpersonal relations early in the troubled post-1968 period and later about assertive discipline and classroom management. They do not remember the workshop of perhaps no more than two years before at which "a black woman came and talked specifically about black children." "I'd forgotten about it, you know what I'm saying," said one black teacher, and others, also present, had no recollection of it at all. Yet once

I got them thinking about such workshops, teachers would say that discussions of strategies for effective teaching and counseling minority
students would be useful and welcome:

I think we have to be concerned about such matters. You have to look at your
personnel [RHS students] and react somewhat to it. Yet, at the same time,
you want to guide that personnel to be able to fit into the large world they're
going into, which is primarily English-speaking and middle-class ethics.

To the extent that teachers were willing to hazard a guess as to
whether the different ethnic groups held variant views about the mission of the high school, or what it should do for their children, their
guesses lacked an ethnic focus. None claimed to know with any certainty
what parents saw as the functions of schooling. Black and nonblack
teachers and school board members saw a common ground: parents
want their children to be able to read and write; "to be better than I am";
"to be able to cope once out of school, whether they're going to college
or to work"; and to graduate. "I would hope not," responded one teacher
to my question about whether the ethnic groups had different expectations. She alone had seen the implication of a yes answer. She realized
what a problem teachers would face if they had to deal with different
parental aspirations. I think she also resisted the implication of the question that ethnic groups might harbor idiosyncratic aspirations.

When teachers saw variations among ethnic groups, they related
them to the level of academic expectation parents had for their children,
and ultimately to the socioeconomic status of the family. They couched
these variations in comparative rather than ethnic terms, observing that
some groups seemed to want more from school than others. Not surprisingly, they felt that blacks and Mexicans wanted less from the school
relative to whites, Filipinos, and other Asians; wanting less meant they
did not connect schooling to attending colleges or universities. All parents were thought to want their children to live better than they did.

Seeing a bright side, one administrator thought that ethnic groups
were less concerned than they used to be about the fair "treatment of my
kid" and more concerned about what the school can do to raise their kid's
test scores. Local-born teachers made a distinction they thought necessary for understanding the expectations of black parents: blacks from the
South were "a lot different" from those who had lived in Riverview for a
generation or two, the latter being far closer to nonblacks in their views
of schooling. The former are possibly those a special-education teacher
was referring to in her discouraging observations:

The black students—for a lot of them it's real hard to understand that they
could better themselves. I talked to a couple of girls. These were the ones

that had problems with pregnancy. I would tell them, "You've got a lot going. You've got a mind that if you can get inspired, there's a whole world out there for you to try anything you want." They don't understand. It's like I'm talking to them in a foreign language. It stems from, I guess, just the kind of people who have been around you.

Finally, teachers further parted company in their reported awareness of differences among ethnic groups, some saying there were differences, but they did not know what they were, and others saying they just did not know of any: they saw none, they had not thought about the matter, or it was too complicated to make generalizations.

Consistent with their limited consciousness of what parents want them to emphasize, teachers readily see a fit between parental views and their own views that reflect academic but not ethnic considerations. Such an outlook supports a school structure, common throughout the country, with markedly varied curricular alternatives (recall the continuation school and special-education classes, as well as the track system, all mentioned earlier). The alternatives chosen usually derive from a judgment of how well a student can do in academic terms, and sometimes in emotional or physical terms. It is a judgment based primarily, though not exclusively, on the standard yardstick of grades and test scores, and on the pervasive perspective of one-country-therefore-one-school. Teachers and parents seem comfortable with this arrangement, although teachers can, when pressed, identify numerous ways that students differ because of ethnicity. Before discussing the latter point, I want to present the standard yardstick in the words of Reva Gerald, a highly articulate white teacher.

There are no sorts of stylistic differences or fine tuning in my teaching because Mexican kids are different from Filipino kids. I would hate to get into that with the kids. Just like I would hate to say, "Well, because he's Mexican, I have to make allowances for his academic achievement."

My values are my values. Kids have to accept that and it doesn't matter what their values are. I don't perceive things, or allow myself to perceive things, as racial. I just don't think that that's what we can afford to let ourselves do. I mean, they have to learn to adjust to whatever you tell them.

I had a class, maybe 20 or 25 percent black, and they almost all failed. Was it because they're black? No, because they didn't study, didn't do homework, because, because. Why can't—why don't those kids do better? I was upset about it. I wasn't going to pass them because they were black. They still have to perform. If they were white kids, I probably wouldn't have paid attention. When they're black, I think you're aware, but I'm not going to do anything different.

No, I wouldn't change my behavior. I would try to change their behavior. If you would do your homework, if you would come to class, if you would not be late, if you wouldn't sleep in class—do all these things and you'd help yourself. It's really hard for me to say it's a racial thing. I think you go back to economics. But you can't solve the problem by treating the kids differently.

Reva Gerald did not formulate her views about how best to respond to RHS's ethnic diversity by virtue of her pre-service teacher training, her in-service instruction since coming to RHS, or her knowledge of the preferences of Riverview parents. She and her colleagues have mostly been left on their own to devise a point of view that fits their sense of how teachers and schools should function. She would have been much less on her own in the 1960s and 1970s, when vocal, visible advocates of ethnic consciousness in Riverview and beyond brought home to legislators and educators an awareness of ethnicity and its implications that at present exists in the general sensitivities of educators but not specifically in their classrooms.

Today, teachers are free to create a school in generic terms that provides one basic type of ladder for all students. Elsewhere in the country, the ladder differs in terms of its components (displaying regional or subcultural variations), but most tellingly in terms of its height. Continuing with this imagery, though the ladder always is an American ladder, leading to American places, it does not lead all those who climb it to the same heights of power, wealth, and opportunity. That RHS teachers safely provide their version of the American educational ladder rests on the contentment of ethnic parents with their children's school as a minimally ethnic place. Riverview parents, characterized by both strong and weak commitments to ethnic maintenance, seem almost of one mind on this point, when they think about it at all. Thus, RHS parents do not contest the education their children's schools offers; if they do, it is to have them do better what they usually do, not something different.

White parents from inside the American mainstream speak of the school's contribution to citizenship, orderliness, job skills, and to "just being American." Respect for other cultures—this is conventional wisdom in Riverview—does not translate into special instructional offerings. People should be allowed to be whoever they want to be in ethnic terms, says a white teacher: "He can be a black man and everything, but he's got to put the correct answers on the paper and he's got to learn to read the correct words and that's got nothing to do with if you're pink or green." Black men and women agree: "I think we should all be Americans. Give me the space, if you will, to be as black as I want to be. I don't think the school should force anybody away from their heritage."

The Curriculum and Assimilation

Black parents, far more than others, thought that RHS could have special, optional courses in history and literature, for example, and support cultural groups for students, such as the current Black Student Union. They want schools to be responsive to student needs and, above all, to avoid promoting a cultural homogeneity that would undermine a student's ethnic identity. "Carry students to the maximum of their potential" is how one black father put it. He acknowledged the impact of this intent as an endorsement of the white culture, saw special ethnic courses as the school's support for a don't-forget-who-you-are-if-you-want-to-remember ideal, but left the matter at that. The "at that" decision is neither impasse nor indecision, but, rather, parental recognition of the school's predominant orientation to serve the process of becoming American, both for the sake of students and that of the nation.

Sicilians, nowadays most like other Americans to whom once they were strangers, emphatically endorse this orientation and often vociferously oppose bilingual education. They think it endorses a foreign language and, accordingly, gives aid and comfort to persons residing in America whose avoidance of English-language learning and usage casts doubt on their loyalty; learning to speak English demonstrates loyalty. Such views are expressed by Sicilians who are red, white, and blue to a fault but speak Sicilian, go often to Sicily, have mostly Sicilian friends, regret it if their children do not marry Sicilians, belong to ethnic organizations, participate in ethnic activities, are active in the Catholic church, and anticipate with joy their annual nostalgic old-neighborhood reunion. On this occasion, they so reconstruct their ethnic microworld that it approximates going home again.

Although individual Mexican and Filipino parents differ widely in regard to the extent of their attachment to ethnic identity, they join black and white parents in believing that schools are not the place for promoting ethnic pride (nor, indeed, for undermining it). That obligation belongs to the home. Ethnic courses are acceptable as elective offerings, as is due recognition "of black heroes or Mexican heroes" in American-history and other courses. Students need to be made "aware of all the differences in every background." Do too much of this, however, and you detract from what schools were "originally set up to be." What seems to come through in parental statements about RHS is their endorsement of it as an assimilating institution that recognizes local and historical ethnic contributions, heroes, and festivals, and clearly does not belittle ethnicity.

What comes through the statements of RHS educators is that none of them doubts the necessity of acquiring the skills, knowledge, and norms that conduce to participating in the nation's economic, political, and social life. Nor does any RHS teacher doubt the necessity of Americanization. This means, as I perceive it, the development of such feelings of attachment to the nation, its symbols, history, and well-being, that one's pride, identification, and support are commensurate with the needs of citizenship. RHS has occasion to think of this possible outcome of schooling since it annually enrolls many newcomers to America.

Teachers and parents are not actively at odds over (nor in complete agreement about) assimilation, that is, the extent to which a person should lose all vestiges of and commitment to the ethnic component of their identity. To be fully assimilated is to give no place to meaning and behavior that derives from ethnicity; it is to be unhyphenated American. The lack of full accord in this matter seems to have no practical consequence at present, since teachers and parents have much the same outlook.

The issues of assimilation, Americanization, and ethnic maintenance are not elaborated in school documents or clarified in school meetings. Thus teachers are left free to follow their own leads. None say, "Thou shalt assimilate," even though some might wish to. Ethnicity is remembered as too potentially explosive to encourage even the most doltish to try that tack. More than the lessons learned from the recent past, most teachers on principle support the idea of ethnic maintenance, but not as a school task. Respecting ethnicity is a different issue. Such disputes as exist, and none are either at or close to the surface at present, relate to the robustness of the school's efforts in pursuing the ramifications of ethnicity for curricular and extracurricular activities. With the memory of the last decade's failed special courses in black or Hispanic history and literature still reasonably fresh, few teachers endorse this means of recognizing ethnicity. A better-supported view is that ethnic learnings are essential for all students in a multicultural community and society and, therefore, they should be duly reflected in existing social-studies and English courses. Just what "duly reflected" means is moot.

Given the nature of school life at RHS, students can find support for a variety of possibilities. Although RHS is an emphatically American place, it does not purposively engulf students in a tide of assimilation; still, students could get the idea that that was what was intended by daily classroom experiences that imply: "This is the way. Fit in. Join the crowd." Going all the way and becoming culturally indistinguishable carries the Americanization process along with it, of course. But it is no less viable for a newcomer student to acculturate and to develop those loyalties that Americanization entails, while maintaining elements of ethnic distinctiveness and attachment. It is also possible to acculturate and maintain one's ethnicity without ever developing those loyalties. But since the latter combination would be stigmatized, it is not one that students would be likely to make public.

If students fail to acquire the means, such as linguistic and social-interaction skills, for participating in the school's routine academic and social activities, teachers would no doubt advise remedial action. Otherwise, RHS teachers do not inquire, nor does the school formally urge them to learn, to what extent their students have assimilated, Americanized, or maintained their ethnic identity. The school and the teachers are not indifferent to these processes, but they have never developed the habit of actively tracking them. A prevailing laissez-faire outlook masks how strongly teachers feel:

To live effectively as Americans in an American society—that's *exactly* how I feel. That's what my job is. That's it exactly. If you're coming to this country, learn our language, learn our ways. Now, go ahead and have your annual or monthly or whatever get-togethers. Protect your culture. Do it outside of the school.

This teacher's sentiments seem directed primarily to immigrant newcomers, rather than to blacks and Mexicans, who are Americans in an American society but who may, by prevailing standards, place themselves outside the societal mainstream where several types of opportunity are found. Doris Washington, who never misses an occasion to bring ethnicity into her classroom, speaks to this point:

If you go in for a job, there are certain things you have to say and ways you have to act. When you have to answer the phone, you've got to sound a certain way. My husband does that; he purposely does that. We have to know that. Minorities have to know that. But at the same time, we can't forget the other part [being black], because it's still part of us. When we get to our own groups, we don't sound white. You get kind of two personalities going there. I think it can be balanced. I think it's hard for the kids to realize they have to have a good brand of standard English, and also know how to behave a certain way. It's the only way to be able to progress in this society.

Her white colleague Sarah Lindsey comments on the same point: "I think a happy medium is needed. I think we need to get students to appreciate other people's differences." This is her concern for all students, not just for newcomers or minorities, one that RHS teachers readily acquire from the exceptionally prominent fact of the school's ethnic diversity. "Learning to get along," as she puts it, may be at best an abstract principle at schools with a more homogeneous population in ethnic or class terms than RHS. It is hard to be opposed to getting along. At RHS, however, the principle is clothed with meaning; it is embedded in every day's walk down the corridors, lunchtime lounging on the quad, classroom encounters, and gym locker arrangements. Sarah Lindsey thinks that you don't teach students to get along; they learn it by absorption.

Lindsey's "happy medium" is what she calls "assimilation." Somewhere between appreciating ethnic differences, getting along with others, and retaining one's ethnic identity is the hard fact that Washington refers to when she speaks of sounding and acting a certain way. Lindsey specifies learning to follow directions and to take criticism "without becoming hostile. If they [an unspecified 'they'] don't know the rules of the Caucasian world, they're going to have problems." The unspecified "they," I surmise, refers to black and Mexican students since they are most likely to appear as if they have not learned those rules of the "Caucasian world" that facilitate getting a job. In the course of becoming and remaining a college-prep student, minority students learn to look, dress, and talk in ways that reassure their mentors that they are on the road to success in the Caucasian world. Teachers are less sanguine about the much larger group of minority students in the non–college-prep track.

Black Doris Washington and white Sarah Lindsey (with no particular ethnic affiliation) are two of the many models that RHS educators present to students for how to "wear" their ethnic garb. Overall, teachers present a bewildering array of models. Washington, as she says, "has kind of two personalities" and Lindsey has only one. Their fellow teacher, Sicilian Rick Norino, represents one more variation of having two:

That's fine to be proud. I am to some extent proud of my Sicilian heritage, but I don't let it come out where I let it affect the way that I teach or the person that I am. I'm not going to be bogged down in that. When I was younger, there weren't the divisions. Somewhere along the line we polarized kids to think of themselves as ethnic groups.

Being black, Sicilian, or plain white offers different possibilities for thinking about the ethnicity of one's self and others. For different reasons, Washington and Lindsey would not speak of being "bogged down." Norino's ideal, one that many teachers share, is for "kids to be proud of their ethnicity, like I am. Put it in place, not only in school, but out of school." Norino's closest friends are all Sicilian.

Teacher Lil Donaldson's close friends are black. She has still another view of ethnicity and of holding "two personalities":

Your roots, where you come from, it'd be wrong for me to deny those cultural things that carry with us through history. But I think we are arriving at a new generation of Americans. Younger blacks, I think they are more just melting in. This is a national thing. Our distinctiveness is just slowly crumbling. We're blending in more. It's a good thing. Of course, I'm an old culturalist and I want my children to know their culture.

I did not hear teachers discuss cultural crumbling. I did not expect to at this time in our history when there has been a muting of the topic, on the one hand, and priorities given to noncultural issues, on the other.

English teacher Sam Thierry observes that perhaps there was a need to emphasize ethnic pride during the 1970s, but his belief is that now "we need more assimilation. Therefore, I would rather teach a course called American literature and make clear to the students just what American means. It means black, Chicano, native American—all this kind of stuff." Thierry's view of assimilation departs from traditional Anglo models and resembles more the effect of a melting-pot blend. He and many teachers and students like the image of RHS as a melting pot, though they do not believe that melting has occurred to the point of obliterating differences among groups. Assimilation, not taken kindly by advocates of ethnic maintenance, assumes a broader, nontechnical form in Thierry's more incorporative version.

Thierry teaches a subject (English) that over the years has been touted as a place for integrating the literature of non-Anglo Americans; Ted Bishop (in vocational education) does not. Thus, they have been socialized to think differently about the nature of their subject matter. I see Bishop expressing the teacher's hard view of schooling, one that has a "let's just get on with educating kids to be Americans" focus. His "hard" view should be seen against two personal facts: he fully accepts the intermarriages and progeny of members of his own family, and he has a warm, easygoing relationship with students from all ethnic groups. Interestingly, RHS teachers may be wrong-headed, by some lights; very few were wrong-hearted. Their professional side often reflected fairly traditional views of the function of schooling; their personal side more often reflected the impact of being daily immersed in a multiethnic environment. In Bishop's words, RHS should be a school like any other school in America, notwithstanding its ethnic diversity. "Nationality and heritage, all that kind of stuff, I don't think schools should have to be bothered with it. Leave it at home. You don't mess with that stuff at school."

In fact, most teachers "don't mess with that stuff," and they mean not to. They comfortably, unapologetically acknowledge that the intent of schooling is to assimilate. A Hispanic teacher, resigned to the school's doing whatever it does, sees bilingual education and other means of recognizing ethnic group interests and needs as subject to bandwagon effects. He recalls the former emphasis on bilingual education, sex education, safe driving, and assertive discipline, and the present emphasis on computers, academic achievement, and improved test scores. The center stage of school life is a shifting scene. It has shifted away from ethnicity.

Linda Thompson's is the last of the teacher perspectives I will present to show the variety of models available to students as they proceed through their adolescent identity formation.

Teachers should present to students the standard in America to the best of our ability. At the same time, students should be able to be themselves. So, if students come into my room conversing in Vietnamese, I don't think it would be proper for me to say, "Ah, none of that." That is telling a student he should not speak his language, he should not be proud of it. But if he were to give a speech in my class, I'd definitely require him to speak English using the proper speech rules and regulations.

To survive, students should be able to switch from their native ways of doing things to American ways. If they take their native ways into society, they would be shunned. So, I think students should be bilingual and bicultural. I think for us to expect students to replace their home culture is to ask them to negate it. We can ask them in a very tactful way to add to it so they can survive to compete with everyone else. While we're teaching students proper English or the proper way to relate, we don't make their native way look bad or substandard.

I think my family expects me to talk like I've been to school. They wouldn't want me to talk as I did when I was growing up. They'd think my college experience was a waste, that their money was ill-spent. They expect me to speak and carry myself as if I'm a professional woman. They can see I'm still proud of myself. I haven't adopted someone else's ways and culture to the point that I've lost my identity as a black American.

Generalizations of "Color-Blind" Teachers

Most RHS students are not part of the ingloriously labeled "wetback" and "FOB" ("fresh off the boat") groups who for lack of time and experience have not yet developed the skills to fit in. Undoubtedly, students look different, in terms of color, hair, face, and size. Their last names not yet changed or anglicized, students appear different on paper, too.

I needed to know if their teachers thought they also were different in ways that had implications for their professional work. At first, teachers had little to say in response to this query. Claiming to be "color-blind," by which they meant, in their own words, that "kids are just kids," they therefore saw no student attributes based on ethnicity that had consequences for the selection of subject matter, methods of teaching, and the like. If, of course, students had limited English proficiency, then they needed special assistance. Otherwise, their students, for all practical purposes, were alike, varying, when they did, in academic ability and achievement, not in ethnic terms with academic implications. Teachers offer different reasons for their color-blind behavior, saying there is nothing they know about students as members of a group that requires any particular response from them as teachers; moreover, they would not allow any opinions they might hold about such groups to affect their responses, lest they run afoul of the local ethnic organizations that are watchdogs of "equitable"—translated as "uniform"—conduct by teachers.

As long as teachers could interpret my questions to mean, "Did they discriminate?," always seeing discrimination as negative, they were loath to do what I failed to realize I was asking them to do: generalize, with the risk of stereotyping close at hand.

In time, generally after a second or third interview, my request to be informed about what RHS students were like produced responses from the teachers. They were not eager to characterize a group. They could and did generalize, quick to clarify that their grand sweeps never, never included everyone. And I believe them because the diversity of student behavior and achievement at RHS defies hard-core, narrow generalization.

Generalizations are the short-hand vignettes by which people live. They save us from examining each case of a class of persons, events, or things. The saving may come with a cost: we may wrongly value a particular object and we may do injustice to a particular person. Teachers know the costs and still generalize, as do we all. They do not do so glibly. It is as if they had buried the understandings they had acquired over the years (possibly embarrassed by them). But upon them, for better or worse, they act almost instinctively once they are past their early years as novice teacher. One fourth-year teacher at RHS recalls how he felt when he first arrived on the job, free of generalizations, and unsure of himself.

I started out very fearfully. I remember the first time I talked to a couple of blacks. I didn't know what to say or how to behave or what. Hallway supervi-

sion—it was the most dramatic thing for me. I didn't know what to do. If I don't follow through [when someone misbehaves], what will happen? Here everyone is kind of loud and rowdy and pushing. I guess with blacks or some other people, if you don't know their culture or language, you just have to get involved [get to know them] where you feel comfortable and then do more and more and more.

His older colleague Sylvia Messina will not even think about what she has learned about her students when I ask her to think of me as a beginning teacher at RHS who comes to her for advice. What she tells me, however, is revealing. She acknowledges the "cultural differences" of students,

but I don't think that has to be a part of your teaching. I think they'll eventually teach you what those things are. I do know what they are but I don't know what they are. Maybe I just operate like with radar, where I stay out of situations. I don't find myself challenged by whatever color. I only teach what I think is true. My classes could be one-hundred percent white.

While some teachers held fast to the position that "I can't make any generalizations that I can support," others with no fewer years in service as a teacher at RHS felt they could generalize. They joined the non-generalizing teachers above in being able to characterize student academic performance, having most to say about black, Asian, and Filipino students, and least about Mexican and white students.

Here is the picture teachers presented about their students. Asians, which include students from South and Southeast Asian nations, are polite, respectful, formal, and obedient. They received uniformly high praise for their academic performance; though quiet in discussion, they always do their homework, work hard, want to succeed, and are attentive and persistent. White students seem to defy generalization. Filipino students were closer to other Asians than to non-Asians; yet, being more Americanized, they were less docile, formal, and obedient. While participating more in discussion and being active in asking questions, they did not exhibit the same intensity for academic success as Southeast Asians. They stood with the other Asians, however, in having high academic aspirations.

Mexican students, generally formal, polite, and well-behaved, had relatively low academic motivation and high drop-out rates.

The problem is national. We've got a tremendous problem of Spanish-surname kids dropping out. I'm not saying they're dumb. I've had some brilliant Spanish-surname kids. Brilliant. As a group, they don't seem to be motivated academically. I'm sorry if this sounds racist; it's not intended to be.

Teachers who felt they could generalize, most readily described black students. They were "laid-back," kidded more, liked physical contact, took criticism poorly, sought attention, and were rebellious and bold. Black girls were singled out as loud and aggressive, with a chip on their shoulders. Academically, black students had the desire but lacked foundations for learning, needed extra help, had short attention spans, and were hampered by speaking in black dialect. This picture does not apply to the small group of college-prep students. Burt Borman's graphic image of black kids is not that of all teachers about all black students, but it seemed to capture what many were expressing:

These kids come out of a totally different environment than I do, and they react so totally different. They may be from the project, living in the midst of drug dealing. I wouldn't know a drug if I saw one. They come out of a no-father, maybe drunken-mother family, where I wouldn't know such parents. I mean, I'm saying, I don't think I feel the blackness. I don't know what to feel to feel blackness, but I really feel that this poor kid—my God, what a home life he has! What a slice of life he has seen that I've never ever thought of. I think I feel this, but I don't think I feel, "Hey, this kid's black, so let's teach him different." That's never crossed my mind.

Repeatedly, whatever the question I asked, the issue I raised, the advice I sought, teachers depicted black students, relative to all others, in the most disparaging terms. That there was a disparaging reality was not generally disputed; that it existed was a matter of consternation and despair to teachers, students, and parents. Shirley Grinder, stalwart member of the black community and long-time Riverview resident, has had four children graduate from RHS; several of her grandchildren are there now. She believes in education, presses its virtues upon her kin, and rushes to school if teachers request her help. She verifies the disparaging reality, shares the consternation and despair, and devoutly wishes that it would cross the minds of Burt Borman and his colleagues to "teach them different." Teacher insistence that they look at individual not group differences seems fair and rational until Shirley Grinder says, in effect, that there is a group problem. Black children are singled out but not for the type of attention that would promote their academic success. The many existing special programs are for problem students, not for the mass of black youngsters who dominate the school's lowest academic track. Is it easier to work with students who are not black because "black kids are too noisy, too aggressive, too loud?" I ask her, incorporating in my question the adjectives most frequently used to describe black students.

That could be a real threat to people; that might cause people to back off. It's easier to work with those kids who are quieter and who take care of their school work. Black kids are surely not quiet. No, they're not. I know that.

A child comes to high school, gets good grades, he's no problem. That kid's going to make it, OK? Those are the kind of children I see our counseling staff latching onto. These kids over here who are not doing too well, they kinda go unnoticed. They don't get the nurturing by the staff, by the counselors, by whoever, along with what the parents give them.

Mrs. Grinder is mistaken. Black children are certainly noticed. It is what brings them to the notice of teachers that makes a difference. Greg Torezza says he is aware of Filipino students in his classroom because they really want to learn. They do their homework and they ask questions. And the way they ask,

it's more soft, you know, than the black. The black population is more demanding; they look more for confrontation. I had a complaint from a black girl who talks and talks and talks. She doesn't realize that I'm giving her lots of breaks. After a couple of times, I said, "Please be quiet." Then she starts complaining that I make her be quiet and not the rest of the class. She is aware that I let some other people talk more than I let her talk. In a way it is true. The reason is she's so loud.

Mr. Torezza would say to Mrs. Grinder that he wishes he could be party to the academic success of his black students, only it is to nonacademic incidents that his attention is most often drawn.

Explanations of Academic Achievement

When some black students at RHS in 1968 went on a rampage after King had been assassinated, persons inside and outside the school system conjured up explanations; the "riot" was too traumatic to go unexplained. It took the passage of time and the press of other issues, not the discovery of a satisfactory account of this locally unprecedented event, to divert attention and energy from the fruitless search. The poor academic achievement of minority students does not hit home as does a riot, though its consequences are no less momentous. Pursuing the play of ethnicity, I wondered if I would hear it evoked as the basis for understanding why these students did poorly in school. Clearly, something about Asian and Filipino students drew them toward academic achievement. Whites were too diverse to generalize about; they stretched across the continuum of academic success during the high school years and afterward. Mexican and black students excelled as soaringly as anyone else, only so much less frequently as to create the impression among

RHS educators that most of them lacked whatever it was that enabled other groups to do better.

I spent an afternoon with Mexican community leaders who were meeting to consider the painful issue of high Mexican student dropout rates. Their talk soon turned to the remarkable successes of Southeast Asian students. Often as poor as the Mexicans, often as deficient in English-language skills, how could they do so well? Where did they get their extraordinary desire and persistence, and were there transferable lessons that Mexican families could and should learn? Not surprisingly, no one looked to biology as an explanation; moreover, no one took refuge in economic facts; having noted the welfare backgrounds of successful Asian students, they could hardly do so. That left cultural factors but they seemed not much more tractable than biological factors. Confused by their inability to pinpoint satisfactory explanations for their children's relative lack of academic success, the leaders' talk drifted toward other topics. The meeting ended with expressions of need to learn about this and that, and, of course, to continue discussing the problem since it was certainly not going to disappear.

A comparable meeting at RHS attended by an ethnically diverse group of educators would sound somewhat different. I never attended such a meeting, and I am not aware that meetings at which the problem of minority achievement was formally addressed were ever called. I visualize what would be said at such a meeting because I asked individual teachers to comment on the academic performance of their students. Unlike the Mexican leaders, RHS teachers steer clear of cultural explanations, realizing that they smack of a racism that they do not feel and would be loath to be identified with. Teachers evoke economic explanations, connecting money to the creation of home conditions that disable children academically. They mean to avoid accounting for poor academic success by connecting it with ethnicity. They are not saying, "This is how black people are" but rather, "this is how poor people are." Teachers have reservations about their own speculations and they sometimes disclose them. Here is a veteran white teacher:

I'll put it this way. A lot of the teachers like to feel that our SAT scores are low because students don't have the right home environment. They're afraid to say this because it's a hot topic. When I push on this, then it's "they are welfare people. They don't encourage their kids to go on. They don't make them come home and do homework. They don't check on the kid." Primarily, the feeling is— "because they are black." There might be something to it; I don't know. I really don't know. I didn't have anybody in high school telling me about college. I didn't know what it was about.

Left unsaid is the conclusion that, "I was poor and had no encouragement. Therefore, if I could do it, then why can't they?"

Teachers extrapolate from their own lives to people they see as similarly situated but who end up profoundly dissimilar. They also
extrapolate from the lives of other community ethnic groups, such as the
Sicilians. Teachers recall that Sicilian children had low academic aspirations as recently as the 1950s. They followed their parents into fishing
and mill work. Parents did not reinforce academic achievement. And, so
the story goes, if the Sicilians or some other group can "make it," why
not—? Teachers do not in fact linger on their extrapolations or, for that
matter, on any explanations for minority failure because they daily face
the problems of individual students, not of groups. Like firemen, they
have to put out the fires of cut classes, tardiness, homework not done,
inattention, failed tests, lest a conflagration occur. And by regularly
dealing with individual students rather than groups, some teachers
come to the personal understanding that it is not socioeconomic status or
ethnicity but what is happening to a particular child that is truly important. Says a Mexican teacher:

You've got to understand the kid, where he's coming from. Their ethnic
background, what class they belong to—it's not important to me. Has the
student been abused? Is he really drugged, having a hard time—the family
disorganized, you know, the mother married the stepfather's brother? These
things really affect the child more than socioeconomic background or ethnic
group. I don't have any prejudices toward any group.

A white teacher extends this conception. He emphatically looks past
social class and ethnicity to a student's classroom behavior, as if to say
that somewhere there may be a background for this child, but here is the
existential reality that I see and deal with.

I don't label Johnny as being a certain socioeconomic group or a certain ethnic
group. If I think that way, I'm not aware of it. Hey, Johnny's a pain in the ass, or
Johnny's a good student. Johnny can read or can't read. Johnny's got a foul
mouth. Johnny's a wiggler. These things I catalog to paint my picture of Johnny.
I don't normally ask a child what their mother or father does. I may want to
find out is the home broken, is the parent overwhelmed with children, what
kind of conditions are they living in.

One week earlier, this same teacher had told me that a high percentage
of Riverview's long-term residents were poor and that when he teaches
his students he tries to keep their background in mind.

A smooth consistency is typical mainly of the responses of subjects
who can rehearse their answers or who are asked questions only once so

that we have no way of learning what they think next week. I interpret the apparent inconsistency of the teacher quoted above and of many of his colleagues as their reaction to difficult questions that they do not discuss in the ordinary pursuit of their professional work. To be sure, they offer explanations of what is undoubtedly an all too common fact: the disproportionate failure and poor academic achievement of black students. They point to deficits that derive from poverty, ethnicity, language disability, home life, and particular problems rooted in uninterested parents, low motivation, low intellectual ability, and the like. Almost invariably, the more teachers puzzled over the academic behavior of their students, the broader and more inclusive their responses became, until what was a simple picture emerged as a very complex one in which, when pressed, they could even weight the factors in their explanatory schemes, saying X is more serious than Y and Z.

No teacher looked at the capability of teachers as a possible factor for understanding students' academic behavior. In this respect, there is reason to believe that the low expectations teachers have for all students — not just minority children—may be relevant. Consider the observations of students and teachers.

Although teachers do not like low student achievement, they were not taught as teachers in training, nor did they learn as teachers in practice, to look inward at self and colleagues for possible explanations of student behaviors. To do so would compel them to ask, "Is there anything within my means and that of my colleagues that could be done to redress this persistent problem? Am I we—however inadvertently, part of the problem and not the solution?" Our learned disposition to look outside ourselves for the sources of problems may be psychologically sensible, freeing us of guilt and from the need to accept responsibility. Teachers do not learn to make certain distinctions that would help them rethink their involvement in the problem: factors beyond their control may be causing the problem, not one but many factors may currently operate, in some instances the problem may be truly unsolvable. This said, what then can teachers reasonably manage to do, individually and in concert? Do they need to acquire a new understanding of the problem, new perceptions of student success, new pedagogical skills, new instructional materials, new supports from administrators, counselors, or other protagonists outside the classroom? Clearly, more of the same teacher practice leads to more of the same student problems, thereby creating a cyclic phenomenon that continues unabated unless broken. I did not see or hear a commitment to break the cycle.

Generally, students thought their teachers were undemanding, that they could do reasonably well (get Bs and Cs) without much work. RHS graduates complain, for example, that they spent two years in honors English and still found themselves having to take "bonehead English" as college freshmen. Generally, teachers thought their students did not work very hard, were unwilling to work hard, and came from homes that did not encourage them to work hard. Teacher Harry Frank is explicit about his teaching orientation:

I go very slowly and tell students exactly what I want. I didn't always do that, mostly the last ten years or so after we lost a lot of students with the situation in the sixties. The number of intelligent students—I don't think they're there—just aren't as many as maybe fifteen years ago. It used to be that I would come into class and I didn't put the terms on the board. I didn't go through the test with a class. I could say, OK, we're going to cover this chapter. Now, I put things on the board. I think the books have slowed down [got easier] quite a lot, too.

Harry Frank's assessment of his students and his consequent slowing down has its counterpart in classrooms throughout RHS. By his classroom practices, Frank confirms what his colleague Al George heard from a school district administrator on the occasion of discussing the high school's low test scores. George was told that the school suffered the handicap of enrolling a high percentage of students who were minorities from welfare homes, and that "such groups always score low." This assessment angered George.

As soon as I heard this rationale that, well, we don't have good stuff to work with, I thought of a guy I used to work with. He had a theory that you don't make chicken salad out of chicken shit. In other words, this administrator was saying the same thing to me: "You know, Al, what are you expecting to get, chicken salad out of chicken shit?" My answer is yes. I think we can get chicken salad out of what we have here if we find the way to do it. I don't think the district is sincerely interested in doing that.

Ethnicity in the Curriculum

In light of educators' views of universalism, assimilation, and color-blindness, their conduct could not be expected to take ethnicity into account as a fact of consequence. I watched them at work in their classrooms and read their documents and textbooks. I do not take seriously what most schools have available in the manila folders of their filing cabinets, the papers that can be trotted out to show inquirers interested in their schoolwide and subject-matter objectives. Since such

documents are usually manufactured in response to some external demand, their validity is about as enduring as a blink, and they seldom
bear much relation to what actually goes on in the school's classrooms. I
expected to find a best-foot-forward listing of objectives that would indicate—at least on paper—the school's curricular awareness of its ethnic
diversity. This was not the case.

The document that most comprehensively covered the entire high
school curriculum was called *Student Expectancy Objectives: Grades 9–
12*. With one minor exception, only the social-studies department listed
objectives that reflected consciousness of ethnicity, and these were of
the type that could have been found in any high school located anywhere. The exception was the English-as-a-second language list that
contained as the last of forty-five items the "expectancy" that "The learner will compare and contrast democratic principles and institutions with
their own cultures." Other references to culture reflected a concern for
the socialization of the strangers who typically take this class: "The
learner will play typical American games that enhance culture-based
learning," and "The learner will participate in the democratic process in
group work by using voting and other American principles."

Even if the statements of student expectancies fail to operate as or-
ders, or even general guidelines, for teachers, they stand as fair
indicators of the school's intention of being in the curricular mainstream. As much as RHS teachers and administrators accept ethnicity as
a fact of their professional lives, it does not carry compelling implications
specific to their instructional ends and means. Unable or unwilling to
see America as a multiethnic society, teachers do not see the utility of a
multiethnic or ethnicized curriculum. Thus it is not what they have
failed to implement but what, because of other value commitments,
they have failed to visualize that might be at issue here.

Each subject within the social-studies domain had its own list of expectancies; each, except for economics, had at least one that related to
ethnicity. The social-studies department as a whole had forty-five of its
own expectancies, including the stipulation that learners "will chart the
contributions of key people and groups which shaped the U.S."; "will
demonstrate an understanding of the impact of multiculturality upon
the U.S. and upon California"; and "will outline the importance of civil
liberties and the protection of minority views." Only one of the expectancies—generously interpreted—incorporated in any of the individual
subject-matter listings came close to responding to what I think of as the
process of strangers becoming friends. The one example, found in the
United States history set, wanted learners to be able to "cite gains by
and continuing problems facing Blacks, Indians, Hispanics and Handi-

capped Americans." Such a statement is a la mode, like sprinkling oat
bran on your salad or dessert, but I think well meant by RHS educators,
their attention drawn to the "continuing problems facing" minorities.
But curricular fiat could never be as potent as daily experience in Riverview and Riverview High School in informing students about "gains"
and "problems."

Teachers of all subjects thought instantly of social-studies classes as
the most likely place to find content that recognized ethnicity in American life. So I watched social-studies instruction, examined social-studies
textbooks, and interviewed social-studies teachers. Teachers recall a
time when they stressed ethnicity more than they do today, attributing
the change in emphasis to the quieting of their students: when students
displayed their ethnicity more prominently, teachers reflected it more
robustly.

I think right now we're in a—you know, the pendulum. I think now we're in a
period of not necessarily covering up, but trying to bring together, trying to
find common elements. We're in a period of reconciliation compared to the
emphasis [in the past] of differences. So, you go with the flow.

The ethnic flow has abated, teachers think, but has not been
stemmed. Teachers point to the shift of content in current textbooks,
compared to those of the past, though they do not rely exclusively on
them for their ethnic-oriented subject matter. They clarify that their
textbooks are selected for their readability; treatment of ethnicity was
not a consideration. The world history text (A. O. Knownslar and T. L.
Smart's *People and Our World* [1984]) has not departed radically from
the traditional western focus of such books: the index shows that in 730
pages, Africa has 23 subheads (as does Poland), Mexico 11, and France
44, with another 11 devoted to the French Revolution. The index of the
United States history text (A. F. Graff's *This Great Nation* [1983]) shows
black Americans with 30 subheads, plus "see also names of individuals";
Hispanics, 3 (with Mexican-Americans listed separately on four different pages); Native Americans, 27; discrimination, 6. Other pertinent
topics have only page references: immigrants and immigration, a total of
20 pages, civil rights movement, 10, Asian Americans, 5, and Chinese
Americans, 4. In addition, the book contains ten one-page biographies;
five are about ethnic minorities and four about women.

Since ethnicity is neither prominent in the textbooks nor embedded
in curricular guidelines that carry any strong force, teachers give no particular attention to ethnicity. Extra-credit assignments offered teachers
occasional opportunities to encourage exploration of special topics that

would appeal to one group or another. Another was the assignment to go home and query parents about the first members of their family to reach America or, as one teacher did when studying stereotypes, to have their parents tell them what they knew about different ethnic groups. The presence of ethnic students is not ignored; it just is not ordinarily tangible in ways that induce teachers to make an instructional response. Teachers do not go out of their way to emphasize ethnicity, and there is no pressure from any source to do otherwise.

After social studies, English is the next most probable subject to include an ethnic component, but the reality is not much different from social studies. Publishers also have modified the literature books teachers use to reflect a broader ethnic spectrum, though English teachers say that "We didn't look at what they had to offer in terms of stories for the different racial groups." The 1977 edition of *English Grammar and Composition*, by J. E. Warriner and F. Griffith, differs vastly from the original 1948 version. It has ethnic sprinklings: for example, "Harriet Tubman was a woman . . ."; "My aunt and uncle, the Giovannis . . ."; "Mr. Sato as a senator . . ."; "Judge Perez, dignified in her long black gown . . ."; and a ten-item exercise drawn from Maya Angelou's *I Know Why the Caged Bird Sings*. Worksheets available to English teachers are in the same mold. An entire worksheet on verb-and-subject agreement has a Hispanic cast to all its examples: "Mexican Americans (is, are) . . ."; "California, Arizona, and Texas (was, were) once part of Mexico"; "Gonzales and Garcia (is, are) . . ."; and "Chicanos and other minorities (has, have) . . ." Such ethnicization of instructional materials is inarguably fairer to the human diversity in Riverview and the nation. Students seem to ignore the ethnicization, however, perhaps because the point of the exercise is mastery of a particular element of English grammar—verb and subject agreement—and not mastery of the ethnic reference in the substantive frame created to facilitate this learning. The ethnicized frame does not guarantee any better learning outcomes:

Teacher: "Pedro and his brother are going out to play basketball." What will you substitute for "his brother"?
Student: "He."
Teacher: Yes, that's what you'll say on a test. How would you say it otherwise?
Student: "Pedro and him."

The English department at RIIS contains more minority teachers than any other department; perhaps for this reason its teachers are more attuned to including ethnic-related experiences in their teaching. Ethnicity, however, was not a theme among the English faculty, a commitment to be honored, so to speak, whenever an opportune moment arose. Still, manifestations of ethnicity turned up in various forms.

One expression is in a teacher's awareness of student behavior that has implications for how she teaches. Linda Thompson was particularly alert to language factors that caused problems for students in mastering English expression. For example, her black students omit an *s* at the end of verbs and plural nouns; Spanish-speaking students "have trouble with sentence syntax," and Orientals don't use articles correctly. "If a teacher is aware of these things, she can be more diligent in her teaching," says Thompson.

Teachers borrow rapping, a song form popular with black students, to teach parts of speech. Ms. Angelotti invites students to combine their understanding of a noun or a verb in a rap that they compose. Here are some examples:

> Here's a couple of nouns I'd like to put in your head,
> I'm telling you boy they'll knock you dead;
> I'd like to say that these nouns are fresh . . .

> Here's a verb that I think you'll respect,
> It's a part of speech such as "protect" . . .
> Now listen to what I'm telling you
> Cause I know I'm correct
> Take it from me
> Cause I'm the best.

Angelotti adopts rapping in terms of a principle that I did not often hear articulated. She explained that since she and most of her RHS colleagues were middle-class whites, they needed to draw upon examples of "materials, methods, and contents" that would insure that their black students felt included. Though her classes contain more than just black students, and I am convinced she wishes all her students well, Angelotti's examples almost invariably are about black students. She arranges for her students to visit a classroom where black students will be role-playing candidates running for political office; they also visit the leadership class whose members run student government. "I want the blacks in our school to learn not to be afraid to get up in front of everybody and to pay their fees [dues] and do their number," she explains.

Accompanying Angelotti's unequivocal commitment to black students are feelings of—what to call them?—timidity, ambiguity, ambivalence, that black students engender in her. Though not new either to teaching or to RHS, she discusses having been nervous in anticipation of her first-period class the day before. It was more than first-day-of-class jitters for her. Because the class contained black students it was, therefore,

slightly intimidating for me because until I get to know the blacks in the class, and until they get to know me, they're hard for me to handle. Yesterday, I had an older black boy in my class who is very outspoken. I knew he was going to start testing me right away and I was edgy. Guess what he said? It's a classic case. Minorities know how to read body language. They're experts on it. I hadn't said more than four minutes' worth of things when he burst out with, "Hey, man, she looks nervous." I said to my class, "Do you think I look nervous?" And Stacy, who's one of my favorite black kids, said, "Well, yeah, you're swinging that thing on your desk, and you never swing that thing."

Flora Mast, Angelotti's colleague, thinks immediately of her class reading *Black like Me* when she is asked about ethnicity in her classroom. She sees something universal in this book's account of the experiences of a white man disguised as a black man: a story of the discrimination experienced by women, the handicapped, as well as minorities. English teachers often require their students to keep a journal. While reading *Black like Me*, Mast has her students write in their journals what life would be like if they changed their skin color.

Interest in Martin Luther King surfaces each year about the time of his official day (January 15) and during Black History Month. The recognition may be as thin as a bulletin board display in the hallway or a three-minute loudspeaker announcement tucked away between reminders to return report cards and to attend the afternoon's pep rally. Facing less competition from the clutter of other stimuli are the lessons on King that Angelotti arranges. They include listening to a tape recording of King, journal writing, class discussion, and filling out special worksheets that she has prepared, all of which might not amount to much without her zeal for the topic. She thinks that since young people mostly hear pabulum, they are unprepared for the intensity of King's voice and message.

Right after they hear him, they're stunned. They can neither talk about nor write about him. They haven't processed it yet. I have them listen to King at the end of the period. The next day, I teach them that King did not operate in a vacuum. He was influenced by Gandhi. I want them to know something about Gandhi; that gives my American students a window on Asia. It will give my Indian student a reminder of her own cultural tradition and its influences on America.

I feel strongly about this unit on King, so I tie it to their school. I say, "you need to know that right now you and I are living out history in this classroom." They just look at me when I say this. They don't know what I'm talking about. "Right here in this room we are all studying together. We have the potential to be friends together, to get to know each other and like each other. This is what King died for." They were just emotional. Nobody said anything.

Angelotti's unit on Martin Luther King grows out of her sense of values as they impinge upon what all American children should feel and understand. From year to year, the unit changes; the students are different and they elicit something different from her. But her values hold fast.

Some of the most powerful classroom moments occur unblessed by planning; good teachers are prepared to seize them. I watched Doris Washington do this one late April afternoon, near enough to the semester's end to believe that the school year would not be interminable. She was tired and annoyed. She had assigned students a summary to write of *The Contender*, a story her sophomores had been reading. Students fidgeted, unable and unwilling to settle down to the task. Her curt, "Class, I'm not in a playful mood today," finally worked. It produced silence so enduring that she had trouble pulling them out of it to discuss what they had written. She got them back when she began to question a white student's reluctance to read aloud the word "nigger" as it appeared in the story.

Prompted by Washington, black and white students alike eagerly identified the names they had been called—"nigger," "spear chucker," and "black-burnt marshmallow," on the one hand, and "honky," "redneck," "pecker wood," and "white bread," on the other. No Mexican voices spoke up. The students spoke intensely, often with anger, but they had no object close at hand to fasten on. Nobody present had called them names; both black and white students had been victims of name-calling. Besides, the white man was long since dead who had been responsible for the light skin color of the black girl who said, "I'm the color I am because of whites having sex with black people." The lesson came close to home after a white student touched off this exchange:

Student (white): "Why is it OK for two black people to call each other nigger, and I can't?"
Student (black): "Because you aren't one of us. You aren't our color."
Teacher (black): "I don't want to be called that."
Student (white): "You don't have to be black to be called a nigger."
Student (white): "I've been called nigger before."
Student (Filipino): "A black guy called me nigger the first time I went to gym."
Teacher: "To my brothers and sisters in this classroom: if this Filipino boy

wonders about this, we have to think about the words we use, about these put-downs."

For their journal assignment that night, Doris Washington required the students to write about name-calling.

Washington felt that in past years she had had time for including more ethnic content in her teaching. Now, she says, with "education in such hot water," she needs to devote more time to the basics. There is so much that she has to do, "I don't have that exploratory kind of time any more." Neither do her co-workers, though they are much less naturally inclined than she is either to plan or to capitalize on an ethnic moment. About the time of my study, and more so thereafter, California schools received state mandates to orient their curriculum toward university and college admission. This orientation, combined with increasing attention to school scores on state and national tests, underlies Washington's reference to hot water. Accordingly, neither internal nor external circumstances favored an ethnic orientation where one might predictably have existed.

In the rest of the school's curriculum, ethnicity is present as a trace. Science teachers may note the ethnic identity of scientists whose names appear in their textbooks, but beyond English and social studies, publishers have not made an effort to ethnicize their textbooks. Biology teachers provide an opportunity to discuss sickle-cell anemia "because it's primarily a black disease." The home-economics teacher has taught a unit on "foreign foods" because her students were "diversified"; this unit is not taught every semester. A music teacher shows the film *Black Music in America*, and sees it not just in musical terms but also as an opportunity to talk about the contributions of different people to the development of music in America. A vocational-education teacher monitors with whom students sit when he organizes small-group work because he does not want them to "get into the habit of working just with their own." And a physical-education teacher includes soccer among the alternative games she will offer because so many of her nonnative-born students requested it. If teachers generally could see no special implications in ethnicity for the selection of their subject matter, they could, almost without exception, cite instances of taking account of ethnicity. To do this, teachers need no mandate, no agreement among fellow teachers in the same department.

Ethnic considerations do not necessarily stop at classroom doors. The large extracurricular segment of school life is where many teachers relate to students as club sponsor or coach. As mentioned earlier, RHS has three different ethnic clubs of long standing, one each for Filipino, black, and Hispanic students. None is limited exclusively to members of the ethnic group for whom the club was formed in the first place, and none is assertively ethnic in addressing issues of identity or of separateness. Some teachers, however, think of them as organizations that "breed political undertones" and thus are not "good for the country."

The realm of cheerleaders and their related promoters of pep is devoted ostensibly to the cause of stirring the crowd to cheer the boys on to victory. When in the past this noble cause was the sole domain of white students, it was one more place where nonwhite students could be reminded that they were strangers at RHS. Those days are long past. If ethnicity is present at half time during a football game, when the cause of pep is served by twirlers, dancers, cheerers, and the marching band, it is in the relatively sexy, jiving, fluid movements of the performers. Their style is most strongly manifest when set beside that of the usually all-white, stiffer performers from other schools. Observers of the RHS style say that it derives from the presence of black students.

Ethnicity in Counseling and Discipline

Beyond RHS's classrooms and extracurricular activities, I also looked for the play of ethnicity in the practices of counselors and in the conduct of discipline by teachers. The five counselors closely reflect the ethnic identity of the students: there are two men—Sicilian and Mexican; and three women—black, Filipino, and white. They are sensitive to ethnicity when relating to students, as demonstrated by the responses of one of the five to my questions.[1]

Because of our multiethnicity in this school, I think that the role of counselor is very demanding. Minority parents expect, because of their past treatment, that they're going to get the shaft. They immediately become very defensive. In any situation at this high school, race usually comes into the picture: that teacher is racist, that counselor doesn't understand black kids or white kids or whatever.

I know I speak different to different kids. A black student from the project came by yesterday. We've become very close. When I speak with her I speak in a much different manner than to other girls. Totally. I was speaking slang in many ways, which maybe a lot of people disapprove of. I find it establishes good rapport with my kids. And if students from my own ethnic group come, I'll slip in a few words that show I speak their language. When two Mexican girls came in—they were newcomers—my whole mental state changed. I

1. In the interest of confidentiality, I will identify neither the gender nor the ethnicity of this counselor.

have three students who work for me, each from a different ethnic group. Two are American-born, but one is a mod and the other is very conservative. The third one has been in this country for about four to five years. I handle each one of them very differently.

I don't know if the differences are due to ethnicity. Maybe if we were talking ten or eleven years ago, I would've said yes. Now, I see myself as trying to reach a student as an individual. There has to be some consideration of their ethnicity, in some respects, but I don't think it's a major factor.

Counselors observe that over the years they have seen students become more like each other, as the traditional ethnic family has given way to contemporary American forms—both parents working, less supervision, and more freedom. Still, they and the teachers can look at the distance between their lives and that of their students and conclude, "It's a whole different culture. For me to talk to them, it's like someone from another planet." So, even if they feel that they must concentrate on the individuality of students, and that ethnicity is not a major factor, they knowingly make distinctions based on a student's ethnicity.

Whatever the frame of reference is—counseling, teaching methods, instructional materials—teachers begin by avowing their respect for the individual child before moving on to identify perspectives they draw from students' ethnicity. They respond similarly when they discuss discipline. Like teachers everywhere, RHS teachers have to establish an appropriate level of control without making it their main priority. Priority belongs to their lessons. Control at RHS, teachers say, requires knowing that there are generalizations about students that stand not as directives but as useful guides.

"Number one, with all kids you're consistent. Always," says Ron Roberts, the first of three white teachers I cite here. He states what must be among the most common bits of wisdom educators extracted from the post-1968 period. "You deal individually, not with an ethnic group, but I think if you have a little background . . ." This said, he can make the characterizations that he has found useful: Mexicans are shy, and need stroking and individual attention. Deal with their fathers. Blacks are the same, but you must not "tolerate any insubordination." Be aware of their backgrounds. They won't look you in the eye, and do not expect them to. Deal with their mothers. He advises against yelling at Mexican or black students and for keeping contact with their homes. Roberts does not cover the range of students either by gender or by the extent of ethnic diversity present at RHS. Nor does Al George, who gives a summary overview of the "minority student" in terms of what he sees as his own stance in the event of a disciplinary situation. To him, minority students invite more disciplinary action and they demand more of his patience: "If anything, I may take a little more from a minority student than I would from a nonminority student." He goes on to discuss a current example of a boy in his class from whom he takes more "because I know how far out he is in terms of being stretched tight." Sarah Lindsey elaborates her views more extensively than Roberts or George. "In handling a Mexican-American situation, you don't yell at the guys," because to do so is to compound the problem. "They do not accept authority from a woman." Black kids require politeness, "since if you're rude, you'll get rudeness back." In addition, you should not touch a black student because they do not like that. In contrast, Filipinos are relatively easier to control because they are more responsive to authority. "Tell them to stop and they just do."

Like his white colleagues, Mexican Greg Torezza excludes white students from his description. He concentrates on black and Mexican students, with a brief comment on Filipinos. If his class contains many black students, he anticipates that they will be noisy and create discipline problems. In response, he becomes stricter and prepares himself for their verbal and physical aggressiveness. "Don't get into a discussion. Just write a referral and send the student out," Torezza advises. Mexican students are very verbal but he finds them much more tractable. He can yell at them knowing that they will remain respectful and not get physical.

Lil Donaldson makes reference to all the ethnic groups, including whites. I do not know if she does so because she is black, a woman, or just an alert observer. In any event, she, too, generalizes about students. "Oriental students," by which she means all Asians except Filipinos, are very sensitive to criticism, so "you have to be a little bit private with them." See them after class because "they are not ones for open embarrassment." Mexican students are also private but if you get into a "reprimanding" situation with them, "they may be a little outspoken because they've been Americanized." Filipinos strike her, as they do many teachers, as easy to handle: "They have a tendency to kind of draw back" if you say something to them. "They kind of hold their head down and that's it." She doesn't think there is an easy "that's it" with black and white students, remembering that she has been in "verbal wars" with them. However, she does see them as different. White students will get "hot under the collar and be embarrassed"; a black student "may really verbalize and say, 'Oh, Mrs. Donaldson, hey, back off me. You know, chill out or something.'" She ends her observations as many teachers begin: "Through all the mixture, they all become Americanized. They don't go heavy toward that cultural thing. They just don't. Not here at Riverview."

It is easy to match the views of these five teachers with those of five others (albeit, none of them minorities) who claim not to see generalizable distinctions among students by ethnic group. Such teachers offer various explanations for their position: they are color-blind; making distinctions gets them into "racist stuff"; distinctions are harmful to the students because outside of school there is only one law and they are not going to be disciplined according to their ethnicity; and they respond in terms of what students deserve and not who they are. The beliefs of this set of teachers are those of the majority. They say in effect that the right way to teach or discipline or relate to students is right for all students. In short, they hold to a universalist perspective and modify it in response to what they believe are the personal, as opposed to collective, attributes of students.

Universalism in Practice

Riverview High School is a veritable academic maze. It abounds with tracks and alternatives and affiliated schools intended to serve a student population that varies widely in academic interests, performance, and aptitude. This maze of programs—some of them opportunities, others traps—amply testifies to Riverview's and California's awareness that one type of education does not fit all. That these programs fall short of their intended goals does not, I believe, cast doubt on the intentions and good will of Riverview's educators. If intention and good will sufficed to make a difference in promoting academic success, RHS would be eminently successful, but this is another story. What I mean to underscore is that while RHS is committed to finding the means for achieving academic success, it has no comparable commitment to finding a place for ethnicity in its school. Whether it should be so committed is a serious issue for those who value multicultural education (see, for example, Lynch 1983; Gollnick and Chinn 1983; Modgil, Verma, Mallick, and Modgil 1986; and Banks 1981). Meanwhile, RHS's multitude of academic options has no ethnic counterpart inside or outside these options. The closest it comes to ethnic alternatives is in its bilingual math, biology, and social-studies courses, in which a regular, monolingual teacher is assisted by a bilingual Spanish-speaking aide, and in its two-year offering of English as a second language. These courses essentially acknowledge only the linguistic not the general cultural variability of students. The courses are grudgingly accepted, not by the teachers who teach them but by most others who, failing to see value in them, believe they waste time and money.

As I observed in regard to the statements of curricular expectancies developed for all RHS courses, there is little in RHS's documents to suggest that it is an ethnically stratified school. Only the availability of a Spanish-language version of the student handbook of rules and regulations suggests that RHS has a large (20 percent of the total) Mexican subgroup. Otherwise, in official terms—that is, in terms of what school documents prescribe and what teachers do—ethnicity at RHS is a fact of no notable consequence. What counts is what pays off. "Standard English is the 'cash tongue' necessary to make one's way in a culture dominated by that tongue" (Freedman 1985:28). Similarly, I think of a "cash curriculum" as prevailing at RHS; it leads to instruction with a supposed market value.

Accordingly, the voices of ethnicity are soft, peripheral, and not so much denigrated—RHS educators know better than to do this—as downplayed. In light of the school's universalist thrust, just how these voices are downplayed and played is complex. Listen to these pairs of voices. They contain a "yes" to the school's universalist thrust, and often a qualifying "but" that acknowledges ethnicity:

Even though you can see different colors, they're all the same to me.

It's important to know what's important to the students. You can't be good enough at this.

You want to guide your clientele to be able to fit into the large world that they're going into, which is primarily English-speaking and middle-class ethics.

You know, it's still an English class . . . but when I deal with new words, I try to have them figure out what languages they come from.

The way that I was raised, an Italian student is no more interesting to me than a student of any other ethnic background.

There's a kid whose mother was stabbed to death at a bus stop with him standing there. That's going to bring to your classroom a different kind of child than one whose parents walk out of a health club.

Notwithstanding the qualifying buts, the yeses carry the day. When I asked students who they thought their school experience encouraged them to be, they answered, "an ordinary American." And that was OK with them: "Like, they're here to teach you. See, the teachers don't teach you to be a certain color." Students do notice some teachers talking differently to students of their own ethnic group, and remember being called on by teachers when a subject came up that related to their home

country, as when President Marcos of the Philippines was being un-
seated. Otherwise, what they hear in their education is the sound of
universalism.

That indeed is what I heard when I sat in classes throughout the
school year. I was most vividly aware of the universal for the first time
while sitting in a home-economics class where the names and faces of
students testified to the class's ethnic diversity. The lesson focused on
the "correct" way to set the table for breakfast, lunch, and dinner, depending on what foods were being served. For buffet meals, students
learned that they could use their imagination about where to stack the
dishes, silverware, and napkins. Otherwise, students learned that there
was a right way to do things. There were no social-class or ethnic or personal standards to consider that controverted the right standard, though
both teacher and students certainly knew they practiced other ways.

Students had long ago learned, by inference, I suspect, rather than
by direct instruction, that the school-taught way either was "correct,"
or, if not, not worth contesting. I never heard a hint of reproach from
students to the presumptions and assumptions behind their classroom-
learned knowledge. Although our students learn to resist rules and regulations, having acquired a keen sense of what is fair and unfair, they
learn much less well to resist what is ethnocentric in any part of their
school's curriculum. How to set a table—whether indeed there even are
occasions that call for setting a table, and, if there are, how it is done, for
whom, and with what variations: these considerations would have produced a strikingly different home-economics lesson for the day.
Learning about the cultural embeddedness of what is correct strikes me
as much worth learning, and not inconsistent with a school's basic commitment to universalism. Mastering the concept of cultural relativism is
not a school commitment.

I was struck again by the promulgation of the universal when I
watched the work of students in stagecraft, one of several courses available in the performing-arts area. Students acquired and used vocabulary
and skills to make the sets used for school plays. As in the cooking class,
stagecraft students were ethnically diverse and, as happens at RHS, students sorted themselves out in pairs and groups, sometimes by ethnicity
and sometimes not. Students were being taught how to build sets in the
best way the experienced teacher knew how. I doubt that students knew
of any alternative ways, as students in the cooking class certainly did in
regard to the conventions of dining. Neither teacher sought instructional opportunities by capitalizing on their students' ethnicity; they did
not explore the matters of cultural diversity and cultural relativism. Nor,
for the most part, do their fellow teachers, each of whom, as befits their

subject, promotes student learning of the appropriate language, knowledge, and skills in the spirit of *the* best way. This is what I have been
calling universalist: within a particular setting, there is one best way for
everyone. Where variations exist, they arise from the academic stratification I referred to as RHS's "academic maze"; they can be thought of
as variations on the common theme of universalism generated by the
different qualifications of students for academic achievement. Thus, although the school experience represents induction into a new culture
for some students and into the mainstream variant of one's own culture
for others, all are undergoing a generally homogenizing process. The
process falls well short of full homogenization because of student resistance, on the one hand, and the diversity that teachers model, on the
other. No less consequential, moreover, is the fact that the homogenizing occurs in a school located in an open society where orthodoxy does
not reign. Custom, norm, modus operandi there may be, but there is no
party line and none is sought. The library is large, its choice of books
uncensored. The homogenizing is the process of socialization to fit students into American society as educators construe the process and the
fit, with the silence or nonprotest of parents and students interpreted as
implying assent.

The universal further operates in regard to school rules and regulations. Punctuality is punctuality, teachers assert. There is no Filipino or
Hispanic punctuality at school. It requires the ingenuity of students to
find ways to make punctuality work in personal, nonuniversalist ways;
beating the "system" is a national pastime of American adolescents. And
the universal operates in regard to what RHS honors as the basis of
achievement. It is demonstrated talent that will admit a student to honors classes, the school play, and the football team. The competition for
entry into the school's several opportunity structures is open to all,
though not all desire entry, nor have all had the same chance to acquire
the prerequisites of achievement.

Teachers consistently affirmed their attachment to the universal no
matter what questions I asked: "Is there anything I could learn about the
professional life of teachers from studying teachers in Riverview that I
couldn't learn from studying teachers in Crawford or Fairview?" "If you
were teaching in a school where the students were middle-class and
white, would you teach any differently than you do now? "Is the cultural
background of students ever a fact in any way in your work as a student?"—meaning, are they aware of ethnic differences with implications for their work as teachers? Teachers concede the obvious: they
"learn a little bit more about working with ethnic groups in a "low-bud-
get community," where there is less parental pressure, fewer students in
college-prep classes, simpler textbooks, and a need to be careful about

the level of your language. Tom Bernardo captures the spirit of the faculty's universalist response to these several questions:

What I do is tell them [the students], in different ways I tell them, we've got all these different backgrounds, but you've got to come together. You've got to come to my way and not me to all your ways. Each one is treated the same, is what I'm trying to get across to them. I'm not going to treat you differently because you don't understand the language too well, except I'll listen a little harder. You've got to learn to come to me and say, "I don't understand." I won't slow the class down because of you.

Doris Washington captures the dilemmas of the particularist spirit:

I remember at the beginning of the year I read this one girl's essay. She didn't belong in college prep but she wanted to go to college so bad. She described what it was like walking home, drug addicts around, stepping over people. She really expressed her desire to get out of that. I waited a long time before I moved her out of college prep. I felt like if I moved her out, she may not make it out of there. I didn't want to kill the drive.

When I'm grading papers, sometimes I don't even look at the name; I just do the grading. Then I have to go back and look at the names. It takes me a long time because then it's like, you know, I don't want to kill this person's effort. Am I going to give the grade the student deserves, or what?

The teachers' universalist perspectives rest on what in some places would be considered an unenlightened view of schooling in multicultural America. However, not feeling unenlightened, they defend their monocultural orientation. Hispanic student Jesse Garcia endorses their perspective. RHS educators infer that they have the approval of their clients and they can safely proceed with implementing their state's decrees to make high schools more academically rigorous. Garcia would not contest these decrees:

The teachers, they don't take away your culture, you know. When you go to school, you grow up with the ethnic groups; you grow up learning about them. Other schools just grow up with theirselves. Here, they don't ignore your culture. They respect you for who you are. They don't really ignore it, but it's not like a big deal. It's just like, you know, you're here to learn. If you want your ethnic thing, you should go to the clubs. You're not supposed to get it in the classroom; you walked in with it. You already got it. Why do you need it reinforced? You've got your values and your thing and you're here to learn. You learn the ethnic thing from your family.

Jesse Garcia, his parents, and their white, black, Filipino, and Asian counterparts do not press for an ethnicized school. To them, the school is not ethnic territory where behavior they deem appropriate at home and

in a few other places should prevail. They want such opportunities as the
school offers to be open fairly to all; their community organizations insist
on this being the case now and remaining so. Otherwise, they seem to
be satisfied if teachers don't ignore their past and present contributions
to society; don't offend them by behavior that violates their norms of interaction, for example, in regard to forms of address, volume of voice,
physical contact, etc.; don't knowingly deny them the chance to succeed; and don't insult them by inappropriate reference to their
language, food, or ethnic group.

Accordingly, in avoiding such proscribed behaviors, teachers are acting on the understandings they have acquired from the school's informal
process of socialization for proper behavior. The result of their avoidance
is that ethnic students are not made to feel invisible by teachers' gross
assumption of student homogeneity. Such an assumption, once rampant
in Riverview and elsewhere in America, was prominent in textbooks and
other instructional materials. At this peaceful time in RHS's history,
school district officials believe they and their teachers are taking due
heed of ethnicity and its ramifications. By seeing no reason for doing
more than they do, and no demand for greater effort, they conclude that
they meet the educational mandate of community, state, and nation.
Unwanted invisibility by outrageous assumption no longer prevails.
Riverview's ethnic groups have been satisfied by a degree of visibility
that compares favorably with that of the past. From no source currently
at work are they being urged on to greater and different expressions of
ethnic visibility that would challenge the status quo. And teachers, despite considerable skill in fine-tuning their interpersonal behavior with
students from several ethnic groups, deny differences among these
groups that would call for a difference in their pedagogical response to
them. More than this, they believe that they are never even unwittingly
discriminatory in their response because they are color-blind. By di-
vorcing learners from their ethnicity, teachers feel they shield them
from the injustices of past times. The acceptance of color-blindness as a
virtue keeps teachers from seizing upon differences rooted in ethnicity
that could affect academic achievement. I do not believe, however, that
the teachers affirm color-blindness for any but well-intended reasons.

6

Riverview High School's Students: Ethnicity and Identity

Riverview's adolescents are coming of age in an era when ethnic identity is relatively unballyhooed, but in a place where ethnic organizations remain reasonably strong and the community's annual round is marked by ethnic occasions. If acute ethnic awareness is a matter of remembering the recent past of black activism and Hispanic protest, ethnic identity is not a dead issue, but what kind of personal issue it is for RHS students remains to be discussed. What should be noted at once is that most parents do not belong to any of the community's ethnic organizations. Moreover, most students do not participate in the annual events that these organizations sponsor, and few belong to their high school's ethnic clubs. Thus it is not in the formal, collective expressions of ethnicity that I will examine the ethnic identity of RHS students. Rather, it is in their self-representations, in what they said about their beliefs and ways of doing things over our many months of tape-recorded interviewing. Underpinning these interviews is the general question: To what extent, if at all, is ethnicity a fact in the students' lives?

A focus on the self-representations of individual students does not deny the basic fact of ethnicity's collective nature. As much as individuals may, in some sense, do the picking and choosing of ethnicity-based behaviors, there inevitably is a collective context: home, neighborhood, and peer group (ethnic and otherwise) provide points of reference and departure and offer reinforcement.

For most children there are family members who say to them: We are such and such—Italian or black or Hispanic or Filipino. (Or, contrariwise—and in Riverview, very rarely—family members who say nothing.) Exactly what this means varies substantially from home to home. But since parents typically address the matter of ethnic identity in the definitive terms of "you are a ———," students are not really free to

171

make unencumbered choices: their ethnic self-identification is always made within the context of their families' self-identification.

Children adhere to and depart from the manifestations of ethnicity they experience at home. We see their responses at school where the attractive force of their own ethnic group operates side by side with that of other ethnic groups, as well as with the many social and interest groups that have no ethnic orientation at all. It is a truism of identity, including ethnic identity, that we are not left to define and shape ourselves as we alone see fit, for there always are others who have their own views of us: their expectations influence our behavior; their questions are reminders, at least at RHS, that who we are in ethnic terms is a matter of general interest. Alicia, for example, does not make much of her Mexican heritage, but when students teased her, calling her a "beaner," she not only was annoyed, she wished that she had some heritage other than Mexican. Ethnicity is a fact with implications.

Of course, the ethnic aspect of a student's identity is not the only one that matters to RHS students. As shown below, several aspects operate simultaneously:

The ethnic (from Alex, a Puerto Rican male):

Students want to know who you are. They do because they—when they first see me, they think I'm Mexican, but they just ask me to be sure. And it's not just Mexicans. It's everybody, because mainly they think I'm Mexican. I'm Puerto Rican. When you first meet students they don't really talk about it. But once you get to know them, they get to wonder, "Are you . . . ?" "No . . . ." Sometimes, some students here, you can't tell if they're white or if they're Italian. They got the features of Caucasian but when you ask them—"No, I'm Italian." "What?" "No." That sort of stuff. But we don't really talk about race.

The American (from Scott, a white male):

I consider myself an American, just American. Other kids, like, they might say Mexican-American. They'd always put, like, American in it. At least part American.

The person (from Pete, a black male):

I just act as a person. Sometimes I have to ask myself, "Why do I have to act a certain way?" I don't have to act a certain way just because I'm black. I mean I get mad at myself for not really being myself, not necessarily black. You should let your manners, the way you act, be determined by what you feel is right, and not something else.

These three perspectives and more are available to students as they wend their way through the thickets of adolescent identity. In fact, Alex observes, they "don't really talk about race," which is to say that matters of ethnic identity seldom are a topic of teen talk. They grapple with interests of more urgency. Still, the overwhelming presence of ethnic diversity everywhere in their school and community has ethnicity abutting their routine events and social interactions. Consequently, Puerto Rican Alex is invited to put straight who he is in this school where Puerto Ricans, other Hispanics, and Filipinos may, because they look alike, need sorting out so that others can keep them straight. Except for the newest of newcomers, most students are one or another type of American in this community of abundant hyphenation, where the identifier to the left of the hyphen—Italian, black, Mexican, Filipino—is bathed in the pride of, "Don't ever deny who you are. Be proud." This is axiomatic at RHS: one acclaims one's ethnic identity, however little meaning it has for the conduct of one's life. To fail to acclaim it is to misbehave.

The identifier "American," placed invariably to the right of the hyphen, is not embedded in similar axiomatic wisdom. To be sure, it is fully acceptable to be just American, sans hyphen. Being American is an undisputed fact of student identity. But the rawness and recency of more than a decade of ethnic-oriented distress disinclines students and educators to do anything that possibly could be interpreted as slighting ethnic identity. Misinterpretations were rife when ethnic consciousness was heightened by the daily events that occurred throughout the nation.

If this now multimotivated disinclination leads RHS students not to "really talk about race," they nonetheless are conscious of their own and other's ethnicity. Thus, while Pete prefers the identity of "person," he is mindful of his black self, which somehow he means to distinguish (downplay? separate?) from being "a person." And while white Scott unhesitatingly acknowledges himself as American, he is quick to mention someone's ethnic identifier—Mexican; he could not do otherwise at ethnically stratified Riverview High School.

We began our interviews without apprehensions that students would see ethnicity as a sensitive issue, or that they might be reluctant to discuss themselves and others in such terms. It was not sensitive and they were not reluctant; their words filled our notebooks. I present them below in the same order that in chapter 2 I presented their adult kinsmen: non-Sicilian white, Sicilian, black, Mexican, and Filipino. Since the conglomerate group I call "non-Sicilian whites" is not, as are the others, an identifiable student ethnic group, I will comment only briefly about them. This list of students contains the additional entry of "newcomers," a varied group of Filipinos, Mexicans, and southeast Asians. To return to a distinction I've made before about newcomers, I would point out that as a group they stand as strangers to all other students whose acculturation locates them somewhere within the group of friends.

Non-Sicilian Whites

Gone are most of the families of the coal miners and other Welsh settlers who were so important in the early days of Riverview's history. Gone, too, are most of the other white families whose historic contributions to Riverview's commerce and industry are recorded in the files of the *Daily Herald*. The children of remaining non-Sicilian white families compose a minority group at RHS. Even when their children are combined, as they are, with Sicilian children, they are a minority in a numerical sense: there are fewer white than nonwhite students.

At RHS, non-Sicilian white students are a diffuse group marked by color and by their mainstream-American, in contrast to ethnic-American, ways. Lacking an ethnic basis for group formation, they sort themselves out in terms of interests, academic achievement, and social class, just as the nonwhite students do. What they do not do is wall themselves off on the basis of color, their own or that of others, although some certainly hold prejudices that dispose them toward white peers.

I asked the white students if being white made a difference in any way they could think of. It certainly did not for grades, how teachers treated them, popularity, getting elected, etc. Being white, they thought, conferred neither advantages nor disadvantages in the formal circumstances of the school's academic and nonacademic affairs. One exception relates to the local scholarships available to graduating seniors. Since most of the organizations giving money have an ethnic affiliation, non-Sicilian white students felt that they failed to get their fair share as judged by academic merit. Things were not equal for them, they said, because they were not "ethnic." Another exception is the programs that help minority students gain access to college. White students indicated their unhappiness at being ineligible for these opportunities. This was particularly true for poor, academically aspiring white students.

In the school's informal circumstances, being white made some students feel different. This happened, for example, when a white student was in a setting where most others present were black. And it happened to white students whose complexion made them stick out. Gary Taylor said he felt like a minority at RHS:

All the time, constantly, yeah. Because we get noticed, especially if you're blond and blue-eyed. There's not many of us. We walk around and you don't see anybody else like yourself. Everybody [else] is different. Everybody considers me a white boy, so I get called white boy all the time. Yeah, even by white kids because I'm a stoner [discussed below], or because my hair is longer and blond.

Gary said that one thing he thought he should not do as a white student is "act like you're better than other people." His comment is interesting in light of what black students also learn about behaving correctly: they are advised not to act "uppity." This point, most strongly articulated by black students, is conventional wisdom at RHS for avoiding trouble.

I asked students if anything happened at school to remind them that they are white. Here are two responses, first from a female and then from a male stoner. "It's pointed out to you [that you are white] every minute of the day, practically. You're walking down the hall—'White stoner.' Sometimes I wish I could paint myself black." "It happens every time I see a black person. They're always calling us niggers and talking about Africa and stuff."

The stoners are a small group of white males and females, perhaps twenty or so in number, reputedly racist, who take drugs, and meet daily in the same location in back of one of the buildings. There they smoke, play heavy metal music, and just hang out. Stoners are readily identifiable by their appearance and musical taste. To other white students, they may be considered acting "too white," in that they do not fit in with the vast majority of other white students whose musical preference is for soul.

In subsequent sections, I will describe the responses of Mexican, black, and Filipinos which indicate their accommodations to life at RHS. That the accommodation is not just in one direction is clear from the reports of white students:

The way you talk, how you act, your moves—you just change a little bit from going to school with people. You talk different when you're around certain people. I can tell I'm doing it. Just to kinda fit in, you do it to fit in. Like if you're in English and talk a certain way, and you're at woodwork, you talk a different way because it's a different level of people in each class. I go out of town, I have to change a little bit because they don't understand some of the words you use. You say, OK, it's time to start changing your lingo. You got to start talking like the white guys. Living in Riverview, it's just a fact of life.

If nothing else, students at RHS have a range of ethnic and nonethnic groups they can try to identify with as they face the adolescent challenge of finding themselves. This challenge takes them to ethnic groups or to nonethnic groups (e.g., mods, new wavers, stoners, preppies, jocks), sometimes to both. Students, so to speak, can "join" different groups at different times because group boundaries are usually permeable (except for stoners in regard to blacks) to those wishing and able to fit in.

Sicilians

In this and subsequent sections about students who classify themselves as having an ethnic identity, I refer to them, as they also do, in a short-hand way as "Sicilian" or "Mexican" or "Filipino." I do not add, as they will upon being questioned, the "American" tag that by a hyphen connects them to their ethnic label.

RHS students of Sicilian descent know their family origins are in Sicily. Ethnic consciousness in Riverview is too intense for them not to know, but nowadays they are most likely to identify themselves as Italians. Unlike the generation of their parents and grandparents, they are mostly absorbed by the group I have designated non-Sicilian whites; neither they nor other students perceive them as a distinct group. Unlike the way it is for other ethnic groups, RHS contains no Sicilian "places" where Sicilian students congregate either as a social group or in a class or club. Italian is taught, but it is also taken by non-Italian students; the Italian Traveling Club is an extracurricular activity whose students—at best, five of thirty-five were Sicilian or Italian—rarely go to Italy.

Sicilian students, like their parents, range across a continuum from high to low degrees of attachment to Sicilian identity. Typical of the third and later generations, they retain a smattering of Sicilian words, the accidental byproduct of talk among relatives of the grandparents' generation. They hold fast to Catholicism, intimate family ties, ceremonial ethnicity (e.g., grand Christmas dinners), and a disposition toward the strong male role vis-à-vis females. Females conscious of this disposition may go so far as to reject the prospect of having a Sicilian husband, even as they remain strongly identified with being Sicilian. One Sicilian student, Audrey Lippi, described her reservations about her male compatriots in terms of mobility:

Italian guys in Riverview, they want to stay here. They're comfortable with their life here, you know. I like this town; nothing against it, you know, but it's just small, really closed in. The guys want to stay put. They want more blue-collar work. They seem to have old Italian values.

On the matter of marriage, Sicilian parents nowadays are more prone to express concern for a Catholic than for a Sicilian mate; if they articulate an ethnic preference, it is more likely to be for their daughters than for their sons. Their children seldom articulate any preference at all. The children's ideal is for a happy marriage, the ethnicity of the partner unspecified. They know that their parents are likely to endorse their conception of the right match unless it is with a black person.

Attachment to ethnicity potentially focuses one's attention, but its capacity to do this diminishes as ethnic identity declines. Sicilian students are not likely to know the names of the great Italian-American boxers of the past, nor, if they happen to learn about them, do they care particularly about them. News from Italy in the American press may catch the eye of a few, fewer certainly than those who will take note of an Italian-American dignitary, a Mario Cuomo, for example. Italy, psychologically, is distant as regards its daily news, though it still appeals to some as a place to visit. Mario Cuomo is psychologically closer.

If Sicilian students are not particularly attuned to reckoning who of their ethnic group has become a "success," a type of calculating perhaps more the practice of older persons, they are mindful of not being just white. "I'm always Italian," asserted Audrey. "I won't forget it. I remind people, I think, because of the environment we grew up in. I had to show everybody that I had culture, too." She is saying that since all other students are somebody in ethnic terms, she would have felt left out not to be an ethnic somebody. She expresses her ambiguity as she recalls that all the other ethnic groups stand together. "I don't think Italians back each other anymore because they're getting too Americanized. But I'm not saying that's bad. I could still be back on the island somewhere [where her grandparents were born]."

Audrey and her many Sicilian classmates readily recite the I'm-proud-of-who-I-am litany. I believe they mean it. Nonetheless, they are just occasional ethnics, with the occasions for expressing their ethnicity decreasing markedly from generation to generation, even for the more orthodox, whose parents are more insistently attached to Sicilian ways. For students, the once relatively expansive Sicilian preserve in River-view has been reduced to moments—Christmas celebrations, Columbus Day, grandparents' visits. It remains to be seen if, as adults resident in Riverview, students will join any of the several Italian organizations where the preserve is more intact because action in concert with fellow ethnics is the norm.

In the meantime, Audrey Lippi does not keep her ethnicity straight. Here she is in company with most of her fellow students. Ethnicity is not like a room containing objects to be set in place and once they are placed, order prevails. In the case of ethnicity, we must speak of shifts of meaning and also of inconsistency and contradiction, as befits human behavior. Neither parents, school, friends, nor ethnic organizations request Audrey to sort out her feelings and behavior as a Sicilian, an unthinkable invasion of her privacy. She does not think to do so herself. What I know of her ethnic orientation results from an interview that allowed her, so to speak, to focus more on this orientation than she ever had before, and perhaps more than she ever will again. This too is true of the other students whose ethnic orientation I present in the following sections.

Mexicans

If Italy shared a border with the United States, some young Sicilians might be more like some young Mexicans in their attachment to native country and language. Also, Sicilians would have to deal with the presence of many newcomers, such as the legal and illegal "wetbacks," as students ungenerously refer to them, who serve to remind the more acculturated Mexican-American "oldtimers" of exactly whom they do not want to be mistaken for. Someone else's newcomers may be merely funny, the butt of poor jokes; one's own newcomers are an embarrassment whose culturally unsuitable behavior invites distance and rejection, not kindness.

The nearby Mexican border means that going "home" is relatively easy. In fact, many Mexican students spend their summers and other times of the year in the villages of their parents and grandparents. There they experience a renewal of being and feeling Mexican, two states of consciousness that interest me as I explore with students their ethnic identity. Mexican students must work out a behavioral configuration that encompasses a Mexican and an American pole, each of which attracts its own cluster of ethnic manifestations.

Vangie Mendez, reflecting on being Mexican at RHS, observes that though her best friends are not Mexican, she knows many Mexicans; they are just not among her best friends. This circumstance strikes her as needing explanation: "Because my family, you know, when I'm at home, I always speak Spanish with my parents and grandparents. So, it's like I really don't need it." The "it" she refers to is speaking Spanish as a basis for finding comfort in a relationship, though, had she thought about it, she might have added that she does not need the intangibles of comfort that many find with others who were raised as she was and with whom there are numerous shared experiences, understandings, and values. Vangie acknowledges that she finds it neither harder nor easier to be with Mexicans. It is just not a necessary condition for her personal relationships, though it may be for her brothers and sisters and also for others who were raised as she was. Since children are obedient or recalcitrant, closed or open to change, they are differentially receptive to the mainstream American world of opportunities and circumstance.

I asked many students to tell me the ethnic identity of their best friends and other important persons in their lives. I believe I learn something of importance when respondents tell me that all or none of their best friends are from their own ethnic group, but I further believe that RHS's tangled ethnic web precludes drawing ready conclusions from what they tell me. Art Sandoval's personal life is a case in point. His parents are so attached to Mexico that they plan to return there when their children have completed their schooling. They return every few years to visit Art's grandparents. In an otherwise Mexican-oriented life, including a Mexican girlfriend, Art has only Filipino best friends. His steady social contacts are Filipino males. Having spent his life entirely in the United States, he has the English-language facility, dress, and social skills to associate with any RHS group. He chose an ethnically oriented group of Filipinos (the Filipino hoodies, whom I will discuss later). Art, like Vangie, does not need Mexican affiliations at school to satisfy his social needs. A very Mexican place awaits him at home, a place in which he is comfortable. He has sorted out the requirements of accommodation to school and home; from place to place he switches language and other behavior as needed. Does he feel bicultural? "I feel Mexican-American, but about 80 percent Mexican, a lot more, because I only talk English here at school."

Felipe Garcia has two close Mexican friends, though one of them is not very Mexican, and many more non-Mexican friends. He explains this by "the situation I was in." Specifically, he was interested in sports and academic success, so his friends were drawn from athletic and college-prep students, "where I don't think there's many Hispanic kids." Thinking that he had gone too far in depicting himself as non-Hispanic, he added, "You have to understand me, you know, because all my friends know that I'm Hispanic, and in my house we speak Spanish."

The homes of many students also are tangled ethnically. Take the case of Sylvia Baca's younger brother. He wants to be white, Sylvia says with disappointment. "He goes, 'I'm not no Mexican. Don't even talk to me at school. I don't want my friends to know that I'm Mexican.' My parents think he's joking. He's not." Sylvia, in contrast, has only Mexican friends, goes occasionally to the Spanish mass, speaks fluent Spanish, and wants her own children to be bilingual. "I'm really proud of being Mexican," she says, but when I asked her what was important to know about her if I wanted to know her well, she placed being Mexican low on her list, preceded by her plans to go to college, her school activities, and her hopes for the future. Rarely did any student we interviewed rank "being Mexican" high on their list of salient personal qualities. Future plans, gender, interests, occasionally religion—these and other attributes took precedence when we asked students to sort out what they saw as their important identifying characteristics. I imagine that the set of characteristics and their rank order will change in time, since I believe that what I have been learning from RHS students about ethnicity is not necessarily what I'd learn if we asked them the same questions in ten, twenty, or thirty years. Perceptive students are aware of this. Maria comments on several younger friends who, by her standards, appear to be strongly Mexican.

It's sort of like a phase. It's like everyone has been through it. Because, like, I used to be like that. I don't know what it is. It's like you're into being Mexican, or something. I was like that in the eighth grade. I had no other friends but Mexican, you know. I hated everyone else. And just everything I said, you know, just had to do with that. It's funny because everyone—lots of other people go through it, too.

Most Mexican students live in accordance with a linguistic map that directs where they will and will not speak Spanish. It includes places where they must speak Spanish, however begrudgingly, as with their elders and others who speak little or no English; where they may speak Spanish, as with parents and others who know English but remain much more comfortable in Spanish; and where they will not speak Spanish, as with siblings and friends who, even if they know Spanish, mutually insist on English. Where things count most for Mexican students, at school and with peers, Spanish lacks the cachet of English. They try to use English everywhere they can, notwithstanding their projection that should they have children, they think they'd want their children to be able to speak Spanish. They think this about a hypothetical future, while in the present they often resist speaking Spanish in the home places where it is natural to do so. Paradoxically, speaking Spanish is the behavior of strangers. To adolescents, speaking English is irresistibly a prerequisite for becoming and being a friend.

My Spanish, it's OK, I guess. I only speak it when I have to. You know, when people come over that don't know English. My mom, mostly I talk English to her, but sometimes, you know, when she don't understand me, I speak Spanish. Mostly, I speak English. I don't know. It's better. I like it, yeah.

It is easier for students to learn how to traverse their linguistic territory than the general ethnic territory of school and community, because the latter is a more complex "place." There, English is spoken and unambiguously esteemed. Furthermore, their color, appearance, and accent often may complicate or preclude their passage into the ranks of deracinated Americans, unlike the Sicilians for whom being just American suffices. Such passage closed to them, Mexican-American students deal with the worlds separated and joined by their hyphens.

One household's hyphenated loyalties rode the streets of Riverview on the back of a van that had pulled up at RHS to collect students for the ride home after school. The bumper stickers were arrayed as shown in the illustration. The Mexican students who use the van carry about a mobile celebration of the American football team, the American military, and the Mexican state of Chihuahua, undoubtedly the original home of the van's owners.

```
                    ┌─────────────────┐
                    │  Dallas Cowboys │
                    └─────────────────┘

┌────────────────┐  ┌─────────────────┐  ┌──────────────┐
│ Para gente buena│  │ The few, the proud│  │              │
│   CHIHUAHUA    │  │     MARINES      │  │  Chihuahua   │
└────────────────┘  └─────────────────┘  └──────────────┘
```

One school of thought advises celebrating the two worlds joined by the hyphen because it sees richness and opportunity in having two cultural wellsprings to inform and shape one's life. Appreciating the potential richness and opportunity, however, may be possible only when there is no tension or conflict between the two cultural realms. When values and behaviors are postulated in contrary either-or terms—the parent-preferred chaperoned dates for females, and no dating at all until they are eighteen, or the student-preferred unchaperoned dates for females beginning at age thirteen or fourteen—then students see little to celebrate in their Mexican world. For such students there is a war to be fought and won, the hoped-for victory to be chalked up on the American side of their identity. Americans date young, Americans speak English, Americans don't have to accompany their parents to the supermarket and translate for them. In many important ways, Mexican students find it easier to be American. Yet family and peer group admonish, "Be proud of your heritage," and thereby hangs their tale of ambiguous, diffuse identity.

The family, of course, has a powerful pull. Its particular ethnic orientation is the source not only of the conflict over the proper conditions of dating, but also of the embracing warmth of tradition and memory:

When I go home, my mom's in the kitchen making food. I can smell that. Then my dad sometimes has this Spanish music blasting. They talk in Spanish. So when I go in there I automatically feel the atmosphere of it. When I come to school in the morning, it's mixed. There's a lot of different atmospheres, so I can't really pinpoint one.

The school does not have the affective web of the home, that ineffable combination of mother, mother tongue, aromas, warmth, and love, but it is the prime arena for establishing oneself as an acceptable adolescent, which at RHS entails many behavioral patterns, most of them differing markedly from the preferences of many Mexican homes.

Accordingly, senior Jack Ramos says that when he sits in class he thinks about being someone else.

Sometimes, I would be in a black culture. Or an Italian. I just don't know why. I'll see, like, a couple of my black friends talking about how their family treats each other and I wonder how it feels. Sometimes, I think about that. I get these funny feelings.

Earlier Jack had told me that he feels 100 percent Mexican and 100 percent American. "I'm proud of being Mexican but I speak English, too, same as everybody else." With his "same as everybody else" comment, Jack marks a special impetus that drives adolescent behavior. He means, of course, to be the same as one of the acceptable groups of somebody elses from which students can choose.

Junior Rita Mendoza expresses comparable sentiments. She, too, has thought about what it would be like to be of a different ethnic group, and has some uneasiness about being Mexican: "I guess there's some things that . . . the way my parents are, you know, they don't really know me. I don't think they know me the way I really am." And who is the daughter that her parents do not really know? "When I think about myself," Rita says, "I don't feel like I'm different from anybody else. I mean my nationality." Feeling different from non-Mexicans, Rita's parents do not know the self of their daughter who feels just like "anybody else," which is to say the self of Rita who feels American. Rita's mother is like Lupe's, whose "mother is always saying marry Mexican, Mexican, Mexican, a Mexican born here." The "born here" qualification of Lupe's mother indicates her preference for an Americanized Mexican. Thus, being American is acceptable if it is an attribute of a Mexican, a distinction that may not be perfectly clear to Lupe's brothers and sisters. Lupe believes her mother is reflecting some unpleasant experiences with her Mexican-born husband, whose behavior she sees as typically Mexican male. Lupe's mother presses her own ethnic blend upon Lupe as the ideal.

Gina Perez combats her parents in a way I never heard any Mexican male student articulate. Both of her parents were born in Mexico; she is the first generation of her family to be born in the United States. Gina's parents want her to go to church, be active in La Raza, the student Hispanic organization, date Mexican boys, and have many children. Each of her parents' specific concerns is anathema to her. Feeling branded as Mexican by these concerns, she struggles to clarify who she is and can be, at the price of being uncomplimentary to those who inescapably are "her people."

When I grew up I was kinda, like, I saw Mexican as low. I didn't want anyone to think of me that way. So in school I never ever associate with Mexicans. I don't even think of going out with one. Mexicans totally turn me off. A lot of Mexicans look at school, "Oh, God, I don't want to go." Mexicans are known to be really lazy. I want to go to school. I look at myself as wanting to be someone more than what a Mexican would settle down to. And here I am from two full-blooded parents, you know, that come from Mexico. I'm proud of being a Mexican, but I consider myself more a white Mexican than a Mexican. I don't know if that makes sense.

Gina fights with her parents. Vangie is past that point with her parents. They have never told her she must marry a Mexican, but she knows that she must not bring home a black boyfriend or they'd "kick me out. To them it's something big. I guess they grew up like that. To me it doesn't really make no difference." In this view she has much company among fellow students.

Ethnic parents of the immigrant generation tend to hold fast to the orthodoxy of in-group marriages, particularly for their daughters. They struggle, usually unsuccessfully, to preserve this pillar of their ethnic edifice. When they relinquish it, as they do under pressure from their Americanizing children, they open a door to more and more relinquishing. When they resist marriage to a non-Mexican, they do so in the name of holding fast to ethnic sanctity. Failing in this, they face the array of persons their children may possibly bring home. Then they resist marriage to particular non-Mexicans in the name of social class and other notions they use to define social desirability, race being one of the prime notions.

Michele Gomez, who spent her first ten years in Mexico and her last six years in Riverview, is at peace with her parents. She has not reacted against things Mexican because her parents have not demanded her conformity to things she cannot accept. Her observations sound mature and reflective; she lacks the tension that characterizes Gina's presentation of herself. Her words have a matter-of-fact tone of realism as she says one need not be ashamed of where one came from as one adapts to the needs of living in a new society. Old ways, which she says she tried at first to retain, don't work.

I live in America so I have to act like an American. I do have a feeling for Mexico; that's where I grew up, you know, but that's all. Some kids from Mexico say they don't want to learn English because I'm not American. I go, "If you don't want to be an American, you don't have to consider yourself *all* American. You can act like everyone else and just feel good for what you are, you know."

Feeling "good for what you are" is conventional wisdom at RHS; it is an ideal that is not limited just to students whose ethnic attachments complicate the matter of coming to terms with who they are. The attachment, however, often an entanglement, adds a complicating dimension to the quest for feeling good, but primarily as it relates to managing disjunctures between the demands of home, school, and society.

At school, non-newcomer Mexicans basically see being Mexican as a fact of little consequence, as I learned when I asked students if being Mexican affected their life in and out of class. Specifically, did being Mexican make a difference regarding the grades they got, how teachers treated them, being popular, getting elected to office, who'd they vote for, what clubs they'd join, success in sports, getting in trouble, getting their share of what the school had to offer? Overwhelmingly, students saw little or no relationship between their ethnicity and any of these points: it was neither helpful nor unhelpful to be Mexican. Did they have to compromise their feelings as Mexicans or did they have to give up any part of who they were? Again, overwhelmingly no. But many recalled times in class when they were conscious of being Mexican because the teacher had asked them to help out a newcomer with language problems, or had called on them to explain something that related to Mexico or to Mexicans in America.

They also recalled feeling sensitive about being Mexican when someone made a remark that stereotyped Mexicans. One of the surest ways to antagonize students, regardless of the strength of their ethnic identity, is to stereotype their group. Says Rudy Tiscareno:

I like to be me. I don't like to be taken as a whole group. Like some people stereotype—all Hispanics do this, all Hispanics do that. I want to be an individual, also. I'm part of the group which has certain characteristics, but I also have some characteristics that set me apart.

Academically successful Mexican students take especially hard the stereotype of Mexicans as ignorant and lazy, and the surprise they see in non-Mexicans who observe them being successful.

In contrast to the uniformity of the stereotypic picture, students lay out the variety of types of persons who share the designation "Mexican." "I don't pay attention to color, all the different shades of lightness and darkness," begins senior Teresa Rodriguez, though she has paid enough attention to have noted that Mexicans vary by color, a basis for social distinctions made by Mexicans and non-Mexicans alike. "I pay attention to their personality," she adds, liking them for what they do or don't do. Teresa continues:

Some Mexicans are really mod and new-wavers. Some are dressed like they came from the slum. There's some smart Mexicans, some stupid Mexicans. It's all mixed. There's rich ones, some poor ones. A lot are poor. And then some Mexicans act like they're white. Yeah, wannabes, you know, want-to-bes. A lot of whites act like they're Mexican, though.

Teresa easily categorizes her fellow students as she does herself. She admits to being a wannabe,[1] and it is a white American that she wants to be. She goes to Mexico regularly. When she is there, she says about Mexicans, "They're my kind of people, but I would hate to be like them." She clarifies, however, that "I'm not like a total American. I picture Americans as you go out and do whatever you want, but, you know, I'm held back because of my parents and living their tradition."

Teresa's friend Rudy, also in college-prep, says in response to my question about whether it is necessary to act white to succeed, "You got to conform. Most of the people that are up in the high classes, like, you know, competing, like, in college-prep classes, they conform more to the white, you know, the proper English, etc., the dress." Rudy is heading in a direction that distances him from many of his fellow ethnics. He has had to reject invitations—to get high, for example—that did not fit his sense of self that is "thinking ahead," "striving for the future," and "planning to live in a better place." Another thing to point out, he concludes, "is that the ones that are striving ahead tend to conform more." Rudy's very Americanized parents refer to "playing the game," rather than "acting white to succeed," explaining that you can't get a decent job without proper English:

You can't go to a job interview and say, "Hey man, I want to get this job, man." You have to make eye contact. I've been trying to tell the kids, you know, I guess it's a matter of playing the game. It doesn't hurt. I think you can do it within reason, you know, without sacrificing your principles.

On the face of it, Mexican students are, except for newcomers and a few with distinctive hair, makeup, and dress, much like non-Mexican students in appearance and comportment. They fit in and they belong.

---

1. I will discuss elsewhere the phenomenon of wannabes.

Behind their generally successful accommodation to the school's social life (their high dropout rates indicate less successful academic careers) are a welter of issues they need to settle. The issues derive from the bicultural nature of their lives. The character and extent of their involvement in each culture is highly variable, but increasingly favors their American side. As adolescents, the two cultures are represented for them by home and school; for some, a barrio neighborhood is an additional ethnic factor; for all, the larger community and American society is the encapsulating reality. The deck is loaded in favor of becoming American. Still, the students' primary socialization is at home, where parents, themselves variably responsive to the imperatives of acculturation, have the first chance to establish what language is spoken, what food is deemed tasty, how male and female roles are played, what the proper relationship to authority is, how one should feel about being Mexican in America—in short, the impact of home, as Teresa put it, is toward "living their tradition."

The impact of the world outside is toward "being the same as everyone else," being just a person, which is to say, being American. Where homes have not been substantially Americanized, the students are conscious of the tension between the ties of home and the powerful pull of conformity to school and society. Students learn they can cash in on their ethnic identity, in that it provides special access to some academic and occupational opportunities, but they learn further that non-Mexicans honor being Mexican primarily as a nominal designation. As a defining designation, it is a condition from which to withdraw, as they see in the generally negative response of society to the most Mexican Mexicans in their midst—the "wetback" newcomers—who know the pain of being a stranger.

There are no evangelists as such saying to the Mexican side of each Mexican-American student, "Cast out the old man of your sinful Mexican self so that you can be born again as a new man, an American man." But there might as well be. From school and community, students learn not to reject their own (and other's) ethnic self; but what they learn to honor is chiefly what is least consequential about that self—food, music, and pageantry.

Blacks

Who students learn to be and who they are allowed to be interacts with their own sense of who they are and mean to be. They bring the outcome of this process, the complex jumble that is their identity in general, and their ethnic identity in particular, to the multitude of circumstances of

their lives. Different aspects of their identity are evoked. The point is
that ethnicity, black or otherwise, is not a fixed set of attributes, or even
a varying set of attributes that is differentiated simply in the usual ways,
that is, by age, gender, socioeconomic status, etc. It does vary by these
facts, but also, for individuals with a given life history, as the events and
circumstances of their lives change. This is Okamura's "situational ethnicity" (1981). Ethnicity, then, is a configuration, like those that emerge
from the assembling and reassembling pieces in a kaleidoscope. With
each turn of events, different attributes of ethnicity emerge, but, unlike
a kaleidoscope, the pieces do not necessarily remain the same.

Yolanda Scott is knowingly different from situation to situation.
When she is with her Filipino friends she does not "really act black,"
though she does not think she acts Filipino either. She prefers to think
that she acts "just like a human being." When she is with black people
she tends "to act like black people. It depends on your surroundings."
"Acting black" (or Mexican or Filipino, for that matter) is not a term I
made up. Though hard put to elaborate on it, students could use it certain they would be understood. Black students had other ways of stating
how one could act, as in "you're acting your color" or "you're acting like a
nigger." Muriel Ross's mother used both expressions when she wanted
to communicate the undesirability of something Muriel was doing; both
are pejorative, never to be mistaken for a compliment. How "acting
black" is construed depends on the context and tone of voice in which it
is uttered.

Michele Williams, sophomore, sixteen-year-old mother of one child,
and full-time student determined to graduate from high school, fits well
the stereotype of the tough black because she, by her own admission,
loves to fight. In fact, I don't believe she reinforces any stereotype.

For a month now I've been putting off fighting this girl. See, when she went
and started that trouble with me, you know, that made me real upset. If we do
fight, it won't be nowhere around this school. Then I won't have to get suspended for it. Everytime I say I'm not gonna fight her, she brings more lies up
and, see, by her doing that, it's just making me even madder. I just want to get
her.

All the sophomores like to fight. I mean, I even like to fight. I try to stay
away from it, but I tell you the truth, I do like to fight. It's just in my blood.
That'd be my best subject if I had that in school.

If you're the same color, try to stick together instead of fighting. That's
what I tried to tell Latrece, but she don't look past that. So, only alternative I
have is to fight. Ain't gonna be no talking, until after the fight. I tried to explain it to her. I just said, well, how we should be together, friends, united,

close. M. L. King wasn't saying his dream for nothing. He meant something. Like he said he would like black and whites to walk together. I feel we should walk together, too.

See, some white kids are prejudice against other whites, and some blacks are prejudice against other blacks. They just jealous of their own color. I couldn't be jealous of my own color because I like my color; I wouldn't give it up for nothing. Some kids is just like that. Some kids around here, they're white, but they're trying their best to be black. I don't know what's so special about black people, though, except they a little darker than white ones. A lot of black kids want to be white. They be trying to talk like they white, sophisticated and all that.

Students such as Yolanda Scott, whose social and academic life regularly includes persons from different ethnic groups, become adept at fitting in. The breadth of their personal accommodations promotes not bicultural but multicultural competencies.[2] Warren Thomas also is such a student; his accommodations begin with his father's side of the family, which contains "black, white, Mexican, Indian, and Chinese," and, in the view of his divorced mother with whom he lives, is "watered down." Warren is definite about never wishing to be anything but black, but "sometimes," he says, "I have to act black."

Sometimes I have to say "I be going, yeah, what about it." I have to talk that way so I don't get talked about and beat up. Like, say, I go downtown. If I go there talking like I am now [to me], they, you know, will just stare at me saying, "Look at that nigger trying to act white." When I'm around them I'm going, "Yeah, what's up man? You know, what it is. How it is." Then I go around whites and say, "Yeah, hello."

Half the time I just walk normal black, but when I get around, you know, like my all-black hoodlum friends—well, they aren't friends of mine, I just know them—I just kick back. "What's up, man," and I dip. I dip. The old term for it was the quote "pimp walk." That means, like, to walk laid back, to one side, and you dip. That's weird because I be going, "Dang, I gotta go through all these changes just to fit in."

Like my best friend, he say, "Warren, are you black or are you white?" I change, others change also, but they don't notice it because I don't tell them. Around different people, you have to act, you know, a different way.

Warren notices not just because he is particularly observant, but also because he has lived in Riverview only for five years. Thus, he does not

2. DuBois (1903/1969) referred to the dual consciousness of black Americans. Even if the separation between blacks and whites is not as great as when DuBois wrote his book, sufficient separation persists so that blacks are aware of the duality of their lives.

take for granted what longer-term residents have grown up with all their lives.

The reactions that Warren gets to the way he acts are not uncommon; black youth learn early about the hazards of crossing cultural boundaries. Regina Hodges picks up on the concept of the "wannabe" to clarify how she behaves. Knowing the sometimes negative connotation of being a wannabe, she distinguishes "wanting to be white" from "just acting white," trusting that she will be taken as an instance of the latter. She is sensitive to the distinction because she is accused of wanting to be white and runs the risk of being labeled an Oreo. They are the black-outside-white-inside persons who behave, says Regina, as if they are ashamed of being black, who look as if "they're trying to lose their culture and that's something we're trying to hold on to."

From comments on Oreos, Regina moved on to discuss the reactions her behavior elicits from her grandparents.

My grandparents say I act like a white person, that I talk proper, and all that stuff. I do act black [she says emphatically]. Sometimes, I'm in certain moods and certain places, I'll act white. I don't know the difference; I just act. When I'm conservative, they say I act white. I don't know the difference. I can tell when I'm acting black: I have a good time, most of the time. Like most black people, when they're having fun, they're loud, they laugh, they joke around a lot.

In their [her grandparent's] day, when they were growing up, they have education, you know, but they still say, "I ain't" and "I isn't." You know, those southern accents. Like, I can say them [the "accents"] and then I can not say them. I can talk proper and I can talk slang if I want to. They think by me, I be talking white, then they say I'm being a little ritzy or I'm being proper, around white people too much.

I wonder if it is just an adolescent Regina or a Regina socialized by the cultural mix of Riverview's schools that separates her from her grandparents.

Regina also makes her own distinctions between acting black and acting appropriately in boy-girl contacts, between being a guy and being a black guy, between always looking at color and sometimes not. She had recently met a young man who appealed to her because he did not "act like a black guy."

He just acted like a guy. He didn't act like a black guy, 'cause if he would've come up like a black guy saying, "Hey, mama, what you doin'?" I'd say, "None of your biz. Get along." He came acting like he had manners. He was cultured and mature. I don't look at color—sometimes, certain ways. It depends on how the black guy acts toward you. If he act like a black guy toward you, then you have to act like a black girl towards him. If he acts like just a guy or a person, there's no problem.

Warren's peers and Regina's grandparents communicate their sense of unacceptable behavior. Warren and Regina have their own standards, feeling right about certain ways of acting and talking that they realize represent departures from norms to which other members of their group subscribe. Each spends hours daily in the school environment where these other standards have deep-rooted currency. Each keeps company with whites, an unaccustomed fact to their detractors, and each makes a distinction that is lost on their detractors: acting and being white are not the same. Regina articulates the distinction:

You know, like, if you have a black friend and you all of a sudden never see her with anyone beside a white friend, and she prefers hanging out with white friends—that's one thing. Black kids just hanging out with white kids—that's another thing. I hang out with a lot of white kids. It's nothing. You wouldn't classify me as a wannabe because I never want to be white. I mean, I was with them 'cause they were my friends.

In the social space of Riverview High, the naturalness and ease of cross-group contact—what students refer to as "mingling"—erodes the limiting conventional wisdom of "don't act better than you are," and it defies the place-keeping dispositions that develop under segregated living. I asked Warren if he ever felt he lived in two worlds.

Well, I try, you know, just to bring everything together in one. Like, before I used to. That kinda, you know, made everybody notice that I wasn't black. I tried to be white at the time because most of my friends were white. According to all my friends, I was too polite. I was all polite and people was wondering, "Is cuz black or is cuz white?" What is cuz? I'm going, "I'm black. Why man, why?"

Students in Angelotti's English classes are expected to correspond with other students whom they have not met. Ninth-grader Lucy Washington writes to Angela, her pen pal.

Hows everything been? Fine I hope. I'm black. I like 2 Dance, Model, Sing, And Play Basket Ball. What things do you like 2 do. Whats your race? Yes I like Music Soul, Pop, very little rock . . . . Do you like 2 read Books? I read books every day, and every night.

Lucy writes lightly about being black, placing it as one of a number of identifying characteristics in an overall jaunty-toned letter of the type juveniles write to each other. There is no rank ordering of characteristics here, though when I asked black students about the importance of being black if someone wanted to know them well, they did not rank it highly. In comparative terms, blacks ranked their ethnicity higher than Mexicans. Low rankers were more eloquent, as Becky Thompson makes unequivocally clear. No, she says, it is not necessary to know she is black.

I mean, I figure if you know what your race is, you shouldn't walk around wearing a T-shirt saying, "I'm black and I'm proud." I think it's so stupid. Of course, everybody have to be proud, but, you know, skin color—it's not really a big thing. We don't think about it. You're black, you may be aware of your color. You know what you are and just get on.

Would she tell her own children about being black, I asked her, since Becky has a baby.

I probably would just say there are different races and try not to make them feel lower than we have to be. I wouldn't want them to dwell on that subject. I wouldn't say, "Sit down kids, we're gonna talk about Africa today." No way.

Nonetheless, Becky is very much aware of being black. In the course of our several meetings, she said that she knew it was harder for a black than a white woman to get a job: "That's the only thing that bothers me when I graduate, if that [being black] will be held against me."

When Lucy's ninth-grade classmate Tricia Morgan wrote her pen pal, she described herself and closed with a postscript: "Oh, I hope this doesn't bother you but I thought you would like to know I'm Black, and it's nice to know you." Is Tricia also saying to her pen pal, "I hope you think it will be nice to know me even if I am black"? Tricia's letter has that edge of anticipation that derives from the certain knowledge that even in the best of places, being black may "bother" people.

Black parents do communicate to their children that they prefer black mates for them. "My mother," she says, "'Warren, grow up and marry a nice sister.'" "I go, 'Sure, Mom,' whatever." Black parents may be so distressed by their child's nonblack boyfriend or girlfriend, that the child will hide the romance, as does Warren. He believes his mother would "have a fit" if she knew. The "girls of my race" also are not happy with Warren's white girlfriends, for it has become so common for black males to date nonblack females that many black girls feel resentful and deprived.

My sense from black students is that most black parents, less expressive than Warren's mom, are not explicit about their preferences. Their children, to the contrary, generally feel that it is not necessarily best for them to marry another black, even though they most probably will. Parents operate out of several commitments: ethnic, which says our people should marry each other because they're our people, and practical, which says out-group marriages cause trouble. Students operate out of a commitment to happiness that says what is happy is right, and happiness is possible without ethnic congruence between mates. What to be happy about is one way to think about the outcome of the shaping impact of age and ethnic groups.

Tommy Kenwood, RHS senior, says that his parents raised him to act in certain ways that he thinks of as "black customs." These related generally to believing that "we're all created equal and everybody got an equal chance." Tommy took this to mean that he should treat all people the same and that he should "never let no one put you down" and not "try to be better than no one." Many black students have acquired the same understandings. I infer this from their comments and also from the observations of black students who see themselves as somehow departing from black norms. John Carter is such a student. A junior high teacher told him that everyone had a "fair chance" to improve themselves, "no matter how poor you are." "I thought about that," said John. "And I tried to think of anybody I knew who couldn't live a better life if they tried. And I couldn't think of one person." Still, John did acknowledge that chances for whites and blacks were not equally fair.

If black students won't party, drink, or take drugs, and if they speak "proper" English, get good grades, and hang around with white students, they invite the opprobrious, "Look at that nigger. Who does he think he is?" Traci Barnes describes the extent to which students will go to apply pressure (see Fordham and Ogbu 1986 and Fordham 1988).

Sometimes you'll be in a crowd—they'd go buy wine coolers at lunch, stay late, and come back late to school. They'll pay your way, sometimes. They offer to buy you beer just so you can be with them. They'll offer to buy you weed.

Cynthia Franks says she gets pressure from both directions: from blacks who don't like her being smart and from whites who think she's supposed to be dumb. Bill Compton says he get abuse from black girls because he doesn't dress and walk black enough, and his friend Roger says it is possible to be "too black," a designation he gave to the "super black hoodlum" who was unacceptably tough, rowdy, and macho. Their classmate Elaine Morgan spoke of the personal reactions she got from friends when she was acting "all rowdy, all crazy and loud." "My friends just say, 'You're acting just like a black person.'" Black students spoke more often of the problem of stereotyping by black than by white students.

Ray Thomas stays comfortably within the boundaries of black norms at RHS. He is in the general or noncollege-prep academic program and he is on the track team. Excelling in sports never invites the negative reactions of students from any ethnic group. Ray does nothing that other black students interpret as acting better than he is or as putting others down, unlike Carey, Lashann, and Traci, who do. They are upwardly-mobile seniors who say: "My goals are higher than theirs [other black students]." "There's that group—they don't have any intentions or any goals. They're kinda intent on living right here."

As early as the seventh grade Carey decided that he did not want to end up like his father working in one of the local factories. He is going to college. A year or so ago, thinking that he might be hurting his chances, he changed his behavior.

I started acting up when I was hanging around all my black friends and my grades were slipping. I decided I had to move away, still be friends with them, but move away so I could keep my grades up. Now I just hang around with them at lunch or brunch. Most of them aren't college-prep students. With my white friends, I'm in class and everything.

As a college-prep student, Carey spends all day in classes that contain mostly white students. There is no academically oriented black group. Thus, college-prep classes separate their few black students from most other black students. (The same is true for Mexican students.)

Carey acknowledges that he lives in two "worlds," is comfortable in each, and plans to retain his dual associations. The two-worlds school experiences of Carey and many other students remind them of being black. College-prep Rhonda Tracey is reminded when she sees pregnant ninth-grade black girls. These girls take her back to her own days as a freshman, a crossroads time when she and others were either resisting or adopting behavior that would set the course of their lives, possibly forever. Rhonda was born while her mother was still a high school student. She is further reminded about being black when she sees talented black athletes fail to play on the school team because they cut class and generally neglect their academic careers. Such behavior reminds Rhonda of her father, who got an athletic scholarship but never attended college because there was "no one telling him to go." To Rhonda, lost opportunities is a hallmark of being black.

Rhonda is so adept at fitting in with her nonblack friends that when she does something that reminds them she is black, they take notice—as does Rhonda.

Some of my white friends get offended when I talk about being black. They say, "Oh, everything has to be black." Things like that. And I say, "Well, I can't help it, I was born that way. And it's going to be that way until I die."

This is the sound of the mature, nearly-ready-to-graduate Rhonda. She often appears to her white friends as if, in some sense, she has lost her blackness. Not thinking of Rhonda as black, they take umbrage when reminded that she is.

At the beginning of her junior year, Rhonda recalls, "I found myself not being myself," in that she was acting less black than she meant to be. This was coincident with getting a driver's license and finding herself more and more in the company of white students outside of school. If Rhonda's white friends are sometimes bothered by her behavior, her general-track black friends, those she has kept as she moved her life over closer to the college-bound and their aspirations, are "confused" when they see her with her white friends: "Like how can I be so black and yet be with them? They don't understand."

In a school with several hundred black students I would expect to find a range of responses to any questions I ask. And that, of course, was the case when I invited students to reflect on the impact of being black in regard to the grades they got, how teachers and students reacted to them, their chances of being elected to office, how they voted, feeling self-conscious, popularity, etc. It was rare for a student to indicate that being black made a considerable difference in any of these instances; most often they said it made no difference. "As a black student," I asked, "would I get my fair share of what RHS has to offer?" "Yes" was the answer I almost invariably received, elaborated by one student this way: "You'll always feel comfortable being black in Riverview, I think, because it is so mixed up with races. There's not, like, one specific race that rules everything."

Black students who take exception to the generally sanguine picture of life at RHS for black students are those with a particular consciousness of being black. Dennis Mackey is such a student. He thinks that being black makes a difference to the "high society people" who "think they're better than somebody else." Attuned to what he believes are the perceptions of such people, Dennis says, "I just try to make us look good. I try to do better to make us look good, but not trying to go out and make us look better than anyone else." He also tries to "make examples" for other blacks. Because Dennis feels obliged to alter his behavior in the presence of white people, he categorizes his behavior as compromising himself as a black person. Not wanting to do what "would make us look bad," he holds back, not saying what he would otherwise say if black—

instead of white—people were present, but, he adds, this does not happen often. Carey feels that he can be more black at home than at school, because at school he feels obliged to speak proper English; at home, he can speak any way he wants. Many black students feel otherwise. Preferring to speak proper English, they find themselves chided for speaking a style of English that black adults and peers interpret as "trying to act better than us."[3]

When I asked students if living in a basically white country created confusion about their black identity, they answered with a virtually uniform no. They were clear about being black Americans. Africa did not signify to them what Mexico signifies to many Mexican parents and students. One black senior explained that he did not feel "related" to Africans.

They have nothing to do with me. A more intellectually active black might think "These are our people." Personally, the South Africa thing, I feel bad for them, but not really because they're black, but because they're human beings.

Many fewer were clear about whether they needed to act white if they hoped to be a success. Some students responded with an unqualified no. Some thought that just being themselves would suffice for success, possibly unaware of the extent to which they had mastered several behavioral registers that they applied in different situations. Darryl Anderson preferred to redefine the terms, so that it was not a matter of whether he had to act white, but of whether he had to act "kind of proper." And he thought he did. "In some cases you might have to act white," conceded one student, but she explained that:

I think you should just be yourself, and if employers can't accept that, then they're not worth it. People should keep their cultural background. If their boss doesn't like it, then that's discrimination. If God wanted everybody to be the same, he would have made them all one color.

This is easy for her to say because except for her color there is nothing about her language and presentation of self that could stereotype her as "black." Her sense of being black is unalloyed; her conduct allows her to operate in the two worlds—insofar as they are distinct—of black and white.

3. In Ferguson's notion of diglossia (1964), there is a high and low version of a language, with prestige generally attached to the high version even though the low version is the one children learn as their mother tongue. For blacks there is a high and low version of English. The low version, the so-called dialect, slang, or black English, often is their mother tongue. When students replace it with the high version, or proper English, they may be alternately complimented or criticized, depending on where they are.

None of the students overtly addressed the complexity of being black. To do so would entail a capacity to stand back from oneself that is seldom within the competency of adolescents (and not particularly common among older persons either). Students differ in their degree of self-awareness. Benny Hogan ranks among the most astutely self-aware students I interviewed. I quote him at length, as I do Beth Robertson afterward, because they so strikingly indicate the complexity of their ethnic identity. Benny, a Riverview native, is a senior, a fine athlete, and undecided about post-graduation schooling, knowing only that he does not now plan to attend college and he wants to live in Riverview.

I know I'm black, but people here kind of have the idea they have to act a certain way because they're black. So, sometimes I ask the question of myself, "Do I want to do this, but I'm not doing it just because I'm black?" Like they expect you to not dress a certain way and not act a certain way because you are black.

A lot of times when black people talk proper, other blacks see them as wanting to act white. That isn't necessarily true. I think you should take pride in your speech and use proper grammar. It's not necessarily black or white. If you get into the habit of "y'all this and y'all that," then when you get in an environment where you mean to use positive speech, you won't be able to use it.

If you're black and you're talking to a white person, you want to show them that you have intelligence. If you use proper English, that's the easiest way to show you have intelligence. Actually, I like to speak proper English. I don't consider it white man's English. It's just English. Actually, I like to speak it myself because it shows I have accumulated some knowledge over the years. With my friends I say, like, "Ain't you comin' over?"

Actually, I think, deep in my unconscious, I'm speaking proper now because I don't have any classes anymore where you really can use your intelligence. So, I just like to use it.

When I think of who I am, I mean [it] in a religious not a racial sense. Black or white, it doesn't make any difference because I just see myself as Christian. I think my first—well, I really wouldn't say my first obligation is to be a Christian, but to be a good person.

Benny might be speaking from an adolescent stance of "I want to be me so don't hem me in with conformities—unless they're of my own choosing." But he also might be speaking from a black stance that would use precisely the same language, taking exception to conformities that derive from black adult expectations about being black. He concludes by opting for the universal category of Christian, and instantly changes that choice for the even more universal one of "good person." Benny comfortably speaks both "slang" and "proper" English, though he feels intellectually challenged in the domains that call for proper English. Knowing he is intelligent, he likes to feel intelligent, which is how he felt in the college-prep classes that he dropped in his senior year.

Beth Robertson, another Riverview native, is a sophomore about to complete her second year in the college-prep track. Beth, somewhat less articulate than Benny, is much less likely to go off in her own directions from the point of a question I asked. Nonetheless, she speaks comfortably as she expands on her written response to questions I had previously asked her.

AP: I see that of your three best friends, one is black, one is white, and one is Italian. If I'd given you five spaces, would you have included a Mexican and a Filipino?

BR: Not a Filipino. I have Filipino friends, but they're not my best friends.

AP: You say that influence of your ethnicity on what clubs you join is both helpful and unhelpful.

BR: I guess that question is asking me does it matter which groups I join because of my color. I guess, yeah, because I know next year I'm gonna join the Black Student Union.

AP: OK, so that's an influence in a helpful direction, would you say?

BR: Yeah.

AP: And it's unhelpful?

BR: Because it's like the club is set up for black people, right? But then it's unhelpful because I don't feel like I should be in a club just because of color. I think it would be helpful to me, like telling you that there's no limitations to what you can do because of your color, and learning about black people. Something that can help me better myself.

AP: I would have guessed that someone who felt as you do would have blacks as best friends.

BR: I guess I'm pretty unusual. It's just real important to me that you would know that I like being me. I'm proud to be me. It's just like saying that I have to be me. My friends, they're from different ethnic groups, but they know how I feel.

AP: But who you are does not seem to influence who your choice of friends is.

BR: Right. Because people are people. It doesn't matter to me what color they are. I'm black. I'm different. People—if I like them and they like me, it doesn't matter at all, the color, just as long as we relate to each other.

Beth presents the varied picture of one who has grown up in a stable, integrated school and community. Two of her three best friends are not black. She intends to join the Black Student Union, looking forward to getting support there for the notion that color is not a barrier to the progress of black students. She feels somewhat uncomfortable about the union's single ethnic focus because she goes beyond her own ethnic group for ordinary social contacts. Having made several references to color in its possibly negative or constraining capacity, she concludes with the universalist pronouncement often heard at RHS that "people are people," and, accordingly, that color is not a factor in her social affairs.

Black students make their way toward self-identity in a social setting where being black bears considerably less stigma than it does most places in America.[4] Though not free of the horrors of stereotyping and rejection, their lives at RHS allow them easy access to nonblacks, from casual contacts to becoming best friends and partners in romance. In doing so they risk the accusations of "wannabe" or "acting uppity" by ethnic fellows who, not sharing their cultural journey, react with varying degrees of antagonism. These fellows base accusations of "acting white" on perceived modifications in speech, dress, walk, and social contacts, reserving their strongest condemnation for those who appear actually to reject being black in favor of being white or Mexican or Filipino. But as black students modify their behavior, they open doors to friendships otherwise closed to them.

The doors to friendship open in many directions because unlike the situation in the earlier days of Riverview, a single ethnic group no longer defines acceptability. Acceptability appears to have been taken over by mainstream American forms of behavior that at RHS are also shaped by generally favored black preferences in music, dance, fashion, language, communicative style, and "being cool" (Stanlaw and Peshkin 1988). No other ethnic group has been comparably influential, notwithstanding that blacks compose a minority (about one-third) of the total student population. No other ethnic group confronts itself with such an array of admonitions: acting ritzy, sophisticated, or proper; acting black, your color, or like a nigger; acting better than you are, white, or uppity. And, therefore, no other ethnic group displays so extensively the ambiguity of identity that characterizes students at RHS.

Filipinos

Some Filipino students have parents who attended RHS and grandparents who live in town or in the vicinity. Most of the students, how-

---

4. Peter Murrell's (1989) concept of resilience, developed under conditions of dual socialization, comes to mind.

ever, are the first members of the Filipino three-generation families to be born in the United States, though some arrived as young children. Their families generally enjoy economic success, while retaining linguistic, familial, and cultural ties to their intermittently visited homeland. If returning "home" is more difficult and less frequent for them than for Mexicans, Filipino memories of home are vivid to the parent generation as they mediate the tensions, for themselves and for their children, between remaining Filipino and becoming American.

Filipino parents, having benefited from the economic opportunities that often result from schooling, ardently support their children's school efforts, expecting that more schooling is better than less and that financial rewards are its natural payoff. Since Riverview's Filipino parents model the schooling–economic benefits connection, their children cannot doubt its feasibility. Accordingly, Filipino students attend school understanding the economic promise of America and being American.

Much as they have acculturated, Filipino parents have not fully shed their traditional cultures. Just what resistance they face in transmitting to their children those aspects they still cherish became clear when I spoke to Alex Ramiro. Alex came to California from the Philippines as a preschooler, so his first-hand memories of any other land and life are vague. He is a senior, expecting to attend a community college after graduation. In the course of many hours of discussion I asked him to talk about what he found to be the most fun at school.

For myself, it's a lot of fun going to the football games and really getting into the spirit of the school. You know, win, win, win, and beat Corinth. Even though you're not on the football team, it feels like it when you're cheering for them and they win.

Clearly, Alex has become a full-fledged Tiger, a RHS Tiger. Schools may be instrumental to his parents, means to vocational ends; to Alex too they may be this, but they are also more. Alex enters the intimate recesses of American culture and society when he wears the mantle of spirited school fan. Being a fan takes one into the realm of friends; entry and acceptance requires passing competency "tests" of linguistic, social, and other behavioral skills relating to fitting in. Alex fits in. In Riverview, Americans look like people named Ramiro, whose parents speak an alien tongue, when they want to. With a Ramiro admitted, the rank of friend becomes still more inclusive.

The parents of Donna Rodriguez keep a tight rein on their children. Part of their strictness is attributable to tradition, but no small part derives from their fear of the risks that children run in their adopted land of the free which, to their taste, is too free for American adolescents regarding drugs, sex, and rejection of authority. The Rodriguezes do not have such children, nor do their children want to be such children. Still, the young Rodriguezes must deal with strong parental constraints. In doing so, they sound somewhat like many Mexican students, and not at all like any of the black students to whom I talked. Many Mexican and Filipino students seem to be in the process of working out a relationship with their parents that relates to ethnic-based matters. Donna takes an active hand in molding the process. In the course of discussing her family life, she refers to several of the issues that arise in the matter of shaping the identity of Filipino students.

I don't think I'd be comfortable there [the Philippines] because I've been raised here all my life and I got so used to America that I want to stay here. I don't consider the Philippines as my home. I do because I was born there, but it'd be hard for me to get used to it. I would say this is my home more than that. I was born there but I'm used to the traditions here.

I feel like I'm half and half, sort of, because when I go to my house I'm back to the Filipino way. When I'm here [at RHS], I hang around Filipinos, but then in class I talk to all different kinds of people. On weekends, I'll hang around different crowds, different ethnics.

At home my parents talk to me in their language, but then, for some reason, I feel I sort of trained them to get used to my surrounding, like what time I have to be home, independence, you know, independence as a teenager. I trained them because before they'd give me, "You can't go out till you're eighteen." I've gotten them used to that boys call me and we'll talk about homework, their girlfriends, etc.

I feel about 80 percent American and 20 percent Filipino. My parents, I think they're 70 percent Filipino and 30 percent American. Opposite to me, yeah, because they don't forget. They're used to what they grew up with. When I get married and have a future, I'll probably raise my kids the way my parents raised me, but around the environment and traditions of America. I think they'll be somewhere, I think, 90–10, mostly American.

Donna tempers a substantial degree of traditional filial respect with her qualification that "We're living here in America now. You gotta get used to it here." So far she has managed to find her way between the poles of both perspectives. The Philippines is home, but she is at home in America. Tagalog is her parents' language; English is her language, technically not her mother tongue, but it has acquired this status. Daily ties of intimacy attach her to the non-American roots of her identity; daily they are overlaid by her astute management of her parent's wishes for her and by her abiding intent to be an American teenager.

For cross-cultural childrearing, there is no Dr. Spock to guide Filipino and other ethnic parents. The theories have not even been articulated that would support the airing of controversy. What prevails is experience, but it is experience contested by Americanizing children, ethnic neighbors, and spouses. The messages from mainstream America are clear: become American; if what you retain of your tradition is quaint, tasty, and entertaining, then you are OK; keep private what is not quaint, tasty, or entertaining.

Such messages do not square with the fact that Donna Rodriguez's parents only know one way of being parents. Donna, literally, teaches them variations on their parenting themes. Donna is an uncommon young woman. Mostly, Filipino parents manifest one of several different models, including continuing conflict with their children, indifference, differential strictness for their male and female children, or shared ideals that are primarily American, Filipino, or a blend. In any event, Filipino students undergo a comparatively uniform socialization experience at school, whereas they come from homes with varied patterns of socialization regarding their identity and its ethnic component.

Jeff Hilado's home is Filipino in language spoken, food served, pictures hung on the wall, and persons visiting. Jeff's parents have never talked to him about being Filipino, they welcome to their home Jeff's non-Filipino girlfriends, and they "just let me be what I want to be." Yet his mother, a resident in America for twenty years, is "not used to being here" and wants to return to the Philippines to live.

Billy Salazar, American-born, a junior in the college-prep track, has Filipino-born parents who, he says, try to instill in him a Filipino identity. Billy is pleased that he speaks Tagalog. His cousins can speak to their parents only in English. This strikes him as wrong: Tagalog is the proper language of a Filipino home. Because of their experience with his older sister "who married a Caucasian," his parents have relaxed their expectations for in-group marriages. On the one hand, Billy has not turned away from his Filipino identity: "I get a sense of great feeling of my country" on the occasions when Filipinos organize a cultural night, and "I'd like to go back and see my ancestors." On the other, he says his parents are not particularly intent upon sustaining Filipino ways but that they are so strict he tends "to lean more toward the American pole than the Filipino pole because I don't like the Filipino pole at all." In response to a question asking if he felt he was a different person at home and at school, he said, "No, it doesn't really cross my mind."

On the face of it, Billy appears full of contradictions: he has great feeling for his country—the Philippines, and he endorses Tagalog as the language of home. Then, he does not like the Filipino pole at all and he believes himself to be no different at school than at home. I believe that both sets of statements are "true" for Billy in some sense that Billy may not be able to clarify. I believe that the Billys of RHS live in a swirl of commitments and dispositions that may never get sorted out unless precipitated by the demands of a romance, a family crisis, or an aversive event either here or in the Philippines. In the meantime, he expresses no need to sort out his feelings. Experiencing no conflict, what is there for him to sort out?

Alex Ramiro sorts things out between home and school. "I'm more relaxed out here at school," he says. "I think I get really tired at home," where there is "a lot of respect, you know, so when they say 'jump,' I say 'how high?'" Indeed, there is a lot of respect at home, demanded by parents who for all their easy access to American culture through their considerable linguistic fluency do not relinquish their strong, traditional authority that demands respect for parents and family. This is a recurring theme among Filipino students: "I've got to respect my elders" and "We never forget that family has first priority."

The lower incidence of parent-child conflict among Filipinos compared to Mexicans may be attributable to the fact that while both endorse strong parental authority and familial respect, the Filipinos do so in a more Americanized context. Thus, there is less for Filipino children to war with their parents about, though Filipino girls, like Mexican girls, often chafe at dating restrictions. Parental preference for a Filipino mate has succumbed to the reality that children marry according to their own choice, so that personal taste, not ethnic orthodoxy, is the applicable measure. "My parents like him," Billy says about his sister's non-Filipino boyfriend, "and gradually they're seeing that it doesn't matter. Their daughter's happy." Ethnic orthodoxy is not a condition for love to emerge. Love eludes conditions and boundaries. Riverview's non-Filipinos see Filipinos as candidates for friendship and for love, and Filipinos hold reciprocal perceptions.

"I'd like to learn my own language," said one Filipino student. "I'm so embarrassed because I don't speak my language," said another. Both of these fluent English-speakers refer to Tagalog as their language. "When I was little I knew the language really well, but I came to the U.S. and I didn't need the language any more. So when, like, elders, they talk to me I just say 'yeah,' 'no,' 'I don't know.'" This particular student is not embarrassed by her inability to speak Tagalog, she is indifferent. Others try unsuccessfully to speak Tagalog: "I can understand it, but it won't come out of my mouth." With at least one generation of Tagalog-speakers present in their lives, often two, Filipino students grow up conscious of the language; it figures in their lives in the variable ways suggested above. Some say they would gladly sign up for courses in Tagalog if RHS offered them, possibly motivated by the feeling of being left out when the family congregates at a grandparent's home: "They're talking and you can hear your name in it." Current student interest in such courses could prove no more durable than it was in the 1970s when RHS taught Tagalog and then dropped it after enrollments declined. I never heard either parents or students argue that maintaining a Filipino identity necessitated acquiring facility in Tagalog. In the absence of such a commitment, and notwithstanding the romantic notions of some students that they want their children to know Tagalog, the determining fact about language and Filipino identity may be, "I didn't need the language any more."

In the matter of locating themselves on a Filipino-American continuum, students unhesitatingly know where they are. Very few feel more Filipino than American. Still, the Philippines is not just another country in the world: they return too often, have too many relatives there, and see too much of the Philippines in their parents' lives to be blasé about "home." This home, however, is not where they live and only tenuously where their heart is. Of course, they avow loyalty—"I think I should never, like, disregard myself as being Filipino." They even feel shamed by those who deny they are Filipino because they were born here. Alex thinks this is true of many students. And there are attachment reminders, as, for example, from parents who make clear their desire to die only in the Philippines. Students make an invidious comparison between the Philippines as a place to visit, even a place that catches their attention in newspaper stories, and America as a place to stay because it delivers on the promise of a good life in material terms. "When we came over here," says Sol Ignacio, "we started up over. And now we're not going down; we're going up." The stability and certainty of the economic well-being of Riverview's Filipinos reinforces the wisdom of their parents' decision to migrate; the acceptance of Filipinos by non-Filipinos provides the backdrop for the students' easy move into the mainstream of American society. Upward mobility has characterized the lives of Riverview's adult Filipinos, and their children garner a disproportionate share of the school's academic and nonacademic honors.

Filipino students at RHS constitute about 12 percent of the total enrollment of 1,600. They rank among the school's most academically and socially successful students. They are segmented primarily into four groups: college preppies, hoodies, new-wavers, and "FOBs," the newcomers whom Filipino students say are "fresh off the boat." Outside these four groups are some Filipino students who are "generic white Americans" and thus "hang out with any social group," even becoming a wannabe. "Mostly all my friends are Mexican," says Rudy Serrano. "Sometimes I wish I was Mexican like them so I won't have to be different."

The hoodies are an older group of males and females whom the preppies accuse of specializing in drugs, drinking, and sexual promiscuity. A few years ago, when hoodies were more prominent in the school, a preppie student said in reaction to them:

I had to pull away from that stereotype. I had to prove to the Filipinos and to the other students that I can become something other than that. I had to work hard. I think I still have to prove myself, maybe because I'm a woman, maybe a colored race, but I still have to prove I'm not the stereotype they put me in.

I found no current support for this proving-oneself perspective, and certainly none to indicate that there was anything resembling the pressure to conform that black students get from black peers and adults. I found no equivalent among Filipinos of the proper-nonproper dichotomy that academically successful black students know so well.

In the reactions of the non-hoodies to the hoodies, I see sentiments akin to those that old-timers have to newcomers. The sentiment is shame, on the one hand, and some fear, on the other, that non-Filipinos will judge them on the basis of persons from whom they feel substantial distance. Sally Toro expresses her shame at the hoodies.

Other people look at them and say, "You're wasting your life." Being a Filipino you say, "Why do they love to do this to their ethnicity? Why are they showing other people—shame, that's the word. Why are you going out every weekend and wasting your money on drugs, on drinking, on girls?" They'll just get a girl, how do you say, just pop her and drop her.

Filipino students want most to be taken only for the friends they mean to be and usually are.

Sally wants to avoid being mistaken for the type of Filipino that Terry Camperos describes himself to be. Terry considers himself to be friends with the Filipino Sallys of RHS; he does not downgrade her lifestyle; it is one that, in terms of academic success, he could have been part of. But his associations since ninth grade have been with hoodies, though this is not a label he would use. Typically, when he describes his and his group's activities, there is no particular ethnic dimension to it; he does not volunteer that his group, like the Filipino newcomers, and totally unlike the mainstream, academically oriented Filipinos, speak Tagalog among themselves.

The girls who stand opposite us on the quad, they're changing with the times. They dress more modern. We never change. We wear leather jackets, lots of jewelry, a cross, blue jeans. They used to hang around with us, but they started changing. We're more wild, have more fun. When we're out there all together, we're wild. School, we don't take it seriously, not really. Usually at the beginning [ninth grade], but not really. I was in college-prep. Too hard work.

Weekends, I sleep late, wash my dad's car, go out with my girlfriends. We all go to the mall. We drink some; no drugs. People think we take drugs. I just let them think what they want. I drink. Sometimes before school, sometimes during school time. That's when I don't go to school.

I think we're more closer, me and my friends, than any Filipino group. We don't start trouble, but if someone starts trouble, that's when we fight. We don't want people pushing us around.

Within each of the three non-newcomer groups, students vary by the extent of ethnicity in their identity. Each contains those who can speak unself-consciously of Filipinos as "my own kind," as well as those who can say, "Then you have the American people like me, who have no accent, and they still go along with their ethnic background, like *lumpia* [an eggroll type of delicacy] and stuff." Each group differs in its degree of involvement in the school, and in the Fil-Am Club. Hoodies are much less likely to belong to the Fil-Am Club; in fact, the club, like its black and Hispanic counterparts, does not thrive. Born in the 1970s of heightened ethnic consciousness, the clubs have uncertain agendas, and therefore uncertain membership. For example, at the Fil-Am Club's first meeting of the new school year someone suggested that "we've got to go out there and show them who we are, that we're Fil-Am and proud of it." Alex Ramiro, present at this meeting, said that that did not appeal to him. Apparently, it did not appeal to the other members either. The club did not have a good year.

Filipino students do not relish doing things that call attention to themselves as Filipinos. Since the FOBs have this effect, non-FOB Filipinos ignore their ethnic newcomers and hope that they will soon fit in. Frank Doloban tells a story about newcomers. One boy, he says, hooked up with a non-Filipino group, while some others joined a Filipino group. At the end of the year, the one boy had "almost lost his accent and got almost completely Americanized. While these other kids who hooked up with Filipinos who'd been here longer, they still have their accents, dress funny, still act like they're Filipinos." Frank approves of Americanizing, the faster the better. His friend Alicia says, "If I meet them [newcomers] through a circumstance, I'll be their friend, but I won't make a special effort to meet them just so I can show them the ropes."

The feeling that is associated with "my own kind," "my language," and the Philippines as "home," does not translate into students accepting responsibility for their ethnic newcomers. There is no established means to do this; students do not seek to find means. "Last year," says Sally Toro, "our Fil-Am Club sponsor told a couple of us to approach them and ask if they wanted to be in our club. I guess none of us really got the chance to, because we don't go to the cafeteria [where the newcomers eat]. We stay outside."

The FOBs are strangers; that they are Filipino strangers counts for little or nothing to the Filipino friends. The latter have paid their dues by Americanizing to the extent that they are fully functioning participants at RHS. Having Americanized, they are free, insofar as pressure from peers and parents is concerned, to be as Filipino as they see fit.

When Filipino students Americanize, they do not think they are acting white; nor do they think they have to act white to succeed either at RHS or in America. Their relatively easy, unrestricted passage into the American mainstream has left them without that feeling—expressed by Mexican and black students—of taking on the guise of white people. Filipinos, apart from color and facial structure, look and act as if they are white Americans. That they have a Filipino identity is evidenced both by the observations of non-Filipino students that Filipinos are the most cliquish of all ethnic groups and by the readily observed fact of their clustering together during all the free times throughout the school day. Shared identity obviously facilitates their social relations, though the comfort of kind does not restrict them from mingling freely with non-Filipinos.

Today's Filipino students at RHS may be the last generation that will experience a cultural gap between home and school. To be sure, their homes fully endorse the school's academic mission, even revel in its interschool athletic competition, but their homes remain Filipino places such that students are mindful of the differences. Valerie Novator reflects on the differences: "When you're with friends who like you, who you like, no one really cares what you are, but when you go home, your parents there are Filipino, so that's the way you live." Valerie's parents were born and raised in the Philippines and, in ethnic terms, they care who she is. Similarly, Rudy Serrano "feels like a Filipino" when he's around other Filipinos. When he is not, "I just feel like myself, a person like other people." Students acknowledge being aware of their ethnic identity at school on those very few occasions when teachers take a count of Asian-Americans or ask a question about the Philippines that they get called on to answer, and also when other students tease them about eating dogs. Another time, recalls Alex Ramiro, is "when I see one of the new kids come in that are Filipino. That kid is a reminder I looked like that once. I used to act like that, with a big question mark on my face."

Clearly, Filipino students see themselves as students at RHS, not Filipino students. This is not to say that they have discarded the hyphen, for by their own accounts they remain Filipino-Americans, but the left side of the hyphen is not a preeminent fact. When I asked them my long list of questions about being Filipino at RHS, they basically discounted the importance of their ethnicity in the range of circumstances that exist at school. Does it matter for grades, dating, relations with teachers, popularity, getting elected, etc., I asked. No, unimportant, does not matter—these were the answers I generally received. They do not feel self-consciously Filipino, they feel just as they imagine other students feel, and they think the school is as much theirs as anyone else's. Their experience at school is a prelude to being absorbed into the mainstream of American life. It would take rejection from institutions outside of Riverview for them to begin to feel otherwise.

I close this section on Filipino students at RHS with a long first-person account of Rita Romaga, a junior, who has lived in the United States since she was four. Her Filipino-born-and-raised parents are professionals; Rita is a mod. I do not think her choosing to be a mod represents a victory of something over something else. Nor do I think that she or the mods are the wave of anything. I am attracted to the honest, joyful, quirky person who so unguardedly said, in effect, I am what I am, I may not be that person tomorrow, but I like whoever I am today. The Filipino-born adolescent Rita sounded prototypically American to me, though I can easily imagine the rejecting tut-tuts of those whose prototypes must have fewer quirks.

Everybody says, "Oh, you're a mod." The first thing I do is get a little angry because, I mean, I don't label myself as anything. When people go, "What are you?" I'll say, "Myself." I'm just Rita, you know. Sometimes I can be a mod, a radical mod. I'll come out of the bathroom with all this stuff on my face and my uncle says, like, "Where are you going? It's not Hallowe'en." And, then, sometimes I can be a thrasher. And sometimes if I go all out I can be a stoner. It depends on what day it is. I have a lot of friends in every group. Or I could just go out and handle it normal.

My friend Sam told me I might be at a disadvantage because people stereotype. They think mods are too busy wearing black and doing all that makeup and their hair to do their studies. Well, that isn't true because I'm in college-prep and I've got a good grade point average.

My friend came over after dinner one night before school began. I had this long hair and that night he shaved my head only on one side. My mom was watching; she thought it was fascinating. My dad said I looked like him when he was in the army. At times I think they think I'm kind of weird. Most of the time, they know I'm normal. Sometimes my dad is kind of tripped out about how I go to the Salvation Army to buy clothes, and I don't beg them to go to Macy's. "You'll get a skin disorder," my dad says. "Wash it again." "Dad!" you know. I'm basically normal with a little touch of jazz here, spontaneity there, color here—whitewall with paint splatters on it.

Rita cannot say, as does her friend Ray, "I don't like the Filipino ways. My parents, they try to drive it in me." At this time in their lives, each is allowed to deal with the fact of their ethnicity in very different ways: by ignoring it, Rita goes her way; by rejecting it, Ray goes his. During their high school years, their ethnicity is not salient.

The Newcomers

Asian people, Vietnamese, whatever, there's quite a few of those coming here now. They don't even try to learn English. They just talk that language. They're not trying to adapt.

—RHS Student

I want to make new friends.
But nobody understands me.
They are laughing and laughing at me because they think I'm talking so
    funny.
Some girls and guys say you are talking too fast.
So they don't understand me.
Some day they will understand me.
Some day I will be your friend.

—Yong Chu Sim, RHS Student

Newcomers congregate in and around the building where the English-as-a-second-language (ESL) classroom is located. This room is their heartland, their port of call. Here one teacher and two aides gently and sympathetically minister to and teach all those whose English-language disability places them together and, thereby, separates them from other RHS students. The longer students remain in the ESL program, the longer they remain strangers, comfortable in their refuge but kept distant from the central life of their school. In their free moments, ESL students—the newcomers—transform the room and the nearby lawn, steps, verandah, and tennis court into ethnic places where English is not spoken. Mexican boys play a soccer type of game with a tennis ball that they kick over a tennis net. A group of blue-jean-clad Vietnamese, two boys and two girls, play hackensack. Standing in a circle, they project a small ball-like object from person to person by tapping it with some part of their shoe. Otherwise, at RHS, only the stoners play this game. After school, a group of Vietnamese girls sit on the lawn chatting over magazines, their attention on clothing. They and the other newcomers are concerned to learn the sartorial ropes of RHS. They soon do, mastering what "designer" signifies in regard to clothing long before they master English.

Whatever their national origins, the newcomers, marked by distinctive hangout location, accent, and, at least for a while, appearance, are the newest members of RHS's ethnic mix. In fact, a door stands open for them to join their predecessors; reassurance of this fact derives from the many who already have done so. They see them signing yearbooks when they are passed around each fall and participating in the other ritualistic diversions of the American high school. Passage into the school's academic life is relatively easy; passing into its nonacademic ritual life is definitely not. Competence in spoken English is a key. So are personality factors. All newcomers want to cease feeling like outsiders; most will want to join their predecessors in becoming friends.

The passage to joining them takes an emotional toll, though it is comparatively easy for Teresa Gomez and comparatively hard for her friend Lizbeta Tavarnol. Both are Filipino, both are in their second year as ESL students. Teresa, however, has made contacts with non-ESL students; Lizbeta's only friends are other Filipino girls. At the end of her second year, Teresa wrote the following essay about her experiences at RHS for her ESL class.

At first week here I was so boring but later I got a lot of friends they are mix. But most of them are Filipino. My first week here I'm going to the Americans [white students] to develop my vocabulary but some of them was teasing me always. And I know I'm so sensitive so I'm going out with black and Mexican. They are almost like Filipinos. About the American's I'm still going out with them but not like my friends now. At lunch we're waiting for each other. We have words to remember "One for all, all for one." About the assignment if somebody needs help we're try to help if we can. Mostly when personnel problems come, we're try to solve or forget so he or she can't think to do something wrong. Mostly our problem is about the love life. Because teenager was too much involved in this topic. For me to stay here in RHS was so memorable. It's up to somebody if she want to have a lot of friends. Nobody can help to me except me myself.

In the course of our interview, she painted a more mixed picture, taking comfort from black students who befriended her and pain from the established, oldtimer Filipinos.

They call me FOB. I don't know what's that. Fresh from boat. I don't know what's that. Sometimes walking in the hallway they are there with friends. I don't feel like to go there because they look at you. I just pretend I didn't see them. I gonna go with my friends, black people.

Lizbeta Tavarnol is less bold and less confident than Teresa. She, too, would like "to be just the same with them." Meanwhile, she is offended by "people hugging and kissing" in public; holding hands is the extent of public affection that she condones. She dislikes the litter in RHS halls; students at her Filipino high school were fined for littering. Expecting to be helped by the settled Filipinos, she is disappointed that they ignore her. Being settled and accepted seems like a distant dream. Though confused about who she is and means to be, she has no desire to return to the Philippines to live. "Sometimes I'm walking around" and she says to herself, "'I am Filipino. How come I'm here walking around in the United States?' You know, I said, 'Oh, God, I don't believe I'm in America.' And then I saw blue eyes and then I said, 'Uh huh, I'm in America.'"

Lizbeta is particularly sensitive about speaking English. She feels that her linguistic disability fuels the ridicule she gets from oldtimer Filipinos. Having spent the first fifteen years of her life speaking only Tagalog, she is distressed to find that her language has no legitimated place in American life. Her distress is enhanced by her unrewarded efforts at speaking English. Her most severely disturbing language encounter was with Gloria, a fellow Filipino, an older newcomer (in the U.S. four to Lizbeta's two years) who took to calling Lizbeta's parents to report Lizbeta's supposed misdeeds.

I said to her [Gloria] I want to talk to you after school. She said OK. And then I speak Tagalog. She's a Filipino. She said, "You don't know how to speak English." I said, "Oh yeah. You don't know who I am but I know who you are." She said, "Oh yeah." I said, "Fuck you, motherfucker—I said that!" Then she said, "You're a fucker." "I'm not afraid to you, girl," I said.

But, you know, sometime if she with Filipinos I said, "Hey, girl, speak Tagalog. You're talking to Filipinos." She speaks better Tagalog than English.

Lizbeta and Gloria will soon learn additional forms of English expression to address the matters of concern in their relationship with each other and in their presentation of self in American settings. Meanwhile, unwelcomed by other Filipinos, the newcomers establish their own pecking order within the general social context of Riverview High

School. The ticket for newcomers joining its American core is to cease being obtrusively ethnic; for newcomer students to be accepted as one of the many versions of friend they must relinquish some of their ethnic behavior. This, typically, is a problem for parents who vigorously protect what they visualize as the proper blend of behavior. Parents often try to impose their own version upon recalcitrant children who feel constrained by their parents' conception. Neither the familial homeland nor the familial language will tug the children's heartstrings as it does their parents'. As long as students remain outside this core, they are subject to the behavior-shaping laughter, ridicule, and scorn of its unsympathetic insiders. Once inside, this particular form of cruelty ceases; in the meantime, it is powerfully instructive.

Most students are within the core, having made the passage to the status of friend at an earlier point in their lives. Most need to construct an identity that blends elements of the ethnic and American. The degree of need is highly variable, as the students indicate, depending at least upon gender, and upon familial and individual personality factors. What students generally seem to seek, when they seek at all, is a way of being ethnic that does not call attention to themselves. They want an accepted way of being an American black, Mexican, Filipino, or Asian. Students acknowledged no concept of being too American. In contrast, they did speak of being too black, Mexican, Filipino, or Asian, attributing excess to the "FOB" or "wetback" or "nigger," their fellow ethnics who, in their opinion, are insufficiently acculturated. In fact, students may not even know what their attachments are until later in life when the process of self-shaping is more settled, and when they are crowded with many fewer ethnic and nonethnic alternatives from which to select.

Non-Sicilian white Sally Barron believes that what was true of her parent's generation will not be true of her own. Sally knows life only as a young woman and thus cannot appreciate the tenacity of primordial affiliations, but as a keen observer she makes some judgments about the possible impact of having grown up in Riverview. She believes that the process of parents' transmitting their ethnic culture to their children is harder than ever.

When our generation grows up, because we've been exposed to all the different races, it's going to be hard to say, "Hey, you're this or you're only this and this is what you're going to do." Especially with marriages, you know, marry only an Italian or a Puerto Rican. It would be hard for our generation to raise our kids like that because we're not exposed to that type of thing.

Sally is saying, in effect, that one may never cease to be nominally Italian or Mexican, but given the nature of life in Riverview and Riverview High School, it is uncertain what consequences, if any, will follow from this nominal fact. It remains to be seen how many RHS students will come to adult life believing, as one black woman, a forty-year-old Riverview native, did, that she can never be very close friends with someone who is not black. To her, ethnic congruence is a condition of intimacy. To RHS students, given their ethnic mingling, ethnic congruence is not.

7

The Children of Riverview's People:
Strangers and Friends

On the well-scrawled desk I occupy at the back of the English classroom, one graffito stands out. It is a three-line dialogue; I don't know if the lines were written on the same day.

"I love Geraldo Tomaso," wrote Geraldo's unnamed lady love.

"Don't you think you should make sure you ain't relatives?" replied her unnamed respondent, a sneer and taunt implied.

"I'm sure we're not relatives. My dad's white," wrote Geraldo's lady love matter-of-factly, affirming his place in her circle of friends.

Much of my inquiry with students was to learn about the boundaries of the status "friend"—by which I mean the full range of social contacts from the most trivial to the most intimate—as they knew and experienced them at RHS. Their one-liners flew glibly: "Lunchtime, you see, everybody mingles," I was told early in the school year by a white girl. "Mingle," I soon learned, was the verb of choice to characterize the close contact among students from different ethnic groups. Visual impressions confirmed that mingling was indeed common. Was it as common as a mixed group of black, Mexican, and white boys thought when they told me that at RHS, "you're a student, not a racial group. You're not a black Tiger [the school totem]," as if to say that Tigers come only in one color. "We all look all the same color, really. Not, 'Don't hang around there, you're a black,' you know."

How much of what I heard about the extent of mingling should I trust, particularly when it is what I would prefer to hear? Is it just the expansive flush of good will that spills out as images of idealized social interactions? I interview Teresa Martinez, Puerto Rican, now a junior and a student in Riverview only since her freshman year, asking her what I ask all students: Who are your friends?

"Whites?"

"Yes."

"Mexicans?"

"Maybe. Some of them are edgy. They, like, look at you, like, you ain't Mexican, you shouldn't be around. Or they'll start roasting you, or something. You gotta start tripping with them."

"Filipinos?"

"They don't really care [who, ethnically, their friends are]. They're just like us."

"Blacks?"

"They don't care. They usually just start talking before you talk to them. They come up to you and say, 'Who are you?'."

"Do they ask you if you're black?"

"Yeah, a lot of them do. They say, 'What are you, a mixture?' Some whites and Filipinos, too. When I'm not talking, they go, 'What nationality are you?'."

The mixed group of boys discuss the unimportance of color, while Puerto Rican Teresa Martinez describes her experience with fellow students who need to know who she is in ethnic terms. They want to be able to place her, and when they do they will extend her differing responses, most positive from those least like her, and least positive from those (Mexicans) most like her. This is the world as Teresa sees it. I wonder if the reactions from the Mexicans she mentions are to Teresa as Teresa or as Puerto Rican? I wonder similarly about the reactions to Teresa by students from the other ethnic groups.

When I posed a question to black sophomore Pam Reston, she responded with a longer answer than I expected, as if to set things straight. Her intention seemed to be to shut down my interminable questioning with a general statement to cover all cases. "Listen up," she seemed to be saying, "here's how things stand at RHS."

See, like one teacher tells us, Riverview is totally different from the real world outside, like what you see here is not what's gonna happen in the real world. I disagree; I think it is pretty much the real world. But here you *would* find it like this: you go out with whoever you want to go out with. It doesn't matter. Nobody would look down at you if you did or if you didn't.

Color doesn't matter, you can be friends with anyone, you can date anyone without repercussions—have I stumbled on a social utopia at RHS? Is it the adolescent counterpart of the gastronomic melange that was available for a recent Fourth of July celebration in Riverview? The newspaper ad announcing the occasion listed donors and donations:

Group	Food provided for sale
Young Men's Institute [Italian]	Calamari fillets
Sons of Italy	Albonetti sandwiches and sfingi [fruit fritters]
Black Cultural Political League	Ribs
McGlothen Memorial Church [black]	Ribs
Spanish-Speaking Cultural Center	Burritos, tostados, hot dogs
Greek Orthodox Church	Gyros and Greek pastry
Seventh-Day Adventists	Corn dogs and tacos
Kiwanis	Soda and pop corn
Loyal Order of Moose	Hamburgers and beef tacos

Mingling and Ethnic Peace

It was not long before one definite picture of Riverview emerged from the invited and uninvited recollections of adults I spoke to who had lived in Riverview before and after 1980: Riverview had changed for the better. Their assessments were comparative and unequivocal. From 1968 to 1980, there certainly were times of ethnic hostility and tension, of group sensitivity and exclusivity. Before 1968, there was the stasis of constrained friendliness and bounded place:

I didn't date their sister, and they didn't date mine, but we had something in common [sports]. It superseded race because we were doing things together. Today, it seems to go beyond just doing things together. It seems to be a sociality type of an affair.

Though the particulars may vary in small details, Riverview adults from all ethnic backgrounds affirm, while not necessarily approving, that "sociality" prevails at RHS. Both adults and students commonly refer to the current state of social affairs as a "melting pot," clarifying, however, that "melting" has not fully occurred, that is, ethnic distinctions have not disappeared. Melting pot is a positive label meant by its nontechnical users to be a commendatory designation of positive interethnic associations. Several persons chose other metaphors. A Mexican man saw RHS as a grand salad:

You have lettuce, you have tomatoes, you have cukes, you have onions, whatever. You chop 'em up and throw 'em into a bowl. You toss it and it's very good; it tastes very good together, but each one still has its distinct taste to it.

A Sicilian man thought that more than simple mixing had occurred:

It's like you're making a minestrone soup. You put a lot of different ingredients in it and you get something unique from it. You don't taste carrots and you don't taste beef and you don't taste onions. You taste it all. I think that's what is happening here today. . . . It goes beyond their own ethnic identity.

I do not challenge either of these observers. Both know that RHS contains multiple social realities. Neither they nor I can establish a single dominant reality at RHS. Both also know that ethnically homogeneous social groupings persist, and that some members of those groups also relate easily to nongroup others, at different levels of contact and in different ways, as I will describe below.

Some mingling arrangements are seasonal. During the basketball season, the players see each other for hours every weekday after school. "Everybody gets a lot closer during that time," says one of the girls on the starting five. But wander the lawns and sidewalks during any of the open times before, during, and after school and you see ethnic flocking. During one such time, I watched eight black males and females sitting on the railings that line the ramp entry to a building. Someone's radio played a song that moved all the students to its strong beat. Black students congregate daily at this same spot at the same time. At a classroom window overlooking this ramp two Mexican boys spoke Spanish as they gazed at the scene below them. They are in one of the rooms of a building where RHS newcomers feel most comfortable. The black students and the newcomer Mexican students are but two of the many ethnically homogeneous pairs and groups that position themselves predictably throughout the school. Their conduct is fully within the norms of RHS, as it would be anywhere in the country.

What is not routine nationwide is extensive mingling. Here is what it looks like in Riverview. In class, a white boy, a Middle Eastern boy, and an oriental girl sit head to head for ten minutes discussing computers and the special terminology that surrounds their use. A Filipino girl and a black girl review a story in preparation for a forthcoming test. Just short of the end of a period, black Desmond, restless, moves aimlessly through the aisles formed by the movable desks. He bends his body to avoid getting hit by a black boy, continues on to the desk of a Mexican girl where he stops and grabs her notebook. She begs him to let go. When she reaches for her notebook, Desmond holds her hand. She does not pull it away. He continues his wandering. He takes a light swipe at the shoulder of a white girl, getting a swipe back in return. In student-government class, a senior black girl listens to a sophomore white boy get berated by teacher and students for a position he had taken. The girl knew he was wrong but didn't like the dressing-down he was getting. She scolded students and teacher.

In classrooms students both surreptitiously and with their teachers' tacit approval use this academic setting for occasions of a nonacademic nature. When this restructured time is added to that available within the school's numerous nonclassroom settings, students have extensive opportunities to pursue their social interests:

In friendship—While fellow students sit clustered in twos and threes to analyze myths, a black girl and a Mexican boy discuss her tribulations with the parents of her white boyfriend. Their teacher preoccupied with grading papers, a Mexican girl and the black boy in front of her talk for half the period. It is the talk of seniors—jobs, postgraduation schooling, relationships. Elsewhere, three students, two black and one white, discuss the movie *The Color Purple*. The black boy invites the white boy to see the movie with him over the weekend.

In teasing—Teasing in ethnic terms can be risky. If you don't know your teased partner well, you may ignite the explosive latent in every ethnic tease. Here are examples of ethnic teasing that had no repercussions. Said a white boy to a Mexican boy, "You're gonna be the lamest, dumbest, stupidest Mexican—" On the outdoor basketball court at lunchtime, a black boy closely guarding a white boy says to him, "What you gonna do now, white boy?" A black girl removes the hat of a white boy and places it on her head. He tells her, "Take off my hat. You'll get Afro-Sheen all over it."

In affection—In Beginning Acting, a black boy leads the class in Simon Says, a game they play to develop their ability to concentrate. For some reason, he abandons the role of leader and takes a seat facing the group. A white girl, who moves when she shouldn't have, leaves the game and comes over to the black leader. She hugs him and rests her head on top of his. In the course of a history class, a white boy lays his head back on the desk of the black girl behind him. First, she touches his hair, as if just to feel what such hair is like. Then she touches it in several places, more in a fondling way. The boy lifts his head off her desk without reacting to her touching.

In romance—At a Friday night basketball game, two couples enter and take seats in the stand. The girls sit in the seats immediately below those of their boyfriends, the white girl leaning back against the legs of her Filipino boyfriend, the Filipino girl leaning against the legs of her black boyfriend. During lunch, a longtime steady couple—she is Filipino, he is black—make their way to the stairs outside the science classrooms; this is their usual stopping place to talk and to hug.

Students confirmed that what I had been observing were not isolated events. Their confirmation did not imply that they were participants in the mingling, or that they approved of all its manifestations. Furthermore, it did not indicate that it was the only norm of social interaction at RHS. Students were, however, definite about its existence. Though they are not practiced in talking about mingling, and they have no stock phrases to speak of it, their point is clear: "My friends are white, black, Mexican," says a Mexican boy. "They're mixed and stuff. I don't really think of that [their ethnicity]. I don't think of that at all," he says emphatically. Being a Filipino is just like "being any other person," concludes a Filipino boy, which is to say, of course, that he sees no limitations in ethnic terms on whom he can associate with. A black girl elaborates the point: "Nobody tries to downgrade you 'cause you're black. And nobody makes you feel lower than what you have to do. And everybody just seems to socialize. And nobody just singles you out, or anything." In the same unqualified language, a white girl states, "Everybody mingles. Nobody goes by race."

This splurge of adolescent hyperbole overstates but does not misrepresent the circumstances at RHS: in the students' eyes, they are individuals first, not members of a group. They know that avoidance, rejection, esteem, trust, affection, and the like can be one's reaction to anyone, notwithstanding their ethnic affiliation. Ethnicity does not exclude one from any personal response, however positive or negative.

In short, prejudice of the type that will foreclose a student's social opportunities is minimal: RHS is a place of friends. Most students date within their own ethnic group. What is different at RHS is that students readily acknowledge that it is thinkable to date anyone. It is common enough, and sufficiently accepted, to be sanctioned as a norm.

"You got to be a nice person and stuff" is how a Mexican student captured the primacy of personality attributes over group affiliation. Students advanced similarly universal grounds to account for what, given national taboos and norms, remains the thorniest expression of ethnic interaction—cross-ethnic dating and serious romance in general, and between black and nonblack persons in particular. Male and female students from each of the school's four major ethnic groups placed the decision of who was an acceptable companion for romance in the familiar language of personal taste: who is attractive, who you like, who has a good personality, and the all-inclusive "if you're a person, you're a person." The disposition of students to date and marry persons outside their ethnic group eventually is accepted by parents, whose early reactions range from reluctance to enraged rejection. By their decisions, students help resocialize parents and other adults in whose lives ethnicity had created boundaries, their ethnic identity not yet merely a nominal designation.

"It's no big deal," students frequently said of the ethnicity of dating partners, as they earlier had said about ethnicity as factor in their own identity, the conduct of their lives, and how others treated them. A Filipino boy draws this matter-of-fact conclusion about ethnicity:

It is kind of funny when you think about it because I'm Filipino and I don't just pick Filipino people. It's how it ends up, I guess. My sister in the seventh grade, she got going with all different kind of color boys, like Mexican, white, Filipino. And my brother, he's Filipino, so far he's been with two Mexican people.

The least common cross-ethnic pairing is between black girls and nonblack boys. As a result, black girls are the only students who, as a group, take issue with the drift of black males to nonblack females, resenting the abandonment and the loss of dating partners. Black boys think otherwise. "Let's say I was a black guy and I was dating a white girl. Would my friends tease me?" I asked a student. "No," he answered. "They'd probably be dating white girls, too." I never heard a black male object to the school's open dating.

A black senior volunteered an explanation of the dating situation, indicating that "black guys go after white girls because they don't give them any shit," and it is this same "shit" that makes black girls unappealing to nonblack guys. He accounts for the toughness of young black females by portraying the model of black mothers.

Historically, the black woman has been like the backbone of the blacks. She's starting to change a little bit, but she's traditionally the one to keep the kids in school, and she works. When there's a need, the black mother sacrifices to make sure that her child gets it. She sorta feels as though I don't really need this guy, so I ain't gonna take no shit off of him.

Whatever the explanation, black girls are the least likely group to participate in the romantic mingling.

Earlier, I referred briefly to a social phenomenon at RHS that students call the "wannabe." This is a person who wants to be of an ethnicity other than his or her own. Wannabes are an ordinary phenomenon, but not a common one. Significantly commoner is ethnic borrowing in regard to dialect, music, dance, and the like. Wannabes transcend borrowing by their overall adoption of the behavior of another ethnic group, so that they act as if they were someone else.

RHS oldtimers recall wannabes from thirty and more years ago. "There was one black kid, we always called him the black Italian because he hung around with Italian kids, spoke Italian. Maybe you got thirty or forty or fifty now that do that." I'm not convinced that the only difference between today and the past is the numbers. The "black Italian" may have been identifying with a more socially "desirable" group. Today, RHS is like an ethnic cafeteria: choice abounds. Thus, students can invent their identity by selecting from an array of nonethnic affiliations (mods, thrashers, new-wavers, stoners, etc.), and of ethnic affiliations, as well. The trying on of selves does not favor the predictably esteemed whites; the trying on occurs in all directions, no less towards the traditionally less-esteemed minorities.

Non-wannabes hold mixed views about those who become wannabes, none strongly stated. Neither students nor teachers cast them in pathological terms, at least none stronger than what is connoted by rebellion. They were just what some students became: the choice was theirs to make, though most did not make it. Set in the context of the school's considerable ethnic mixing, wannabes just go a few steps beyond what is typically done. And as with other circumstances at RHS involving ethnicity, wannabes are not a cause for "commotion." Here is what a black teacher thinks about them:

I don't think anything about them anymore. I mean, I probably thought about them when I first started teaching because I was all black—problack—everything black then. I don't think about it now because this school is so much like that. I mean, there are so many students like that. One thing about the kids here is those that are wannabes are so strong, they don't care [what others think]. I've never really heard, you know, any commotion or any big thing about it.

In the course of being a wannabe, students transform what is transformable about themselves, and which they see as necessary for acceptance by the group they want to receive them. Being accepted hinges more on the aspirant's intentions and commitment to hanging out with the target group—doing what they do—than on the exactness of their transformation. A Mexican girl commented on the attempt of white girls to look Mexican:

They wear their eyeliner all the way up to here beyond the eyes. Dark eye shadow. Dark, dark lipstick, practically black. They wear a black eyeliner around their lids. Blush—it's a heavy darkish color, just a line going up their cheek. They'll have their hair long, and the top cut and curled. The bottom's cut and just straight. The front part's cut and it goes back, somehow.

Disliking wannabes, she says, scornfully, that she can pick them out from a group of girls. They try to get the makeup right, but "it doesn't work." By the detail of her description, we learn how carefully she had observed the elements of the wannabe's hoped-for correct appearance.

Not surprisingly, the most troublesome ethnic shift is from white to black. White girls who make the move, said a white boy disparagingly, "they hang out with the blacks, braid their hair like the blacks do—those little bitty braids. They dress like them and act like them. They go out with the black guys." A black student has a more positive reaction to white boys who want to be black. Though he doesn't endorse the idea, he does not join other students who think it's "horrible" and that people "should be satisfied who they are." He says he knows blacks who don't want to be black and whites who "are trying to act black."

I don't think nothing of it. I'll be friends with them and everything. I know a lot of people who are very convincing, and they're all considered black. Well, they're not all black, but I consider them just like me. I treat them just like normal. It's just how they act. I don't treat them like black people. You don't treat a black person and a white person different. Well, sometimes when it comes to certain things, but I always treat them as my friend.

And from one more black student, who responds to wannabes in terms of particular white boys, we get further perspective on RHS's smallest "minority" group:

They, like, follow our fashions and try to do things that mainly you only see black people do. They just fit into that. They're our friends, and we don't think nothing bad about them. There ain't nothing they could do about being white and wanting to be black. That's how they want to be, and that's how they are.

It is beyond my study of ethnicity and RHS to explain why some students become wannabes. Students offer various explanations: the wannabes grow up where most everyone in the neighborhood is of another ethnic group, they are more readily accepted by another ethnic group, or they have a boyfriend or girlfriend in another ethnic group, which is the beginning of their crossover. A white junior, Donna Thomas, talks about her own wannabe orientation:

When I first was here I wished I was black or Mexican, just to fit in. That's how I thought it was. I thought I wouldn't be called names, pushed around. I thought at the time it was just because I was white, but then I realized that black kids get pushed around, too. I wouldn't ever want to change. Then, I really did. I've heard more black kids say, "I wish I was white" or "that guy makes me wish I was white." It's when a black girl sees a gorgeous white guy. But then the next thing you'd see is a gorgeous black guy walking down the street and he looks at the black girl. That makes me wish I was black.

What I do not hear in these explanations, or in the characterizations of wannabes that anyone makes, is the intent that anthropologist DeVos writes about as "disguising the stigma of a disfavored family background [so that] appearance and behavior are consciously changed into socially acceptable forms, in order to be considered part of a more desirable social group" (1975:27–28). To be sure, wannabes move to a "desirable social group." The point of special interest here is that all ethnic groups are "desirable" candidates for receiving and generating wannabes. The effects of extensive mingling and the roughly equal status of the ethnic groups in social terms makes it thinkable to redirect one's identity in any direction. I would need to know much more than I was able to learn about who becomes wannabes, the process of becoming a wannabe, what is the nature of their life as one, how they are received, etc., to speak more definitively about them. Not knowing all this, I remain impressed that traditional stigmas do not operate to preclude nonminority groups from receiving minority students as wannabes, or minority groups from being attractive to nonminority students who are wannabes.

In short, mingling at RHS operates in these terms: all social interactions that elsewhere ordinarily happen within an ethnic group routinely happen at RHS across all ethnic groups. The result has been the emergence of a moral "code" that guides social interactions:

1. "Don't trip off color," which is to say, don't make decisions, positively or negatively, on the basis of color.

2. Claim but do not assert your ethnic identity. Pride is fine but ethnicity is not a big deal.

3. "Prejudice is not cool." If you have any, best keep it to yourself, and this includes name-calling that shows disrespect and rejection of others.

4. Social interactions, from casual contact to serious romance, can be within one's ethnic group, across ethnic groups, or both. No single style prevails, no way is better than another.

5. Be yourself, without pretense, particularly about being better than anyone else.

6. Students are more like than unlike each other. Differences exist, but they matter less than similarities.

Other Indicators of Ethnic Peace

The nature and extent of mingling testifies to the calm that parents and educators believe has settled in at RHS. I looked for other indicators.

For example, were there "racial" fights as there had been throughout the 1970s? There certainly were fights at RHS; mostly they were between black girls. I never saw or heard about a racial fight during my entire year of fieldwork. Teachers and students said such fights were so infrequent as to be anomalous, and had been for years. When a fight occurred between students of differing ethnic groups, it was a fight with nonracial causes.

Fighting is just one possible manifestation of ethnic strife. It may be curtailed by rigidly enforced regulations and careful, systematic policing. As a legacy of the 1970s, the deans, the principal, and the assistant principal always wear walkie talkies. Ethnic antagonism, if it exists, can be seen in "legal" activities of the school. For example, I asked students if there was competition among ethnic groups; their responses were overwhelmingly in the negative. When I asked more specifically if on the occasion of elections for Ugly Man, Homecoming Queen, or class officers, students were inclined to vote by ethnicity, their answers were somewhat different. If anyone did, it was Filipino and black students, but it seemed to have stopped well short of being noticeably bothersome. In fact, a few years ago, the Fil-American Club sponsored a black boy for Ugly Man and he won this most prestigious Homecoming competition for males. The black student was so popular that he probably would have won regardless of his club sponsor. Why, though, did the clubby Filipinos choose a black boy?

I don't know. He just needed a club and we said sure, come on. There's that American side to the Fil-*American* Club. We looked at him as being American. That's where me and my dad think the same. In the old Fil-Am Building downtown there's two flags, one's American and one's Filipino.

It seemed that I was the only one surprised by the Fil-American Club's black candidate; when he won, I expected volunteered reactions to his victory to dominate my interviews with students and teachers. They did not.

Notwithstanding occasional flurries of activity, what seems to be happening to all three ethnic clubs—black, Hispanic, and Filipino—is a decline of purpose. Their membership has been decreasing, attendance at meetings is poor. They lack issues that provide a foundational raison d'être. They seem to have been done in by good social times, and they do not know how to mobilize around other interests, causes, or problems.

The very limited success of the ethnic clubs may be due to the students' belief that their school does not favor one group over another, and that all have an equal chance to succeed. More than just thinking that RHS is generally fair to all students, students and teachers assessed the experience of being a student at RHS as particularly positive because of its ethnic diversity. There may be some overstatement in their views, a reaction to the minority-based stigma borne by the community and the school. Specifically, students and parents approve of the large number of blacks at RHS, notwithstanding the negativism of many parents toward their child's romantic involvement with black students. A white student reported her mother's endorsement of RHS: "My mom wanted me to grow up in this environment because she said it's how life is gonna be. When you get out there in the real world, it's not gonna just be all white people." According to a Mexican mother:

There's blacks that are mean and no good, and blacks that would give you the shirt off their back. There's that of all nationalities; it's a matter of knowing. I think my son is a little richer for having gone to Riverview High, and having grown up knowing a lot of different blacks. He knows there are some to avoid at all costs and some that if you know they were getting the hell beat out of them, you'd go help them.

A white father said his college daughter told him, "Dad, thank God for RHS. Those kids I go to school with have never been associated where there is a lot of minority students. They're very naive." From the vantage point of fifteen years in RHS classrooms, a veteran black teacher confirmed what a black student had said about her opportunity to be with people of more than "one particular color":

I used to feel it would be a little bit of an adjustment when they [black students] found themselves [outside of Riverview] in a mostly white situation, but I think that they could deal with it. I don't see them freezing up around a lot of whites, not knowing what to do, feeling self-conscious.

There are mixed views about whether or not the ethnic experience at RHS might be dysfunctional for black students. The reasoning is that because they are much less likely to meet people outside of Riverview and Riverview High School who are so friendly and receptive, their high expectations will lead to disappointment. Neither the logic nor the reality of this argument found support among blacks. Black students "are getting both ends of it," is how the dysfunctional argument was rejected. As nice as it is to be black in Riverview—"you get to live among people without threat," is how a former RHS graduate and now a parent put it—blacks still face "everyday problems" and they're close enough to the antagonism of nearby communities to not be lulled into a false sense of hope and idealism.

Finally, in regard to the general point of ethnic peace at RHS, I asked students and teachers if they thought there should be more minority teachers at RHS. Teachers, notably minority teachers, said it would be a good idea, offering the predictable "role model" argument. One teacher, a black woman, wanted more women, Filipinos, and black teachers and deans. Moreover, she wanted "outspoken" blacks because all present black faculty, herself included, have "kind of just melted in." Most students seem baffled by the question about hiring more minority teachers. To them, a teacher is a teacher: the issue is not their ethnicity but their instructional skill.

Thus, the universalist premise is extended once more, having been applied by students to friendship and romance, and by teachers to the range of classroom circumstances they face. Its prevalence establishes it as the dominant orientation of the school in the conduct of its formal and informal activities. Its prominence is not the outcome of planning, of explicit, articulated purpose discussed and agreed upon by educators and parents. In its avoidance of ethnic particularism, it safely skirts issues and complications that arise when individuals appear to operate from ethnic group confines, where sentiments of *our* interests, *our* priorities predominate. In its openness, it suggests the promise of anyone's being designated as acceptable. Thereby fairness is established. In its appearance of favoring everyone, no individual, because of group identity, should feel left out, scorned, less valued. Universalism is one version of the American dream. It gets its due at Riverview High School.

The Limitations of Mingling

RHS is not paradise, however; there are constraints to mingling and they take several forms, none of them novel: peers, parents, and teachers name-call, stereotype, and inculcate prejudice. These practices, familiar to all students, exist as a minor subtheme to the major theme of mingling, a ranking that does not trivialize their presence as an abiding fact of life at RHS.

I want to begin with a consideration of attitudes and action directed toward black students, as the group that is most abused, going on to other groups, the order following the decreasing amounts of abuse they receive—newcomers, Mexicans, Filipinos, and whites. There seems to be a correlation between the amount of antipathy directed against a group and the ease of articulating images of that group. Thus, both blacks and nonblacks readily characterize the behavior of black students. No group is viewed as tougher,[1] more uninterested in school, less

1. In this regard, Patchen writes: "Whites tended to agree with blacks in seeing the blacks as more physically tough. Specifically, whites saw larger proportions of blacks than of whites as "good fighters" and smaller proportions of blacks as afraid of students of the other race" (1982:50).

likely to be successful academically, and more rebellious, hostile, pro-
miscuous, and involved with drugs. Stereotypes come quickly to mind:
"If you're in a classroom and something gets stolen, it's, like, everybody
knows it was a black person."

Persons identified with this set of attributes are called niggers by both
black and nonblack students. In general, however, nigger is not publicly
used except in the several nonpejorative forms common at RHS. Black
students do report hearing the word in its most disagreeable sense. That
this is uncommon, I think, is due to its explosive potential, as well as to
its general unacceptability. I shall discuss other ways the term is used
below, in connection with the complexity of social relations at RHS.

The black female–nonblack male relationship is too uncommon to
evoke any mention at all, while the black male–nonblack female is sufficiently common to be mentioned frequently. At its gentlest, the student
reaction to this latter relationship is, "I kind of look at them and think,
'That's kinda weird.'" At its worst, nonblack girls who date black boys
are called "nigger lovers" or "mira." Mira refers to any nonblack girl who
dates a black boy. It is said to the girl in a taunting voice, with three
fingers of a raised hand pointing down in the form of an "M." No one was
certain either of the origin or the correct spelling of the word. "It's like
peer pressure to stay with your own group," said a Mexican boy. He added that it was acceptable for him to date Filipino or white girls, which
suggests that one's "own group" was not necessarily narrowly defined,
though it did exclude blacks.

Reactions of nonblack to black students are shaped, informed, and
moderated by deeply entrenched norms that have developed over years
of continuous contact that often begin before kindergarten. The parents
of both groups live on the fringes of the student subculture, their own
daily experience in the public arenas of life in Riverview seldom jux-
taposing them in intimate or continuing ways. Parents who grew up in
Riverview have had experiences that approximate those of their children. Nonnative parents may learn to see virtue in RHS's mingling, but
it was affordable housing, not the promise of mingling, that brought
them to Riverview. Many come to see opportunity in the high school's
ethnic diversity. Others who see no such thing try to perpetuate in their
children the taboos that support a wall between black and nonblack.
Such parents either remove their children from the Riverview school
system after the elementary grades, or, as most do, leave their children
in school and accept mingling as long as it stops short of romance.

Often both sets of parents oppose the intimate black-nonblack relationship; parental antagonism may be so strong that the children feel
compelled to hide the relationship from their parents. Within the ranks

of antagonized parents, I find different levels of resistance. Black sophomore Rina Carson dated a white boy. Neither set of parents warmly
welcomed the relationship. They were reserved and cordial, adopting
the stance of the Filipino parents whose daughter dated a black boy: do
not openly resist the relationship because you risk prolonging a romance
that in time would die of its own accord. Rina describes the responses of
the involved parents:

His parents were OK. I mean, I never thought they did anything racist. I mean,
they liked me. I went over there and talked and sat with his parents. He came
to my house and talked. My dad is sort of like, "Hmmm, my daughter is with a
white guy." I told my dad, "He's just like a black guy, just a little different." And
he said, "I guess." My dad didn't really say anything else. His parents [her boyfriend's] never really said anything. I mean, they were shocked at first. After
that, they were, you know, "She's a pretty nice kid." After they saw beyond
my color and saw me, they accepted it.

There is considerable distance between the actions of the parents
Rina Carson describes and of those parents who refuse to countenance
cross-ethnic dating. The latter kind of parents are not a homogeneous
group. Here is what a moderate father sounds like:

I remember watching that movie, Guess Who's Coming to Dinner. The statement it made was, "Well, you know, we never did say anything was wrong
with them, so she must of thought it was automatically OK to accept one to
marry." So, I think, then, you should say something to people. A friend is nice,
but I don't think you should go beyond friendship. If you're against that, you
should say it and make it understood. It's up to you to make those points
because you are the parent.

Loving parents try to spare their children the opprobrium of a disap-
proving society, their own disapproval masked by evoking that of
society. The views of the moderate father cited above are not accepted
by his children. They know him, as a native of Riverview, to have many
long-standing relationships with black men and women. He draws a
line—between friendship and intimacy—that his children can see but
not accept. The rationality of their father is supported by experiences
and understandings that they do not share. To them their father's line is
arbitrary.

Moderate black parents reach conclusions similar to those of their
nonblack counterparts, but for different reasons. Tommy Robert is in
this category. His light-skinned grandfather could and did pass for
white; his children could not. They grew up with a man whose life was
replete with an ambiguity that today influences Tommy:

The kid of the interracial marriage will be hit the worst of any kid ever. It'd be worse than being in slavery. In slavery, you knew where you stood. You knew not to say this, not to say that. These kids don't know.

Black parents may start with different reasons but reach the same negative conclusions about who their children should date. One black mother staunchly rejected her son's argument that he didn't date black girls because, among other things, they were too mean. She reminded him that when he was talking about black females he was talking about his own mother. Another black mother couldn't even "understand why God made white people." A third was portrayed by her son's white girlfriend:

I don't have any problems with my parents. [To them] it's the person inside, not the color they are. My [black] boyfriend's mom does not like me. I don't think she ever gave me a fair chance because she has all these preconceptions of what I would be because I'm white. He can't even come over to my house to watch TV, only to pick me up.

The position of antagonistic parents—when not based on unmitigated prejudice—derives from experiences their children have not yet had and may never have. To the children, these experiences are secondhand and remote, lacking the power to inform. The children speak from personal experiences that lead to other understandings. White junior Sarah Curtin replays a conversation she had with her father about her younger sister's black boyfriend.

I tried to talk to my dad because he's really hard-nosed about it. I told my dad, "Dad, you've got to be more open. You've got to at least accept him as a friend, because if you push him away it's going to make things worse." It's hard for my dad because you can't change older people. A lot of parents are like that. They say if you go out of RHS, people look down on that [being with a black person]. It's going to be a problem for you later in life. We're looking out for you.

Adolescent children have many occasions to play the role of instructor to their parents because of the frequency of black-nonblack romances. They also may play the role of clarifier of parental views, views which, in fact, they oppose. As they clarify, they testify to a gap between self and parents. Mexican Tim Rivera sounds mature as he talks about his parents, who might not have been presented so amiably if Tim had been describing the actual case of his sister and a black male.

My dad, he'd be kinda like proud if my sisters married Mexicans. They're [the parents] not prejudiced or anything, but they wouldn't feel right if we were to go out with a black person. The way I feel, they're people, too, the same as me and you. But I guess it's the way they were brought up. Different culture.

The older people whom Sarah Curtin believes "can't change" may already have changed in ways that satisfy them but fall short of their childrens' sense of what is desirable. It is the discrepancy between children and parents that the children seize upon, not their parents' "progress" from earlier-held views of black-nonblack relationships. Riverview native Peter Altagoni sees the ethnic-line crossing of his childrens' lives, thinks they have gone too far, and dislikes the acrimonious discussions he has with his children. He might conclude that "you can't change younger people."

Meeting up with all different kinds of people is OK for my children and for me, too. I have black friends, Mexican friends. It's OK, you have this friendly relationship, but then what happens? You start to intermingle, go a little step further, have a date, and then what? When my daughter graduated, a couple of boys that came to the house were black. My aunts were talking about them, you know. Now, they are a generation behind me, which makes that even more foreign. It bothered me because I felt it was probably bothering them. And maybe it just plain bothered me because of the way I am: can't we get a group of people in here—where's *my* people at, you know? But there's only so much you can do. You can't ostracize your children; I mean, we put them in this town. I have come a long way in my mind. I could have been gone [from Riverview], but I let my heritage hook me and keep me here.

The extreme black and nonblack parents are those whose degree of rejection is so strong that the romance stays at school. The couple invents strategies for meeting each other that involve them in considerable deception and, in time, lead to frustration and distress. These are the over-my-dead-body parents who totally reject what they see as the foolishness of other parents who advise letting "nature take its course." Unlike many RHS students, few RHS parents would claim that they have no preferences at all about whom their children are intimate with; they do not argue that it is the person, not ethnicity, that matters. Many more parents are challenged to see the person behind a black countenance than seek the opportunity to do so. Their children present them with a fait accompli. In Riverview, one does not go to the video shop to pick up *Guess Who's Coming to Dinner*. In Riverview, it is real-life drama year round.

If only a black child is not involved, cross-ethnic hostility drops sharply, though it still exists. A special version is directed to newcomer Southeast Asians, but in terms not of their ethnicity—as yet, there are few instances of their involvement in cross-ethnic relationships—but of their success. Perceived as having done too well too soon, their success rankles many. On the one hand, students believe they are able to "kinda take over" because they have been given "special privileges." On the other, students resent their success, finding it and them beyond comprehension. Southeast Asians stay close to each other, speak languages that no one else knows, and speak English so poorly as to baffle anyone's grasp of their outstanding performance in class, as a dismayed college-prep sophomore relates:

There's one girl, I think she's a senior now, from Vietnam. I think she's acing all her classes. She barely speaks English, and when she does you have to really help her along. She's in my Spanish class right now, and she's at the top of the class. I don't need this, you know. I turn to her for help and I can't understand what she's telling me. There's no way I could learn two languages at the same time. I couldn't afford to put in that much effort. She doesn't think anything of it. A lot of people think, "I'm the one who should be getting the smiles from the teacher, not her." She can't even speak the language. It's just something that she does; it's something that they all have a standard for. That's what's expected of them.

Non-Mexican student views of Mexican students can be as dismissive as those directed at blacks. "If you've seen one Mexican, you've seen them all," says a white boy, with the one type being the thug. "I've never seen one Mexican by herself, or by himself," says a Filipino boy. "They smoke their cigarettes or joints and mostly hang out by the flagpole or by the stairs." On the somewhat more evenhanded side is a white boy's thought that "Some of them are nice, some of them aren't." Those that aren't are the "punks. Just by looking at them you can tell they're punks. Oh, man, fat laces, what they wear, stuff like that—I don't advise hanging out with Mexicans. I've had some bad experiences with them." Different but not much more generous observations are made by a black girl.

There's some Mexican girls that dress nice, but they aren't academic students. They're concerned about dress and partying. There's some that don't speak English. There's some that want to be white. They don't want to be Mexican.

Some of her classmates are Mexican wannabes. More than any other nonwhite group, many Mexicans can pass for white and do, only their last names betraying their ethnic origins.

The animus of non-Mexican students is matched by that of Mexican students, though Rosie Gomez's images contain "smart ones, middle-class ones, and Mexican-Mexican ones, the fresh-off-the-boat" students. She elaborates, however, on what she calls the "trouble Mexicans," who "drink a lot, shoot up, and don't graduate." Rosie's picture of "trouble Mexicans" is similar to those of black students who denigrate fellow black students. It is as if Rosie is saying, "I am not them, the trouble Mexicans. Please keep us straight."

Non-Mexicans do not always keep Mexicans straight. Monica Reyes tells about her uncle who came to Riverview for a six-month visit and rented an apartment from a man who kept entering the uncle's apartment when he wasn't home. When she and her mother protested, the landlord told them, "Well, if you don't like it here, you can go back to your beautiful Mexico." Who did the landlord think Mexican-Americans were? Gracie Lopez had a close white friend at school who, when she heard Gracie speaking Spanish, refused thereafter to be her friend. "Are you Mexican?" she asked Gracie. Gracie said yes and her friend told her that she didn't like Mexicans. For both Monica's landlord and Gracie's ex-friend, Mexican designates stranger. Sonia Salazar learned firsthand about this status as the girlfriend of an Italian boy whose family refused to accept her even after two years of dating. "As a matter of fact," says Sonia, "I was treated like a dog, not like I was part of the family." Her explanation of her boyfriend's family's rejection fixes the blame on her not being Italian, rather than being Mexican, a construction whereby all non-Italians are categorized by Italians as strangers.

Among Filipinos, the group called the hoodies have not contributed to a poor overall picture of the Filipinos because a strong countervailing image always has existed. This image depicts Filipino students as basically well-behaved and academically aspiring. If, as is true, Filipino students bear the brunt of some prejudice, they are basically well received, enjoying considerable social and academic success. A young student of mixed parentage refers to this fact: "I sort of fit in more because people think that I'm Filipino and Filipino is a big thing now in Riverview."

Some non-Filipino parents disapprove of Filipinos as romantic partners for their children. They are not vociferous in their disapproval. In Riverview the appearance of Filipinos as respectable strongly moderates the lingering sense of their being different. A senior girl, born and raised in Riverview, testifies to the prejudice toward Filipinos— "it's not that bad, they don't throw on their [Ku Klux Klan] hoods, but you'll feel some prejudice." She may or may not have heard the voices of the rabid few, who are less anti-Filipino than they are anti-nonwhite:

There's this one girl [says a white student], she's Filipino. I had a tremendous crush on her. My friend, one of the burnouts, sees me talking to her. He says, "Why are you hanging around that fucking bitch? She's got slanted eyes." Actually, he calls Filipinos spoonheads. He talks about niggers a lot, too.

Prejudice, name-calling, and ethnic-oriented hostility are not the common experiences of Filipino students at RHS. It is more the case that non-Filipino students react in different ways depending on which of three different Filipino groups they have in mind. Filipino newcomers, the smallest of the three groups, are classified no differently than other newcomers of whatever nationality. They are ignored, teased, sometimes derided, especially by fellow Filipinos. Filipino hoodies, consisting of both males and females, inspired some fear, as well as some antagonism in those who think the hoodies give the school (and Filipinos) a bad name.

The third group inspires resentment by virtue of its success in both the curricular and extracurricular domains of the school and by its cliquishness: "Most Filipinos are really prejudiced against anyone who's not Filipino." It is primarily girls who are identified as members of this group. Other students see them as too pretty, too smart, and too "hotsy totsy," leading one white girl to conclude that they are unfriendly, rude, and "consider themselves highest of everybody," a designation anathema at RHS. "Then you've got the Filipinos with brains," another white girl says about the same Filipinos, "that want to do something with their lives. And, you know, they're going to mix with the white friends and Mexican friends." She, obviously, is among the white friends with whom they mix; the first girl is not. Unlike other ethnic groups, Filipinos engender antagonism in others more by the perception of their "excess" of virtue than their lack of it.

No one stated or implied that white students had an excess of virtue. With one exception, they did not readily evoke typing, as did the other ethnic groups. The one exception is the stoners. Other "types" were mentioned, but by very few students: there is a group that likes to party and switches boyfriends and girlfriends, and a second that is "academically inclined. They're going to college. They're involved in school activities. If you want to be liked by them, join the student leadership class." A Mexican girl classified white girls as the wannabes, the popular ones, the smart ones, "the ones with blonde roots, air heads," the hoodlums, and the jocks.

Sicilian students may feel distinct, and their families may have a strong sense of ethnic identity. At school, however, they have merged with all the other whites, although several non-Sicilian girls, one Mexican, the other white, have a minority report to submit on this point. Both have Sicilian boyfriends who have already graduated from RHS.

Both of our boyfriends are WASPs, meaning Italians[!]. They're like jealous; we can't even go to the mall without thirty questions. If we told them we talked to some man that was writing a book, they'd say, "Who is he? How old is he? What does he look like? What did he ask you?" Sometimes it's difficult. Their food, they make this spaghetti—it's got green stuff in it. Ohhh, gross. Their parents say, "Have some of this." "I'm not hungry." There's little green specks in the meat. It's not the spaghetti we make; we have red sauce. I don't like real raviolis. I like Chef Boyardee out of the can. Real ones are nasty. When Italians get older, they're all fat. They grow up on pasta and garlic bread with butter and green things.

To non-Sicilians, the shrinking boundaries of Sicilian ethnicity may not encompass much more than food, and an Americanized version of it at that. The palatability of ethnicity to others may reside in its degree of Americanization. As far as I know, no white students attract negative attitudes on the basis of their particular ethnicity, in contrast to their general identity as white. There is some unfriendly use of "honky" and "whitey"; their use is constrained by the same explosiveness I mentioned in regard to the use of "nigger." Name-calling of white students, to the extent that it exists, is usually attributable to black students. They are accused of prejudice by the white students who are stoners. Two girls relate their experiences:

The prejudice in this school is terrible. I'm getting sick of being laughed at because I skate [on a skateboard] or because I listen to heavy metal. Every day at least once I get a hard look from a black. When they walk by they say stuff like, "look at that stoner chick."

If you accidentally bump into one of the blacks in the hall and you say excuse me they'll stand there and make a big deal out of it. They are nice to white people who listen to their music. I mean, sure, the people I hang around with are prejudiced, but why shouldn't they be? They don't go around and treat the blacks like dirt. They keep to themselves about it.

Stoner girls feel notably singled out for abuse because of their appearance, as well as their musical preferences. Other black students confirm the hostility of some blacks who if bumped into by a black student will say, "What's happening?" but if jostled by a white student are "ready to jump down his throat." "Some black people are really into their race a lot," a black girl says in explanation of black hostility.

To find prejudice, hostility, and antagonism at RHS that is rooted in ethnicity no fine-tooth comb is needed. Yet the extent of this negativism is so limited that almost every student who identified it was quick to add a qualifying comment about its rarity, lest I get the wrong idea. Although I see black students as the target of such sentiments much oftener than any other group, it was from stoner girls that I heard tales about receiving the most blatant verbal abuse. Given the nature of cross-ethnic mingling at RHS, it may be that the stoners are more distant from the social mainstream of RHS than any other student group.

The Complexity of Social Relations at RHS

Life appears simple at the extremes where, in fact, nobody lives. When groups have blanket feelings for each other, we think we more or less know what people will do, assuming that their feelings direct their behavior. Of course, nothing and no one are that simple. Contingencies pop up, calculations are made, socialized behavior intrudes, civility dictates, concern for appearances prevails, as may pressure for conformity of some sort. The assumption of freely exercised will—I have a feeling about something or someone and I can, unhindered, act upon it—is absurd. Nonetheless, we can still distinguish relatively simpler from relatively more complex times.

The more complex times of contemporary Riverview and Riverview High School did not begin at an ascertainable date with an identifiable event. Their arrival is discernible when observations such as the following can be made:

The one race that stands out most like a sore thumb is the black, because they say years and years ago you didn't see a black guy kissing on another woman that was not black. Or swatting her on the rump. Or walking down the hallways at school with his arm around her shoulder. It was a rarity here in my days in 1965, where now nothing's really thought about it.

This is Josie Thompson speaking; we have heard her voice before. I often wrote "COMPL" on certain sections of an interview transcript; I put many on Josie's transcript. COMPL is an abbreviation for complexity; it usually meant that I was hearing something paradoxical.

Or, to put this matter another way, I would hold an imaginary conversation with an onlooker to whom I had shown only selected bits of Josie's interview transcript. When they had read the bits, I would ask the onlookers, "Is Josie a racist? Is she a racist at all?" You hear her refer to blacks as the race that sticks out like a sore thumb. Isn't "sore thumb" interpretable as pejorative? She speaks of "a black guy kissing on" a woman who is not black. "What to make of "kissing on"? Doesn't it have a hostile edge to it? "Kissing on," as Josie says it, just does not sound friendly, or as friendly as the act of kissing should be presented. And what would the onlookers conclude if they knew, as I have previously quoted her saying, that she vehemently opposes her children marrying blacks, and if her daughter did so, she would advise her to be sterilized? In light of all this, can an onlooker escape concluding that Josie Thompson is a racist?

I never knew when my COMPL sections would turn up. I did not try to elicit them by any ingenious questioning strategy. Just in the normal course of tracking down how parents, teachers, and students perceived ethnicity as a factor in their own identity, and how ethnicity played out in school and community, the number of COMPLs increased. For example, asking Tina Orsini about growing up in Riverview led naturally to her account of moving away from her beloved hometown to nearby Corinth: her young son was being threatened daily by black boys and she feared he would be seriously hurt. Still all of her social life is in Riverview; she likes the place it was and has come to be, including its ethnic diversity. She has easy contacts with the ethnically diverse individuals she has known all her life. Never does she make a statement about a group; it was not black people she disliked, but the black boys who she felt threatened her son.

Obviously, all-or-none type labels do not fit either Tina Orsini or Josie Thompson; existing labels may err on the side of being too generous or too ungenerous. We lack a vocabulary that would allow easy summation, and it may be just as well that we do. What label could do justice to the Josie whose words I have quoted above, the same Josie whose children have black friends who spend the night at her house, some of whom call her "mom"?

Nor is there a label to fit Debby O'Brien who in the course of several days of interviewing spread over several weeks discussed: (1) a group of girls she called "nigger bitches"; (2) the black boyfriend who, to her regret, got away; (3) how hard it is to identify a student's ethnicity; (4) the prejudice of students from schools around Riverview; and (5) that you do not have to be white to succeed in America, with the exception of "nigger bitches," a type of person whose attitudes will preclude their success.

From just outside Riverview's political boundaries, and also from inside them, Tina and Josie, both Riverview natives and RHS graduates, watch the lives of Riverview's adolescent children. Their children know what the adult Tina's and Josie's in their lives believe. Their young lives have dimensions of complexity that are distant from if not alien to most of those adults. While retaining their ethnic identity—albeit to an ex-

tent they and we may not know with any certainty until they have made
the decisions of adulthood—they overlay it, replace it, add alternatives
to it with the bewildering array of behavioral possibilities that RHS offers. Thus, for example, with regard to the self students bring to school,
we see Filipino boys and girls displaying varying degrees of ethnicity,
depending on their own facility with Tagalog and on their parents' ethnic
attachments. At school, they can associate with Filipino students who
have Americanized to varying degrees, or with non-Filipino students
who form groups around lifestyles (e.g., mod, new-waver, punk, surfer),
sports, interests (e.g., computers, performing arts, journalism), or their
own ethnicity. We see the aforementioned wannabe Mexican boy fully
absorbed in the Filipino hoodie's group; from all appearances at school
he has fully joined them, giving no indication by his associations that he
has a fully Mexican life at home. His two lives are comfortably juxtaposed. He sees no conflict between his dual selves, perhaps because
they are separated by place.

Another Mexican boy belongs to a group of mixed ethnicity which
came together during pre–high school days because of shared devotion
to team sports. He has no dual identity; his family has cut its ethnic ties
and so has he. He sees himself as white. Not so a black member of this
same group, who meets some black students for the sake of activities
(football and student government) and others for the sake of ethnicity,
knowingly touching base "to show I've not forgotten my blood."

White students obtain an education at RHS from the incidental experiences of their daily presence at RHS. It is learning of the sort that
derives from contrasting perspectives, that is, from the chance to see
one's own behavior in the context of different others. Accordingly, in Karen's account of being white at RHS, she comes to a point where she
hesitates to proceed because she fears that she does not "know how to
explain without making it sound racial." What she wanted to say was that
there were clubs—La Raza, Black Students Union, Fil-Am Club—that
she would not join because their activities would not interest her. Karen
worried that I would interpret as "racial" her rejection of these clubs,
whereas she meant to say no more than that these clubs did "things" that
didn't interest her; it was these things and not those people that she was
rejecting by not joining. Learning to distinguish between what people
do and the people themselves is no small learning to acquire.

In Perry's account, he dwells on the presence of non–English-speaking groups of students who make him want to say, "Oh, shut up and talk
to me in English." Language is a wall between Perry and them, and Perry feels excluded, though the reverse is more commonly the case. For
better or for worse, Perry is acquiring some feelings about language use

by virtue of attending a multilingual school, and the feelings may well be negative. Peggy's reaction is not to other languages but to what she calls "slang," the dialect of black students that influences the speech of all students at school. Many RHS students learn for the first time the full extent to which their spoken English is not perfectly standard when they meet other white students outside of Riverview; sometimes they learn as freshmen in college English classes when instructors call attention to the dialect in their speech. Trent says that if he has been around black students for "a couple days I'll start talking like them. When I go to Crawford, my friends they say you talk like a nigger."

Peggy takes strong exception to this aspect of life at RHS. "I wouldn't mind if my own kids went to this school. I'm not prejudiced at all. I don't care what kind of color or nationality my kids grow up with, but at RHS they do talk, like, a slang. Everybody does here. It bugs me. I just like my kids to grow up respecting English." Peggy and other white students at RHS do not have a two-language situation to deal with, as do many Mexican, Filipino, and other Asian students; nor do they have two versions of English to deal with, as do black students. They are more conscious of non-English discourse than most American high school students, and in the ordinary course of attending Riverview's schools they absorb elements of black dialect.

RHS contains many students whose four years on the dance floor of school life involves them in all types of steps with all types of persons. What students learn from "dancing" in their complex social life relates, in one way or another, mainly to black students. I conclude here, as I have throughout this book, that the salience of black students is disproportionate to the 33 percent they constitute of all students at RHS. This salience is reflected in what I see as the major nonacademic learnings of the students.

In general, these major learnings relate to the students' ability to make distinctions that stem not from a priori logic but from daily experience. It is no trick to acknowledge that people are not alike; it is somewhat harder to win the confession that a group I generally dislike contains many likable members. Simple logic, if not some experience, underlies both acknowledgments. Where logic does not lead is to the deeper level of knowing that only ongoing experience can create and support. It is at this level of knowing that groups and individuals are put in proper perspective. Here is an example from a black boy: "I think most whites realize blacks are OK, but not all blacks. Same as us. We realize whites are OK, but not all whites." He concludes, "I think people are OK, but not all people."

In a similar view, a white boy discusses what it was like to be a white boy at RHS. He seems to have worked his way through the tangle of his father's ethnic antagonism to enjoy his school's mixing. He states directly that "your head comes off" if you bring home a Filipino or black girl; a Mexican girl "wouldn't be so bad." Here is the distinction that he learned to make.

I don't understand it [his father's prejudice], but I just figure it's the way he is. I consider myself not prejudiced but racial towards some people. It's, like, prejudice to me is when you don't like nothing [about a group]. OK, it's like you're black and I have nothing to do with you. You dislike all blacks. Then, racial to me is, like, this is OK—*you're* black, so what? I have friends that are black, and stuff. Black boyfriends are OK [to his father]. I can make black girlfriends, too. It doesn't bother my dad except when I'm kissing on them [said in friendlier tone than Josie's] and stuff like that.

In the example of a Filipino boy I see what seems to be the irresistible impulse people have to categorize on the basis of what they presume is hard fact. In one interview he generalized about what black students are like. Their overall desire for attention was his explanation for their being loud, liking large cars, and wearing flashy clothes. He said this quite matter-of-factly, not intending to insult black people—nor thinking he had—but simply to say, "This is how they are." In another interview, I asked him if he could be best friends with someone who is not Filipino. He smiled and said that his best friend is black. Categorizing may be done maliciously—and the result is stereotyping and consequent prejudice—or innocently—and the result is the generalizing we all do to simplify a complex world. Whether malice or innocence motivates, the result may be damaging. The Filipino boy innocently categorizes, his shorthand ordering no barrier to the important act of making best friends.

Another distinction students learn to make is one that many parents hope they will make, for to them it represents the best that can be hoped for under the circumstances of RHS's mingling: friendship is acceptable, but romance is not. The two best friends of a white sophomore girl are Chinese and Mexican, designations she has to think about because, she explains, both are just Americans to her. She never discusses ethnicity with them, and she can't think of anything about them that is peculiarly Chinese or Mexican. Romance is another matter. She would not date "colored" or Mexican people: "I really don't think that's good for me so I don't plan on doing it." This, so to speak, is what she says on the one hand, while on the other she says, later in our discussion, "I don't know what everybody else would call them [ethnic groups], but to me everybody's just the same, whether you like it or not. You're not black, you're not white."

This young lady's best friends are Chinese and Mexican, it is not good for her to date Mexicans or "colored" boys, and, ethnically speaking, "everybody's just the same." None of these three statements is predictable from the other two. Logically, they should be the statements of three different persons. That they are not testifies to the fruits of living in a complex social milieu; consistency is sustainable where one's social milieu does not have RHS's fuguelike interweaving of ethnic themes. From these themes, RHS students learn that anything is believable about individuals of varying ethnic identities because they see a full continuum of their behavior, from despicable to wonderful, and all points in between.

When the observations of both black and nonblack students reveal black students whom they like and admire and others they do not, they may then distinguish between "blacks" and "niggers." The comparably derogative term for the other ethnic groups, "Flip" for Filipinos, "Spic" for Mexicans, "Wop" for Italians, is not commonly used to distinguish between liked and disliked members of these groups. In the usage I refer to here, "nigger" is removed from its sweepingly disdainful use by nonblacks to reject an entire people; its scope is scaled down to embrace a subset of black persons about whom both blacks and nonblacks have a grievance. A black boy refers to the group that he heard was going to "jump" him after a concert as "niggers, hoodlums, you know, thuggish people," and a black girl mentions that when her mother wants to point out behavior that she finds unacceptable, her mother says, "you're acting your color. You're acting like a nigger."

Trent's family has lived in Riverview for nearly fifty years. He mentions this by way of explaining his response as a white boy to blacks, knowing that the school group he associates with, the stoners, has no nonwhite members. Trent readily acknowledges the group's racism, and regrets that his friends can't handle what he calls the "blackness" of black students:

It's really kinda sad, actually, that they can't handle it, you know what I mean? Because I find no problem unless they start punking around, picking on people, pushing them around. Because there's a difference between black people and niggers, I mean a big difference. A black person, you can sit whole conversations with, hang around with, trust him leaving him in your house alone. Now a nigger, you would not trust. You can't talk to one because they're prejudice of you. They'll rip you off. They're usually poor guys. Probably turn out with bad attitudes because their parents are prejudiced toward white people. My black friends, their mothers like me. But, see, I have other [black] friends, their parents see me, they really get stiff and tense.

A young white boy answers my standard questions about his three best at-school friends with the information that one is Filipino and two are black. Away-from-school best friends include his dad, with whom he is so close that his dad offered to help find the "two niggers" that had "jumped" him after school one day. This is the distinction I heard repeatedly: a Mexican girl speaks of her friend Rona as a black, not a nigger; a white girl says "there's blacks, but then there's niggers, too. Black is real clean and down to earth, not smart aleck. Nigger is freaky hair, greasy, always has a smart remark"; a white boy clarifies for his father that certain black students weren't niggers, they were his friends. In a Mexican girl's picture of black students, we never see the terms "nigger" and "black," though she sharply presents bad and good types. The former, as others have described them, are "the hoody ones" who get pregnant, use drugs, speak slang, and are tough; the latter, "the normal ones," don't cut school, speak less slang, are active, nice, easy to get along with, and "get pretty decent grades."

What this Mexican girl has learned to do for the purpose of assessing who she can like and who can be her friend is perceive black students in terms of actual behavior. Her choices derive from those same considerations that ordinarily operate within an ethnic group: social class, interests, personality, and likability. With the basic removal of ethnicity as a social barrier, other factors come into play.

Only the newest students have not learned to make a distinction that is further indicative of the complexity of social relations at RHS. It relates to the use of "nigger" by both black and nonblack students. What has generally happened is that students have recoded a word that elsewhere is customarily the property of blacks; its customary use by nonblacks is as a racist epithet. Because its usage at RHS has changed, nigger has both old and new meanings. Black students are cognizant of both sets:

BLACK MALE: While walking on the campus after school, he hears someone call out, "Nigger, what you doin'?" He stops to see who has called him. He hears another voice answer "Maaan." No one was calling him; the words were addressed by one Vietnamese boy to another. He related this incident with amusement in his voice.

BLACK MALE: "Some whites will call you nigger," he says, "but it's nothing. Ain't really nothing. They're just trying to be somebody." He construes the use of the word by whites in a way that defuses its sting. He thinks it is just the behavior of students who "when they do that they think that they're some-body special."

Here another student has also assumed a defusing interpretation of the use of nigger by nonblack persons. It is the recourse of someone who is "frustrated" and who could not mean what he is saying:

BLACK MALE: It's happened a couple of times [being called "nigger"], but only because, you know, a guy gets so frustrated all he can do is call me a name. I mean, it isn't like he really believed I was a nigger. Like what else can he do? He can't beat me up [this student is very big, as well as very smart]. He can only resort to name-calling.

"Nigger" does not predictably trigger a physical response from those against whom it is directed, although it would be most unwise for non-black students to assume they can indiscriminately apply it to black students. Other black students say, in this regard, that only blacks have the rightful use of this word.

Another young black recalls the lecture that his mom gave him and his black friends about not calling each other nigger because this will encourage "people from another race" to think that "they can call you that name." Other "races" do call him nigger but he, too, has an explana-tion that moderates his response: "They don't mean it whenever they are talking to you like that. They'll call you that because everybody else calls you [that]."

The extension of "nigger" to persons who are not black is fairly com-mon. This student stresses the pronunciation of nigger when he applies it this way:

BLACK MALE: Everybody says like nigger, not nigger but niggah. Like, Mex-icans call each other that, and you don't say [to them], "never use that word." If they say it and it ends nigger, you know they mean something racial. If it's your good friend and he says it to you and he doesn't stress that er, you kind of know—

The more he thinks about it, the more uncertain he is that he can be fully comfortable when a nonblack person calls him nigger, no matter how it is pronounced.

A black girl acknowledges the extended application of nigger to non-blacks, as well as a sense of the word that deflects the abusiveness it carries:

BLACK FEMALE: The students might call you nigger, but then I might look at them and say, "You're a nigger too." And they say, "Well, I'm not black." And you tell them, "You don't have to be black for me to call you a nigger, you know."

She conceives of nigger as the label for a type of behavior, rather than as the character of all persons in a particular group. In her way of thinking, anyone of any ethnicity can be a nigger, and certainly anyone who calls her "nigger" is exhibiting the behavior of a nigger.

Another girl clarifies that nigger has not been so fully recoded that she, as a black person, can presume to hear it in the same way any non-black person would. It is too burdened with historic and contemporary censure for that to happen. Yet, she clearly perceives the word in the way that is peculiar to places like RHS: it has been adopted by persons who are not black, it can be used playfully or seriously, and when it is the latter she can take it in a way that will not damage her:

BLACK FEMALE: Riverview is different because there'll be like two white people and they'll call each other nigger. They're just playing. You can tell when it's being used in a dirty way, and you can tell when it's not. Like, there'll be a whole bunch of Mexicans or Filipinos and they'll go "nigger" [to each other]. You can tell when somebody's using it negatively towards you. It doesn't go unnoticed. You still know that somebody violated you, but you don't sit there and dwell on it because there'll always be people like that.

White students use the word nigger in the variety of ways that we hear in the examples of these several black students. They learn how and when to use it, aware of its safe and unsafe applications. From these examples, I infer that at RHS the word has been defanged to a large extent, one major exception being the practice of both black and nonblack students referring to a subgroup of blacks as niggers. When this union of non-nigger "friends," black and nonblack, demarcates itself from nigger "strangers," they supplant ethnic differences with differences based on social class and on behavior seen in academic and other terms, as when a black college-prep student refers to certain blacks as "thugs" who impregnate girls, sell dope, and "grow up with no hopes, no dreams, no aspirations."

Ethnic Peace Explained

Ethnic peace prevails at RHS; tranquility characterizes intergroup relationships. In the 1960s and 1970s, ethnic distinctions became self-assertive realities. In the 1980s, they were not. Ethnic peace may not be the most accurate term to identify the status quo in RHS because it suggests that peace has been made in ethnic terms. Rather, amicable interactions have resulted because of the dampening and submergence of ethnic-based sentiments in favor of those derived from other personal attributes.

In any event, I see a school characterized by a high degree of mingling, where ethnicity does not operate predictably and sharply to mobilize, separate, unite, empower, alienate, or define individuals. At times, and to some extent, ethnicity does produce all these effects. We learned of black and Filipino students preferring candidates for elective positions based on ethnicity, of birds of the same ethnic feather staying together, of white students feeling alienated because they feel so different from most other students, and of newcomer students whose adherence to their subculture defines their behavior to a degree that exceeds that of most other students. But we also have learned of the lack of competition, hostility, and tension between ethnic groups and of the view students profess that ethnicity is not a big deal, that people are just people. In short, the conditions of contact among students are of a type that promote harmony and well-being.[2]

I should try to explain how this situation of peace has come about, emphasizing at once that it is not a mere absence of conflict that I have in mind, but interethnic mingling, an infinitely more positive state of affairs. I want particularly to identify events and circumstances and contingencies that seem to be antecedent to the consequence of ethnic peace. This explanation is by way of saying, "Here is what happened in the country and in Riverview and Riverview High School." What I cannot say is that if you want to see mingling in your school, among your students, here is what to do; nor can I suggest that if conditions approximating Riverview's exist in your community, then you might expect comparable outcomes. I don't register these caveats because I think I have encountered a singular case, or because I see no virtue in attempting to generalize. I simply prefer a more guarded presentation that takes the form of "Here's what I have learned," rather than "Here's what I predict."

Over thirty years ago, Gordon Allport wrote in his classic study of prejudice that "Ethnic labels are . . . 'labels of primary potency.' These symbols act like shrieking sirens, deafening us to finer discriminations that we might otherwise perceive" (1958:175). In Riverview and Riverview High School, "ethnic labels" most definitely do not operate as "shrieking sirens," but that they do not is not because of any program of formal instruction. As a teacher said, "I don't think you can teach it. I

2. Schofield usefully reviews the literature on this topic and the conditions in Wexler, the school she studied. See the section of her book she calls "Contact Theory: A Perspective on Improving Intergroup Relations" (1982/1989:9–29).

think you just have to live it. I've seen people try and force things, and it doesn't go." How RHS students have learned to behave and believe is critical, and this is what I focus on.

Lamar Robinson, prominent black community leader, locates the explanation for mingling in factors beyond any conscious decisions:

It was nothing the town did. It was just something that was happening nation-wide, and then as it settled in the nation it settled in town, also. There was nothing the school did or nothing the parents did. I think that everybody just settled down and said, "We're the same and we go to school. We just have to get along," and they started getting along. I don't think it was anything that anybody taught them or anything they weren't taught. They just realized we go to school together, we might as well get along.

I believe that Robinson rightly credits national conditions as important for understanding what happened in Riverview. These conditions provide the necessary backdrop for what goes on in towns and schools across the country. I believe, however, that Robinson's analysis does not do justice to other circumstances and decisions that facilitated the getting along he refers to.

A contributing demographic circumstance is that no single ethnic group is in the majority at RHS. The exact numbers are not consequential; moreover, they change from year to year. Estimates for the year of my full-time residence in Riverview (1985–86) were black, 33 percent; white, 33 percent; Mexican, 21 percent; and Filipino, 12 percent. By virtue of these numbers, students from any group need not feel they are attending someone else's school. Newcomers and stoners may have this feeling, but it is due to their behavior, not to their ethnicity.

More important than the percentages, of course, is who the students are in other terms—social class, for example. For decades the major local occupations were fishing and blue-collar factory work; newcomer Mexicans and blacks joined Sicilians in the factories. As noted much earlier, most of the non-Sicilian white elites departed, leaving behind ethnics who lived side by side in the old part of town. Some meaningful number of persons from each of the four ethnic groups still live in Riverview today; they had the experience of being neighbors and school friends. If their relationship was generally at some distance from the breadth and depth of mingling characteristic of their children, they had still advanced beyond the tightly bounded stranger-friend categories that preclude people's getting to know each other and feeling a measure of affection, if not of intimacy. Such racism as existed in past years, notably before 1968, was not harsh, divisive, or alienating.

Racism in Riverview was modified after 1968 by the exodus of non-black families who were frightened by the 1968 "riot" and subsequent racial disorder. Their departure left behind a somewhat more economically homogeneous and less racist group. By virtue of their decision to stay (for whatever reason), the surviving group was more inclined to make the best of life in Riverview. The "survivors," who felt abandoned by their departed family members and friends, experienced anew Riverview's we're-in-it-together sentiment that derives from the stigma Riverview's neighbors impose on it.

Here is what a Sicilian survivor sounds like, one of those who grew up with non-Sicilians and remained in town to raise his children there. It would have been easy for him to flee; he had the financial means and the encouragement of many people he'd known for a lifetime.

When I grew up, we were all down there—blacks, Mexican, Chinese, etc. When I went to the Navy, I was on board ship with about seventy southerners, half black and half white. When I'd be friendly with blacks, the southern whites would warn me I shouldn't do that. Within one week of being in the Navy, I learned about prejudice. I don't understand the people who were raised like me and who left Riverview because of the blacks.

Such white survivors joined nonwhite ethnics to change the political and educational order in Riverview by voting out the Sicilians and non-Sicilian whites who had controlled the city council and school board as their private preserve. They had been not so much hostile to minorities as unresponsive to social change. Important indicators of a new Riverview became evident in the first-time-ever election of nonwhite ethnics to political office; the defeat of a proposal to establish a second high school (which would have effectively created a minority ghetto school at one end of town and a middle-class, basically white school at the other); and the promulgation of the sense that political opportunities were open to nonwhite persons. A new order had begun in Riverview!

The fact of a single high school joined another circumstance of enduring consequence. When open housing became a guiding principle in real-estate brokerage and home building, nonwhites joined whites in dispersing themselves throughout the town. Riverview's resulting residential integration has meant that children naturally attend school from kindergarten to twelfth grade in ethnically mixed classrooms.

For a time in the 1960s and early 1970s, busing was necessary to insure integration in the city's elementary schools. Since the late 1970s, "when the neighborhoods mixed," said a school board member, "there was no need for busing for integration, just for transportation." A current

RHS high school teacher, a graduate of the school over twenty years ago, has watched the changes that resulted from integration. It has been a long, slow process, but eventually, she says,

once the little ones got into the high school, our racial problems dropped dramatically because they had all grown up together. There was no reason to be scared of anybody just because they were different. We have a real peaceful racial environment in this school. We didn't always have one.

Nonetheless, the remaining ethnic ghettos of poorer minorities and newcomers create far from ideal conditions for mingling in a few of the elementary schools and in one of the two junior high schools. These conditions, however, are mitigated and soon overcome by the impact of attending Riverview's single high school.

With very considerable reinforcement from state and federal legislation and agencies, the elected political and educational managers of Riverview are basically alert and responsive to the interests and needs of all their constituents. They are strongly moved by the linking of state and federal money to ethnic accounting. The managers got the habit of being sensitive,[3] and the once-disempowered people got the habit of standing up and being counted and of thinking that in relative and absolute terms they had joined the establishment. As needed, they took advantage of the new laws and the nearby civil-rights office for protection and appeal. These external supports strengthened the impetus for fairness and justice.

In practical terms, the new-order school board members hired a high school principal and, in time, two superintendents who were determined to run a high school and a school district in which ethnic peace prevailed. This principal and the second of the two superintendents are Riverview natives, graduates of RHS, survivors, and skilled managers of their multiethnic establishments. They join Riverview's nonwhite groups in the support of affirmative action and in the operation of schools that communicate openness and opportunity to all children. Their success is clearly reflected in students' comments that they get their fair share of what the school has to offer. The intent to be fair, and the perception of it as reality, contributes to ethnic peace.

A central concern of the school district's leadership during most of the post-1968 period has been to create conditions conducive to ethnic peace. On the one hand, ethnic leaders grew tired of years of protest and confrontation. I had heard this as well from leaders outside of Riverview

3. See Metz for a brief but useful review of the literature on "interracial relations" (1983:207–10) and the "special characteristics" of the magnet school she studied which support good relationships (1983:213–15).

when I was searching for a research site. On the other, administrators, teachers, and students eventually developed the requisite skills for sustaining salutary relationships across ethnic groups. A black teacher recalls the feelings of the 1970s:

Ten years ago, God, it's like night and day. Then we were in the attitude of black pride, Hispanic pride. It wasn't really the blackness in the kid, the whiteness in the kid, it was just the old prejudice that showed up in the seventies, in the sixties. When you had to "burn, baby, burn," the blacks got an attitude, the whites got their attitude. What happened [finally], I think, parents said, "Hey, wait a minute. I can be proud but I don't have to burn down the building. You can be proud but you can't cuss the teachers out and you can get As and Bs.

The responsiveness of the school board and its superintendent is inferrable from the comments of a major black community leader:

When I'd go present a problem to the superintendent of schools, I'd want him to look at me and say, "Well, here he is presenting this problem to me and he wants something done about it. And if I don't deal with it, he's going to have the board room filled with people to support him," which I don't like to do, but I've never had to do that.

And the responsiveness of the high school principal is inferrable from still another black leader: "You know a lot of people criticize him over the years and think we ought to have a black principal. I've stuck with him because he's sensitive. He cares."

Perhaps most important, the availability of the school board to Riverview minorities has blunted the emergence and exacerbation of problems that can result from parents' feeling that they are neither heard nor understood. In its entire history, Riverview's school board had as members only one Mexican (in the middle 1970s) and one black (from the early 1970s to the present). Because the black member and a longtime (for sixteen years) Sicilian board member are active participants in Riverview's largest black organization, the black community feels it is "represented." But so does the Mexican community. A Mexican community leader explains that the black and the Sicilian are their "friends on the board," and the superintendent "I think he listens and he's willing. He tries to negotiate issues and problems; I have not heard of any serious problems with the high school since then [1980, when there was a three-day Hispanic boycott]."

For all RHS educators, a lesson learned from the 1970s that stands high on the list of words to the wise is to be consistent in the treatment of all students so that there is no basis for a claim of discrimination. This claim resounded in the school halls during the 1970s. Between cases in which outright favoritism was manifest and others in which an attempt was made to leaven the school's response by considering the circumstances, students and parents found the basis for charging discrimination. Consistency became, and remains today, the canon for applying school rules, especially as regards matters of discipline. One parent lavished high praise on a high school administrator who epitomized consistency:

The kids used to say about him—he don't care if you're black or orange or brown or white. If you did anything wrong, you're out. In the old days it was more a case-by-case basis, where some kids would get into a fight and, because of the circumstance, nothing would happen.

RHS's hard-earned lesson about the virtue of consistency overpowered the contrary message ethnic groups often delivered—about understanding their culture and taking account of their differences, because the differences were often closely connected to the group's dignity. Still, if educators leaned toward the rewards of consistency in dealing with infractions of school rules, they had not been deaf to the messages asking them to take account of ethnic groups and their interests. If the messages were ignored, the results could be strikes, boycotts, riots, and relentlessly long meetings.

Another lesson learned was to avoid the impression of favoring one group over another. "You had to balance," said a district-wide administrator. "You had to balance Columbus Day, which was an Italian thing, with Martin Luther King Day. You can't take one or the other." The notion of balance was passed on to teachers in those many school matters where choice existed, though no one ever thought it applied to participants in athletic competitions.

If the high school, regrettably, cannot offer all children roughly equal opportunities for academic success, it cannot be faulted for interfering in the success of any child. It continually seeks out the hard-to-reach children and introduces alternative programs to minister to their needs. Many children, mostly of minorities, regularly fail. Since parents and students do not blame the school for this failure, RHS enjoys an atmosphere of good will, as do the city's political agencies. This good will is rooted in, among other things, the high school principal's recollection, quoted in a 1984 newspaper account, that "Riverview is still recovering from the riot. I think people still remember and fear that happening again." Remembering and fearing have been beneficial to ethnic peace.

In sum, the social order in Riverview that preceded the civil rights movement was relatively gentle but highly circumscribed in regard to the rights and opportunities of nonwhites. The changing political mood of the nation combined with specific pieces of legislation such as the Model Cities program to crack open the old social order. People who had never had to deal with each other in matters of finance and power, were required by law to meet and talk. As one participant in this process observed, "I would say that the process [of dealing with each other] had a big effect on the political system, because it never went back to the way it used to be. Whether it did a lot about solving the social ills of the community is another thing."

This is a major irony: control of the political process as it relates to the city and the school system shifted from an entrenched circle of oldtimers to a new group of skilled people with a strong sense of social responsibility, while the economic disparity between have and have-nots remained—and still remains—enduringly harsh. Blacks and Mexicans are quick to point out that Sicilians still vastly outnumber them on city and school district payrolls. They are not pleased with the sensitivity of police officers to minority offenders. And they see their children dominating the statistics of failure at school. These disparities do not lead them to mobilize within their ethnic organizations, as they did in the 1970s. Accordingly, the organizations do not heighten ethnic consciousness in ways that are, as earlier they had been, reflected in the social interactions of RHS students. Ethnic peace—at a price—is thereby served. This outcome is not the work of peace-at-any-price advocates, but, I reason, of ethnic leaders who are disinclined to agitate, as they once did.

The new order in city and school governance persists and by remaining in place becomes a factor for promoting ethnic peace. Indeed, a begetting effect occurs: the more officials in office grow accustomed to being attentive to the needs and interests of all Riverview's citizens, the more does attentiveness become the norm in what the officials do and what the electorate expects them to do. The continuation of this process is facilitated by the prominence of an able, relatively moderate leadership among the nonwhite ethnic groups.

Here is what the voice of moderate leadership sounds like. It is Lamar Robinson's, reflecting on his one-time vociferous resistance (including the filing of an injunction) to the closing of a school in his predominantly black neighborhood:

What I've learned over the years, I'd say it was a justifiable closing. It was the school that had the lowest enrollment. At the time, I didn't look at it that way. I just looked at it—they're closing our neighborhood school, and busing all our kids to white schools. I didn't like that. Hindsight, I can see where you have to close the school with just that many kids. It's not profitable to operate.

And also reflecting on the election of black candidates:

I never believed that you run a black just to be running a black for a political office. I don't feel a black person should run for a position unless he's totally qualified for that position, number one. Number two, that person has to be electable.

And, finally, reflecting on his conception of leadership:

It's been my experience over the years that when I negotiate with anybody for anything, I don't use threats and demands. It's more effective to deal that way than to make demands and embarrass them in a public meeting. I'd rather sit down in their living room and say, " This is what I'm concerned about. It's a need [for which] the community wants and deserves [your attention]."

Such leadership softened the encounters that brought officials and ethnic leaders face to face. As their respective skills—on the one side, listening, and on the other, communicating—sharpened, the likelihood of mutual trust and negotiated resolutions was enhanced. This trust, a fundamental element in Riverview's ethnic peace, was based on the belief that those who ran the school district were persons of good will, their intentions in the right place, their behavior commensurate with their intentions. For example, a critical, thorny issue in the 1970s, by no means resolved today, was the hiring of minority educators. The administrator in charge of recruitment took minority-group members with him on his recruitment trips so they could see firsthand the lengths to which he went to find and hire minority educators. Eventually, these community persons "just disappeared, they didn't want to come anymore." They became reassured that he was working as responsibly as they would want him to.

Riverview's white adults, not least those who are natives, became accustomed to working with and relating to Riverview nonwhite adults in ways that were necessary for mingling to develop, as it eventually did at RHS. Adult mingling has been facilitated by the failure of the city's nonwhite groups to unite to outvote whites in city and school elections. While this failure clearly limits their political success, it prevented a siege mentality from developing among whites that could have encouraged further white flight and promoted dysfunctional defensiveness among those who remained. Ethnic interaction among students exceeds what is wanted or welcomed by many Riverview adults. For the most part, RHS students inhabit a social terrain that has no exact adult coun-

terpart. Yet, if there was no adult constituency for it, if the students' social patterns had no sanction from outside the school, they could not
prevail.

That adult constituency has been slow to develop, for the outlook of
most adults has not been forged in the crucible of thirteen consecutive
years of positive proximity at school, if not of several years before school
began. Adults simply have far fewer occasions to be linked across ethnic
groups in shared endeavors. There is multiethnic coalescing around
elections, since no single ethnic group has the numbers, on its own, to
win an election. There is further coalescing of a usefully continuous sort
around school events, particularly sports. Football has the major multiethnic team and, accordingly, its large audience of adults is most
ethnically diverse. Indeed, the high school is the only community institution with the capacity to attach all people to it. Its causes, events,
and teams inspire the mutual affect of caring and sharing. Adults support
and cheer on these causes, events, and teams.

One afternoon, I watched RHS's outstanding girls' baseball team.
The RHS stands were filled with engaged, outspoken fans. RHS was
playing archrival Corinth. The two teams offered a striking contrast in all
respects, Corinth's side all-white, from spectators to coaches to players.
As if for the benefit of a researching observer who would take comfort
from such things, three preschool boys, one black and two white, played
in and around the RHS bleachers, fully oblivious to the baseball game.
The boys wrestled, had mock fights, and ran around in keeping with
some little game of their own making. Then, as if following a script, the
boys stopped wrestling and stood up. The black boy stepped between
the two white boys and put his arms around their shoulders. Together
they walked off to a new play area. Score one for mingling.

The adult mandate also derives from the group of former RHS graduates who remain in Riverview as residents and parents. Having
undergone the experiences of a multiethnic school and community, they
have developed skills and insights that are the special province of insiders. A Sicilian man, in his thirties, relates his observations of the non-
Riverview manager of the store in which he works, fully aware of what
he knows that his manager from nearby Corinth does not:

At work, there's this racial feeling going on between my manager and two
black people. He really doesn't know how to talk to the blacks, where I grew
up with them and I know. He'll give them an order and he'll say twice, "Do
you understand, George?" as if he's a dumb nigger. I can see the expression on
George's face. He goes, "Yeah, I understood it the first time." And the manager may call a person, "bro," but the black guy says, "I have a name." I warned

the manager last night. I said, "Hey, you'd better just watch yourself. You've got to respect everyone's culture."

A school-based adult constituency for student mingling has emerged from the district's moderate success in hiring nonwhite teachers, counselors, administrators, and nonacademic employees, and from hiring so many Riverview natives in all these positions. Riverview natives, by virtue of their own upbringing and schooling, are personally and vicariously accustomed to a degree of mingling that cannot be matched by outsiders. Outsiders may learn to be at ease with the prevailing norms; if not, they learn to be quiet about their antagonism to them.

Josh Pearson's years as a Riverview resident give him an ease with students that would be hard for an outsider to acquire. He is in special education. In the anecdote below, he demonstrates this ease, and he also indicates the type of socializing opportunity that has potential as a begetting effect.

There are days when the kids are always teasing me. Today it was "How does it feel, Mr. P., being the only white person in the room?" I laughed and said "I don't know, I didn't even notice that. How does it feel to be black?" They said it feels a lot different. We discussed that. That's always gonna be in students' minds. I seem to be able to talk about it.

The more Pearson has these experiences, the easier it is for him to respond to them and communicate to students that they can question him in a certain way, which thereby engenders more such experiences for Pearson. Like the students, RHS teachers work in a peculiarly ethnic milieu, their eyes and ears daily accustomed to the sights and sounds of the culturally unique setting the school represents. Whatever their personal values about the merit of ethnic mingling, they see it as a natural aspect of school life.

Teacher accommodation to this reality means that they offer no counterperspective to the social status quo. In their classrooms they proceed, as I have indicated, in accord with an implicit notion of universalism. In practice, this means that they see their instructional role as the preparation of students for working and living in a society that does not apply varying standards based on ethnicity to anyone. This they assume as both reality and ideal. This homogenizing orientation of teachers reinforces a comparable orientation operating among students, parents, and other community adults to mute ethnicity as a factor in public and private activities. RHS's ethnic clubs are weak; the city's ethnic organizations do good work on behalf of "their people" but not much in the spirit of enhancing ethnic awareness. The consciousness raising of the 1970s seems to have been supplanted by concern for educational and economic issues that focus on the fate of ethnic people but not on the intensification of their ethnic identity.

Within RHS, several circumstances conduce to the establishment and perpetuation of ethnic peace. I have already mentioned the contributions of the principal, the board's hiring of nonwhite teachers and native-born Riverview teachers, and the socialization of all teachers for maintaining at least a public posture of respect for all ethnic groups. An outcome of the school districts' successful hiring of nonwhite educators in all positions except for the superintendency is the promulgation of the idea that ethnicity is not a barrier to employment. This is the principle; it can be learned by students and teachers and parents from the media. What they know from daily life at RHS is the reality of this principle, that, indeed, it is a normal, natural occurrence, one marked by no special comment or ceremony. At some level, therefore, adult mingling is as normal as student mingling. Because adults of a range of ethnic identities are present in their lives, students expand their conceptions of who can exercise legitimate authority in their lives. Thus authority, like friendship, romance, and trouble, transcends ethnic boundaries. Black, Mexican, and Asian teachers organize, control, reward, punish, instruct, and comfort, just as white teachers do.

Students receive a similarly expanding experience from their peers. Since it is highly probable that students from all ethnic groups will occupy the places of honor, responsibility, and authority throughout the school's curricular and extracurricular programs, students thereby further learn the normalcy of ethnicity serving neither as barrier nor precondition to achievement. The open society is not an abstraction to RHS students. The higher probability of minority students failing to enter the cherished places of achievement, such as the college-prep track and student government, in proportion to their numbers, seems barely to dampen the belief of these students that RHS is their school as much as anyone's. Why this is so, I speculate, results from two conditions. First, students, educators, and other adults believe that black and Mexican students do less well in school compared to whites and Filipinos because their parents are less supportive of schooling. By so believing, the schools are not blamed for their failure. Second, black students are generally content with the school because they have a dominating presence that lifts them into the school's limelight. For example, listen to the school's nonblack valedictorian talking about acting black: "I can talk black, I can act black, if I want to. It just comes naturally, their movements and everything you know. I don't know why." As a writer remarked, "In the mingling and jostling of peoples, there is more stylistic exchange" (Bell 1975:43). Black students, I am suggesting, have disproportionate social power, which combines with the odd case of distinguished success to act as a sop for their overall modest academic achievement.

In fact, the prominence of black students is translated into the belief by students from all ethnic groups that black students are in the majority at RHS, the estimations ranging widely between 50 and 75 percent. Ed Barker, a young student of mixed ethnicity, figured that the school was more than 50 percent black and less than 50 percent white; he seemed to start off on the right track. He left it immediately: "I'd say about 70 percent blacks, and about 45 or 50 percent whites. Mexicans, I'd say about 20 percent, and, well, Filipinos are probably like 30 or 40 percent." His reactions to the numbers are one more factor in the cause of ethnic peace: "Blacks overrule the whites. That's all there is, is blacks around here. But I don't mind because I get along with all of them. So, it's like cool for me."

Notwithstanding the assumption of a black student majority at RHS, nonblack students do not feel overwhelmed or defensive. There is no ethnic derby of any type that has students competing from within their ethnic groups. Mingling is the abiding fact. It rests on the experience of one's eyes and one's personal associations. Concrete cases have been elevated to principle—"Actually, I don't think it's the race that matters, it's the person themselves." Ethnicity is overriden by individual attributes: "You just mix and it's natural; you don't notice it." The strength of knowing a person as a person, rather than as a member of an ethnic group, inhibits stereotyping, even when it could easily happen otherwise. As in the case of a black boy who describes the disaster of his black friend who got beat up, his nose broken, by white boys from Corinth. All white people don't do that, he clarifies. "It could be anybody who do stuff like that." And in the case of a white boy who speaks of the anger he and his friends feel toward black boys who "take away their white girlfriends." He, too, clarifies: he and his friends are not mad at blacks in general, but "a particular black."

As students become friends and carry their friendship beyond the confines of the school, they visit each other's homes, meet parents who speak little or no English, and see various expressions of cultural differences. These differences stand as characteristics of home life and adults, not of one's friends. For one's friends are like oneself, preparing for the same tests, doing the same homework, cheering on the same team. Tigers only come in one color at RHS. The assumption among students is of similarities; they see and value each other acting the same.

Where the practice and principles of mingling do not prevail, an acquired civility does. Students learn that "you can't really be prejudiced. If you are, then no one's gonna like you, really." Being prejudiced, "That's not the thing to do here, you know. You'd probably get into a lot of fights that way." Prejudiced people "at school they just kinda swallow it." Which is to say, as one black teacher did, "You've got to live with these people every day." And having to live with people every day results in a modus vivendi. It complements mingling to provide a firm foundation for ethnic peace. Both processes socialize new students; the behavior of older students provides models for both. Mingling begets mingling; ethnic peace begets ethnic peace. The impetus for civility among students is powerful; the impetus for mingling is even more powerful.

Though I have been writing about civility and mingling as contributors to ethnic peace, I cannot specify which, strictly speaking, came first. There surely has been an interactive effect, with more of one promoting more of the other. Of the many other factors antecedent to ethnic peace that I have identified, some are distinctive for being what I see as controllable, that is, they relate to decisions that the public or some group has knowingly made. Controllable factors include the election of a majority of school board members with an orientation toward responsiveness to all students, opposition to favoritism in school district hiring, support for affirmative action, and selection of administrators favoring a certain type of school. School board members and administrators intended to establish and perpetuate ethnic peace. Intention, too, is controllable, although it is not tantamount to reality.

Outside the school, major contributions to ethnic peace came from the quiet mood of the country following years of disturbance and from state and federal legislation that offered funds and facilitating structures for attaining the goals of the civil-rights movement.

How much weight to attach to contingent factors—Riverview's particular configuration of ethnic groups, its large post-1968 exodus of white families, its blue-collar economic base, and its denigration and stigmatization by neighboring towns—is beyond my calculation. As is the contribution of what I have called the begetting effects, so that once a certain type of event occurs, it facilitates more of the same. As are also certain ancillary, one-of-a-kind effects: for example, when a white teacher's sister married a Filipino and the marriage succeeds, the teacher will not look at Filipino students as she did before this marriage. Filipinos are now not just nice kids, lively students, or disciplinary problems—all possibilities within the category student—they are located in the category of friend, which encompasses the intimate act of marriage. This teacher's words about the marriage are instructive: "I never really paid attention to that until my sister married a Filipino." Then she began to realize, "they're really—I learned something. I appreciate Filipinos more." What is a singular, attention-demanding event for this teacher is, in its adolescent equivalent, a powerful and ordinary set of events for RHS students. They are too common to stand out, as does this marriage for the teacher.

I often visited the advanced acting class. I liked the atmosphere, the activity, the students, and the teacher. One morning when the teacher went to answer his telephone, the students spontaneously broke into song. All knew the words, a form of adolescent mastery that will never again be so important in their lives. The students share pieces of the same cultural fabric—clothing, music, language, hair styles, movies, events, as well as the time and place of school. They form and re-form groups based on variations of the themes drawn from their common cultural fabric. On another morning in the same class, the teacher was waiting for the next student to volunteer to perform; he reminded them that if a volunteer did not come forward within the designated time, he would penalize all students. The teacher's system made the students cheer each other on; it made them very conscious of being in the same boat. RHS students seem generally to be mindful of being in the same boat. I think this awareness is instrumental for promoting ethnic peace.

8

It Can Happen Here: Friends and Failures

Most migrations begin with lone migrants . . . who later bring their wives and children. As they become permanent residents . . . they recreate their traditional culture.

—Jacqueline S. Mithun

The ethnic lines were there, but it was always, "We're from Riverview" because the whole world was against Riverview, and it still is.

—RHS teacher

It is one thing for a white child to be taught by a white teacher that color, like beauty, is only "skin deep"; it is far more convincing to experience that truth on a day to day basis.

—Supreme Court Justice John Paul Stevens

You [Peshkin] spend a lot of time on ethnicity, but that's fine. I hope your book isn't going to be all about ethnicity, because to me that's not a very big issue. Maybe because I'm here and it's not a big issue here.

—RHS student

What is it like being a black student at RHS? It's fun—I like being black. Everybody is human beings. We're no different—the only thing different is our color and color only. We are all the same. We are all people.

—RHS student

As I come to the end of this book, I am reminded of the first book I wrote in what is now a series of studies of American high schools. The setting was rural, midwestern Mansfield. I was struck by the sense of community in Mansfield that encompassed young and old residents and made its high school instrumental to the survival of community. I chose to tell the

257

story of community and its powerfully sustaining sentiments, which meant that I did not tell the story of those who for different reasons lived outside the compass of Mansfield's social blessings.

As a complex place, Riverview and Riverview High also contain stories I have chosen not to tell, as well as many others that I'm not even aware are there for the telling. I choose to tell the story of a school and community that transcended a decade and more of ethnic strife to become a place of abiding mingling. By creating a narrative with this particular orientation, I mean to make more readily imaginable what I believe is both ideal and necessary for American society.

Multiethnic Riverview has joined rural Mansfield and fundamentalist Christian Bethany Baptist Church as a setting for my exploration of the school-community relationship. I called the rural study *Growing Up American*, a title also applicable to the study of the religious school and its community. I could as well give it to Riverview and RHS, for they, too, are about growing up American in several of its current variations. Because of local control, and the prerogatives it provides our cities and towns and villages to put their own stamp upon their local schools, our schools differ. Because these schools are located within the same larger society, subject to the same nationalizing impositions (e.g., from tests, textbooks, schools of education, federal legislation and money, the media), they also resemble each other in respect to subjects taught, authority relationships, and emphasis on sports and extracurricular activities, among other things. I asked students, teachers, and parents, "Is RHS different in any way because so many different cultural groups send their kids to this school?" This question, modified to fit the rural and Christian fundamentalist settings, was the same one I asked in Mansfield and Bethany, and the same one I will ask when I go next to explore the school-community relationship in another setting. It considers, in effect, what ways, if any, it matters whose children attend a particular school.

The epigraphs that introduce this chapter capture my sense of Riverview and its high school. As Mithun says about migrations in general, Riverview was settled by people who followed the arrival of one "lone migrant" whose testimony brought in others of similar ethnic identity. Thus, Riverview's history is of successive and overlapping waves of newcomers, their descendants staying on in Riverview in sufficient numbers to maintain its multiethnic character. Each group's "traditional culture" simultaneously was "recreate[d]" and underwent assimilative change at a pace reflecting the group's opportunity to move from being strangers

to becoming friends. Internally, this was the picture. Externally, Riverview received the contempt befalling communities that are home to
minority residents; its citizens, accordingly, developed what a teacher
termed "the whole-world-against-Riverview" outlook. This outlook engenders an edge of toughness to the performance of RHS football
players, a tone of defensiveness to the talk of residents in matters involving comparisons between themselves and their wealthier, whiter
neighbors, and mixed ripples of anger, shame, and vexation that their
town should be so unfairly stigmatized.

Riverview's neighbors do not usually get close enough to see the special quality of Riverview High School's social interactions. And if they
knew about it, they might not find it admirable, unlike Justice Stevens,
who would. By his dissent in the 1986 Wygant v. Jackson Board of Education case, he indicated that he interpreted the equal-protection clause
to sanction preferential treatment for black teachers when their district
had to lay off teachers. The legal issue aside, Justice Stevens's words acknowledge and applaud the essential fact of RHS: its students learn the
"truth" about color on a "day to day basis." The daily experience at RHS
is the basis for a student of mixed Mexican and white ancestry wanting to
be sure I understood that ethnicity is "not a big issue here," and for a
black student to affirm in her English class essay that she likes being
black and "we are all people." How incredible that her observations are
noteworthy! How further incredible that the odds so highly favor her
becoming an academic failure! The wonder of RHS is that despite the
school's location in a society where color remains an "obsessive theme,"
it has so little consequence there.

In Retrospect

Committed to following the play of ethnicity, I began my journey
through Riverview and Riverview High School. Ethnicity was the yardstick by which I measured whether I wanted to stay where I was, listen
to what was being said, finish reading the documents I had collected,
and even whether in research terms I thought I was having a good time.
Ethnicity brought me to Riverview; it had the ethnic diversity I sought
as the condition for my study. Moreover, it has had this diversity for decades. Notwithstanding the influx of white newcomers to the town's
many new housing developments, Riverview will remain a place of ethnic stratification for some time. This reflects the demographic facts of
contemporary California and the emerging facts of the United States.
We once were overwhelmingly a nation of people from Europe, which

meant that when newcomers learned to act and speak "properly," most could become interchangeable parts with those citizens whose ancestors had arrived earlier. A basic fact today is that most of our newcomers do not come from Europe, and they do not look like their European predecessors. Will these newcomers become interchangeable parts with the already Americanized Americans? At RHS, they have.

To follow the succession of Riverview immigrants—Welsh, Sicilians, Mexicans, blacks, Filipinos, non-Sicilian whites, and Southeast Asians—I spoke to the oldtimers, those who if there were an ethnic faith to keep would be its keepers. Their ethnic faithfulness stretched from near indifference to ethnic identity to gastronomic and festival-holiday observations to concern for history, endogamous marriage, etc. If they so chose, they had ethnic-based memories sufficient to "keep the 'wolf of insignificance from the door'" (Saul Bellow, quoted by Morrow 1988:100).

Among the many questions I asked ethnic elders were always some that related to marriage; I wanted to learn who it was OK to marry. I reasoned that a preference for ethnic orthodoxy in marriage would be an important indicator of a person's commitment to perpetuating ethnic identity. Of course, I quickly learned of mixed marriages, a Sicilian male to an Irish female, for example, and of the adaptation by the non-Sicilian wife to Sicilian ways. After all, Riverview for decades was a Sicilian stronghold, with little chance locally to reinforce being Irish. I learned further that in the marital sacrament honored under mixed ethnic conditions children could see daily what they would eventually personally realize: love refuses containment by ethnic boundaries. In time, parents accepted marriages that they had first disapproved, using the sweeping, American rationale of, "As long as they're happy." Meanwhile, my questions stimulated respondents to considerable reflection about ethnicity in general. When I learned of the traditional objections to cross-ethnic marriages, and recalled other facts about who (in ethnic terms) occupied the major elective and appointive jobs in city and school affairs, I adopted *strangers* and *friends* as central concepts to shape my story about a multiethnic community.

Not all former newcomers told the same story about their experiences of coming to and settling in Riverview. One element they did share related to how their predecessors in Riverview received them: as newcomers, they were the strangers. They learned the language and acquired the interests, skills, and behavior that would facilitate acceptance by those who were the self-fashioned gatekeepers of who is American. The seeking newcomer and the gatekeeping oldtimer converged on issues of acceptance: to what extent could and would the former adapt

American ways, and to what extent could and would the latter accept the adapting newcomers? Only diehard gatekeepers thought that the newcomers were too hopelessly distant from themselves ever to be accepted as American friends. Most of the people who received the newcomers were ordinary, wary neighbors whose reservations about the latest newcomers in their midst would erode with each manifestation of the newcomers' becoming like themselves. When their reservations had a basis in religion (being Catholic) or color (being black), the erosion was less certain.

One thing certain about past and present Riverview newcomers is their unwavering devotion to America. Some parents and grandparents may want to die and be buried in a natal home; they are, however, loyalists in their adopted home. Though Asian and Hispanic elders don't always merge seamlessly with more fully assimilated peers, the behavior and unaccented English of their American-born children joins them to Americans of European origins in all but appearance. Thus one learns anew at RHS what Americans look like.

The as yet unsocialized RHS newcomers are subject to the shaping behavior of their peers; they receive powerful incentives to learn the American ropes, to fit in, to be accepted, to acquire, in short, the appearance, behavior, and language of friends. Only newcomers seem moored in their ethnic identity.[1] As newcomers, what else do they know, what else can they do? This condition seems to be temporary. In time, they see the same three avenues open to them as to their more culturally settled predecessors. They can locate themselves within their ethnic group in one of its acceptably Americanized versions; they can make a temporary ethnic crossover, as do the wannabes; or they can associate with one of the nonethnic, lifestyle or interest groups which, except for the stoners, are open to students from any ethnic group. These three options are not mutually exclusive.

About the time of my residence in Riverview, California and other states were entertaining measures to install English as the state's official language. Californians passed the measure in 1986 by popular vote, with an almost three-to-one margin. From inside Riverview I found no warrant for what animated so many people throughout the country: a threatening ascendancy of non–English-speakers. The English-first-and-only sentiment feeds on experiences, fears, and impulses that do not square with the realities of the city and high school in which I lived and worked. Informed by the stories of elderly Riverview Sicilians who,

---

1. For American cases see Schofield 1982/1989, Patchen 1982, and Metz 1983; for an English case, see Hewitt 1986.

like the Japanese, had been interned during World War II, I concluded
that the mentality of English-language-only pushers smacked of the in-
ternment camps.

Still, the rush of newcomer students and their predecessors to Americanization seems unduly hasty. "Don't give up so much so fast," is how I
personally responded to the pace of their retreat—at least in the public
arena of the high school—from ethnicity. In what I'm sure is a further
instance of projection, I would think how unpropitious the circumstances were for reflecting on the place of ethnicity in one's identity.
"What is happening to my heritage?" is not a question that youth are
prone to raise. They come closest when they regret, as some do, their
minimal facility in Tagalog, Spanish, or Sicilian, languages with currency in their family circles.

RHS's ethnic potpourri does not encourage thinking about ethnic
maintenance. Students call upon other students to clarify their ethnicity; there is this type of need to know. Beyond this identificational
interest, students downplay ethnicity, preferring to be known in their
adolescent world by other markers of personal and collective identity.
Student groupings by ethnicity, when they occur, are rooted in the students' greater familiarity with and ease of access to their ethnic others,
not in a principled consciousness that has them wittingly seek out their
ethnic kind. Within Filipino, Mexican, black, or white (stoner) enclaves, students find language and behavior traits that are peculiar to
that group. Given the openness of groups of all types, the fluidity of
movement among them, the range of nonethnic behavioral alternatives
they offer, and the homogenizing influences of in-school and out-of-
school experiences, I do not attach much weight to these convenient,
comfortable enclaves as places for ethnic maintenance.

As I reflect on the conduct and self-characterization of students and
their parents, it seems likely that what they retain from their subcultural
heritage is reflected in these concerns: Do we have access to the education we need and are we rightfully visible in the education we receive?
Do our people get their share of elective and appointive offices? Do our
people get their share of jobs? Is our music and dance being sustained?
Can we buy the ingredients we need for our special dishes or the dishes
themselves? This amounts to shareholder, festival, and gastronomic ethnicity. It is a group legacy that does not demand much from a particular
individual; it is a legacy that intrudes few obstacles to Americanization,
and that expects little from the institutions that serve them. Thereby the
passage from stranger to friend is facilitated. In Riverview, the last European group to decline to these limited manifestations of ethnicity are the

Sicilians. Riverview residents do not single out any other local white group by name; Riverview whites (excluding Hispanics) simply blend into a large, undifferentiated group called "white." Non-European groups are advancing down the same path of combined absorption, on the one hand, and limited but situationally variable ethnic expression, on the other.

I have not done a study of the acculturation process of newcomers, let alone a study of the socializing impact of schooling on the children of newcomers. RHS does contain newcomers, a small subgroup of Southeast Asians, Mexicans, and Filipinos, but it mostly contains children who have attended American schools since kindergarten and spoke English when they began school. My interest in ethnicity is in circumstances where children hold fast to at least their nominal ethnic designation and where either parents or grandparents or both were born abroad. I wondered how ethnicity would be played out in the formal and informal affairs of the school: Would it be a fact of any consequence in shaping the life of the school? Would RHS be different in ways that could be attributed to ethnicity?

If RHS is different, and I think it is, the differences are perceptible in a community where a black mother tells her daughter, "White folks in Riverview got more soul." And they got it, the daughter explains, from black people: so white folks are not snooty, you can talk to them, and they dance better than other whites.

The differences are further manifest in several facts: That racism lacks status at RHS. That ethnicity neither allows nor bars access to the school's goods. That no group arrogates right, authority, superiority, or privilege to itself on the basis of ethnicity, notwithstanding that black taste and style predominate in many nonacademic matters. That the permeable boundaries of ethnic groups permit the ethnic-identity shifts of wannabes. That ethnic-group territoriality is so slight that students have little opportunity to learn defensiveness or to acquire the habits of caution, resistance, or reservation in their relations with others.

Following the 1960s, events outside Riverview compelled Riverview residents to take account of ethnicity. State and federal legislation, a response to the pressures of urban rioting and a powerful civil-rights movement, led to ethnic accounting. As a condition for obtaining money, school districts kept track of whom they hired and whom they taught. Specific programs attuned school districts to the needs and interests of students, not merely by ability, gender, age, or social class, but also by ethnicity. Riverview's black minority, always a central fact in the stigmatizing of the town, became—and remained—the central fact in the

school district's attention to ethnicity. Nonetheless, the ethnic picture at
RHS is not the simple one of blacks and nonblacks, because the nonblack group contains several other ethnic groups which might be
expected to see themselves in distinct terms. I wondered, therefore,
about the mandate RHS educators received from its seemingly culturally diverse parent constituency. Would RHS be ethnicized in some
way? Or was the physical appearance of diversity overlaid with cultural
uniformity so that the school would be primarily like schools anywhere
in the country?

I heard no endorsement for an ethnicized curriculum from within
Riverview's ethnic groups. General opinion held that ethnic maintenance, such as it will be, is the business of the home; the school has
other things to do. This rough-hewn division of labor between home
and school did not mean opposition to ethnic clubs or to the occasional
integration of ethnic-oriented elements into English and social-studies
instruction. But neither parents nor community ethnic organizations
had sufficient interest or concern to determine if the instructional program actually included ethnic-oriented elements. Parents, teachers,
and students related RHS to necessity (compulsory attendance) and
opportunity (jobs and further schooling), and thus to its function as an
American school that could have been located in Maine or Minnesota.
Parent and educator support for hiring more minority teachers, the
English-as-a-second-language classes, and whatever ethnic-inspired
pedagogical accommodations the school makes are motivated by interest in promoting the school's universalist orientation. That is, they
help students to succeed in school, not to be more firmly ethnic.

RHS educators consciously draw upon knowledge of their students'
ethnicity in minor ways, minimally cognizant of the depth of the cultural
understanding they are acquiring from daily experience at RHS. They
don't realize how much they know because what they know they have
learned slowly and unconsciously, not by formal instruction. They do not
foster their students' ethnicity, nor are they hostile to it. Respectful understanding and quiet appreciation of it rather than neutrality would be
their stance. RHS teachers generally operate as if they had read and accepted as dictum: "We don't need diversity in the American classroom;
we need uniformity" (Rodriguez 1981:45).

Teachers claimed, often emphatically, that they are color-blind and
"kids are just kids." They explained that what matters is the students'
varying capacities to learn, not their varying ethnic identities. Solving
learning problems necessitates not ethnic knowledge but pedagogical
knowledge, abetted by sensitivity to home and personal conditions that
could exacerbate the problems. By claiming that "kids are just kids,"

teachers save themselves from explicitly asking, "Does student ethnicity constitute a fact with instructional consequences?" Paradoxically, they do not think to reconcile the considerable sensitivity and insight they have about students from different ethnic groups with their color-blind outlook. Were they truly color-blind, could they have developed their cultural sensitivity? Their ostensible unwillingness to label the lore that they daily act upon derives, I think, from their historically fostered caution to avoid any appearance of prejudice or favoritism. Declarations of color-blindness signal this avoidance. It also draws upon what they see as irrefutably sound: success in American society generally does not have an ethnic component, nor, therefore, does the formula for establishing a fitting school for Riverview's youth.

Down the street from Riverview High School, so close that students often walk there for lunch, is Tony's Snack Shop. It serves different clienteles throughout the day. Each weekday morning, from about 7:30 to 9:00, Tony's is claimed primarily by male, Sicilian, Riverview natives, many related by blood or marriage. They drink coffee, eat calamari omelets, tell stories, and mull over the events of the day—from baseball to family to city council business. They are linked to each other, to Riverview, its history and its future, and to being Sicilian. Each has a family, a life beyond their shared space together, a connection to other worlds, large and small. At Tony's, however, they are rooted in the particularisms of community and ethnicity, which for them merge readily.

The men who create this ethnic time and place each morning at Tony's snack shop did not learn to do so at RHS; nor will their children and grandchildren learn to do so there. Tony's Snack Shop and Riverview High School contribute different but useful understandings and values about affiliation, community, and social interactions. At Tony's, adults alert to the status of their ethnic group in Riverview life discuss and debate where to stand on issues bearing on the well-being of their ethnic group. In addition, they daily reinforce their mutual connectedness, which begins in shared ethnicity and expands to other concerns by virtue of shared space, history, and friendship. At RHS, students attuned to mingling learn to look past ethnicity as the basis of affiliation, while acquiring experiences that join them to other generations through pride, commitment, and expectation.

Teachers generally forgo opportunities to promote ethnic consciousness in their classrooms. Such promotion is not part of their socialization. An English teacher's preoccupation with the universals of subject-verb agreement need not have kept her from drawing attention to the Hispanic context of all the examples. But on the one hand, such attention could be no more than curricular tokenism, and tokenism is

never more than a step in the right direction, and often an insultingly
small one. On the other hand, if such small curricular elements prolife-
rate, they could communicate through the school's cognitive domain
what is strongly apparent in its social domain: everyone counts. Thus,
when the prose, poetry, and pictures that constitute a student's high
school education routinely refer to our society's cultural and human diversity, then this diversity becomes eminent, and the cause of
legitimation and counting for something is promoted (at no cost, as I see
it, to efficacy). A sensible curriculum surely lies somewhere between
Rodriguez's "uniformity" and the recommendation—fitting, perhaps,
for a less culturally complex setting—that "appropriate education
in a pluralistic society would begin with the development of programs
that use the cultural contexts of the population served by the schools
to determine the values, goals, and content of education" (Epps
1974:179).

The foundation for mingling at RHS is the students' compulsory presence in public schools that serve all of Riverview. Though many students
and parents question the merits of the academic program at RHS, no
one doubts the distinctiveness of the school's social experience. Many
parents disapprove of this social experience. In social terms, RHS prepares students for a world of friends their parents never bargained for.
As a group, students surpass parents by a light year in their easy legitimation of others as friends. Such legitimation counters the
dehumanization that permits assaults on life and dignity by neglect, dis-
enfranchisement, and ignorance.

In mingling, students acquire experience, understanding, and skill
their parents neither endorse nor personally possess. Mingling represents a significant incidental learning at RHS. If it required a
widespread parental mandate to exist, as does the school's universalist
orientation, its perpetuation would be in doubt. Parents fail to see mingling as the social counterpart of the school's curricular universalism.
Being able to make it anywhere in American political and economic life
does not extend to making it anywhere in American social life. The
breakdown of social exclusivity, with its enlightened view of stranger
and friend, continues in spite of parental dispositions. In fact, it continues in spite of the dispositions of many RHS educators who accept
without cherishing student mingling.

At RHS, ethnicity is not a barrier to achieving goals or to establishing
any relationship. This is one part of what by the title of this chapter I
suggest can happen here. I mean to acclaim its happening. I wish I knew
how to make it happen where it does not. What happens at RHS is sin-

gular; because it also occurs in other American schools (Schofield 1989/1982, Patchen 1982, Metz 1983), it is not unique. I believe, however, that RHS's mingling is sufficiently uncommon to warrant highlighting it, saying, "Look here, this school is special. It has a priceless stock of social capital. Its mingling is an enviable good."

Tracking down ethnicity has led me to a complex place of cross-ethnic warmth, affection, love, loathing, and rejection, where nonblack students abhor persons they call "niggers" and have blacks as their best friends, a fact that, along with others, signals the recoding of color and ethnicity I have mentioned before. For social interactions, color and ethnicity do not predictably connote either acceptance or rejection. And since they do not, students generally are spared the onus of defensiveness that hostility engenders. The absence of ethnic defensiveness seems to have had two results. It has created the open boundaries that encourage the phenomena both of widespread mingling and of identity-seeking wannabe-ism. It has also led to blurred identities. Students are not uncommonly confused about who they are, but they are relatively free to select behavioral elements from their school's cultural grab bag. But by minimizing ethnicity as a factor in the composite of their own identity, they thereby enhance their school's universalist thrust, surely unaware of, probably unconcerned by, what they may be forgoing in regard to ethnic maintenance.

Indeed, ethnic maintenance is undermined by the "soft weapons" (Kramer 1986) of tolerance, good will, acceptance, and, above all, mingling. Students, therefore, are not so much wrenched from their ethnic souls as they are subjected to a continuous barrage of eroding experiences that result from the ordinary events of school life. Because students wish to become friends, they learn "to predict one another's behavior . . . accommodate to it and articulate their own behavior with it" (Berreman 1975:97). By this process, the school is mainly closed to ethnic behavior, leaving its expression to home, and sometimes to neighborhoods. It also is closed to students confronting "an alien turn of mind" (Geertz 1986:269), as would be the case if students were cocooned in their ethnic casings. Permeable ethnic boundaries permit a degree of mutual fathoming of fellow students' behavior. RHS students, sadly, are more effectively educated by the school's ethnic diversity than by its academic program.

The triumph of RHS is that students learn that individuals from every ethnic group merit acceptance and rejection. They know that students from each ethnic group merit every attainable position, achievement, and honor: admission to West Point, winning a scholarship to the University of California at Berkeley, election as Homecoming Queen, earning the grades to be valedictorian, making county-level, prize-winning speeches, ad infinitum.

In reality, a principle of substitutability operates, whereby this year's Filipino class president can be replaced in next year's voting by a white, black, or Mexican student, or this year's Mexican homecoming queen can be replaced in next year's voting by a Filipino, white, or black student. Substitutability is a fundamental fact of life at RHS. It occurs in the general absence of ethnic competition, unqualified by the effects of an ethnic division of labor that would distribute students to this or that domain of school activity. The one area that follows ethnic lines, (though not by plan) is the boy's basketball team, which is composed almost exclusively of black players.

What else happens at RHS is contained in what I have been calling the statistics of failure: black and Mexican students are disproportionately high in the ranks of dropouts, suspensions, expulsions, and assignment to special programs, and disproportionately low in test scores, eligibility for college-prep classes, and college attendance. That RHS keeps company in this regard with many American schools does not lessen the harshness of its failure.

In 1968, a local group, working under the designation "Black Achievement Project," prepared a manifesto. Its eleven-item "List of Demands" was prefaced by these words: "We cannot wait any longer to participate equally and fully in every realm of school life. We must be included in the school, we will not remain invisible. We have to be recognized now." When black Sarah Cartwright came to Riverview in 1944, she said "it was dried fish, French-type bread, and spaghetti," her way of characterizing the primacy of Sicilians in Riverview affairs. "Things have gotten better since then," Sarah concludes. And since 1968 they've also gotten better in the schools as regards the fullness of black participation in all of school life and their recognition. The school's outstanding failure has to do with the academic achievement of minority students. The failure occurs under conditions basically devoid of ethnic slurs, closed doors, overt racism, and discrimination. Thus it goes on unmitigated either by an angry, aroused public seeking redress, or by lists of demands, organizational protests, packed school board meetings, administrator bashing, and lawsuits. The failure is known and noticed; it is not perpetrated by indifferent educators. It results from hard-core ignorance of what to do to enhance the ability and willingness of students to seize opportunities available in the school experience.

This failure conjures up the specter of a permanent underclass, a society divided, and the like. Several years ago, a group conducted a restudy of racial conditions in America. The occasion was the twentieth anniversary of the renowned Kerner Report of 1968. The 1988 findings were disturbing:

America *is* again becoming two separate societies, one black (and, today we can add Hispanic), one white—separate and unequal. . . . [As] Roger W. Wilkins has said, "The problem is not a problem of a defective people; the problem is a problem of a defective system" (*Education Week* 1988a:17).

This failure also generates the language of "at risk" students. Inventing language to name this failure and highlight its ramifications leads often to hideaways, those instructional corners of special programs that educators fashion for students failing mainstream classes. These programs lead students to a high school diploma, whereas one of RHS's conventional academic tracks might not. For students grown accustomed to failure special programs also afford them some degree of success, though seldom to the extent that they return to regular classrooms. The one sure contribution of special programs is that they reduce the heterogeneity of classes in the mainstream academic tracks.

Minority students abound in hideaways, placed there by the school's filtering processes, which are devised, we must assume, out of concern, not cynicism. Students are assigned to one of the many academic compartments attached to the school, the school district, or the county. These are widely dispersed and so, consequently, are the students, dispersed everywhere, in fact, except to those settings where students and teachers mutually value academic accomplishment. The right label—at risk—and the dire forecast—a society divided—serve to alert and alarm. Unsupported by sufficient commitment and knowledge, they generate flurries of reform that stir the dust for a while but ultimately produce little of value, least of all the massive effort needed to overcome the failure of minority students.

Hideaways contain those students a school defines as special problems. More disturbing are the school's vast majority of students in the mediocrity of its general academic track. They disturb more because they enjoy no special programs and are significantly more numerous. In Powell, Farrer, and Cohen's term, they are the "unspecial" (1985). They seldom rise to academic levels above the school's mainstream track; they seldom get special attention. When they are added to those who are special at the negative end of the academic continuum, the total includes most minority students at RHS. The brilliant successes of a few minority students are a bright ornament. They offer solace to educators who are annually reminded that to be fair, they must interpret their students' scores on normed tests within the band of schools containing high percentage of poor minority students. This is cold comfort. Students from schools with high percentages of minority students are not protected after graduation by membership in a special band; they are not viewed in any special perspective by the rest of the world.

In its own historical perspective, RHS has made commendable progress. In a general, absolute perspective, RHS has the "problem of a defective system." Perhaps nothing less than declaring it defective will suffice to clear the way for fundamental, sustained exploration of how to reconstruct the status quo. This is a harsh judgment. I direct it not at Riverview High School overall, but at those aspects of it that contain its core of minority students. Although RHS educators, administrators, school board members, and parents are perpetuators of the status quo, they did not invent it, did not select it from an array of pedagogical possibilities, and do not callously maintain it, indifferent to its consequences or the opportunities for reform. All of these local agents of the prevailing curricular practices are embedded in an interlocking system that includes teacher unions, textbook publishers, accreditation associations, state departments of education, and federal agencies, as well as parents and educators grown accustomed to expecting too little from too many of their students.

Perhaps RHS parents and educators are so accustomed because of the school's "mingling" and its ethnic peace, and because of the school district's deserved reputation for meaning well and trying hard. The school is party to enough good will to blunt the anger and resentment that in other circumstances minority parents could direct at it for their children's record as academic failures and, at best, modest achievers.

The good-will-fostering deeds of many educators deserve mention. They take varied forms. I will include examples drawn only from teachers who work with the "unspecial" majority or whose performance affects all students. The list, of course, is incomplete. It contains: Teachers who voluntarily teach only general-track students, unrelieved by the college-prep sections of their subject with their bright students who allow teachers to be on task most of the time. Teachers who plan instructional sequences to discourage the blight of teen-age pregnancy in courses where such instruction does not naturally occur. Teachers who stand on the campus outside their classroom building in the interim between classes, chatting and joking with students who never realize that the teachers' vigil is in response to a "riot" of more than ten years ago that they feel could have been averted. Teachers who come to school early and stay late, making themselves available to any students who seek help. Bilingual teacher aides who when they are not teaching keep their doors open to the many Spanish-speaking newcomers whose newness leaves them outside the pale of friendship. All of this and more contributes to the students' sense of being cared for, to their parents' sense that their children are in good hands. This sense is not misplaced. But the laudable conduct of these many teachers is by choice; it is piecemeal and uncoordinated. It is not part of a system that puts it in concert with the behavior of all or most of the other teachers. These good deeds are beneficial but well short of a program that encompasses the school, persists from year to year with certainty, and grows better because it is organized, grounded in an articulated conception of ends and means.

The fact that some things truly work at RHS, that things of value occur there, mitigates against sentencing it outright as defective. What a victory it would be to maintain those features that deserve respect and to reorient its approach to students so that a promising future for minority students became an event of high probability.[2]

In Prospect

ETHNICITY

In the several decades since 1968, Riverview and Riverview High School have experienced ethnicity as a dynamic mass that has expanded and contracted in size, shape, and intensity in reaction to circumstances both inside and outside an ethnic group. There is no ethnic midden for those elements that apparently have lost value, such as language, for some persons, and certain ritual practices of marriage and religion, for many others. The capacity of the newly faithful to revive elements that once seemed abandoned forever is considerable. What is abandoned is not on a midden heap but in what you might call an ethnic checking account, which the faithful can draw upon as perceived needs arise. Riverview's ethnic organizations, now given mostly to raising money for various good causes and ceremonial displays, could, if necessary, return to their defensive postures of the past, as when the Mexican-American Political Association sued the Riverview school district.

The ethnic account contains the potential to mobilize one's fellow ethnics for some cause that affects the well-being of "our people." It contains friendship ties for students to draw on of the type that we may have

---

2. Many schools around the country are seriously involved in reform efforts of various types. Among the most promising is one known as the "Comer Process," named after its creator, James P. Comer of Yale. His approach involves the resocializing of students and the establishment of effective working relationships between educators and parents (Magner 1990). For another plan, see the report on results of the Quality Education for Minorities Project (1990).

only with persons designated as "our people," as in the case of the black woman who acknowledged that her very closest friends had to be black. The ethnic account contains the basis for feelings that underlie one's tender spots, as when a Mexican-American woman, otherwise living and looking like any other American, expressed her anger at the federal government's treatment of undocumented Mexicans. Mexicans had not and perhaps never will become a mere *them* to her. Her American *us*, informed by a sort of phantom ethnicity, retains a sensitivity and concern for the fate of her Mexican own. She did not extend the same sensitivity and concern to the dispossessed of Southeast Asia, Haiti, or Central America. Ethnicity's sticky web attaches us beyond our capacity to disentangle ourselves easily and permanently.

The play of ethnicity in social terms reveals a school of students whose general adolescent interest in their personal identity overpowers their concern for the place of ethnicity in that identity. Adolescent need for peer acceptance and approval stifles the ethnic aspect of their life; it may await adulthood, if ever, for resurrection and revitalization. Adolescent interest in the more palpable matters of current activities and future jobs and ambitions cause them to rank ethnicity low in the list of attributes that may be important for someone, a possible friend, to know about them in order to understand them. This judgment reflects not only adolescent preoccupations, but also how little they know and understand the impact of their own ethnicity in shaping the person they have come to be. Filipino senior Tom Aguyat observes that for close friends one does best to stay with one's own nationality. Less than five minutes later he says that he does not think of himself as different from Mexicans, blacks, etc.: "Everyone has been Americanized." But his my-people orientation for close friends is possibly a lifelong distinction he will make. Tom may feel best believing that he has been Americanized like everyone else; he may neither seek out nor need that degree of self-awareness necessary to understand how ethnicity operates in his life.

What Tom and his fellow students do not deliberate is how far they can go in becoming mainstream Americans and still feel at home at home. When parents and children dispute the boundaries of how far they can go, each group finds allies among its peers to support its own case. In such conflicts, I see more truces than resolutions, more avoidance than clarification, each group accepting what strikes it as inevitable. The at-home feeling, derived from the intangibles of language, behavior, posture, mood, and attitude, and from the tangibles of the ethnic souvenirs of childhood, is too taken for granted by adolescents to warrant their articulation. We know, however, from the histories and biographies of American immigrants, that the requisites of getting by, making it, being accepted, and fitting in can lead to cultural distancing at odds with feeling at home at home. "The emissaries of the public and private agencies were bent on improving the immigrant to a point at which he no longer would recognize himself" (Handlin 1951:283), and, therefore, neither would the folks at home. RHS's ethnic students seem headed in the same direction.

RHS students reveal a pronounced disposition to be, as one student said of himself, "a person just like other persons." This stance seldom precludes acknowledging one's ethnic origins, as when I asked students which of three possible identifications, for example, Mexican, Mexican-American, or American, they would select. The hyphenated middle choice was the usual preference, except by those white students with too-mixed or too-attenuated ethnic backgrounds for hyphenation. The local social situation rewards nominal ethnic identification—"I am a Filipino" or "I am a Mexican"—as does that in the larger society where prospects of academic and occupational opportunity are sometimes contingent upon ethnic identity. Both situations necessitate a minimal withdrawal from one's ethnic checking account. One's parents are prone to be both larger depositors and users of the resources on reserve in this account. They tend more to seek the security and comfort of "connections with the past" (Kilson 1975:261), caring more to keep their ethnic future from dying. Their adolescent children can find security and comfort outside the confines of ethnicity, leaving largely untouched this element of their ethnic accounts. For now, they lack "an ear for the music of its revelations" (Fischer 1986:230–31); "they don't go heavy toward that cultural thing," as one RHS teacher said of student interest in ethnicity.

While coming to terms with the ethnic component of their identity, some students acquire self-hatred; it is not confined to black students who join white students in rejecting "niggers." A black girl, Rae Thompson, provides an example from an incident in one of her classes. The class had heard an announcement inviting Latino students to an all-expenses-paid conference. Fellow students urged their classmate Carlos to take advantage of this conference. Rae recalls that Carlos said, "Latinos, I don't want to be up there with all those SA's." She went on:

SA—that's like a derogatory term for a Mexican. To me, that's just like a black person saying I don't want to go to a conference with all those niggers. Carlos hangs around with white guys and black guys. I can see him succeeding and then, you know, forgetting the rest of the Latinos that aren't making it, and he, like, blames them for being poor.

Carlos may be among those with ethnic scars of the sort that newcomers develop subsequent to the ridiculing they receive for language, appearance, and behavior that sets them apart. And of the sort that both

newcomers and second-generation students acquire as a result of resisting the entreaties of their more ethnically orthodox parents.

Adults notice the diminished attachment of their children to ethnicity, especially those with vivid memories of the attachments of their
own parents. "We'd just been talking about that at our cultural committee," said a Filipino woman. She and her friends were reacting to the
virtually total absence of adolescent children from a recent Filipino-
American Association affair. Similarly, second-generation Sicilians recall the frequent *che bergogna* admonitions of parents who by their
"what an embarrassment" rebuke were communicating that a transgres-
sion of Sicilian propriety had been committed. "Seventy-five years ago
che bergogna really meant something." With each generation, children
find less that is embarrassing by ethnic standards.

In the recent past, before Sicilians departed their intact ghetto at
Riverview's north end, neighborhood, church, home, peers, ethnic organizations, and work brought them together. Many of RHS's black and
Mexican students still live in ghettos, but as run-down enclaves of the
poor they lack the completeness and the stability of the old Sicilian settlement. Black churches and Spanish masses reinforce ethnic identity.
RHS does not because other factors for activity, affiliation, and success
operate there: talent (what you can do) and taste (who and what interests
you), not ethnicity, are preeminent. Parents implicitly acknowledge
these other factors when they dismiss grandparental opposition to their
children's behavior by saying, "That's the way they are." This translates
as, "Grandparents see the world differently and they are bound to do
so." Parents dismiss their own opposition by saying, "You can't live their
lives." This translates as, "I may not like what my children do but I can't
and shouldn't do anything about it."

The children, for their part, also find language to explain parental beliefs they choose to ignore. Ron Acuna's parents object if he and his sister
have contact with blacks beyond the level of friendship. "I guess that's
the way they were brought up," he says to explain what they believe. He
and his classmates arrogate the right to reject what their parents believe
and do, unaware how much of their parents' outlook they may have internalized, awaiting only the right situation to become manifest. In the
meantime, adolescents hone their judgment to insure passing their
school days in minimal jeopardy of being singled out by peers in unacceptably ethnic ways. They want to lead taunt-free lives, to be perceived
as OK. At RHS there is no OK status for being actively ethnic, as there is
for being one of many American variants, none of which sanction wearing one's ethnicity prominently.

As adolescents follow their elders in retreat from ethnicity, they further attenuate the concept of "good Sicilian" or "good Mexican" or "good Filipino." They endorse other characterizations—good person, citizen, student, American—all without an ethnic qualifier. Ethnic organizations can honor their person of the year, recognizing individuals who have served well the cause of the black or Filipino people, for example. Such recognition is not equivalent to a general, known category of "good black" or "good Filipino." These are not ideal ethnic identities to aspire to. At RHS, students frequent a broadly inclusive place of good persons, of friends, as I have been using the term.

Notwithstanding the homogenizing impact of RHS and its corresponding dampening of ethnic expression, the play of ethnicity is and has been sufficiently robust to inform students, teachers, and parents of the nature of ethnicity and its potential: a parental protest made with the enlisted aid of the NAACP, a chance for certain scholarships and instructional support, a pride in the salience of one's skill in music, dance, and talk. Today, the informing is, I believe, largely at a tacit level.

MINGLING

At Bethany Baptist Academy, the fundamentalist Christian school I studied some years ago, students frequently heard their mentors cite 2 Corinthians 6:14: "Be ye not unequally yoked together with unbelievers: for what fellowship hath righteousness with unrighteousness? And what communion hath light with darkness?" Bethany Baptist Academy was determined that its students shun the nonfundamentalist children of unrighteousness and darkness as unsuitable candidates for close association. In fundamentalist terms, the apostle Paul would be no friend of RHS's mingling.

"Unequal" cross-ethnic yoking is rampant at RHS. It is a stable aspect of school life, independent of any particular configuration of ethnic groups, the impetus of particular student leaders, or the encouragement of a special set of teachers or administrators. To be sure, all three are supportive factors, but mingling is embedded in the school's social structure so that each new wave of freshmen is socialized with appropriate behaviors, beliefs, and values.

Will there be mingling after graduation? Which is to say: How tied to the circumstances of RHS is this phenomenon? A definitive answer lies beyond my data, but not beyond my speculation. Today in Riverview and in American society there is no principle that argues against mingling. Nor is there exhortation of the 1960s and 1970s type, that of the so-called new ethnicity with its enhanced ethnic consciousness, to impel minorities and nonminorities to return robustly to their ethnic account.

Thus, RHS students are free to mingle. In the absence of their school's special, supporting, circumstances will they continue to do so?

Of Benny Rivera's three best friends, one is black, another is Italian, a third, like Benny, is Mexican. He knows all three from school. Ted Robinson, black newcomer to Riverview, has a black, Filipino, and Mexican as his best in-school friends and three blacks as his best out-of-school friends. He knows his three black friends from church. Sally Thomas is white, an athlete, and longtime Riverview resident. During the school year, her good friends are her ethnically diverse teammates. During the long summer vacation, her circle of friends is ethnically narrower "because when we're here at school we plan things on the weekends. Everybody does it." And in summer when she is away from school, everybody does not.

In short, the circumstances of school facilitate mingling; the circumstances of summer and church do not. This suggests that the perpetuation of mingling, in contrast to the conviction that it is perfectly acceptable, depends upon circumstantial factors, such as who, in ethnic terms, is present where one lives, works, plays, and goes to church. A black teacher voiced another consideration. She reasoned that though students "feel safe in school" they will go into "little [ethnic] cubbyholes" when they get out into the working world because then there's uncertainty and "you get that support group that you need from your own." Her assumption is that "your own" may be defined one way in adolescence and another way thereafter. I do not believe that mingling at RHS reverses a student's conception of "your own." It does, however, expand the conception of how much like one's own the own of others can be. RHS's moral code endorses the notion and practice of social inclusion unfettered by a priori tests of ethnic suitability. Thus, custom, belief, and practice at RHS encourage mingling, but circumstances may be the most compelling facts to shape the extent of postgraduate mingling.

And already in Riverview the circumstances are changing. In 1987, the more than fifteen hundred new homes under construction were expected to bring about 850 additional students into the city's public schools. The building of new homes and apartments has continued since then; their purchasers are primarily white families whose work at some distance from Riverview increases its status as a bedroom community. Dotting the city are new neighborhoods with people whose concerns are safe water, fast transportation to work, properly located garbage dumps, and schools attuned to securing high test scores, the standard, shorthand measure for academic goodness. These white newcomers move to Riverview because of the relatively modest price of its housing (modest because of the high percentage of minority residents), not because of its rich history and "interesting" ethnic diversity.

Riverview's white middle-class newcomers represent the city's basic demographic change. A Filipino adult, thinking about the implications of the newcomers' presence, knows that change is imminent "but I don't think they can change the one thing Riverview has, which is a lot of people living together. They're going to have to mingle with the rest of us." How accurate she will be remains to be established. Will the newcomers' children, often raised apart from such mingling realities as Riverview's, constitute groups with countervailing orientations that are harder to discount than those of the nonmingling stoners? Will they provide havens for other RHS students who, while civil under current conditions, have not bought into the norms of interethnic intimacy? The prevailing social order in RHS that I have been applauding is not flimsy, but neither is it so fixed on bedrock as to be proof against determined battering. The prevailing respect for ethnicity in Riverview is distant from the concerns and priorities of the ethnically nondescript white newcomers. They may have little regard for what I see as the major unresolved issue of RHS, its academic underachievement.

COMMUNITY AND CURRICULUM

In the rural and fundamentalist Christian settings of my earlier studies, the high schools function as community-maintenance institutions by their many activities that draw people together, by serving as an object of deep, widely shared attachment, and by inculcating the major values of community adults. In demographically larger Riverview, the high school has relatively less importance as a focal point for community energy, affect, and activity. Nonetheless, no other institution approximates the high school's capacity to unite local people. It not only is the alma mater of many residents, it also, by virtue of its sixteen hundred students, connects to many others—parents, relatives, friends, and neighbors.

Unlike rural Mansfield and Christian Bethany, where the fit between school and community rests on a core of conservative political, economic, and religious values, the product of midwestern village and church orientations, the fit in multiethnic Riverview focuses more on the school as means for meeting various expectations: academic expectations (manifest in the school's many academic niches, which indicate the school's intention to find an academic place for everyone); Americanizing expectations (manifest in the school's universalist orientation); and athletic expectations (manifest in the school's devotion to success in football competition). It is these expectations, more than a distinctive core of values and beliefs that classrooms reflect and reinforce, that define the fit. As do most high schools outside of urban areas, RHS incidentally fosters Riverview's sense of community. Also incidentally, it provides occasion for a moral code vis-à-vis ethnicity to be fostered among students. This code may prove to have enduring consequences for individual students; it does not appear to be an element in the fit between school and community.

In Mansfield and Bethany, the employers hired educators whose lives and beliefs verified that they belonged in such schools. In Riverview I identified no community-based value structure underlying the selection of educators and the shaping of instructional content. Thus Riverview's school administrators are freer to select teachers in terms of their instructional qualifications; in addition, they focus on tolerance, more than on intellectual capacity, for working in a multiethnic school and community. This concern goes beyond ethnic accounting, that is, the hiring of designated proportions of Mexican, black, or Filipino persons, to include white persons who can fit in a school that has not ethnicized its curriculum, but where ethnicity is in the air—the complex, tangible (but sometimes intangible) entity that runs through the social fabric of the school.

Job-seeking educators need demonstrate neither interest in nor ability to contribute to a curriculum that is multicultural in any of its several suggested forms (see Banks 1977 and 1981; Gollnick and Chinn 1983), or that has been ethnicized. At RHS, as almost everywhere else in the United States, plans for multiculturalism or ethnicization are not explored and rejected as unworthy, they are ignored. The well-being of students, community, and society is not construed as hinging on their implementation, though our universities have aroused debate by their compulsory courses in non-Western civilizations. Only 11 percent of the legal immigrants in 1985 were European; by 2050, Americans not of European ancestry will be the majority (Codrescu 1989:32). But the increasing presence of non-Western people in America seems not to stir policy makers to reorient the curricular thrust of our schools. In the past, when the new and different people were eastern and southern Europeans, and at present, when they are Latin Americans, Asians, and Africans, the thrust to Americanize predominates.

This thrust appears to "work" for most students who are not black or native American; it is perhaps premature to judge how it will work for Mexican-Americans. Again, the circumstances of black students is highlighted, as it has been, if only by omission, throughout our history. For no American group has been so continually and abysmally excoriated. President Lincoln, reflecting the Northern sentiments of his day, invited black leaders to the White House in 1862 to discuss returning all American blacks to Africa. He told them, "You and we are different races. We have between us a broader difference than exists between any other two races" (quoted in Gates 1986:3). The implications of Lincoln's conclusion, and those following the views of less charitable persons, demeaned, depressed, and denied blacks.

Resistance to blacks' claiming their identity and rights as Americans remains entrenched in our society. Joseph Califano, who held high office in the administrations of Presidents Johnson and Carter, writes revealingly on this point:

During all my years on President Johnson's staff, I cannot recall a single personal call from a member of Congress asking us to step up civil rights enforcement for blacks; I remember scores of pleas to blunt such enforcement. . . . [Under President Carter] our vigorous enforcement of civil rights laws on behalf of women, Hispanics and the handicapped met with relatively modest resistance; similar action on behalf of blacks often sparked fierce opposition (1989:28).

Nicholas Lemann, who calls the fate of blacks in America "The Unfinished War," agrees with Califano: "Race remained, and will remain, one of the obsessive themes of American life" (1989:68).

UNITY AND DIVERSITY

In light of Califano's and Lemann's observations, Riverview High School emerges as a special place, far from utopian but at least with a solid whiff of it in the air. When one's experience is firsthand, social realities make concrete what are the too easily articulated abstractions of high-minded principles and understandings acquired at a distance, that is, acquired vicariously from the media, from literature and the movies, and even from classroom instruction. As in the case of Gina, a white woman featured in a recent report on Milwaukee, who grew up in an all-black neighborhood with only black friends. One day she visited a nearby Lutheran church with a primarily white congregation: "I remember that . . . I was astonished to see so many white people" (Schell 1987:60). And in the case of RHS students for whom the faces of a Rodriguez, Ruiz, Chu Sim Pham, Pizzagoni, Siino, Hines, and Washington are daily fare. As also in the case of a white mother, Lydia Morgan, fifteen-year resident of Riverview, who says about her adopted city that "you don't have to be afraid of somebody because they're poor or they're black or they're yellow." I asked her how she came to view Riverview this way. "Probably just from seeing our children grow up in the school and around these people, the friends that they've brought home." As finally in my own case when after almost a year of full-time residence in River-view I returned home and, like Gina, was surprised at the unaccus-tomed look of people around me. I'd grown used to being surrounded by people of every color and tint. It felt unnatural to be in relatively mono-chromatic surroundings.

At RHS, cautionary lessons, lectures, and preachings do not produce principles of tolerance and brotherhood, which then create mingling. To the contrary: principles follow mingling. In the process of mingling, strangers become friends; in the concreteness of being together, prin-ciples are engendered and clothed with meaning. Principles come to life in the integrated conditions of RHS. While the category of strangers shrinks, the antithetic category of friends expands. The school's integra-tion undermines the insularity that inclines us to see as friends only those who look like us. Such a perspective punishes the innocent, de-humanizes all, and plants the seeds of mutually destructive conflict. The experience of RHS undermines insularity. For this it merits applause, but not so thunderous as to drown out the complaint of a local Chinese restaurant owner. He told me about his younger daughter, an academ-ically successful student at San Jose State University. "She is 1 percent Chinese," he said. "Only the skin. The rest is American." By abandoning what has been called the "particularities of life—the ethnic, religious, cultural affinities" (Will 1988:76), she discomforted her father. As, in the course of assimilation, the students' abandonment of family pride and respect for elders and authority discomforts parents and educators. Lik-ing both the open door of mingling and the "particularities of life," I, too, am discomforted. At RHS, some students are growing up American, while others are becoming American. If in the process the latter become just like the former, the cause of national unity is served, albeit at the too-high price of uniformity.

I suspect that uniformity is the inevitable consequence of ethnic per-sons perceiving that social and economic success in America comes most surely to those who assimilate. Individuals, accordingly, are hard pressed to sustain their distinctions, unless they are of the type that can be eaten, applauded, or worn. The Lebanons, Northern Irelands, Sri Lankas, and Sudans terrify us and persuade us that unity demands uni-formity. Paradoxically, a fair share of the dynamism of American society has always emerged from the diverse talents of its recent immigrants. This dynamism struggles in the face of the fearful, who by seeing virtue and security only in the settled are discomforted by reminders that we are a nation in process, a nation still learning what colors Americans come in.

In 1990, when our television sets showed pictures of Americans chanting "freedom now" in unaccented English in support of Lithuania, we heard no dissenting voices from other Americans decrying this behavior as unseemly, as smacking possibly of a strain of un-Americanism for favoring a foreign territory. Many of the chanters were native-born Americans, not "suspect" naturalized citizens. They stood in the streets and yelled slogans for a country they'd never seen, promoting its right to be independent. To be sure, the chanters should not learn to chant and sloganize in our schools. What children learn in our schools, however, should not be destructive of people who chant, or their right to do so.

I see the chanting as one expression of ethnicity. I believe that our schools should teach about ethnicity—what it is, how it operates in the life of fellow Americans, how it changes, what forms it can take—so that students may learn about ways of being American without blinders or adherence to any orthodoxy. Flag, anthem, and Fourth of July are safe; the chills are there. I want comparable force and heart behind understanding and respecting human difference, deviance, and idiosyncrasy.

The school year at RHS ends as it begins with memos and reminders and menus placed in teachers' mailboxes. In June, students can lunch on burritos, bagel dogs, and cheese pizza, served with tater tots, orange wedges, and ranch beans—the unabated play of surface ethnicity. The prose that accompanies the June menu warns students about swimming calamities and the dangers of the sun's rays. The June menu sheet finally proclaims what must be among the most momentous statements that any society can make: "This is an equal opportunity program [the one that provides federal support for school meals]. If you believe you have been discriminated against because of race, color, national origin, age, sex or handicap, write to the Secretary of Agriculture, Washington, D.C. 20250."

A major portion of the history of our nation lies behind these fine words; a major portion of our future may be invested in clarifying their meaning and promoting their implications for the conduct of our nation. As I construe them, these words say that though you may feel certain others are strangers, you may not legally treat them as if they were. You may not assign prerogatives to those whom you designate "friends" and deny them to those whom you designate "strangers." In its practices, RHS does not ignore these words. Tucked away in the corner of the June menu, and there only because of federal requirements, the words, like the warning on a cigarette package, lie inert. The positioning of this extraordinary statement on a menu assures that it will get less attention than the pineapple tidbits and pudding pops with which it shares the page.

Teachers close the year with three days of final examinations. Seniors graduate at 6:00 p.m. on Thursday and prepare for their "all nite party," their last all-class roundup until they begin the postadolescent succession of fifth-, tenth-, and fifteenth-year reunions. Teachers mark papers and prepare to submit grades that are due on Friday. They must heed the last day's necessary humdrum message from the principal's office: "Clean all counter tops in your classroom, remove all mail from your mailbox, turn in your keys to Jean." They also receive an end-of-year message from the teachers' union president:

The classroom teacher is a key to the intellectual and occupational preparation of individual citizens who, collectively, determine the quality of life in America. . . . The classroom teacher deserves the deepest respect and admiration of the citizens of this community.

The grandeur of determining "the quality of life in America," for which teachers merit a large measure of "respect and admiration," surely stirs fewer teachers than the principal's requests and the note they found in their mailboxes on the last day of school. It was left by an unidentified wag with a bite to his humor. Under the heading "Not So Trivial," the note informed teachers that it would require four hours a day, above and beyond their regular school day, to devote just two minutes per student to reading their work (quizzes, rough drafts, homework), if they had a student load of 120. Increasing the load to 150 (a more probable figure at RHS), raises the four to five hours. The piece ends exclaiming "Now we know why we look forward to June 13, 1986," the last day of school.

As a nation, we have barely begun to realize the intent of the government's message inscribed on the school menu. As a nation, we have not yet learned how to organize schools so that teachers receive their community's "deepest respect and admiration." As a nation, we have yet to take seriously the implications of the "Not So Trivial" two additional minutes.

I have focused on ethnicity in this book not because I believe it is the most powerfully determining characteristic of the people whose lives I came to learn about and understand. That ethnicity has significance in its own right I am persuaded, though separating its significance from social class, age, gender, interests, and aspirations is more than I can do. Social class shapes and distinguishes, and ethnicity does the same, but not as distinctively at this time in the students' lives as it may do later. Ethnicity is present without being determining. Like an unseen hand, it leads and guides, but always in the company of other factors.

Lincoln Steffens returned from his 1930s visit to the Soviet Union to declare that he had "seen the future, and it works." His eternally sprung hope had led him to exuberant excess. When in 1982 I searched for a multiethnic community for the site of my research, I was not in quest of the future. Moreover, my enthusiasm for Riverview High School stops well short of compelling me to make prophetic declarations. Still, not discounting its academic failure, I found much there that pleases and gives cause for optimism. In Riverview and Riverview High School, I see the natural experiment of an ethnically integrated community and school. In 1974, Thomas Pettigrew asked, "Shall Americans of the future live racially separate or together?" (1974:1). In Riverview, the answer is "together." I see there its victory: friends, not strangers, come in all colors.

White people rarely mean to offend. In fact, they hate it. They are just so narrowminded that they sometimes forget that there is anyone else out there.

—Martin Mull and Allen Rucker

White folks in Riverview got more soul.

—RHS parent

Appendix

In Search of Subjectivity—One's Own

We cannot rid ourselves of this subjectivity, nor should we wish to; but we ought, perhaps, to pay it very much more attention.

—A. P. Cheater

Introduction

A dictionary definition (*Webster's Third New International*) takes account of subjectivity as "the quality of an investigator that affects the results of observational investigation." This "quality" affects the results of all, not just observational investigation. It is an amalgam of the persuasions that stem from the circumstances of one's class, statuses, and values interacting with the particulars of one's object of investigation. Our persuasions vary in time and in intensity.

Though social scientists generally admit that subjectivity is invariably present in their research, they are not necessarily conscious of it. When their subjectivity remains unconscious, they insinuate rather than knowingly clarify their personal stakes. If in the spirit of confession researchers acknowledge their subjectivity, they may benefit their souls, but they do not thereby attend to that subjectivity in any meaningful way. This paper will argue how and why researchers should be meaningfully attentive to their own subjectivity.

This appendix was written during and after my year of fieldwork in "Riverview," and before I had begun writing the present volume. A slightly different version of the paper appeared under the same title in *Educational Researcher* 17,7:17–22, © 1988 by the American Educational Research Association, and is reprinted here by permission of the publisher. I would like to thank Liora Bresler, Golie Jansen, Maryann Peshkin, and Carolyne J. White for their helpful comments on drafts of this paper.

I hold the view that subjectivity operates during the entire research process (Peshkin 1982b). The point I argue here is that researchers, notwithstanding their use of quantitative or qualitative methods, the nature of their research problem, or their reputation for personal integrity, should systematically identify their subjectivity throughout the course of their research. When researchers observe themselves in the focused way that I propose, they learn about the particular subset of personal qualities that contact with the subjects of their research has released. These qualities have the capacity to filter, skew, shape, block, transform, construe, and misconstrue what happens from the outset of a research project to its culmination in a written statement. If researchers are aware of the personal qualities that have been activated during their research, they then can at least disclose to their readers where self and subject became joined. And they will at best be able to write unshackled from orientations they did not realize were intervening in the research process. [1]

Awareness of Subjectivity

Subjectivity is not a badge of honor, something earned like a merit badge and paraded around on special occasions for all to see. Whatever the substance of one's persuasions at a given point, one's subjectivity is like a garment that cannot be removed. It is insistently present in both the research and nonresearch aspects of our life. As conventional wisdom (see Reinharz 1979:141; Stein 1971:143; Freilich 1970:568), this view of subjectivity takes its place among other usually unexamined maxims of research, such as "rapport is good," "random samples are wonderful," and "informants can mislead." According to the same conventional wisdom, our subjectivity lies inert, unexamined, when it counts, that is, while we are actively engaged in the research process.

I became acutely aware of my own subjectivity in the course of writing *God's Choice: The Total World of a Fundamentalist Christian School and Community* (1986). The research I did for this book continued the studies I have conducted since 1972 on the community-school relationship in different environmental settings. Long interested in the concept of community, I looked at the nature of community in the fundamentalist Christian setting of Bethany Baptist Academy. I had previously done so in rural Illinois (1978; 1982a), and most recently in multi-ethnic "Riverview," California, the locus of my pursuit of subjectivity in

1. Mary Lee Smith (1980) makes a similar point in her sensitive, insightful paper written about her awareness of self in the course of two research projects.

this paper. But as regards my awareness of subjectivity at Bethany, I began writing chapter 1 of *God's Choice* no more and no less alert to my subjectivity than most of us ordinarily are, but then I was forced to confront it in a way that I never had before.

What I encountered was this. "Mansfield," the village site of previous research, was no more nurturant as a community than was the community I studied at Bethany, and Mansfield High School contributed no more to promoting a sense of community than did Bethany Baptist Academy. Yet I found that in writing of the community and school at Bethany I was not using the strongly positive terms that had come so easily to mind in describing Mansfield. Struck by this differential generosity, I knew that "I had indeed discovered my subjectivity at work, caught red-handed with my values at the very end of my pen" (Peshkin 1985:277).

Having stumbled upon my own subjectivity in this way, I drew two conclusions. First, I decided that subjectivity can be seen as virtuous. For its existence underlies a researcher's making a distinctive contribution, one that results from the unique configuration of the writer's personal qualities joined to the data he or she has collected. Second, I decided that in subsequent studies I would actively seek out my subjectivity. I did not want to happen upon it accidentally as I was writing up the data. I wanted to be aware of it in process, mindful of its enabling and disabling potential while the data were still coming in, not after the fact. Here are the results of what I did.

Subjective I's Uncovered

Throughout eleven months of fieldwork in Riverview High School I pursued my subjectivity.[2] How did I know when my subjectivity was engaged? I looked for the warm and the cool spots, the emergence of positive and negative feelings, the experiences I wanted to have more of or to avoid, as well as when I felt moved to act in roles beyond those necessary to fulfill my research needs. In short, I felt that to identify my subjectivity, I had to monitor myself in order to sense how I was feeling. When I sensed that my feelings were aroused, and thus that my subjectivity had been evoked, I wrote a note on a five-by-eight card, the researcher's friend. Perhaps equally or more useful, Smith (1980) kept a diary to document her "feelings and reactions": for example, she wrote about "spinning into the realm of the irrational" (p. 8) and "a weight on

2. Dale Minor also refers to the subjective I: "Maintaining the fiction of the reporter as an eye without an I is not in the best interests of sound journalism" (1970:196), as does Krieger: "The subjective 'I' of the author is hidden in the book." (1985:321).

my chest and a tightening of my throat" (p. 9). I preferred to record my
sensations as I was experiencing them, a matter of personal taste, as is so
much of fieldwork procedure.[3]

The results of my subjectivity audit are contained in the following list:
(1) the Ethnic-Maintenance I; (2) the Community-Maintenance I; (3) the
E-Pluribus-Unum I; (4) the Justice-Seeking I; (5) the Pedagogical-
Meliorist I; and (6) the Non-Research Human I.[4] These discretely characterized I's are, in fact, aspects of the whole that is me. They are no
more truly discrete than the organs of my body are independent of each
other. These I's comprise a subset that emerged under the particular
circumstances of Riverview High School. In another school, a different
subset would possibly emerge, even containing I's that do not overlap
with those I learned about at Riverview. That I's may change from place
to place I call "situational subjectivity." By this concept I suggest that
though we bring all of ourselves—our full complement of subjective
I's—to each new research site, only a subset of our I's will be elicited by
that site and its particular conditions.

The appearance of the Ethnic-Maintenance I was no surprise, since I
knew of it long before I went to Riverview. This, of course, is my Jewish
I, the one that approves of my own retention of ethnicity. In fact, being
Jewish shapes my life. When I saw ethnic-maintenance behavior in
Riverview, I identified with it; I got a warm feeling from it. I saw people
doing something that I realized I do myself, and I valued it.

In the course of trying to understand ethnicity, I encouraged Jessie
Pacheco, a Mexican woman, to tell me when she feels most Mexican.
She described Cinco de Mayo and other celebrations. "On such occasions," she said, "I wear clothing that I never wear at any other time of
the year. I walk into the large meeting hall," and her eyes opened wide
as if she actually saw herself as she spoke. "I walk into that room and I
see my people." "My people"—I know what Jessie Pacheco means when
she says this. While I do not have occasion to wear such special clothing,
I could truly walk into that large hall with her and feel what she feels.

When I met Barney Douglas, a black man, and heard him describe
the Black Cultural League that he himself founded some twenty years
ago, I relived with him his causes. They were causes conducted on be-

3. Sociologist Susan Krieger presents another subjectivity auditing procedure worthy
of careful attention (1985).
4. The names selected for each of the first five I's were ones I thought best fit the particular sentiment I had been perceiving and that I described in the account I kept each
time a sentiment was evoked. The sixth one, the Non-Research Human I, is taken from the
distinction anthropologist Morris Freilich (1970) makes between the human and research
self.

half of his people, including the celebration of "Juneteenth," an event that we do not hear about in the North. It is June 19, or thereabouts, the time in 1863 when blacks in the South realized that the Emancipation Proclamation had freed them. Barney Douglas organizes Riverview's annual Juneteenth celebration. It is a picnic-carnival affair held in a large park. He, like Jessie Pacheco, can come to this park, see the faces of his people, and be satisfied that something central to his life is being perpetuated. I identify with Douglas when he does this. Finding the Ethnic-Maintenance I, as I have indicated, was no surprise. I sensed it often because Riverview, being the multiethnic place that it is, contains many Jessie Pachecos and Barney Douglases.

The distorting hazard of my Ethnic-Maintenance I is that in valuing the behavior of those who chose to perpetuate their ethnic identity, I may ignore the lives of those who chose not to. Thus, I could perceive the school through one set of meanings while failing to give credence to the meanings of people whose concerns direct them toward assimilation.

Given that I study communities and their schools, it also was no surprise to encounter the Community-Maintenance I. I felt this one in various places, perhaps nowhere more strongly than at Mario's Snack Shop. Although I just happened upon it one day after a long morning walk, it became a place I stopped for coffee every day thereafter for two months. Mario's is the meeting place for descendants of old families, the Italian fishermen who came to Riverview decades ago. Riverview remains an Italian community in many ways, to none more so than the regulars who gather at Mario's Snack Shop for coffee and talk every morning.

The talk of the regulars ranged from nostalgia for golden days past to review of issues and opportunities extant in their town today. Clearly, they saw Riverview as *their* town. These fierce loyalists had sharp words for old friends and former neighbors who fled from Riverview to nearby towns when times were bad following Martin Luther King's assassination. The talk of the men at Mario's took me back to the midwestern village of Mansfield, where I had first discovered my attachment to community and concern for its survival. Two tables of farmers sat every day in Mansfield's only restaurant. An important sense of community was perpetuated there, as it was every day at Mario's Snack Shop, and I reveled in it. The subjectivity of the Community-Maintenance I was engaged each morning at Mario's.

By letting the Community-Maintenance I direct me, I tied myself to the Riverview of native oldtimers, a substantial, visible group but far from being a majority. Most particularly, however, this subjective I distracted me from Riverview's continuing flow of newcomers, whose agenda was low on nostalgia and high on political housecleaning for the city and on significantly improved test scores for their children.

I uncovered the E-Pluribus-Unum I, and experienced it every day, during all the before-, between-, and after-class times at Riverview High School. The visual impression of the school captivated me from the first time I went there to the last. Its sea of faces comprised a student population that was white, 33 percent; black, 33 percent; Hispanic, 20 percent; Filipino, 12 percent; and the rest American Indian, Vietnamese, and others. I had never seen such diversity; indeed, it did not exist to the same degree anywhere else in the community. One could see a semblance of diversity in any of the large, local supermarkets, but nowhere other than the high school was every variety of Riverview human being assembled daily for some seven hours. This was one fact.

The second fact was that this heterogeneous human lot was not simply there in the same physical setting, it was there in the way local people called "mingling." Students referred often to mingling; teachers did, too. I needed to verify whether what I thought I saw—kids from the different ethnic groups truly being together—was my hope springing eternal or something that was really happening. So, in the course of interviews with numerous students I asked about cross-group social interactions. They were a reality. To be sure, black students hung out with other black students, and Filipino boys bunched together over here and Mexican girls over there. There was ethnic clustering, what one would expect to find anywhere, because birds of an ethnic feather still flock together. But, in addition, an ordinary, routine fact of life was the mingling: any type of interaction that could take place between students of the same ethnic background took place between students of different ethnic backgrounds. All the time and with everybody? No. Riverview is not Utopia; there are still problems, still elements of prejudice, fear, and hate. These exist.

Nonetheless, I saw students together in ways that I found wonderful. I uncovered my E-Pluribus-Unum I, and one more manifestation of my subjectivity. It is somewhat contrary to the sense of the Ethnic-Maintenance I, but for now I do not mean to reconcile my I's; I just mean to note those that I have identified.

At a later time, however, when I am ready to create my narrative about Riverview, I will need to decide how to present the "stories" that can be derived from maintaining ethnicity, on the one hand, and from mingling, on the other. More than this, I will need to be cautious about overstating the magnitude of mingling among Riverview's sixteen hundred students, for verifying that it exists in general—a matter I find personally satisfying—is not equivalent to establishing that it is an abiding fact of student life in particular.

The Justice-Seeking I is one that I learned about shortly after coming to Riverview. In fact, I learned about it and kept learning about it because the events that alerted me to it were commonplace for every Riverview adult and most Riverview children.

One night, for example, I went to a parent-teacher meeting in the high school lunchroom. Ten of us were present, nine parents and me. The woman who presided over this group said, "Well, we don't seem to have a quorum. Why don't I introduce Dr. Peshkin; he can tell us what he's doing here." I discussed my work briefly, asked no questions, and sat down. For the next hour I heard the parents talk about their town and how residents from nearby towns denigrate it and them.

What did denigration sound like? It sounded like this: "My daughter has friends who live outside of Riverview. She can go to their houses to sleep overnight, but they cannot come to Riverview to sleep with her in our house." And also like this: "We go to a shopping mall in the next town over, and when I'm filling out a form of some sort and the clerk sees that I have filled out Riverview, she says, 'What! You're from Riverview? Oh my God.'"

After some months of living in Riverview, I had my own personal contact with denigration. I was shopping in a store in a nearby town. When the saleswoman realized that I was not a local person, she asked what brought me to California. I told her I was from the University of Illinois, living and doing research in Riverview. "Oh," she said, "are you there to study pollution or crime in the streets?"

This denigration stems primarily from the fact that Riverview is the only town in its part of a very large county that has long allowed black people to find housing and live there. Blacks now live elsewhere in the county, but until quite recently they were concentrated in Riverview. Riverview's almost totally white neighboring communities once took pride in forbidding blacks to remain overnight in town.

Because this denigration of Riverview distressed me, I was moved to investigate it as systematically as I could. Throughout the time I was learning about this phenomenon, I knew my sentiments would somehow figure in my writing; I knew, therefore, that I would need to take account of them. While feelings of distress helped focus my inquiry[5]—a positive outcome—they could make me defensive in a way that would not facilitate my analysis and understanding of denigration.

5. Similarly, Erickson writes, "one must not only suppress a sense of outrage while in the field, but still stay in there and take advantage of one's rage, *using it as a barometer to indicate high salience*" (emphasis mine) (1984:61; see also Smith 1980:9).

The Pedagogical-Meliorist I, a new and surprising expression of my subjectivity, emerged while I was sitting in the back of classrooms. Although much of my professional life entails watching teachers at work, never before had this I been aroused, but not because the teaching I'd previously seen was particularly admirable. Mansfield and Bethany were not citadels of academic excellence. The Pedagogical-Meliorist I emerged from seeing ordinary-to-poor instruction given to youngsters who would suffer, I imagined, as a consequence of that instruction.

When I observed teaching I did not like in rural and Christian schools, I confined myself to concluding that I would not want my own children to attend such schools. I never believed that the rural or Christian fundamentalist children would be penalized in the way I anticipated many Riverview High School children would, and that was because I had never before seen children taught who were the poor underclass of America. Of Riverview High School's sixteen hundred students, 27 percent are from welfare families. Day in and day out, I sensed that many would pay a high price at the hands of their teachers. To be sure, I did not believe that if the instruction were better, these children would be catapulted out of the school's low academic track, out of their poverty, and into the good life. But when I saw the performance of many teachers, I concluded that they contributed to the array of complex factors that perpetuate poverty.

As I sat in the back of classrooms, I felt that I wanted to remedy the teaching I observed. This surprised me because among the first things I explain to the personnel at any of the schools I study is that I am neither an evaluator nor a reformer. I come neither to judge whether they teach well or poorly, nor to make them better than they are. I go to great lengths to establish who I am not, so that my behavior can reinforce daily who I am. Accordingly, I am careful to be interested yet nonjudgmental and uninvolved with a school's instructional program. Nonetheless, I found myself judging, and I wanted to be involved so that I could redress pedagogical wrongs. My feelings were engaged, my subjectivity was present, and I frequently thought, "How can I help improve the instruction of those I deem ineffective teachers?"

When I found myself planning with the basketball coach how to promote the academic success of his players, who typically starred at Riverview High but failed to make it to four-year colleges, I realized that thought had become father to deed. In this victory of subjectivity over reason I risked undermining the integrity of the nonjudgmental persona I had constructed to insure teachers' comfort with me in their classrooms. I also risked mixing roles, as when "field workers hope to strike back through their writing" (Glazer 1972:59). Striking back and reforming may be worthwhile endeavors, but they were at odds with the intentions of my research project.

My final I, the Non-Research Human I, is another one I repeatedly experienced. For example, when my wife and I first arrived in Riverview, the Community Women's League invited her to be an honorary but full participant even though its members knew she would live in town for one year only. They took her in and made her feel at home, as did many others. One day my wife and I were walking past the home of a Riverview High School teacher's parents. The teacher happened to be there. We met his parents and spent two hours with them. Times like this were repeated again and again in Riverview, with people saying by the warmth of their reception, "How nice for us that you are here. How nice that you are in our lives."

This particular subjective I softens one's judgment; the others distort in a certain direction. Its by-product is affection, which tends to reduce the distance between self and subjects that scholars presume is necessary to learn and write about a person, place, or institution. Even if affection and dispassion are not antithetical, it still seems probable that affection could block the sharp, harsh light that dispassion usefully generates throughout one's research process. In the large space between feelings of a love affair, at one pole, and of a let-the-chips-fall-where-they-may outlook, at the other, there is ample room for an affection that serves to remind one of obligations to his respondents, and for a dispassion that, like horseradish in the nasal passages, clears his vision.

Other subjective I's may be uncovered when I begin to write, but these are the six I have taken note of to date.

Tamed Subjectivity

An unnamed author wrote in a *New Yorker* column, while reflecting on what he had learned from the then recently deceased writer E. B. White, "I think I half believed that if some editor or reader caught a glimpse of me in the underbrush of my own prose, he would order me out of there forthwith" (April 25, 1985:33). One point of this paper is to say that I have looked for myself where, knowingly or not, I think we all unavoidably are, and indeed belong—in the subjective underbrush of our own research experience. Having found myself there, I can certainly expect when I write about Riverview to find myself as well "in the underbrush of my own prose," where I will continue the process of taming my subjectivity.

Another point of this paper is to demonstrate a procedure that I recommend strongly to all researchers. Perhaps, at some level, all or most researchers are already aware of their subjectivity and its possible impact on their work. I advocate the enhanced awareness that can result from a formal, systematic monitoring of self. Speaking personally—but intending general application—I see this monitoring as a necessary exercise, a workout, a tuning up of my subjectivity to get it into shape. It is a rehearsal for keeping the lines of my subjectivity open—and straight. And it is a warning to myself so that I may avoid the trap of perceiving just what my own untamed sentiments have sought out and served up as data. If so trapped, I run the risk of presenting a study that has become blatantly autobiographical. "Autobiographical" here is meant in the sense that Geertz captures in his observation that "All ethnography is part philosophy and a good deal of the rest is confession" (1973:346) and that Smith acknowledges when she writes, "If this distortion and projection had not been identified I would still have written a reasonably good account, but it would have been too much about me" (1980:5). I also run the risk of presenting a study that has assumed the form of an "authorized" statement. "Authorized" is a term used to characterize biographies that the biographer has been invited to write by the subject or by his or her heirs. The "in-house" stamp of authorized work conveys the sense that the writer not only has permission to write, but also the subject's best interests at heart. By unwittingly assuming the role of special pleader, defender, or eulogist, I may move away from the cooler edges of the world I investigate to its hot emotional core, where hazards of overidentification or going native lie.

It is no point of this paper to say, "Here am I," holier than thou and released from my subjectivity because I have owned up, whereas you, being unrepentant, remain afflicted. The point is this: by monitoring myself, I can create an illuminating, empowering personal statement that attunes me to where self and subject are intertwined. I do not, thereby, exorcise my subjectivity. I do, rather, enable myself to manage it—to preclude its becoming unwittingly burdensome—as I progress through collecting, analyzing, and writing up my data.

For example, when I discovered my lack of enthusiasm for the contributions of Bethany Baptist Academy, I was alerted to the need to avoid the negativism which, unconstrained, would have tainted my intended portrayal of the school in the terms of the fundamentalist Christians who used it. Untamed subjectivity mutes the emic voice. Further, knowing that I am disposed to see—and, no less consequential, not see[6]—in the

6. Rubin refers to "blind spots . . . a product of our self-protective instincts" that lead people to cover "the gaps with smoke screens and fictions" (1985:9).

particular ways directed by each of the six I's, I can consciously attend to the orientations that will shape what I see and what I make of what I see. By this consciousness I may possibly escape the thwarting biases that subjectivity engenders, while attaining the singular perspective its special persuasions promise.

References

Allport, G. W. 1954/1958. *The Nature of Prejudice*. Garden City, N.Y.: Doubleday Anchor Books.

Balliett, W. 1985. "Jazz. Little Jazz." *New Yorker*, December 16: 154.

Banks, J. A. 1977. *Multiethnic Education: Practical and Promises*. Bloomington, Ind.: Phi Delta Kappa Educational Foundation.

―――. 1981. *Multiethnic Education: Theory and Practice*. Boston: Allyn and Bacon.

Barth, F. 1969. *Ethnic Groups and Boundaries*. Boston: Little, Brown.

Becker, G., and Arnold, R. 1986. "Stigma as a Social and Cultural Construct." In *The Dilemma of Differences: A Multidisciplinary View of Stigma*, edited by S. C. Ainlay, G. Becker, and L. M. Coleman. New York: Plenum Press.

Bell, D. 1975. "Ethnicity and Social Change." In *Ethnicity*, edited by N. Glazer and D. P. Moynihan. Cambridge: Harvard University Press.

Berreman, G. 1975. "Bazaar Behavior: Social Identity and Social Interaction in Urban India." In *Ethnic Identity: Cultural Continuities and Change*, edited by G. DeVos and L. Romanucci-Ross. Palo Alto, Cal.: Mayfield Publishing Co.

Bonacich, E., and Modell, J. 1980. *The Economic Basis of Ethnic Solidarity: Small Business in the Japanese American Community*. Berkeley: University of California Press.

Bruner, E. M. 1961. "Mandan." In *Perspectives in American Indian Culture Change*, edited by E. H. Spicer. Chicago: University of Chicago Press.

―――. 1974. "The Expression of Ethnicity in Indonesia." In *Urban Ethnology*, edited by Abner Cohen. London: Tavistock Publishers.

Califano, J. A., Jr. 1989. "Tough Talk for Democrats." *New York Times Magazine*, January 8: 28–30.

California Department of Education. 1983. "Selected Statistics." Sacramento.

Codrescu, A. 1989. "Remade in America." *New York Times Book Review*, April 2: 15. A review of *New Americans*, by A. Santoli.

DeVos, G., and Romanucci-Ross, L. (eds.) 1975. *Ethnic Identity: Cultural Continuities and Change*. Palo Alto, Cal.: Mayfield.

di Leonardo, M. 1984. *The Varieties of Ethnic Experience: Kinship, Class, and*

Gender among California Italian-Americans. Ithaca, N.Y.: Cornell University Press.

DuBois, W. E. B. 1930/1969. *The Souls of Black Folk.* New York: New American Library.

Epps, E. G., ed. 1974. *Cultural Pluralism.* Berkeley: McCutchan.

Education Week. 1988a. "Kerner Report: A 20-Year Review." March 30: 17.

Education Week. 1988b. "'Explosion' in Testing Threatens Schools, Fair Test Study Charges." June 22: 3.

Erickson, F. 1984. "What Makes Ethnography 'Ethnographic'?" *Anthropology and Education Quarterly,* 15: 51–66.

Ferguson, C. A. 1964. "Diglossia." In *Language in Culture and Society,* edited by D. Hymes. New York: Harper and Row.

Fischer, M. M. J. 1986. "Ethnicity and the Post-Modern Arts of Memory." In *Writing Culture,* edited by J. Clifford and G. F. Marcus. Berkeley: University of California Press.

Fordham, S. 1988. "Racelessness as a Factor in Black Students' School Success: Pragmatic Strategy or Pyrrhic Victory." *Harvard Educational Review* 58, 1: 54–84.

Fordham, S. and Ogbu, J. U. 1986. "Black Students' School Success: Coping with the 'Burden of Acting White.'" *Urban Review* 18, 3: 176–206.

Freeman, M. 1985. "On Linguistic Diversity in Classrooms." *Education Week,* November 13: 28.

Freilich, M. 1977. "Toward a Formalization of Fieldwork." In *Marginal Natives at Work: Anthropologists in the Field,* edited by M. Freilich. Cambridge, Mass.: Schenkman.

Gann, E. K. 1963. *Of Good and Evil.* Greenwich, Ct.: Fawcett Publications.

Gates, H. L., Jr. 1986. "Talkin' That Truth." In *"Race," Writing, and Difference,* edited by H. L. Gates. Chicago: University of Chicago Press.

Geertz, C. 1973. *The Interpretation of Cultures.* New York: Basic Books.

————. 1986. "The Uses of Diversity." In *The Tanner Lectures on Human Values,* edited by S. McMurrin. Salt Lake City: University of Utah Press.

Glazer, M. 1972. *The Research Adventure.* New York: Random House.

Glazer, N., and Moynihan, D. 1970. *Beyond the Melting Pot.* Cambridge: MIT Press.

Gollnick, D. M., and Chinn, P. C. 1983. *Multicultural Education in a Pluralistic Society.* St. Louis, Mo.: C. V. Mosby.

Gordon, M. M. 1978. *Human Nature, Class, and Ethnicity.* New York: Oxford University Press.

Graff, H. F. 1983. *This Great Nation.* Chicago: Riverside Publishers.

Greeley, A., and McCready, W. C. 1974. *Ethnicity in the United States.* New York: Wiley.

Handlin, O. 1951. *The Uprooted.* New York: Grossett and Dunlap.

Hewitt, R. 1986. *White Talk Black Talk: Inter-racial Friendship and Communication amongst Adolescents.* Cambridge: Cambridge University Press.

Horowitz, D. L. 1975. "Ethnic Identity." In *Ethnicity: Theory and Experience,* edited by N. Glazer and D. P. Moynihan. Cambridge: Harvard University Press.

Hunter, F. 1953. *Community Power Structure*. New York: Anchor Books.

Isajiw, W. W. 1974. "Definitions of Ethnicity." *Ethnicity* 1, 2 (July): 111–24.

Juliani, R. N., ed. 1988. *The Family and Community Life of Italian Americans*. New York: Italian American Historical Association.

Keyes, C. F., ed. 1981. *Ethnic Change*. Seattle: University of Washington Press.

Kiefer, C. W. 1974. *Changing Culture, Changing Lives*. San Francisco: Jossey-Bass.

Kilson, M. 1975. "Blacks and Neo-Ethnicity in American Political Life." In *Ethnicity: Theory and Experience*, edited by N. Glazer and D. P. Moynihan. Cambridge: Harvard University Press.

Knownslar, A. O., and Smart, T. L. 1984. *People and Our World*. New York: Holt, Rinehart and Winston.

Kobrin, F. E., and Goldscheider, C. 1978. *The Ethnic Factor in Family Structure and Mobility*. Cambridge, Mass.: Ballinger Publishing Co.

Kramer, J. 1986. "Letter from Europe." *New Yorker*, February 17: 67–93.

Krieger, S. 1985. "Beyond 'Subjectivity': The Use of the Self in Social Science." *Qualitative Sociology* 8(4): 309–24.

Lemann, N. 1989. "The Unfinished War." *Atlantic Monthly*, January: 53–68.

Lynch, J. 1983. *The Multicultural Curriculum*. London: Batsford Academic and Educational Ltd.

Magner, D. K. 1990. "After 30 Years, Some Answers about What Makes a Good School." *Chronicle of Higher Education*, April 11: A3.

McKay, J., and Levins, F. 1978. "Ethnicity and the Ethnic Group: A Conceptual Analysis and Reformulation." *Ethnic and Racial Studies* 1, 4 (October): 412–27.

Metz, M. H. 1983. "Sources of Constructive Social Relationships in an Urban Magnet School." *American Journal of Education*, February: 202–45.

Minor, D. 1970. *The Information War*. New York: Hawthorn Books.

Modgil, S., Verma, G., Mallick, K., and Modgil, C. 1986. *Multicultural Education: The Interminable Debate*. New York: Falmer Press.

Morrow, L. 1988. "The Five-and-Dime Charms of Astrology." *Time*, May 16: 100.

Murrell, P. C. 1989. "Coping in the Culture of Power: Resilience as a Factor in Black Students' Academic Success." Paper presented at annual meeting of the American Educational Research Association.

Okamura, J. Y. 1981. "Situational Ethnicity." *Ethnic and Racial Studies* 4, 4 (October): 452–65.

Paden, J. N. 1970. "Urban Pluralism, Integration, and Adaptation of Communal Identity in Kano, Nigeria." In *From Tribe to Nation in Africa*, edited by R. Cohen and J. Middleton. Scranton, N.J.: Chandler.

Parsons, T. 1975. "Some Theoretical Considerations on the Nature and Trends of Change in Ethnicity." In *Ethnicity: Theory and Experience*, edited by N. Glazer and D. P. Moynihan. Cambridge: Harvard University Press.

Patchen, M. 1982. *Black-White Contact in Schools: Its Social and Academic Affects*. West Lafayette, Ind.: Purdue University Press.

Peshkin, A. 1978. *Growing Up American: Schooling and the Survival of Community.* Chicago: University of Chicago Press.

———. 1982a. *The Imperfect Union: School Consolidation and Community Conflict*. Chicago: University of Chicago Press.

———. 1982b. "The Researcher and Subjectivity: Reflections on an Ethnography of School and Community." In *Doing the Ethnography of Schooling* edited by G. Spindler. New York: Holt, Rinehart and Winston.

———. 1985. "Virtuous Subjectivity: In the Participant Observer's I's." In *Exploring Clinical Methods for Social Research*, edited by D. N. Berg and K. K. Smith. Beverly Hills, Cal.: Sage.

———. 1986. *God's Choice: The Total World of a Fundamentalist Christian School*. Chicago: University of Chicago Press.

———. 1988. "In Search of Subjectivity: One's Own." *Educational Researcher* 17, 7: 17–22.

Pettigrew, T. F. 1974. "Racially Separate or Together?" In *Cultural Pluralism*, edited by E. G. Epps. Berkeley, Cal.: McCutchan.

———. 1976. "Ethnicity in American Life: A Social Psychological Perspective." In *Ethnic Identity in Society*, edited by A. Dashefsky. Chicago: Rand McNally.

Powell, A. G., Farrar, E., and Cohen, D. K. 1985. *The Shopping Mall High School*. Boston: Houghton Mifflin.

Quality Education for Minorities Project. 1990. *Education That Works: An Action Plan for the Education of Minorities*. Cambridge: Massachusetts Institute of Technology.

Reinharz, S. 1979. *On Becoming a Social Scientist: From Survey Research and Participant Observation to Experiential Analysis*. San Francisco: Jossey-Bass.

Rodriguez, R. 1981. *Hunger of Memory: The Education of Richard Rodriguez*. Boston: David R. Godine.

Rothschild, J. 1981. *Ethnopolitics: A Conceptual Framework*. New York: Columbia University Press.

Rubin, Z. 1985. "Why We Stick Our Heads in the Sand." *New York Times Book Review,* June 16: 9.

Schell, J. 1987. "A Reporter at Large: Milwaukee." *New Yorker,* January 5: 35–68.

Schofield, J. W. 1982/1989. *Black and White in School: Trust, Tension, or Tolerance?* New York: Teachers College Press.

Selakovich, D. 1978. *Ethnicity and the School: Educating Minorities and Mainstream America*. Danville, Ill.: Interstate Printers and Publishers.

California Dept. of Education. 1983. Selected Statistics. Sacramento.

Seligman, K. 1985. "Wave of Immigrants Rolls In from Philippines." *San Francisco Examiner,* December 29: A-15.

Smith, M. L. 1980. *Solving for Some Unknowns in the Personal Equation.* CIRCE Occasional Paper. Urbana, Ill.: University of Illinois.

Snider, W. 1987. "Study Examines Forces Affecting Racial Tracking." *Education Week* 7, 10: 1, 20.

Stanlaw, J., and Peshkin, A. 1988. "Black Visibility in a Multi-Ethnic High School." In *Class, Race, and Gender in American Education,* edited by L. Weis. Albany, N.Y.: SUNY Press.

Stein, M. R. 1971. "The Eclipse of Community: Some Glances at the Education of a Sociologist." In *Reflections on Community Studies,* edited by A. J. Vidich et al. New York: Harper and Row.

Steinberg, S. 1981. *The Ethnic Myth: Race, Ethnology, and Class in America.* New York: Atheneum.

Warriner, J. E., and Griffith, F. 1977. *English Grammar and Composition.* New York: Harcourt Brace Jovanovich.

Will, G. F. 1988. "Gorbachev, Meet Jefferson." *Newsweek,* December 19: 76.

Yinger, J. M. 1981. "Toward a Theory of Assimilation and Dissimilation." *Ethnic and Racial Studies* 4, 3: 249–64.

Index

303